Mutiny amid Repression

Mutiny amid Repression

Russian Soldiers in the Revolution of 1905–1906

John Bushnell

Indiana University Press • *Bloomington*

This book was brought to publication with the assistance of a grant from the Andrew W. Mellon Foundation to the Russian and East European Institute, Indiana University, and the Center for Russian and East European Studies, University of Michigan.

Manufactured in the United States of America

Library of Congress Cataloging in Publication Data

Bushnell, John, 1945–
  Mutiny amid repression.

  (Indiana-Michigan series in Russian and East European studies)
  Bibliography: p.
  Includes index.
    1. Soviet Union. Armiîà—History—Revolution of
1905.   2. Sociology, Military—Soviet Union—History—
20th century.   I. Title.   II. Series.
UA772.B87 1985   355.1'334'0947   84-48849
ISBN 0-253-33960-X

1 2 3 4 5   89 88 87 86 85

Contents

Tables

Introduction

This study began with the discovery of an anomaly: very large numbers of mutinies in the Tsarist armed forces took place in 1905 and 1906. There were, at last count, a minimum of 211 mutinies between October 17 and December 31, 1905, another 202 in 1906. Long before the full extent of the upheaval in the army became apparent, the evidence appeared to indicate that disaffection among soldiers had far surpassed the level that could be accommodated by the universally accepted assumption—my own assumption—that the principal role of the army during the 1905 Revolution was suppression of civil disorder. And the army had, indubitably, suppressed revolution. My first supposition was, therefore, that with perhaps a few exceptions the mutinies could not have been of much consequence. Presentation of a petition of service-related grievances—the high point of most of the disorders in the army—may have been mutiny as defined by law but appeared to be a feeble challenge to the military order, and no threat at all to the Tsarist regime. However, collation of mutinies with units garrisoned in European Russia in late 1905 disclosed that one-third of the infantry regiments with which the regime presumably crushed revolution had mutinied. Even had the mutinies been of little account individually, their number made them significant. A closer look at the mutinies showed that they were not individually inconsequential, and that they were the tangible issue of a military revolution that went far beyond mutiny and involved many more than mutinous units. The mutinies of 1905 could not be explained away and so presented something of a puzzle. The mutinies of 1906 were positively unsettling, because by 1906 revolution was supposed to have been over. This book, then, emerged from the questions raised by the soldiers' behavior in 1905 and 1906.

The obvious question is how the Tsarist regime managed to survive with its army so thoroughly disaffected. The equally obvious answer—that soldiers could at almost the same time mutiny and suppress revolution—is very nearly the initial question rephrased, but at least points to the critical importance of understanding the soldiers' psychology. One probes collective mentalities gingerly and ever alert for treacherous missteps. My own endeavor moved progressively from inferences that could reasonably be drawn from the soldiers' behavior, to an examination of service in the Imperial Russian army as soldiers experienced it, to exploration of the characteristics of Tsarist society that shaped the army, its officers and its men. The soldiers' behavior during the 1905 Revolution turned out to hinge on features of Russian history far removed from the revolution and even from the army.

The regime's ability to survive widespread mutiny in 1905 and 1906 suggests that its existence may not in fact have rested on its ability to suppress civilian discontent. The mutinies, though noteworthy, would in that case not have been terribly threatening in themselves. However, investigation of the army's repressive role in 1905 and 1906, and of the policing duties that the army routinely performed even in the absence of revolution, underscored the regime's dependence upon the availability of a large and reliable punitive force. The mutinies did pose a potentially mortal threat to the regime, and the regime's survival in 1905 and 1906 thus turned on the psychology of its soldiers.

Russia did not lack for men and women who sought to destroy the regime, and who grasped eagerly at every opportunity to do so. The efforts they made to destabilize and win support in the army—though occupying a minor place in the history of the revolutionary movement—assume importance once it is recognized that there was, even briefly, severe revolutionary discontent in the armed forces. The outcome of the revolution alone tells us that revolutionaries failed to turn the mutinies to their advantage. The soldiers' mentality was one obstacle, but the assumptions revolutionaries made about the soldiers' role in revolution reduced their ability to exploit, and affected the course, of the revolution in the army. These assumptions did not emerge from a vacuum in 1905, but were a product of the intellectual and organizational history of the revolutionary movement.

Finally, and to return to the initial impetus for the study, the mutinies must be accommodated within the 1905 Revolution itself. The Western understanding that the revolution reached its high point in the general strike that wrung the October Manifesto from the Tsar, and that the regime handily suppressed the December insurrections and so brought revolution to an end, does not readily encompass the mutinies that swept through the army after October 17. The mutinies of 1906 do not fit that scheme at all. Finding a place for the mutinies required modification of the prevailing view of the situation in the Russian empire in late 1905, and a rather more complete redrawing of the accepted picture of 1906.

What began as an effort to account for the 400-odd mutinies that occurred in 1905 and 1906 has thus grown into a good deal more than a close analysis of the mutinies themselves. The logic of the inquiry led to a lengthy excursus on the relationship between army and society in Imperial Russia—society molding the army, the army holding society together—detours down some byways of the revolutionary movement, and reconceptualization of the 1905 Revolution. The result, I hope, is a demonstration that the mutinies were not anomalous after all.

I have received generous support for this study from many sources. The International Research and Exchanges Board and the Committee on Fulbright-Hays Fellowships sponsored and funded a year of research in the Soviet Union, and Indiana University supported another year of research with an Edwards Fellowship. I am indebted to Boris Sapir of the International Institute of Social History in Amsterdam for granting me access to the SR Party archive in his charge. A grant from the National Endowment for the Humanities permitted work at Columbia University's Bakhmeteff Archive and the Bund Archive in New York, and the American Philosophical Society provided funds for research at the Archives Nationales in Paris. My gratitude to those institutes is not the less for the fact that I owe even more to Progress Publishers, which employed my wife and me as translators and so provided the opportunity for three years of research in the Soviet Union beyond the year we spent on academic exchange. Only prolonged access to Soviet libraries made it possible to pursue the puzzling mutinies of 1905 and 1906, and to turn what was meant to be no more than an introduction to a dissertation on revolutionary activity in the garrisons in 1917 into the present study.

Debts to friends and colleagues are not so easily measured. Alexander Rabinowitch, who directed my dissertation, has offered encouragement and advice and—most important of all—exhibited exceptional forbearance toward a student who scrapped a dissertation topic when the work was well under way. Ben Eklof was present at the inception of this study, and his interest in it then and since has made the labor seem worthwhile; I have drawn heavily—far more than the footnotes indicate—on his study of peasants, and he offered valuable advice on the manuscript. Allan Wildman, too, provided a critical reading of the manuscript and important suggestions. Bill Fuller shared both his thoughts and his manuscript on *Civil-Military Conflict in Imperial Russia, 1881–1914,* which complements my own work and yielded a wealth of valuable material. Roberta Manning was kind enough to provide a manuscript copy of her fascinating *Crisis of the Old Order in Russia* prior to publication. The history departments of Carnegie-Mellon and Northwestern Universities have provided intellectual stimulation, a truly congenial atmosphere, and the example of their own high standards. The gentle prodding of senior colleagues has encouraged me to bring this book, at last, to completion.

I cannot, without seeming to belittle it, convey the magnitude of my appreciation and indebtedness to Kristine Bushnell, who has over the years tolerated my preoccupation with mutiny and suffered my work to intrude on her own.

Conventions

Dates follow the Julian calendar.

Transliteration is according to the Library of Congress system for the social sciences, except that the unsightly "yi" ending has been changed to "y" in the text (but not in the notes). Familiar names are given in their familiar spellings.

Place names are those in use at the time (thus Helsingfors and not Helsinki, Tiflis and not Tbilisi), except for some Polish cities that were known in both Polish and Russian spellings.

Mutiny amid Repression

I. Officers and Men in the Russian Army

Deeply religious, steadfast in battle, instinctively deferential to his officers—this was the established image of the Russian soldier at the opening of the twentieth century. The central tenet of Tsarist military ideology was that the army served "Faith, Tsar and Fatherland," with officers as intermediaries between the simple soldier and the more distant founts of authority, God and Tsar. This was not mere prescription: Russian officers assumed the men trembled at the mention of God and routinely invoked divine sanctions when instructing soldiers in their obligations. Even observers whose job it was to penetrate the official myths took creed for reality. Analyzing the Russian army's sources of strength, a Japanese military attaché wrote in 1903 that since the Tsar was anointed of God, "to serve the Emperor is the same as serving God: to oppose the command of the Sovereign, or in other words, the orders of officers, is the same as opposing the will of God." Superimposing Japanese myth upon Russian, he added that because of the religious fervor of the Russian peasant soldier, Russians held death in contempt—to die in battle was, after all, to die for God.[1]

Theology aside, almost everyone agreed that the Russian soldier was of surpassing quality—patient, enduring, brave, obedient—the kind of human material yearned for by officers the world over. This image of the Russian soldier had taken shape soon after the Russian army appeared on the battlefields of central Europe in the eighteenth century; foreigners had marvelled at the Russian soldier's barbaric capacity to withstand fire. When General Henry Lloyd wrote that Russian infantry "cannot be defeated, they must be killed," and Frederick the Great remarked that "it is easier to kill these Russians to the last man than to defeat them," they were stating what was after the Seven Years War conventional wisdom.[2] Inevitably, awe of the *furor Russicus* waned as Russia's string of eighteenth-century triumphs ran out in the nineteenth century, and as technological and social change produced new styles of combat and a new appreciation for rank-and-file initiative. Nevertheless, Major Von Tettau, a German General Staff officer who had made a close study of the Tsarist army, wrote after spending two months in the field with the Russians in 1903: "Full of selflessness and loyalty to his duty, nourishing trust in his commanders, *the Russian soldier is material that is scarcely to be found in any other army in the world.*" True, most Russian soldiers were illiterate, but they "do everything with a will, are distinguished by endurance, are unassuming and always satisfied and jolly—even after labor and deprivation."[3]

Both the German and Japanese observers identified the relationship between officers and men as a major ingredient of Russian military strength. Tsarist officers agreed. The model commander was a father to his men, and officers of all ranks were enjoined to exhibit paternal solicitude (and paternal severity) toward their charges. The Japanese attaché took the officers' image of themselves, too, for fact, and believed that military paternalism was a carryover, not at all a bad one, from serfdom: "The Russian soldier is convinced that he and his officer are different kinds of people, that the latter is his lord, and that the officer knows more than he." Officers, in turn, took a great interest in their men, provided both military and moral guidance, and withal, "officers love their soldiers, and there is a firm bond between them."[4]

Foreign officers saw the Russian army much as it wished to be seen, but also as most Tsarist officers, to their subsequent undoing, believed it to be. It is easy enough to point to discrepancies between myth and reality, and to find satisfactory metaphors for the Russian army's weakness in its nineteenth-century practice: whatever the bonds between officers and men, at mid-century Russian soldiers practiced musketry without targets, at the end of the century they marched in boots that disintegrated on the road to battle. Yet even the most fatuous and self-serving myths tell us something important about the Russian army. What needs examining is not the true measure of religiosity, selflessness, benevolent paternalism, and other qualities attributed to officers and men, but what it was about the Tsarist army that produced beliefs so misleading, and so widely shared by Russian officers and their foreign interlocutors.

The Two Russias and the Army

One feature of the Russian army that the Japanese attaché got right was the soldiers' belief that officers and men were "different kinds of people." In 1903, 89 percent of the conscripts were rural in origin; 65 percent were tillers of the soil, 18 percent were classified as "artisans and tradesmen" (and could come either from cities or villages), 2 percent were factory workers. Not all soldiers were Russian, but in 1903 73 percent were Russian or other Orthodox Slavs. In all but the technical units, the typical soldier was a Russian peasant.[5] The connection between the Russian soldier's martial virtues—largely passive—and his peasant background is clear: peasants arrived in the army fatalistic and inured to hard work and hardship.[6]

The officer corps was more heterogeneous. It had never been composed exclusively of the nobility, at least not since the days of Peter the Great. As of 1721, at least 17 percent of officers in the line infantry and cavalry were not of noble origin; the proportion of commoners probably remained at roughly the same level until the end of the eighteenth century, when the Russian army—and the officer corps—expanded rapidly during the Napoleonic wars. By the middle of the nineteenth century, the hereditary nobility supplied only half the officer corps, as it did in 1895, when only 50.8 percent of Tsarist officers (but 97.5 percent of full generals) were hereditary nobles.[7] Yet the invariance of the proportion noble in the second half of the nineteenth century masked a gradual change in the economic status of the noble officers. Due to the impoverishment of the nobility and the declining social prestige of the officer corps, the noble officer was less and less likely to be landed. By 1895, only 35 percent of Russia's full generals owned any property at all (and that usually not property in land); only 15.2 percent of lieutenant generals, 10.2 percent of the major generals on the General Staff, and 5.2 percent of the colonels on the General Staff owned any sort of property. The proportion with sizable holdings was much smaller, and among officers of lower rank the percentage of property owners must have been minuscule. Outside the socially exclusive Guards regiments, the typical officer—whether noble or not—was penurious.[8]

It was difficult to differentiate between officers who were and were not noble not only because their incomes were identical, but also because they shared a common life style. In an attempt to instill noblesse in the increasingly declassé officer corps, military schools in the latter part of the nineteenth century taught the social graces, and for the same purpose the government instituted regimental courts of honor and, in 1894, dueling for officers. Courts of honor and dueling sustained a cult of the uniform that impelled officers to behave in at least some respects like old regime nobles. Moreover, all officers indulged in varieties of social activity—heavy drinking, gambling, and other forms of boisterous behavior—that may with certain allowances be considered characteristic of the stereotypical Russian nobility. For all that, it is misleading to think of Russian officers—even most of those born to the degree—as impoverished nobles, or even as a group with a sense of unity.[9] Officer and soldier were not "different kinds of people" because one was an epigonous noble, the other a raw peasant. The difference was more fundamental than that.

Whatever his lineage, the officer came from Europeanized Russia, the peasant soldier from traditional Russia. This most fundamental of all divisions within Russian society dated from Peter the Great's reign. Peter quite deliberately cut the ties of the Russian elite to traditional Russia when in 1698, just back from Western Europe, he personally took scissors to the beards and loose garments of his startled nobles, ordered that suits of English fashion be hung at Moscow's gates, and commanded nobles and officials to copy them. Western fashion, almost immediately assimilated at court and in the bureaucracy, had by the late eighteenth century become standard even for provincial nobles on their isolated estates. But it was not then or later adopted by peasants, or by much of the tradition-bound merchantry or urban lower classes. So obvious were the implications of sumptuary differences that in the late 1870s the inferior classes were warned off from the fashionable Tauride Gardens in St. Petersburg by a sign reading "entrance forbidden to persons in Russian dress" (this in the capital of the Russian empire).[10] By the second half of the nineteenth century, nobility and elite were no longer coterminus, and not all of those who dressed in the Western manner belonged to the social, political, or cultural elites. Nevertheless, the meanest clerk in an ill-fitting frock coat lived in the ambit of the fashionable aristocratic salon rather than the world of the peasant hut.

Manner of dress, of course, stood for a complex of social and psychological traits. During the eighteenth and nineteenth centuries the domestic architecture, diet, and entertainments of the two Russias diverged in parallel with their dress. So did their language. That the late eighteenth century elite was as much at home in French as in Russian is less important than the fact that the Russian used in official society evolved until it became, as Alexander Herzen noted in 1851, "an undifferentiated flux of noise" to the peasant who had to make sense of it.[11] (The language of the army was equally foreign to the peasant conscript.) Behind the two Russian languages stood different ways of perceiving the world. However many exceptions there may have been, and however misleading the terms may be, the European Russian mentalité was rational and linear in a way that the peasant mentalité—nourished on the closed seasonal cycle and the arbitrary intrusion of the elements— was not.[12]

Not that the Russian peasant or peasant conscript was dull or necessarily illiterate. Indeed, the statistics on conscript literacy in the early twentieth century are impressive: roughly 50 percent of all draftees were judged literate by the army.[13] Even allowing for the fact that the army counted a conscript literate if he could not sign his name but could decipher a few syllables, this is a remarkably high figure given the state of Russia's primary school network—many literate conscripts had not attended public or church schools. Peasants had understood since at least the 1860s that the world was changing around them and that literacy and numeracy were essential for survival, and they had sought education even when formal schooling was unavailable. However, peasants acquired only the minimum of education necessary for self-defense, and they adopted enrollment strategies that ensured the education their children received would not threaten traditional village society.[14]

Russian peasants had always sought to deflect or propitiate the forces that intruded on the village, and they continued to do so at the turn of the century, adapting the village economy to the increasingly dynamic market while retaining the traditional social and economic functions of household and village. Urban goods and items of urban fashion—from galoshes and short jackets (incongruously combined with traditional garb) to brick construction—increasingly penetrated the village, urban names did not. The one reflected the hegemony of city over village, the other the peasants' unshaken sense of separate identity. Indeed, one could gauge the distance between peasant and European Russian by the names they bore: the peasants' Akulina and Fekla were unthinkable in polite society, the Olga and Elena of the city notably unpopular in the village. At the close of the nineteenth century, many peasants still lacked surnames; conscription boards assigned them by fiat.[15] Peasant Russia was changing, just as peasant societies have always responded to pressure from the urban world that dominates them. But peasant Russia continued to stand apart, tenaciously and deliberately, from European Russia. When peasant conscripts arrived in their units, the confrontation between officers and men was a confrontation between two different cultures.

That confrontation continued throughout the five or so years (fluctuating between six and four from 1874 to 1905) peasants served. The cultural schism within the army withstood even the efforts of Dmitrii Miliutin, a military reformer whose interests extended to social and political reform, to transform the Tsarist army into a modern, professional force and to make of the army a tool for achieving national unity. Miliutin served as Minister of War from 1861 to 1881, a period during which first the fresh impression of Russia's humiliation in the Crimean War, and then the stunning display of prowess by the Prussian army, created opportunities for reforms that a deeply conservative military establishment and a hesitant government would otherwise have blocked. Miliutin radically overhauled the system of military administration, attempted to bring Russian arms up to the Western standard, oversaw a revision of the regulations on tactical training, and sought to improve the quality of the Russian officers corps by establishing a new system of officer training schools that could for the first time provide formal military education for all officers and facilitate the advancement of talented commoners. Equally important to Miliutin was to improve the quality of enlisted personnel and eliminate the stigma of servility from service in the ranks.[16]

Prior to the emancipation of the serfs in 1861, military service had itself been a particularly brutal variant of serfdom. In the standing army created by Peter the Great, service was for life, a term later reduced to 25 years. State peasants and the taxable urban population were subject to conscription along with serfs, and in the army they were all enserfed. Length of service alone marked the soldier as a social outcast—if he survived his term he had no home to which to return—while the fact that the children he sired while in service were the property of the army underscored his status as chattel. This was a reality recognized in the rituals and laments with which peasants took leave of conscripts (the conscript lament itself emerging together with the standing army). The conscript's family feasted as if in memory of the dead, the conscript went on a socially sanctioned drunken spree while the womenfolk lamented at home, and finally the conscript paid his last respects to his relatives and friends, each of whom fed him and lamented over him.[17] The earliest extant lament for conscripts, recorded by Radischev in the late eighteenth century, illustrates the motif of loss and abandonment that persisted in the genre down to 1914:

> Child of my heart, to whom are you abandoning me?
> To whom are you entrusting your parents' home?
> Our fields will be overgrown with grass, our hut with moss.
> I, your poor old mother, must now wander the world.
> Who will warm me in my decrepitude, who shade me from the heat?
> Who will give me food and drink?[18]

The conscript lamented not only the loss of family, but also his lot in the army:

> The spring torrents will pour out,
> Our bitter tears will flow,
> During training, parent, during torment.
> They will beat us, unfortunates, without mercy,
> They will beat us, parent, until we bleed,
> Unto death they will beat our miserable heads,
> They will drive us, poor soldiers, through the gauntlet.[19]

"Beaten unto death" was a frequent refrain in the conscripts' laments, "bitter" the invariable epithet evoking the soldier's fate. The songs, sayings, and lore of military service were grim.[20] They were also reasonably accurate, though the folk vision gave little place to the monotonous routine of army life. Brutally beaten, degraded, utterly defenseless, the soldier in the serf era was the lowest and most unfortunate element in Russian society.

If the soldier serf was appropriate—inevitable, really—in a serf society with a standing army, he was no longer appropriate, either socially or militarily, after the Emancipation. The length of service meant, for one, that it was impossible to establish a reserve system: the annual draft was low, the number who annually completed their service lower still, and those mustered out of the army were in any case too old for further soldiering. The impossibility of adding significant numbers of trained reserves to the army during war had contributed to Russia's defeat in the Crimean War, and even before he became War Minister Miliutin urged that service be shortened and a proper reserve system be introduced. Shorter service would require more intensive training, which could best be effected by raising the educational level of the soldiers—by teaching illiterate draftees how to read and write, and by drafting more literates (who because of the correlation between literacy and social class were largely exempt from the draft). For military reasons alone, then, Miliutin believed that service must be shortened, liability to conscription made universal, and soldiers taught to read and write. Moreover, Miliutin had concluded as early as 1839 that more humane treatment of soldiers would improve the army's fighting capacity.[21]

But Miliutin had a broader, though unstated, purpose in urging these reforms. He had come of age when the Slavophiles were preaching that peasants were the bearers of Russian national character, when writers—Turgenev the most illustrious of them—had made peasants fit subjects for literature, and when the spokesmen for "official nationality" had insisted on the virtues of the "organic unity" of the Russian people. National character and the uniqueness of Russian society were the coin of discourse in intellectual circles in the second quarter of the nineteenth century, though the rediscovery of the peasant and the new appreciation for "organic unity" were themselves oblique testimony to the fundamental disunity of Russian society. Indeed, "Westernizers" had argued that only if Russia adopted Western social and political principles would the Russian peasant ultimately be lifted from the mire and debilitating social divisions be eliminated. Though Miliutin associated with Slavophiles and "official nationalists," and shared some of their views on Russian exceptionalism, his vision was more that of liberal Westernizers who looked to the government to steer Russia toward national unity through social and political reform. And just as he hoped that the Emancipation and other reforms in civilian society would make all Russians equal subjects of the Tsar and citizens of a united Russia, so Miliutin wished to use the army for national as well as military purposes. To educate soldiers and to make even the nobility liable to the draft (which was conceivable only if the term of service were reduced and conditions of service altered) would make the two Russias one within the army and foster unity in the nation at large.[22]

Among Miliutin's first steps as Minister of War was to eliminate the most obvious marks of the soldier's debasement. In 1862 he abolished the gauntlet and sharply curtailed corporal punishment. The conscripts of 1863 (the first after the Crimean War) were not required to stand naked for hours awaiting medical inspection but were allowed instead to wear shifts, their foreheads were not shaved to signify they had been taken, and they were not dressed in convicts' garb as they proceeded to their units.[23] Miliutin also went a long way toward turning the army into the school of the nation in the narrow sense. Immediately after the conclusion of the Crimean War, officers began to teach literacy classes in the winter months; the initiative seems to have been taken by junior officers gripped by the same missionary zeal that led their civilian contemporaries to teach Sunday classes for urban workers, but the Ministry of War seconded their efforts. Advocates of educating soldiers believed literacy would improve morale and morality, provide soldiers with a conscious appreciation of their obligations and rights, broaden their intellectual horizons, and even make it possible for conscript NCOs to achieve officer rank. Although in the 1860s not all regiments provided instruction in reading and writing, by the end of the decade reports arriving at the Ministry of War indicated that 50 percent of enlisted personnel were at least able to read, and that 28 percent could write. Military inspectors concluded that these figures were inflated and should be reduced by one-third, but even so the level of literacy in the army far surpassed the meager attainments of conscripts prior to service: in the late 1860s fewer than 10 percent of those drafted could meet the army's minimal test of literacy. Progress in elementary education continued in the 1870s, and in 1875 literacy instruction became mandatory for all illiterate conscripts.[24]

It was more difficult to introduce short-term service, a reserve system, and universal liability to the draft: generals believed that only long years in the army made reliable soldiers, while the nobility fought any loss of privilege. In the 1860s Miliutin circumvented opposition to short-term service by giving soldiers permanent leave after seven or eight years in the ranks; only after 1870 did resistance to the principle of short-term service and universal liability soften. The crucial convert to Miliutin's point of view was a former Minister of Interior, Valuev, who had been in Western Europe in 1870 and had witnessed the mobilization of the Prussian army during the Franco-Prussian War. Even with Valuev's support, it was not until 1874 that six-year active duty and universal liability became law (certain family situations secured exemption, enrollment in an educational institution earned deferment). The length of active service was reduced in proportion to the conscript's level of education because Miliutin believed that the most productive members of society should be permitted to contribute to national development as quickly as possible. Additionally, those with a secondary or higher education who volunteered were rewarded with an even shorter term in the line (as little as a year), and could then qualify for admission to the officer corps. The details of the regulations for volunteers were heatedly contested, because conservatives feared that too many commoners would become officers by this route. But the principle of national unity triumphed over the tradition of class privilege in this matter as in the new conscription law in general. Echoing what Miliutin had long argued, Alexander II proclaimed in his manifesto on universal liability to military service that "The strength of the State . . . is based chiefly on the moral and intellectual qualities of the army, which can be fully developed only on condition that the defense of the country has become the common task of the people, and when all, without distinction of rank or class, unite in the sacred cause."[25]

Miliutin's reforms achieved at least a part of their military purpose—after 1874 the army could be rapidly expanded in time of war—but the reformed army did not foster social cohesion. After Miliutin's resignation in 1881, even schooling in the most restricted sense fell into disfavor. During the 1880s literacy instruction became optional, and by the 1890s had largely been abandoned. Miliutin's successor, Petr Vannovskii (Minister of War 1881–1898) suspected that education was harmful for soldiers, a view shared by many officers. Officers were as likely as not to make fun of soldiers who had the itch to read, and junior officers who continued after 1881 to view the dispensation of enlightenment as a part of their mission were mistrusted by their superiors and occasionally ordered to desist. Even when mandatory courses in literacy were reinstituted in 1902 (and then only in the infantry and artillery), officers satisfied the higher staffs by routinely writing up fictional accounts of classes taught.[26]

Neither Russia ever accepted the notion that in the ranks of the army all were equal. The reaction of the nobility to the 1874 reform was typified by the mass resignation of young nobles without military education who were marking time as junkers in the Guards before receiving commissions. Required under the new rules of service to spend a year in the ranks as volunteers and risk treatment as ordinary soldiers, they preferred to find alternative careers.[27] The young nobles need not have worried. Members of the educated classes who served in the ranks, either as volunteers or under other circumstances, never became a leaven in the soldier mass. Peasant conscripts were suspicious of them, while officers assigned them light duties (in company offices, for instance) and treated them as social equals.[28]

Officers could not treat volunteers as they did ordinary soldiers because, as Captain Anton Denikin (later to lead the Whites against the Reds) wrote in 1903, they could not conceive of soldiers as fellow men.[29] The soldiers' inferiority was codified in military regulations: soldiers were forbidden to smoke in public (or in the presence of officers), to ride first or second class on the railroad (this regulation was adjusted to technological change in 1908, when soldiers were additionally forbidden to ride inside street cars), or to enter buildings where alcoholic beverages were served.[30] Signs in major cities and garrison towns banned "soldiers and dogs" from walking on major streets, in public gardens, or in some cases on sidewalks.[31]

More important than the myriad restrictions on the soldiers' behavior and movements was the mentality that underlay them. Officers addressed soldiers not with the polite "you" (*vy*) but with the familiar "thou" (*ty*), used with animals, children, and social inferiors. When progressive officers pointed out that use of the familiar demeaned soldiers, most officers responded that it had always been thus, while a few argued learnedly that use of the polite form was a Petrine innovation and as such foreign to the Russian village.[32] True enough—and soldiers understood that the familiar denoted their inferiority as members of peasant Russia. Regimental commanders gave newly commissioned officers private tuition in the use of "multi-story" Russian curses, explaining that soldiers could not be made to do anything unless they were roundly abused.[33] The incidence of physical abuse had declined by the late nineteenth century, but there was nothing out of the ordinary in an officer striking a soldier. Striking a volunteer or any other soldier from educated society was, of course, unthinkable. The peasant soldier understood that in the matter of beatings as in the familiar, his inferior standing derived from his social origin rather than his military rank—it was as natural to him as to his officer that he, but not the ex-student, would be beaten before he left the army.[34] These attitudes, deeply imbedded in Russian society, survived the Miliutin and all subsequent military reforms. The reform of military institutions did not alter the character of Russian society, rather it was Russian society—in particular the two cultural systems that coexisted in it—that shaped the army as a social institution, the psychology of officers and soldiers, and the views they had of each other.

The Tsarist Army's Peasant Economy

Some Tsarist officers believed that, whether or not formal education were provided, service in the army "civilized" peasants. As one put it, the conscript's military career began "with a bath and a haircut," then proceeded to "cleanliness and neatness in dress." Conscripts were "taught to speak, look, turn and move with military precision," and they learned new words and concepts—the intricate grammar of the military hierarchy, the catechism of the soldiers' duties and military virtues. In sum, "the wholly rough-hewn and rude peasant conscript receives, in the broad sense of the word, a human finish."[35] The attitude toward peasant soldiers revealed in that statement is one more illustration of the cultural abyss that divided officers and men, but if phrased in neutral terms the proposition is superficially plausible. It accords with the view of military sociologists and modernization theorists that service in the army—an institution with a formal hierarchy, abstract rules, and precisely defined patterns of behavior—instills not only "new habits of dress, of cleanliness, of teamwork," but even "a new personality," "a new sense of identity."[36] But the Tsarist army did not remake the peasant personality, and not just because civilian cultural patterns overrode formal military institutions: the structure of Tsarist military service itself sustained peasant habits and peasant attitudes.

The regimental economy rather than military training shaped the soldier's duties. This was the result ultimately of Russia's relative socioeconomic backwardness, but more specifically of the fact that in the late nineteenth century the government restrained military spending in order to finance economic and social development. Russia's military budget did grow steadily, from 256 million rubles in 1881 (206 million in 1882, a more representative year) to 326 million rubles in 1902, but this represented a declining share of the national budget: from 30 percent in 1881 (26 percent in 1882) to 18 percent in 1902. As William Fuller has shown, the Russian army, with nearly a million men, received in the period 1881–1902 just barely more money than the German and French armies, which were not much more than half as large as the Russian. In 1893, Russia spent only 57 percent as much per soldier as Germany, only 63 percent as much as France.[37] Indeed, it was in the maintenance of soldiers that the greatest economies were made. Striving to achieve parity in armaments, the Ministry of War economized on the upkeep of soldiers and so transferred the financial pressure downwards: tactical units were forced to be, in large measure, self-supporting.

A typical line regiment spent annually up to 5,000 rubles more than it received from the Ministry of War, but the cash deficit was less important than the deficit in kind covered by the liberal use of soldier manpower for nonmilitary purposes. The commissariat provided basic foodstuffs, or money for the purchase of comestibles on the market, but to maintain an adequate diet regiments cultivated their own gardens and orchards wherever feasible, and even kept some cattle. The commissariat provided the raw material for boots and uniforms, but the regiment produced them (in 1907, 12 percent of all enlisted personnel— 150,000 soldiers—spent their duty hours tailoring). Prior to 1906, the commissariat provided neither money nor raw materials for blankets, coats, felt boots, utensils, or other necessities; these the regiment had to produce or acquire on its own. Every regiment maintained workshops staffed by soldiers permanently detailed to production, but soldiers from line companies as well did duty as tailors, cobblers, carpenters, cooks, and gardeners. They also served as stable hands, singers, musicians, church attendants, batmen, and lackeys in the officers' club.[38]

During the eight or nine months a regiment spent in its barracks, forty or more of the one-hundred-odd men in a company spent their time on these duties. Since most other soldiers were on guard or serving as duty orderlies, the total number of men free for the training prescribed in the regulations was low: one officer estimated that on an average day only one or two soldiers, in rare cases as many as ten, were free for drill; another figured five to eight men were available for drill on most days, twenty in exceptional circumstances.[39] Only in the three months of summer camp was an appreciable number of men free for training, and even then roughly half the strength of the regiment was left at winter quarters for sentry duty, barracks repair, and other housekeeping chores. What with guard duty, rehearsals for review, and miscellaneous details, not much time was left for drill even in camp.[40] Military training, clearly, was near the bottom of the regiment's priorities. What training a soldier received was episodic, and it is not difficult to believe a report that, after the four months of intensive post-induction drill a Russian soldier's military skills steadily deteriorated, reaching a low point just before he was discharged into the reserves.[41]

Liberal employment of men for production and upkeep seriously impaired training but still left the regiment woefully short of money to obtain needed supplies. Funds could be diverted from budgeted expenditures to unbudgeted but more pressing needs; though illegal, this was an unavoidable necessity in every unit.[42] Yet the money available for misappropriation was itself inadequate. The only resource a regiment had in relative abundance was labor, so commanders dispatched soldiers to earn money in the civilian economy through "vol'nye raboty" ("civilian work"). After the summer encampment, soldiers spent a month or two working away from their units; part of the money earned went into the regiment's coffers, part the soldiers were allowed to keep for themselves.[43] The detrimental impact of vol'nye raboty on military efficiency was obvious. As General Dragomirov, commander of the Kiev military district, wrote in 1899,

> In July enlisted men are usually off mowing hay, working in forests, on railway lines and on construction in the cities; they ruin their clothing; they acquire an external aspect entirely unsuitable [for military service], they become unaccustomed to discipline and lose their military bearing.[44]

Between 1900 and 1902, serious consideration was given to banning this migratory labor entirely, but regimental finances dictated otherwise. Dragomirov, who strongly favored a ban, concluded that this was impossible—the money soldiers earned was needed to purchase supplies. Another officer noted that he had to issue blankets to his men from the unit's permanent stores, the stores had to be replenished to the regulation level, no money was allocated for this, so there was no alternative to collecting money soldiers earned.[45] The money earned was considerable: regiments acquired an average of 3–5,000 rubles. In 1900, soldiers in the Warsaw military district brought 500,000 rubles back to their regiments, in 1903 they returned with over 600,000 rubles. There being no alternate source of revenue, migratory labor continued, though work that might endanger the soldiers—such as operating agricultural machinery—was forbidden. Only in the St. Petersburg military district were vol'nye raboty banned, in 1900.[46]

The austerity that the Ministry of War transferred to the regiments was in turn passed down to the soldier; as the regiment had to produce its own goods and finance much of its operations, so the soldier paid for much of his kit. Until 1906, soldiers provided for themselves soap, spoons, boot brushes and polish, oil and rags for cleaning rifles, in many units blankets, bedlinen, shirts, and so forth. Some small funds were distributed to soldiers so they could obtain necessities that the army was supposed to issue (unlike those in the foregoing list) but for one reason or another did not; these funds never covered the market cost.[47]

The most burdensome expenses were associated with the soldier's boots. According to regulations, soldiers were to receive two pairs of boots per annum, but since regimental commanders preferred to amass stocks, soldiers had to make do with one pair. And army-issue boots were renowned for their poor quality, lasting no more than three months—they did, quite literally, disintegrate. As one officer wrote, after summer camp and maneuver, "soldiers are in most cases barefoot."[48] That was not hyperbole. Another officer described the Chinese landscape after a Russian detachment marched through in 1900:

> The entire road was strewn with the boots of the 2nd battalion, which had preceded us. These implements of soldiers' torment, specially designed by the commissariat, lay about with only the remainders of soles, like sharks with their teeth bared.[49]

Since soldiers could not get by without boots (were indeed required to keep them in proper shape), they had no choice but to repair boots at their own expense, which could run to as much as 4 rubles per year even if the work were done by the company cobblers.[50]

The cost of repairing boots was alone greater than the soldier's pay. Prior to 1906, a Russian private received 2 rubles 70 kopeks per year (as against 13 rubles in the French army, 36 rubles in the German army). According to one officer's computation, the soldier's minimum annual budget in 1903 was 23 rubles 58 kopeks, producing a deficit of 20 rubles 88 kopeks. Another officer came up with a minimum budget of 10 rubles 86 kopeks by eliminating, among other things, repair of boots (it was the soldier's fault if his boots wore out, he should be expected to pay for repairs himself), tobacco (harmful), and entertainment outside the barracks (soldiers can sing and play games inside the barracks, and they ought not to mix with civilians in any case).[51] The budgets officers drew up tell us as much about officers as about the soldiers' expenses, but all agreed that soldiers needed a great deal more money than they were paid.

Soldiers obtained the money they needed from a variety of sources. They kept a part of the money earned through seasonal labor. Many received money from home, but usually not enough to cover expenses; at least half of the soldiers in a unit were "in need" even after family subsidies. Soldiers also sold part of their daily 3-pound bread ration; officers, embarrassed by soldiers and civilians haggling over the price of bread just outside the barracks, attempted in vain to end the practice. The 30 or so kopeks per month soldiers earned in this way exceeded their monthly pay of 22½ kopeks. As a last resort, soldiers begged on the streets.[52]

As hard as his lot was, there is no reason to believe that the Russian soldier experienced it as special hardship, still less as something traumatic or psychologically disorienting. The psychological burdens were confined to the four months of intensive training after induction.[53]

After that, the soldier's life resembled the familiar peasant routine. Poverty itself was familiar, as was the spectrum of quite unmilitary daily activities. Like the village, the regiment tried and failed to be self-sufficient, and like the village, the regiment had to participate in the market economy. Individual soldiers marketed what surplus they had, but since their surplus was meager they joined the migratory labor force to augment their own and the regiment's income.

Even the seasonal rhythm that shaped life in the village was replicated in the army. Units set off for the summer encampments in early May. Field exercises, the most exhausting part of the annual cycle, ended in late July or early August. At that point, soldiers who had completed their term were discharged from service; a few others were given leave; most of the rest set off in search of work (the number of men present in the regiment fell from 1,800 to about 300). Training was supposed to resume in mid-October, but with soldiers off doing one thing and another no start could be made until mid-November—and then end-of-year holidays intervened. What training there was took place in the four months between the new year and the onset of field exercises, but soldiers spent most of their time doing the chores required to keep the regimental household in working order.[54] Not only was military life as cyclical as peasant life, the modulations of the two cycles were virtually identical.

The Moral Economy: Exploitation, Distance, Incomprehension

The underfunding of the army (or, reading the equation the other way, the excessive size of the military establishment) would by itself necessarily have produced something like the regiment's peasant economy, but the regimental economy also reflected (and shaped) the officers' attitude toward their men. Regiments had been employing soldiers to produce provisions and supplies since the formation of the regular army in the eighteenth century, in that early period as much because of logistical as of budgetary difficulties. By the early nineteenth century at the latest, regiments—taking advantage of the expansion of the market economy and the rising demand for mobile labor—were adding to their resources by hiring out soldiers for part of the year, and by mid-century regimental commanders required companies to earn a specified sum through contract labor. After the Napoleonic wars, Alexander I sought to make a virtue of necessity by converting much of the army into farming settlements ("military colonies"): if soldiers devoted yet more time to production, a larger army could be maintained. In modified form, some of these settlements lasted through the Crimean

War. Even soldiers not in the settlements spent a good part of the year in agricultural labor, helping out the peasants on whom they were quartered. When the army moved into regular barracks in the late nineteenth century, agricultural labor became less common (the regimental gardens remained as a vestigial legacy of the soldier cultivators), while artisanal production became relatively more prominent. But soldiers were still hired out for harvesting, and as new labor markets opened—in railroad construction, for instance—soldiers moved into them, too.[55] Irrespective of the specific needs of the regimental economy, cumulative military practice dictated that soldiers constituted a labor resource to be deployed in whatever way provided maximum advantage to the regiment. While in the early 1900s some officers worried that production cut into training, to most the regimental economy seemed part of the natural order of things: this was the way the regiment had always operated, hence the way it was supposed to operate.

A direct corollary of the functioning of the regimental economy was that officers dealt with soldiers chiefly as units of labor. Because of the authority military regulations vested in officers, the soldier as laborer was indistinguishable from a serf. General Dragomirov observed in 1900 that "so-called 'civilian work' is in essence forced labor, with overtones of serfdom. Formerly the serf-owner hired out his own peasants, now the military commander does the same."[56] Another officer added that not only did contract labor "accustom the commander to view his men as serfs; from this it is but a short step to the use of soldiers as free labor."[57] Short indeed, though "civilian work" was only a contributory factor. The colonel in Saratov who in the early 1900s hired out the men and carriages of his regiment for funeral corteges was atypical only in his inventiveness: colonels all over the empire looked on their regiments as estates to be exploited as they pleased. The proceeds from such operations might benefit the colonel personally, or they might provide money for regimental needs, but in either case soldiers were an economic resource free for the using. Officers of all ranks employed soldiers in their private gardens or as household labor, ordered up household goods from the regimental workshops, and used their men to build comfortable cottages at summer encampments.[58] From appropriating the soldiers' labor it was but another short step to appropriating their money. Officers occasionally pocketed the money soldiers received from home, in some cases they kept the soldier's pay. When soldiers were given money to purchase supplies, they could be required to buy from their commanders, who took a middleman's cut.[59] Even the military press admitted that officers who contracted their men out as labor gangs received kickbacks from landlords (because the going rate for soldiers was about half the rate for civilian labor) or took a cut of the soldier's earnings for themselves.[60]

Appropriation of the soldiers' labor and earnings was essential to the functioning of the regiment, but the exploitation of soldiers went beyond economic necessity. Officers felt free to use their men for personal gain because they considered them not military subordinates but inferior beings. Officers knew in their bones that regulations against theft and graft did not apply to their operations with peasant soldiers to any greater degree than did regulations against abusing soldiers physically. It did not occur to officers to end or conceal their exploitation of free soldier labor because the conventions of educated Russian society did not apply to dealings with peasants: officers had an unquestioned right to treat their men as a servile work force. Soldiers took this rule for granted, too: just as soldiers expected officers to strike them, so they expected officers to exploit them economically. As the soldier proverb had it, "Soldiers' calluses fill officers' bellies."[61] Soldiers translated even the impersonal operations of the regimental economy into personal terms. To them it made no difference whether money earned through *vol'nye raboty* went to the regimental coffers or the captain's private account, no difference whether money budgeted for food was diverted to the gaming table or barracks repair. Soldiers believed that every time money passed through their officers' hands, officers gained and soldiers lost.[62] Lamented the conscripts of northern Russia:

> From the Tsar good food is delivered,
> From the good Tsarina drink is provided,
> Among officers it's at once divided.[63]

That officers did frequently take advantage of their men could only confirm the soldiers' perception that their social inferiority was calculated into every transaction.

If economic exploitation was one of the axes ordering relations between officers and men, social distance was the other. The principal items in the soldier's time budget were economic chores and sentry duty, and neither required the physical presence of officers. The Sergeant Major handled what little training there was while officers tended the books. Not only were soldiers left to themselves, the soldier community was—within the framework of externally imposed duties—autonomous and egalitarian. Neither characteristic is normal in modern armies, and neither would have been possible had there been a proper hierarchy of noncommissioned officers. In the Tsarist army, there was only a rudimentary hierarchy within the soldiers' world, because there were very few long-term NCOs. Miliutin had recognized that the rapid training required in a short-service army depended upon the retention of a permanent cadre of noncoms, but no combination of inducements could persuade Russian soldiers to reenlist in adequate numbers. In the late 1870s, two-thirds of the Sergeant Majors were first-term conscripts, as were almost 90 percent of the other NCOs (corporals *not* included). By the early twentieth century, the Sergeant Major was ordinarily a reenlistee, and in a small proportion of companies one or two of the other NCOs were, leaving the Tsarist army with proportionately fewer reenlisted NCOs than any other European army: slightly more than one per company, as against twelve long-term NCOs in a German and six in a French company. All other noncom slots were filled by literate conscripts given some extra training, but they were NCOs only on paper. The conscript NCO might be a natural leader because of his greater literacy, but ordinary soldiers did not consider themselves subordinate to him in a military sense.[64] Except for the Sergeant Major, who wielded immense power and was the intermediary to the distant world of officers, all the men in the company were equals.

Within this company of equals, soldiers formed groups in the manner of all peasants away from their village. The most informal was the *zemliachestvo (Landsmannschaft)*, a group of conscripts from the same region (induction centers sent men to the same units every year, regiments received conscripts from a limited number of districts, so no soldier was without *zemliaki—Landsleute*—in his unit). The *zemliachestvo* had no formal structure or functions, but it did provide the soldier with his primary set of associational ties and reinforced his identity as a peasant from such and such a district.[65] The *zemliachestvo* was an exclusive group, while all soldiers belonged to the company *artel'*. In the army, the *artel'* was primarily a messing arrangement, but it functioned in much the same way as the civilian *artel'*. The company chose an *artel'shchik*—their spokesman, treasurer, and purchasing agent—who was responsible for obtaining food and sundry other soldiers' necessities with funds provided by the company commander and the soldiers themselves. Within limits, soldiers determined what the company purchased. The company *artel'* did not have production or contracting functions within the regiment as did the *artel'* formed by peasants who left their village in search of work: the Sergeant Major, rather than the *artel'shchik*, was responsible for allocating work assignments. On the other hand, groups of soldiers were frequently permitted to constitute themselves as an *artel'* to search out and conclude contracts for "civilian work," and in that capacity the soldier *artel'* was identical to any *artel'* formed by peasants or day laborers.[66]

Soldiers valued the autonomy and self-management that was customary in the company, and invariably the most detested officers were those who supervised their men closely. It was the fact of officer intrusion in the barracks that soldiers resented, not the results. Units in which officers took an interest in the welfare of their men were the best clothed, the best shod, and the best fed, but that made no difference to soldiers. They preferred—and performed best for—the officer who let his unit run itself, even if they suffered some privation in consequence.[67] Soldiers disliked improving officers for the same reason that peasants disliked improving landlords: they saw in better management only new methods for exploiting them. Since they believed that officers always sought to cheat them, soldiers could make sense of officer intervention in the soldiers' affairs in no other way. Suspicion was suspended only in the case of a very few officers, generally fresh out of military school, who were transparently eager to be decent to their men. But soldiers did not understand these young idealists any better than they understood officers whose main interest was efficiency: to the soldier, the idealistic young lieutenant was a *chudak*, a combination simpleton and eccentric, someone to be treated kindly, even protectively, but not to be taken seriously.[68]

From improving officers to the seasonal cycle, from the *zemliachestvo* to migratory labor, the world of the Russian soldier bore a strong resemblance to the world of the Russian peasant. Whatever the formal tables of military organization and the prescriptions of the training manuals, the soldier spent his time performing chores much like those he did at home, earned money as he had at home, and worked according to the peasants' seasonal rhythm. Human relations in the army were familiar, too. Peasants knew that the world beyond the village was full of snares, that every stranger and everyone in Western garb wished to prey upon the peasant, just as urban, educated, official Russia (the three were the same to peasants) taxed, conscripted, and otherwise arbitrarily exploited peasants. In the army, officers—educated and official Russia by definition—preyed on soldiers, and one had to be on guard against their wiles. Peasants sought to deal with gentry and officials from a distance; soldiers preferred officers not to meddle in the company. By and large, officers played the role peasant soldiers assigned them—powerful outsiders who battened on soldiers but generally did not meddle in the company's internal affairs. The regiment was physically unlike the village, the soldier was far from home and—by the early twentieth century—quite likely in or near a city, but the economic and social structures of military service sustained his peasant mentality.

There were variants on this basic pattern. Life in the cavalry, engineers, and artillery differed in some details from life in the infantry, and the cossacks were in a class by themselves. The Guards variant deserves special mention, not just because service in the Guards had unique features, but also because of their political significance as the core of the capital's garrison. Both the officers and the men of the Guards were exceptional. Soldiers were selected for height and physique (and matched to units by hair color and physical type), officers were chosen for lineage and wealth. Postings in some Guards regiments passed from father to son, all officers had to be wealthy enough to function in high society (an outside income of 100 rubles per month was considered the minimum in the least expensive regiment), and the officers of a regiment could veto a candidate if he did not meet their social standards.[69] Nevertheless, Guards regiments operated in much the same way as line regiments: the same preoccupation with economic chores (Guards regiments had the largest gardens in the army), the same "civilian work" (until 1900), the same seasonable cycle.[70] The cruder forms of exploitation were lacking—Guards officers had no need of the soldiers' pittance—but the soldiers of the Guards provided the same pool of free labor as in the line.

However, Guards officers were not mere exploiters of soldier labor, they also provided patronage. Officers paid for sumptuous rations on regimental and company holidays (only in the Guards did companies have traditional feasts), extra rations and extra vodka or beer on other special occasions, and for the occasional company visit to the brothel. Guards officers bought their men special items of equipment (in the Guards cavalry, for instance, new white gloves for conscripts after they had passed their first test of horsemanship), and they provided Christmas trees and distributed Christmas presents. Guards officers might also give emergency financial assistance to the families of their men.[71] Soldiers in the Guards understood that their officers' munificence was exceptional, but the practice of patronage had analogues in peasant society: periodic manorial feasts and the lord's protection in an emergency as a means to retain fealty, that is, in exchange for the right to control and exploit a subject population. Many Guards officers no doubt had learned this method of treating inferiors on their family estates. So long as patronage was forthcoming, the exchange worked in peasant society, and it worked in the Guards.

If a steady flow of patronage set the Guards apart, so did the Imperial presence. Every regiment had Grand Dukes on the roll, and these royal officers contributed their share of patronage. And, because of the Tsar's traditional attachment to the Guards, and because of rotating sentry duty at the various imperial residences, Guards soldiers periodically set their eyes upon the Tsar himself. The Tsar strolling through the palace might even speak to a soldier, in which case the Imperial words were reported in a regimental order of the day.[72] This physical proximity to the Tsar brought soldiers respect in their native villages, but also some puzzlement. One Guards officer reported (how accurately is hard to say) that even in the early twentieth century his men returning from leave related that the villagers did not understand how a soldier could survive sight of the Tsar, because the Tsar always sat on a golden throne and radiated light so brilliant that to behold it was to be struck dead.[73] The men of the Guards were not so naive as that, at least not after they had lived through their first glimpse of the Tsar, but they were certainly awed, and felt privileged to serve in the Guards. Yet the soldier in the Guards remained a peasant, in his attitude toward the Tsar as in the cycle of his duties and his relations with his officers—a privileged peasant, but a peasant nonetheless.

And so the two cultures of Russia, traditional and European, met in the army, but did not join. The cultural barrier that stood between officers and men transcended the hierarchical division between authority and subordination, and it was impermeable. Not only did officers and men not understand each other, they did not know that they did not understand. Soldiers misread the intentions of efficient and idealistic officers. They understood condescension and exploitation well enough, but not that there might be some purpose beyond personal enrichment in their officers' actions. For their part, the officer who believed that nightly readings from the regimental history entertained and edified his men and who never used his fists, and the officer who believed one had to hit a soldier to get his attention but read edifying tales written in a language closer to the soldiers' own, were equally distant from their men, yet both believed they had established rapport. Officers genuinely believed that the ritual dialogue in which they frequently engaged soldiers—"What province are you from?" "What village?" "Do you have a girl waiting at home?"—established bonds of understanding and trust.[74] While a number of critically minded officers appreciated the defects of the regimental economy, very few found fault with relations between officers and men. Aside from infrequent theft and beatings, they saw—whether writing in 1900 or 1925—only a benevolent paternalism that produced mutual affection. One who did detect a discordant note was the reactionary General Petr Krasnov. In his novelistic account of life in the Tsarist army, *Ot Dvuglavogo Orla k krasnomu znameni (From Double Eagle to Red Flag)*, a soldier of worker background explains to his squadron commander why an officer could never be close to his men:

> "What sort of conversations do you have with the soldiers?—'What province are you from?' . . . 'And your district? County?' 'Are your parents alive?

Your trade?' Just as though you were a magistrate or police officer. The soldier dislikes that. You ought to tell them about yourself . . . . But of course you can't . . . Your life is different . . . And he can't tell you the truth about himself. How could he tell you that he stole twenty kopeks from a peddler, or that he sold a ration of oats to a baker, or jabbed his horse with a pitchfork while he was goofing off?"[75]

In the same novel, one officer remarks: "Horses are beasts, the men are beasts, ignorant. Both are incomprehensible, but strong. Suppose they decide to make war on us?" To which another replies: "Hit them on the snout, nothing will happen."[76] Only in an emigré novel would it occur to an officer even to suggest that soldiers might rebel. Virtually without exception, officers considered their men childlike (or, in the Guards, "simple childlike giants"), naive, sometimes deceitful, nearly always stupid, and utterly dependent upon officers. Were officers wrong? If asked what he was doing or why he was doing it, the soldier could not explain himself. Asked the name of a nearby village, or how to get to headquarters, the soldier replied, as per military formula, "I cannot know" *(ne mogu znat')*, the standard answer to all questions.[77] The soldier's stupidity was writ large—which was just what the soldier intended. Avoiding a direct response, or responding only after careful consideration, was a defensive reaction. The soldier—as one officer at least understood—"has been taught this wisdom by life and discipline. He knows from experience that officers sometimes pose treacherous questions."[78] The wisdom of stupidity was peasant wisdom. As Tolstoy once remarked to Maxim Gorky,

In real life muzhiks [peasants] speak stupidly, awkwardly, at first you can't tell what they're trying to say. That's done on purpose, the desire to lead the other man on is always concealed beneath the apparent stupidity of their words. A true muzhik never shows what's on his mind straight away, that wouldn't suit him. He knows people approach a stupid person simply and guilelessly, and that's just what he wants. You stand revealed before him, he sees all your weak spots at once. He is mistrustful, he is afraid to tell his secret thoughts even to his wife.[79]

Tolstoy exaggerated: not all peasant stupidity was art. There was much beyond the village that was genuinely incomprehensible to peasants, just as there was a great deal about the officer and his world that baffled soldiers. Yet even in this regard obstinate stupidity masked the extent of the soldier's secret insecurities from the officer whom he mistrusted.

Dissembling was not unique to Russian peasants and soldiers, and Russian officers were not alone in being deceived. What made the soldiers' deception of their officers so convincing was that it was not really deception at all. Soldiers were genuinely submissive to their officers, they did behave like devious and dependent children. They endured hardship and risked their lives without audible complaint. Uncle Tom behavior was instinctive to the peasant, and to the soldier who was a peasant in all but dress, whenever he had to deal with the educated and the powerful. Transferred to the army, the peasant method of coping with gross disparities in power appeared as exemplary discipline and commendable deference to paternalistic officers—precisely the traits that Russian and foreign officers identified as the principal virtues of the Tsarist army. There was little difference here between genuine and simulated deference, and the difference if any was irrelevant in the routine of military life. So long as they saw no way to escape the clutches of the powerful, peasant and soldier submitted to the inevitable, to all appearances meekly. Even the soldiers were not fully aware of their deeper urge to cast down the European Russia that oppressed them.

II. Enemies Domestic: Russia Moves toward Revolution

A Brief Socio-Military History of Nineteenth-Century Russia

Cultural dualism was a persistent feature of Russian society, and so of its army, but Russia was scarcely unchanging. And naturally, shifts in the contours of Russian society affected the army—not just its organization, the treatment of soldiers, and the sources of regimental income, but also the use to which regiments were put. In the late nineteenth and early twentieth century, all of the major currents in Russian society—peasant unrest, the growth of the factory proletariat, pogroms, student disorders, the emergence of a mass revolutionary movement—pressed against the army.

It had always been one of the army's functions to contain civilian discontent, from the early eighteenth century deployment of the new Petrine regiments against anti-Petrine rebellions, through the campaigns against the Pugachev rebellion in the 1770s and the Polish insurrections of 1830–31 and 1863, to the use of small detachments to suppress minor but chronic peasant disturbances and occasional major plague and cholera riots. Through the 1860s most disorders involved serfs. Crop failures, the reorganization of land use and labor services by serf owners, rumors of emancipation, rumors that a newly enthroned Tsar would curb the gentry, real changes in peasant legislation that peasants took to be justification for their resistance to the exactions of gentry and officials—almost everything that impinged on the peasantry provoked disorders at one time or another. Certainly peasants had ample reason to rebel, and in the first half of the nineteenth century the number of minor peasant (mostly serf) disorders rose from decade to decade. Yet whatever their cause, they did not pose a threat to the established order, partly because they rarely involved more than a brief confrontation with the authorities, partly because troops were generously employed—in roughly 50 percent of all disturbances from the 1820s through the 1840s—to overawe the serfs.[1]

A more serious wave of serf disorders involving mass flight to the Crimea struck during and immediately after the Crimean War. Unrest was spurred by rumors, first, that service in the militia would earn emancipation, and then that serfs repopulating the Crimea would be freed. Though troops brought the runaways under control, these disorders contributed to the government's decision to emancipate the serfs even in the face of stiff gentry resistance. Talk of impending emancipation triggered hundreds of disorders, and troops were again called out against the serfs—245 times between 1857 and 1860—but the continued unrest impelled the government to hasten emancipation and increase the amount of land alloted to liberated serfs. The most serious wave of peasant unrest, however, came after the announcement of emancipation in March 1861, because the terms grievously betrayed the serfs' expectation that they would receive free of charge all the land they had previously worked. Rumors abounded that the gentry had suppressed the true terms of emancipation, and in the confusion over the very complex legislation and in the wish to believe that the Tsar had granted them "true liberty," there were in the first five months of 1861 in excess of 1,340 disorders (rising to over 1,800 by the end of the year), with troops called out 718 times. Occasionally, troops fired on mutinous peasants, as at Bezdna in Kazan Province, where on April 12, 1861, between fifty-five and seventy peasants died.[2]

Peasant unrest receded quickly after 1861, the incidence of agrarian disorders oscillating around fifty per year (about the same as in the last decade before the Crimean War) from the late 1860s through the end of the century.[3] Most incidents stemmed from the peasants' conviction that they had the right to use gentry-owned forests and fields to which they had previously had access (attempts to survey and properly demark gentry estates often triggered deliberate mass infringements of property rights). The establishment of new administrative institutions also touched off peasant disorders, as for instance when the introduction of "land captains"—local nobles appointed beginning in 1889 to tighten fiscal and administrative control over peasants—triggered rumors that serfdom was being reestablished, and that flogging machines were being employed against recalcitrant peasants.[4] Local officials were usually able to persuade peasants to meet their fiscal obligations and respect property rights (at least for the time being), but when exhortation failed officials routinely summoned troops to the villages in about 20 percent of all peasant disorders. Almost without exception the mere presence of a detachment or even the news that soldiers were approaching brought peasants to their knees.[5]

The incidence of peasant unrest was no more threatening, and the incidence of military suppression lower, than before the Crimean War, but the context in which peasant disorders occurred was very different. Between Emancipation and the close of the nineteenth century, steady expansion of the market for agricultural goods and of opportunities for earnings outside the village triggered a 40-percent increase in agricultural productivity, sustained a 46-percent increase in population, and left 50 percent of the peasantry dependent upon off-farm income for at least part of their livelihood. Peasants did not believe that these changes, or the flood of cheap manufactured goods into the villages, left them better off. Instinctively, they came to believe that the way to maintain the equilibrium of village society was to acquire more land, especially the gentry's land, much of which they were already renting or otherwise working. In the 1870s, rumors of an impending "black repartition" (*chernyi peredel*, the redistribution of all land to the peasants) began to circulate for the first time. As the nineteenth century ended, the conviction that all land—not just their pre-Emancipation holdings—belonged to peasants by right and tradition had taken firm hold in the villages, and within a few years this newly minted tradition would find expression in widespread peasant rebellion. It was characteristic of peasant dependence on the urban world that the rumors originated in the city, which was simultaneously creating the conditions that suggested to peasants the need for black repartition.[6]

The city was the center of the commercial and industrial development that from the 1860s on so unsettled rural Russia, though much industry was in fact plunked down in rural areas to take advantage of cheap peasant labor. Following the Crimean War, the Tsarist government encouraged industrial development, first by facilitating the expansion of credit facilities and the construction of railroads, at the end of the nineteenth century by purposefully employing railroad construction to stimulate heavy industry and by aggressively promoting foreign investment. And these measures were effective. Between 1860 and 1883 the output of industry grew by a healthy 5½ percent annually, the growth rate rising to a robust 8 percent annual average in the 1890s.[7] As industry grew, so did the number of workers in factories, mines, and the railroads—from around 850,000 in the 1860s to almost 3,700,000 in 1900—and the number of strikes. Virtually nonexistent through the 1860s, strikes became ordinary if not very frequent occurrences (20 to 40 a year) in the 1870s and 1880s, and exploded during the industrial boom of the 1890s: over 100 per year by 1895, over 200 per year by 1898.[8]

The volatility of the industrial proletariat imposed a new responsibility on the army. Since strikes were illegal and occasionally involved the destruction of property (rather more often management fear of such violence), troops were regularly called in to maintain or restore order—in about 20 percent of all industrial strikes.[9] As the number of strikes increased, the burden of containing civilian discontent rose dramatically. In the first half of the 1890s, the army intervened against workers an average of fourteen times per year; in the second half of the decade, the annual average reached fifty-two. By the last half of the 1890s, the army was intervening against all types of civil disorders an average of 147 times annually, deploying for this purpose sixteen infantry and sixteen cavalry and cossack regiments every year.[10]

As with peasant disorders, the mere presence of troops at a factory usually sufficed to prevent violence and often broke the back of a strike. But the level of violence was markedly higher at factories than in villages: industrial conflicts accounted for five of the six incidents in the 1890s in which soldiers suffered more than ten injuries (usually bruises). Of course, workers sustained far more casualties than soldiers. In the Donets Basin factory settlement of Iuzovka, to take the worst example, a cossack squadron in August 1892 opened fire on a mob of 5,000 people, killing between fifty and two hundred (the squadron commander set the dead at sixty, wounded at one hundred).[11]

Industrial development meant not only that the army had ever more frequently to intervene in civilian conflicts, it also occasioned minor adjustments in deployment. The cossack squadron that massacred workers in Iuzovka in 1892 had been garrisoned there permanently in 1888 after a wave of strikes, and its only duty was to police the mines and settlements; a second squadron arrived in 1898, after another round of strikes. In a few other cases as well, military units were redeployed to control workers; the 226th Bobruisk reserve battalion was moved to Tsaritsyn after a strike in 1899, for instance.[12] Generally, however, the Ministry of War resisted the pleas of civilian officials and industrialists who called for the redeployment of the army to control civilians. The Ministry rejected a plan in the 1880s to redeploy units in the Jewish Pale to forestall pogroms (though the army nevertheless intervened—not always in a timely manner—against pogroms), an 1896 suggestion from the Moscow military district to garrison two cossack squadrons in the factory settlements of Vladimir Province, and requests from civilian officials in 1899 and 1900 to beef up the permanent garrisons in the

Donets Basin. The Ministry of War regularly claimed that garrisoning was based on strategic principles, that it had no units to spare for permanent control of workers, and that factory and mine owners should raise their own police force.[13]

The Ministry of War was quite properly reluctant to divert troops for strike- and riot-control, and military district commanders were probably correct to rail (as they did every year from the mid-1890s) against civilians for summoning troops without cause and for not appreciating the true functions of the army. Yet the generals did recognize, however grudgingly, that the army had necessarily to help contain and suppress civilian discontent. The staff of the Moscow military district, at least, resolved to gather intelligence on the enemy. As it noted in a request to the Governor of Vladimir Province in 1898, "In view of the fact that the troops of the district are often required to assist civil authorities on the occasion of disorders at factories, the staff of the district has begun to collect information on the latter," specifically on their number, size, and location.[14] Instead of a routine inconvenience, the suppression of civil disorder had become by the close of the century one of the major preoccupations of the Tsarist army.

A high level of social unrest became a prominent feature of Russian society in the 1890s. In the opening years of the twentieth century, peasant disorders and industrial strikes began to threaten the established order. Not only did disorders multiply, they became politicized: the revolutionary movement of the intelligentsia finally made contact with the masses, and this, too, added to the army's burdens. The reasons for the rise of revolutionary sentiment are easy to identify: students and other members of educated Russia knew how retrograde the Tsarist autocracy was by nineteenth-century European standards (the point of reference for European Russians); they believed, for good reason, that the autocracy would not reform itself out of existence and that significant change in the political system and in social legislation could come only through revolution; they were well aware of the miserable condition of the peasants and the nascent industrial proletariat; and with every passing decade the ranks of students and professionals expanded, thus broadening the base for the recruitment of revolutionaries. A relatively small but determined revolutionary movement in the 1860s and 1870s culminated in the assassination of Alexander II in 1881. When Tsarism survived the Tsar and peasants failed to follow the radicals' example, the revolutionary movement went into a decade-long recession, but with the emergence of popular unrest in the 1890s it revived. By 1900, a Marxist Russian Social Democratic Workers Party and a peasant-socialist Socialist Revolutionary Party (which for the time being focused on workers, whom Socialist Revolutionaries viewed as peasants in all but job) were beginning to take shape. As of that point, however, the revolutionary movement was largely confined to educated Russia: revolutionaries were peripherally involved in some strikes, they helped in some instances to focus otherwise diffuse discontent, but very few workers considered themselves part of a revolutionary movement, and even militant workers were notoriously hostile to the intelligentsia. The cultural barrier that separated peasant and European Russians had its analogue in the cities.

Almost accidentally, university students and the army catalyzed the juncture between workers and revolutionaries. The student movement—harassment of conservative professors, demonstrations in honor of tenants of the radical pantheon—blossomed in the 1890s in tandem with the revolutionary movement, and the army was called on to tame unruly students. In July 1899 the government adopted "Provisional Rules" under which students could be sentenced to service in the army, the humiliation attendant upon being treated as a peasant being much the most punitive aspect of this measure so far as students were concerned. Minister of War Kuropatkin liked the rules no better than students, protested against turning the army into a penal institution, and worried that student agitators might spread sedition in the army, but Tsar Nicholas held firm. In any case, the "Provisional Rules" merely antagonized students further. In 1900 a series of incidents at Kiev University culminated in the arrest with the aid of military force of hundreds of students, and the sentencing of 183 of them to terms of one to five years as privates. This triggered yet more protests, one in St. Petersburg resulting in the dispatch of twenty-eight more students to the army, and to confrontations between students and troops that stretched out over the next several years.[15]

It soon became apparent that the army was no place to send rebellious students, not because students had a baneful effect on soldiers but because cultural norms overrode Imperial edict. Kuropatkin visited the Petersburg students just before their train pulled out, and though he told them that they must obey orders, he gave them the right—this gesture indicating how hard it was to think of students in the role of peasant soldiers—to complain directly to him if they were maltreated. A circular from the staff of the Kiev military district urged that the treatment of students be aimed at rehabilitation rather than punishment. Noncoms were not to indulge in "methods and expressions insulting for an educated person," and the students were not to be detailed to work "inappropriate for a cultured person: such work as cleaning out latrines, scrubbing barracks floors, sweeping the streets in front of barracks, etc." Furthermore, advised the circular, students were to be provided underwear, bedlinen and other items that ordinary conscripts had to obtain for themselves. Officers spontaneously invited the students to tea and conversation in off-duty hours. The Tsar himself had a change of heart and pardoned the student soldiers in June 1901.[16]

For the army, the most important consequence of the student disorders was not its unwanted role as a correctional institution but the fact that the student demonstrations brought workers out of the factories: to the army's duty to contain unrest in village, mill, and university was added in 1901 the task of controlling the streets. In some cities, as in Kharkov (December 1901), workers rushed spontaneously to aid students being manhandled by cossacks. Elsewhere, revolutionaries, themselves galvanized by the student movement, instigated joint worker-student demonstrations, or worker demonstrations pure and simple. May Day 1901 saw a number of political strikes and demonstrations (as opposed to the conspiratorial meetings in the woods of previous years), and these were repeated in 1902; troops—cossacks especially—were called upon to clear the streets.[17]

Workers became more militant in their own bastions as well. Excited by the dramatic street violence of the preceding months, in May 1901 Russian workers for the first time erected barricades—at the Obukhov steel mill outside St. Petersburg—in an effort to repulse police and soldiers (at the Obukhov mill, actually, police and a detachment of sailors; the infantry arrived late). In Batum in March 1902, 2,000 workers surrounded the jail and demanded the release of 300 of their comrades who had been arrested for striking; at least eighteen workers died when soldiers opened fire. In Rostov-on-Don in November 1902, 3,000 workers in the railroad shops went on strike, asked for and received the support of other workers in the city (in all, 10,000 Rostov workers struck), and in one confrontation with the army showered cossacks with stones: the cossacks sustained ten injuries, but they killed six workers and wounded an indeterminate number of others.[18] Accompanied by bloodshed or not, the number of strikes rose, from around 200 in 1900 to between 300 and 400 in 1901 and again in 1902, with a corresponding rise in the demand for troops for factory patrol. By 1902, some garrisons kept companies on standing alert for crowd control and had drawn up detailed instructions on the disposition of troops in the event of major disorders.[19]

By 1902, it was no longer just workers who were threatening established authority, but peasants as well. Peasants in the Ukraine, the Volga provinces of Saratov and Tambov, and elsewhere in the south—in almost one-third of the provinces in European Russia all told—rebelled en masse for the first time since the emancipation. Peasants in the affected regions had specific if variable grievances—crop failures in some provinces, conflicts between gentry landlords and hired hands and renters in others—but these problems were not notably more acute than they had been before. Almost certainly peasant activism was a response to the growth of the workers' movement in the immediately preceding years and to increasing contact with revolutionary agitation, at least indirectly; few revolutionaries were in the villages, but they left stacks of pamphlets on the roadside, and seasonal workers brought more home. In the Ukraine, peasants cited revolutionary pamphlets to support rumors that the Tsar had authorized a "black repartition," and they even believed in a few cases that the troops sent against them had been charged with overseeing land redistribution. News of the Ukrainian disorders contributed to unrest in the Volga region, and peasants there drove out landlords and burned their mansions so they could not return. Five regiments—more than a division—marched against peasants in the two Ukrainian provinces of Poltava and Chernigov alone. As in the past the presence of troops usually cowed peasants into submission, but there was some shooting.[20]

Peasants continued unusually restive in 1903, though the number of peasant disorders fell. In that year, workers presented the major challenge to the regime. The tone was set in Ufa (in the Urals) in March, when 2,600 workers from the railroad shops and iron mill struck against the introduction of new workers' registration booklets. Arrests led to demonstrations, window smashing, shooting at police, and a virtual siege of the residence of the mine inspector. On orders of the governor, soldiers fired on the mob: three volleys killed 45 (or 69), wounded 83 (or over 250). In early July, workers in the oil fields and railroad shops of Baku struck, and for a few days public service workers virtually shut down the city. Similar "general strikes" rippled through the Caucasus and Ukraine over the next two months: Elizavetgrad, Odessa, Tiflis, Batum, Nikolaev, and Kiev in July, Ekaterinoslav and Kerch in August. By the end of the year, roughly 300,000 workers had taken part in 1,382 strikes (counting separately all the factories, mines, and depots involved in the general strikes). Revolutionaries seldom instigated either the general or local strikes in 1903; indeed, some strikes in 1903 (as in 1902) were carried out by workers in unions that the police had set up to divert workers from politics. But these workers had seized on the possibility of legal organization to press their demands on management, and revolutionaries were able to give many strikes a political coloration once they were underway.[21]

The surge of worker and peasant disorders placed an enormous strain on the army. Soldiers marched to the aid of civil authorities 117 times in 1900, 271 times in 1901, 522 times in 1902, 427 times in 1903. Although not every case of military assistance to civil authorities involved action against workers and peasants (the military also chased bandits and preserved order at fairs), in 1903 75 percent of the incidents involved action against workers (179 cases) and "civil disorders" (143 cases) and these accounted for 89 percent of the infantry and 86 percent of the cavalry deployed against civilians; in all, the equivalent of 73 infantry and 47 cavalry and cossack regiments, representing one-third of the infantry and two-thirds of the cavalry available in European Russia, took part.[22]

The incessant civilian demands for military assistance appalled the War Ministry and generals in the field and, especially after 1902, they sought to deflect civilian requests for troops. Yet as Minister of War Kuropatkin conceded in 1903, the employment of the army "to maintain the domestic tranquility of Russia" was now second in importance only to the army's mission to defend Russia's territorial integrity against the Triple Alliance. Protection of Russia's southern and eastern flanks was distinctly secondary to those two principal missions.[23] By 1903 operations against civilians were being planned in much the same way as operations against foreign powers. The Ministry of Interior drew up forecasts of its requirements for troops during the forthcoming summer campaign, and the Ministry of War endeavored to supply the necessary manpower. Kuropatkin noted in his diary on January 19, 1903:

> [Minister of Interior] Pleve . . . fears serious agrarian disorders in Poltava Province, also in Voronezh and, in part, Saratov Provinces. In addition, he declares it imperative to station some unit in Viatka. I showed Pleve the report already prepared on the transfer of the 2nd Composite Cossack Division to Poltava Province . . . I then promised to recommend that Viatka be occupied by a battalion.[24]

Even the language of military campaigns—"the occupation of Viatka" (*zaniatie Viatki*)—had crept into discussion of the army's role vis-à-vis civilian society.

The generals' principal lament was that police duties distracted soldiers from training, but they complained as well about the way in which troops were used—too frequently without resort to force, so that mobs no longer dreaded the appearance of troops. There was merit to this charge: how else explain the behavior of workers in Ufa and Batum who ignored warnings to disperse, or in Rostov who stoned cossacks? The generals were also concerned about the potential demoralization of the troops involved in crowd control. As Kuropatkin had reported to the Tsar in 1900: "Dispatching troops to aid the civil authorities has a very harmful influence on them if they are required to use arms or if, to avoid bloodshed, the troops are forced to retreat under the pressure of the crowd."[25] That covered almost all the options—demoralization, in Kuropatkin's view, was an ineluctable consequence of military operations against civilians.

No doubt Kuropatkin's judgment was correct, though the only concrete evidence of demoralization was a certain unpredictability in the soldiers' aim. If they were hemmed in and felt physically threatened, soldiers might loose terrible fire on civilians. Yet in some cases soldiers chose not to do so. One official confided to his diary in 1902:

> A Gendarme general says that one cannot rely unconditionally on the troops. During the disorders in Kolpino, 76 bullets were fired at the crowd (almost point-blank) and no more than 3 found their mark. It seems that the government can still count on the army, but the fact adduced by the gendarme can set one to thinking.[26]

Other official information on the ratio of cartridges expended to casualties inflicted also suggests that soldiers occasionally shot over the heads of civilians, and lends credence to the many unofficial reports of the same. One from Kiev in 1903 had it that a soldier, berated by a worker for the fact that soldiers had fired, replied: "And did we really shoot? . . . What sort of shooting was that. Just think, if we had wanted, we could have smashed the entire mob with one volley. . . . The majority didn't shoot at the mob. Is there really so little room for bullets above them?" (In the incident in question, two volleys by two infantry battalions and two cossack squadrons produced two or four dead, twenty-seven wounded.)[27] Orders issued to troops before they sallied forth stressed that under no circumstances were they to talk to civilians and that, when firing, they were not to shoot in the air, which suggests that officers feared soldiers would do just that.[28] By and large, however, soldiers obeyed orders. Prior to 1905 there was no instance in which they failed to disperse mobs of workers or peasants when told to do so.

Kuropatkin repeatedly implored civilian ministers to adopt policies that would reduce civilian discontent so that troops would be needed less often.[29] Kuroptakin's was the voice of common sense, but his concern was misdirected. The fundamental problem facing the army and the regime was not the distraction of soldiers from other duties, or incipient demoralization in the ranks, but that the wholesale application of military force against civilians had failed to achieve its purpose: it had not checked the growth of the revolutionary, worker, and peasant movements, or their convergence toward a genuine revolutionary crisis. If the army could not forestall revolution, what could? The army had intervened in fully one-fifth of agrarian and factory disorders even before the massive unrest of 1902 and 1903. Peasants, even workers, may not have been able to imagine Russia without a Tsar, but only the routine application of military force prevented them from destroying the social and political order over which he presided. There had never been a peasant consensus in favor of serfdom, never more than glum resignation to the post-emancipation agrarian and factory orders. Naked force—not the abstract force of political theory but force regularly and visibly applied—alone held the Tsarist state together. Overwhelm the army, or eliminate it from the political equation, and the state would disintegrate.

Revolutionaries and the Army

That the Tsar's throne rested on bayonets was a truism to Russia's revolutionaries, so naturally they sought to neutralize the army. In the late 1870s and early 1880s, radical officers established a substantial Military-Revolutionary Organization that at its peak had up to 200 members and aspired to lead at least a part of the army against the regime. Revolutionaries did not then believe that they could recruit soldiers, or that they needed to so long as soldiers obeyed their radical officers.[30] Revolutionaries exhibited no interest even in officers during the 1890s, but the street demonstrations of 1901 kindled new enthusiasm for agitation in the barracks, this time among soldiers as well as officers. A brief note in the first issue of the Socialist Revolutionaries' *Vestnik russkoi revoliutsii* in 1901 observed that revolutionary work in the army, heretofore nonexistent, was necessary because of the army's role in suppressing strikes and agrarian disorders. The Social Democrats' *Iskra*, in a lead article "On Demonstrations" in January 1902, advised revolutionaries to inform soldiers beforehand that demonstrators meant them no harm, and through 1902 and 1903 the SR and SD leaderships periodically appealed to local organizations to address more propaganda to the army.[31]

Revolutionaries on the spot were quite capable of assessing the situation for themselves. The Ministry of Interior's Department of Police reported that efforts to revolutionize the army picked up noticeably in 1902, and in the same year Minister of War Kuropatkin informed his military district commanders that "attempts by political agitators to disseminate propaganda in the armed forces, a comparatively rare phenomenon earlier, have recently become more frequent and are so insolent that it is necessary to turn special attention to them."[32] By 1903, most revolutionary organizations were at least distributing an occasional leaflet in the garrisons, though they directed roughly half of their output toward officers. Indeed, when revolutionaries considered how to organize their prospective following in the army they fell back on the only model at hand: a centralized military organization that could at the decisive moment turn substantial bodies of troops against the regime. And in 1903, SDs and SRs were fascinated by an apparently reborn, but chimerical, officers' Military Revolutionary Organization.[33]

Properly enough, revolutionary leaflets asked soldiers only to turn their weapons away from civilians. The role suggested in the pamphlet-length stories for soldiers was equally modest: with few exceptions, model revolutionary soldiers did little more than read revolutionary leaflets and fire over the heads of demonstrators.[34] Indeed, in 1902 and 1903 the pamphlets revolutionaries most frequently distributed in the army were Leo Tolstoy's anti-militarist writings: *Soldatskaia pamiatka* ("The Soldier's Handbook"), *Ofitserskaia pamiatka* ("The Officer's Handbook"), and *Pis'mo k fel'dfebeliu* ("Letter to a Sergeant Major"). In addition to stressing the biblical injunctions against killing and swearing oaths, Tolstoy made the same points as revolutionaries: soldiers were being led against peasants and workers for the greater profit of gentry and capitalists, yet soldiers were themselves flesh and blood of the people.[35]

Judging from a somewhat atypical case—that of the "Alshanskii group" in the Ekaterinoslav Grenadier regiment in Moscow—soldiers were willing to give these appeals a sympathetic hearing. Though Alshanskii's story changed from time to time, the truth of the matter seems to have been about as follows.[36] The son of a civil servant, Aleksandr Alshanskii was drafted in 1899 and, through his fiancée, fell in with revolutionary students in Moscow in 1901. Under their influence, he concluded (as he said after his arrest) "that a political revolution in Russia, needed to improve the life of the lower classes, was impossible so long as the troops did not pass over to the side of the discontented."[37] With the help of his fiancée and the students, Alshanskii began propagandizing among the Ekaterinoslav Grenadiers. He distributed literature and read some aloud (the indictment mentions *Iskra* and Tolstoy's *Pis'mo k fel'dfebeliu*), and he urged soldiers not to shoot civilians. The five soldiers arrested with him early in 1902 declared themselves Social Democrats at the trial (reflecting the incomplete differentiation among revolutionaries at the time, Alshanskii declared himself an SD during the investigation, but a Socialist Revolutionary at the trial), and many others—including some NCOs—admitted listening to him without reporting his subversive activity.

But there were few Alshanskiis, and randomly distributed leaflets not reenforced orally were unlikely to elicit a response. The best chance revolutionaries had to penetrate the army was through the draft. Social Democrats and Socialist Revolutionaries undertook campaigns among draftees in 1902—holding special meetings and printing special leaflets for them, organizing demonstrations of their conscripted supporters as they marched away—and they repeated these campaigns in subsequent years. The Bund, which had proportionately the largest following and to whom the possibility of infiltrating the army with conscripts presented itself earliest, began these activities on a small scale as early as 1899.[38] In a special leaflet of 1902, the Central Committee of the Bund told Jewish draftees:

> Conscripts, as you go off to serve the Tsar, don't forget those whom you are leaving behind. You are spreading out through all Russia. Take our ideas, our thoughts, the idea of freedom, with you everywhere. Explain to your comrades how they should behave when they are sent against workers, peasants and other "rioters." *One* soldier can do nothing, but *many* can be of great benefit to the struggle for liberation.[39]

With or without special campaigns among draftees, as the revolutionary movement mushroomed in the early years of the twentieth century the armed forces called up increasing numbers of men, mostly workers, who had been exposed to revolutionary agitation. When revolutionary conscripts met, they formed circles, sought contact with civilian organizations, and engaged in reading and distributing illegal literature until circumstances (arrest, discharge, loss of civilian contacts) intervened. Not all such groups managed to locate civilian revolutionaries: a group of SD soldiers that formed in Alexandropol (Armenia) in 1902 spent three years looking for civilian contacts before settling on an Armenian revolutionary organization.[40] By far the largest of the groups of conscript revolutionaries formed in the Black Sea Fleet, where in 1902 draftees organized revolutionary circles, and in 1903 made contact with SD and SR civilians. By late 1903 300—and a year later perhaps as many as 800—sailors regularly attended revolutionary discussion circles.[41] There were similarly active, though smaller, sailor circles in Kronstadt, but the level of revolutionary activity in the navy was exceptional. The navy drafted for the skills needed to run modern warships and so drew on the groups most exposed to the revolutionary movement in civilian society; 15 percent of sailors had worked in factories (as against 2 percent of soldiers), while 70 percent of the naval conscripts of 1902–1904 were literate (as against 53 percent of the army's conscripts in the same years).[42] Not counting the sailors' circles in Sevastopol and Kronstadt, in 1903 SDs had contact with six or so soldier circles, SRs with at least four.[43] No doubt these figures are low by a factor of two or three, but the surviving evidence suggests the order of magnitude: measured against the million men under arms, the revolutionary soldier groups were insignificant.

Revolutionaries had an interest in winning military support, but they were unimaginative in reaching for it. It was, admittedly, difficult to penetrate military enclaves, or to find appropriate tasks for soldier converts to revolution, but the real problem was that civilian revolutionaries were out of touch with the soldier's world. By contrast, the workers outside Moscow who in 1903 persuaded soldiers engaged in railway construction to join in a strike found soldiers both physically and psychologically accessible.[44] The revolutionaries' want of initiative derived at root from a lack of urgent interest. Concern with the army had been thrust on them in 1901, but despite assertions of the need to neutralize the army, and the distribution of the occasional proclamation to officers and soldiers, the army bulked low in revolutionary thinking. Judging by the contents of the revolutionary press, their interest in the empire's thirty thousand students in institutions of higher education outweighed their interest in the one million soldiers by a ratio of 4 to 1.[45]

That is not especially surprising. The revolutionary movement was just past infancy; students were making a visible contribution to it, soldiers not. And all revolutionaries thought of the revolution as fundamentally civilian. Moreover, as of 1903 few believed revolution was in the offing. They had debated at considerable length the role of different social groups in the revolution, but had yet to give much thought to the mechanism by which autocracy was to be overthrown. The more optimistic (or naive) among them asserted that overwhelming numbers, stiffened by armed combat groups, could smother the army in the cities, and that small groups could wage successful partisan operations ("agrarian terror") in the countryside.[46] Russian revolutionaries had not as yet confronted Engels's well-known dictum that insurrection could not succeed against modern military technology. They seemed to hope—as had Engels—that by the time the appointed day arrived the problem of the army would somehow have taken care of itself.[47]

Military authorities took revolutionary propaganda in the army far more seriously than did revolutionaries themselves. In January 1902 the Ministry of War ordered surveillance of all politically suspect conscripts, and in the same year Kuropatkin ordered that a count be kept of courtsmartial for illegal political activity. The statistics demonstrated, if anything, that the level of seditious activity in the barracks was low: the great majority of the trials were for illegal activity prior to conscription (40 of 49 political courts-martial in 1902, 102 of 152 in 1903, 65 of 97 in the first half of 1904).[48] Nevertheless, the number of politically unreliable soldiers was increasing, and in January 1903 Kuropatkin suggested that military authorites inform the political police whenever they noticed anything suspicious, and that they subject soldiers, especially Jews, to close surveillance and frequent searches. Local commanders issued similar instructions, as did the Naval Ministry. During 1903, too, there were high-level military conferences on the problem of revolutionary subversion. The recommended countermeasures boiled down to the obvious: isolate soldiers from civilians, search the soldiers' effects frequently, see to it that officers involve themselves closely with their men.[49]

These measures did not stem the seepage of revolution into the armed forces, if only because the draft of sedition-minded civilians increased annually. Yet prior to 1905, neither revolutionary propaganda nor revolutionary soldiers even began to threaten the integrity of the army. The harbinger of the future was that the obvious remedies against subversion were incompatible with the structure of the army: exhortation could not reduce the distance between officers and men, large parties of soldiers were annually immersed in the civilian economy. The character of Tsarist military society, not sporadic leaflets or the handful of revolutionary soldier groups, rendered the army vulnerable to revolution.

The Russo-Japanese War and the Rebellion of Polite Society

"One may ask: does the government have friends? And one answers with complete assurance: no. Who would be the friends of fools and oafs, robbers and thieves?"[50] So wrote Aleksei Suvorin, a conservative publisher who sat on government commissions, in his diary on November 16, 1904. By late 1904, the government of Nicholas II had few friends even among those whose every instinct was loyalist, and the dry rot of disaffection and irresolution had spread within the government machine itself. The combination of mounting popular discontent and the desertion of the regime by its presumed friends was the classic prescription for revolution.

The emergence of political opposition to the government within polite society coincided with the revival of the revolutionary movement and the beginnings of serious working-class disorders in the 1890s. Professionals and liberal nobles took heart from the ferment: they were no longer hopelessly isolated, and they began to call, at first discretely and then more boldly, for the introduction of some sort of constitutional order in Russia. Not initially very substantial, the liberal movement swelled as the mass discontent of the opening years of the twentieth century created the impression that the government was losing control and might yield to liberal pressure. By 1903 the liberal movement had coalesced into a Union of Liberation, which operated semi-clandestinely inside Russia and supported a newspaper published abroad that articulated the liberal political program. The regime's clumsy efforts to suppress liberal opposition, its campaign to circumscribe the activities even of the zemstvos (organs of local government whose rights were already severely limited) controlled by the nobility, and its style—the Tsar's vacillation in matters of policy, his wife's mysticism and weakness for miracle workers, the prominence of a motley crowd of favorites at court—weakened the regime's hold on the loyalty of conservatives like Suvorin and even the flower of the aristocracy. There was no great public outrage when SRs assassinated Minister of Education Bogolepov in 1901, indifference when they assassinated Minister of Interior Sipiagin in 1902, general approval when they assassinated Minister of Interior Pleve in 1904.[51]

Characteristically, palace irregulars helped embroil Russia in the war with Japan. More importantly, they were widely credited (the retired Guards officer Bezobrazov and his Yalu timber concession especially) with causing the war. In fact, in their pursuit of spheres of influence in Manchuria and Korea, Japan and Russia had been on a collision course for some time, and Russia had gradually (with some rapidity in 1903) built up her military forces in the Far East. The major consequence of the intrusion of Bezobrazov and others of his ilk in Russia's Far Eastern policy was that policy became muddled: the ministers (War, Foreign Affairs, Finance) principally concerned were no longer in control and could not make the concessions that they hoped would at least postpone the conflict. Through violations of international agreements (e.g., governing the withdrawal of the troops that had entered Manchuria during the Boxer Rebellion), a frankly racist contempt for the interests and military capacities of the Japanese, and confusion and indecision in policy formation, Russia gave every appearance of negotiating only to cover a military buildup. Japan resolved to fight before the military balance shifted against her, and attacked the Russian fleet at Port Arthur on the night of January 26–27/February 8–9, 1904.[52]

The Russian army fought the war incompetently, though the Japanese must be given credit for sound strategy. They opened by attempting to eliminate or at least bottle up the Russian fleet at Port Arthur in order to achieve control of the sea. Because their strategy was premised on control of the sea, they worried more about the ill-assorted fleet sent from the Baltic to its doom at Tsushima than about any other Russian operation, and the same worry impelled the Japanese to accept enormous casualties to capture Port Arthur. With full control over the sea lanes, the Japanese could pour men into Manchuria unimpeded. They sought a decisive battle before Russia could move east in force, but they badly overestimated the time it would take the Russians to bring troops from Europe by rail, and in all the major engagements the Russians had a numerical advantage, sometimes by almost 2 to 1. However, the peacetime routine had bred inefficiency deep into the Russian army. At the outset of the war Russian regiments attacked as though on maneuvers, in close order with bands playing. For the first half year or so the Russians fired in volleys, doing more harm to their ears than to the enemy. They worried incessantly about encirclement and broke off engagements timorously at the first setback. The Japanese won a series of increasingly bloody and lengthy battles that culminated in late February and early March 1905 at Mukden, where approximately 600,000 men suffered in excess of 130,000 casualties. The Japanese had hoped that Mukden would be the decisive battle of the war—Port Arthur had fallen, so with troops rushed north they were for a change not significantly inferior in numbers—but the Russians, though routed, escaped encirclement. The balance of manpower then swung decisively in Russia's favor. By the end of the war there were over 950,000 Russians in Manchuria, under 400,000 Japanese. While there was little likelihood that Russian generals could take advantage of their strength, the Japanese could not push so huge a mass of soldiers around, and they had no more men of their own to put in the field.[53] It was Russia's domestic weakness that eventually assured Japan the victory that her army had not quite been able to secure.

The Japanese attack appeared at first to have restored social harmony to Russia: there were spontaneous patriotic demonstrations in the capital, the nobles in the zemstvos forgot their antipathy to the central bureaucracy and pledged full support to the national cause, even worker and peasant disorders sank to the lowest level since the 1890s. Yet the surge of loyalism was brief and weak: indifference was the most common reaction to the war. When defeats ever more humiliating shattered the illusion of Russia's innate superiority, and when the regime continued to veto zemstvo elections and even thwarted zemstvo efforts to assist the army in the field, contempt for the regime swelled to unprecedented proportions in polite society. The liberals' Union of Liberation concluded by April 1904 that chauvinism had yielded to disdain, and that the war offered an opportunity to mobilize public opinion and wrest a constitution from the regime. In the summer and fall liberals worked to achieve some degree of coordination with the revolutionary parties, and in October 1904 met in Paris with representatives of the SRs and six parties of the subject peoples (only the SDs boycotted the conference) to plan a petition campaign against the regime.[54]

The strength of the opposition even in time of war and the rejoicing that followed Pleve's assassination in July shook the regime's self-assurance. After some hesitation, Nicholas appointed as his new Minister of Interior a man of liberal inclinations, Prince Sviatopolk-Mirskii. Sviatopolk-Mirskii began his tenure by proclaiming that his policy would be based on trust, which was manifested concretely in the extension rather than contraction of zemstvo rights, the removal of the civil ban and exile imposed on prominent liberals, and the relaxation of censorship. He permitted representatives of the zemstvos to hold an unofficial congress—which under the prodding of the Union of Liberation called for an elected legislature. In November and December resolutions demanding political reform of a more or less parliamentary character were adopted by provincial zemstvo assemblies where the Union of Liberation was not in control, in the ordinarily quite conservative provincial assemblies of nobles, and even by the Marshals of nobility, who were specifically charged by the government with preventing the zemstvos from concerning themselves with politics. In November and December, too, the Union of Liberation organized approximately 80 political banquets—attended in the main by professionals but including civil servants and a scattering of officers as well—that adopted constitutionalist resolutions.[55] In a word, Sviatopolk-Mirskii's liberal gestures touched off a crisis. As Tocqueville had observed long before, the moment of gravest danger for a conservative regime is when it begins to reform. In Russia in late 1904, the regime's unwonted liberalism signalled its loss of self-assurance and encouraged the belief that more pressure would produce more reform, perhaps even some variety of representative government.

The regime's ardor for reform cooled abruptly. His resolve stiffened by conservative advisors and relatives, the Tsar on December 9 publicly rebuked and stripped of court rank a prominent marshal of the nobility who had dared to forward a petition for a representative assembly, and on December 14 the government pronounced the zemstvo congress and other political meetings—as well as newspaper coverage of them—illegal, and warned that participants, especially civil servants, would be punished. Sandwiched between these two reaffirmations of autocracy was an Imperial Edict of December 12 announcing reforms deemed sufficient to satisfy the public: the rule of law would be upheld, the rights of zemstvos broadened, censorship loosened, religious disabilities lightened.[56]

Even more dangerous to a conservative government than reform is inconsistency. As the regime—internally divided, disoriented, and demoralized by the contempt in which it was held by liberals and conservatives alike—vacillated between reform and repression, defeatism and the expression of subversive sentiments became fashionable (which is not to say that such sentiments were not justified). The temper of public opinion in late December 1904 can be judged from an extraordinary political banquet attended by over 800 persons "representing the cream of the literary and other professions of St. Petersburg and the provinces" on December 14.

The speech of the evening was delivered by Professor Lutugin [of the St. Petersburg Mining Institute]. . . . The war, he declared, was their own crime, because they had not protested against the adventurous policy of the Russian Government. The majority of the professors lectured in the Universities about Russia's interests in the Far East, and none of them informed the youth of the country that the Russian Government was always playing the role of an international gendarme, perpetuating the police traditions of obsolete European States. They never told the students that Russia was the last hope of the reactionary elements in Europe. As to the Emperor's manifestoes, he described them as insolent and tactless.

This daring pronouncement was greeted with the wildest enthusiasm, the ladies waving their handkerchiefs and the men climbing on the tables and cheering.[57]

By late 1904, the goverment had not only lost the respect of polite society, it no longer inspired fear. Lutugin's was not yet the voice of revolution, but his audience was primed.

The army could not win the battles in Manchuria that might have dampened the rebellion of polite society, and the succession of defeats gravely weakened the garrison units in Europe, the regime's sole defense against popular rebellion. As the war dragged on, the army called up almost 1,200,000 reserves in nine separate mobilizations of European corps and divisions. The reserves caused the army problems almost immediately: between the time they arrived at the mobilization depots and their inscription on unit rosters, they were involved in 123 serious disorders, 107 of them during the mobilizations of September, October, and December 1904. The disturbances ranged from simple "mob disorders" to full scale riots, small-scale pogroms, looting, attacks on police and military authorities, refusals to board troop trains, and the destruction of railway property along the line to Manchuria. In 1904, regular troops were called out 67 times against rioting reserves, only 62 times to control civilian disorders, and by the end of 1904 cadre units were being drawn up to protect railway stations in Siberia when troop trains rolled in.[58]

The succession of defeats quite likely contributed to the disorders, as did a confusing system of exemptions from the call-up, but the principal cause was chaos at the mobilization depots. As the Tsarist regime had not seriously prepared for the war that its imperialist policy provoked, so it had no machinery to handle the huge numbers of reserves mobilized to fight the war. There was insufficient equipment and food for them, no provisions whatsoever for the families that accompanied the men to the depots. Reserves were held in limbo for weeks, then dispatched over-hastily into the army, the whole system working by fits and starts. The families hung around until their men pulled out, and reserves beat up officers who tried to prevent the men from visiting their wives except, say, on Sundays. There was no lack of incidents to set off major brawls.[59]

Not only was the army swollen with restive reserves, the use of the European garrisons to feed the army in Manchuria badly disorganized the units remaining in Europe. The 100-odd depot battalions formed in Europe during the war had a permanent skeleton of 140 enlisted men and a revolving complement of 1,000 reserves who were sent to the front as fast as the Transsiberian Railway could handle them. The depot battalions were assemblages of men in uniform, not military units with the cohesion of settled organization and long mutual association, but the line regiments in Europe were in little better shape. Up to 90 percent and more of the cadre personnel and up to 70 percent of their regular officers (mostly subalterns) were transferred to units in Manchuria and to regiments formed during the war.[60] Unhappy reserves replaced cadre troops in the garrison units, but there were far too few reserve officers to replace the missing regulars. In some regiments only one regular officer was left for every two companies, and reserve officers—former "volunteers" who had served brief terms in the ranks—were not the sort to exercise firm control over their men. A regular officer wrote later:

> "Our ensigns [of the reserve], who had nothing in common with military service and viewed it as an extremely distasteful burden, were especially uninterested in the inner world of the soldier. And, after the greater part of the regular officers had been posted to the Far East, only company commanders and ensigns remained in the regiments; there were almost no other officers.[61]

The army was none too cohesive even in time of peace, and the Russo-Japanese war placed enormous strain on the weakest element of the military organism, the link between officers and men. This was more important than the fact that the reserves' anger carried over into 1905, or that reserves—older and more worldly wise than cadre troops—provided in 1905 the initial conduit through which civilian discontent penetrated the barracks.[62] In 1905, regulars would prove as prone as reserves to run roughshod over their officers when confusion and disorganization provided the opportunity.

III. Failing to Contain Revolution: January–October 1905

The Social and Psychological Contours of Revolution in Russia

Bloody Sunday—January 9, 1905, when soldiers shot down 1,000 of the 30,000 workers marching to present the Tsar a petition for labor and civil rights—was an appropriately Russian beginning to revolution. Not revolutionaries but Georgii Gapon, a radical priest who spoke the workers' language and shared their social and political sensibilities, mobilized workers in unprecedented numbers: Gapon's officially sanctioned Assembly of St. Petersburg Factory and Mill Workers had brought 110,000 out on strike between January 3 and January 8. It fit the workers' vision of the social order that, having struck because of the efforts of factory management and government officials to shackle their organization, they sought succor from the Tsar. In the words of their petition, "we are . . . contemptuously treated. . . . We are enslaved, enslaved under the patronage and with the aid of Thy officials," but "Thou reignest in order to bring happiness to Thy people."[1] That liberals, whose banquet campaign of November and December was the spur to the workers' petition, and revolutionaries were unaware of the ferment in the factory districts until planning for the march was under way testifies to the chasm between workers and polite society. The workers' own alienation from educated Russia was expressed by the politically sophisticated members of Gapon's organization who recoiled from the Union of Liberation after one fruitless attempt to obtain the liberals' advice, by the more conservative workers who objected to presenting a petition because they believed they had nothing in common with the intelligentsia, and by the excited workers who on the eve of the march expelled from the Assembly's meeting halls revolutionary "students" who could not pass for followers of Gapon. It was of course entirely characteristic of the regime's attitude toward even nonviolent and naive challenges to the existing order that, rather than accepting the workers' petition, it reinforced the Petersburg garrison with battalions from Pskov and Revel and perpetrated a massacre.[2]

Because of the social tensions that had been building for a decade, Bloody Sunday set convulsions surging through Tsarist society. More workers struck in January 1905 than in the ten years preceding, and some cities suffered small-scale replicas of the Petersburg massacre; by government count, troops killed and wounded about 100 in Riga, over 200 in Polish cities. Polite society denounced the regime at angry meetings and in open letters. Even the discrete and apolitical historian Vasilii Kliuchevskii, occasional advisor to the government and tutor to a Grand Duke, announced in class that Nicholas would be the last Tsar. That was almost Kliuchevskii's last lecture, because students turned classes into political meetings and in February declared the universities on strike. Peasants in February began to attack gentry estates and expel the owners, and the incidence and violence of agrarian disorders mounted as the weather turned warm. The non-Russian peoples rose in both social and national rebellion; indeed, Bloody Sunday resonated more immediately and violently in Poland and the Caucasus than in the Russian heartland.[3]

Stunning in their sweep, the rebellions were as diverse—even divergent—as Tsarist society was ill-joined. No one social group—not the workers who triggered the revolution, not the middle class liberals who provided the political focus for the first nine months of the year—drove the revolution, for none would have had the impact it did absent the action of all the others. Yet if the eruptions in working class, polite society, peasantry, and borderlands drew strength from each other, each group contributed to the revolution for its own reasons, and each moved to its own rhythm.

Least consciously revolutionary were the peasants, who attributed their rebellion to the will of the Tsar but followed in the wake of urban revolution. The rise and fall of peasant disorders trailed the strike curve by a month (see Table III-1), and the crucial determinant of peasant rebellion was proximity to centers of urban disorder: the closer and earlier the strikes, the sooner agrarian disturbances commenced. News of working class disorders reached peasants from kin in the cities, from rural factories, from travelers, and from newspapers and revolutionary leaflets. But peasants did not consciously emulate workers. Village readers and their audience purported to find in the printed words that

TABLE III-1. Workers on Strike, as Reported by the Factory
Inspectorate, and Peasant Disorders, as Recorded by the Department
of Police and Central Newspapers, January–October 1905

	Workers on Strike	Percentage on Strike for Political Reasons	Peasant Disorders
January	443,929	59.2	17
February	293,152	39.7	109
March	73,081	27.3	103
April	104,646	75.2	144
May	220,523	50.4	299
June	155,741	64.6	492
July	152,474	42.6	248
August	104,133	68.3	155
September	37,851	38.5	71
October	518,752	77.6	219

SOURCES: V. E. Varzar, *Statistika stachek rabochikh na fabrikakh i zavodakh za 1905 god*, Spb.,
1908, p. 5 and "Prilozheniia," p. 102; Varzar, *Statistika stachek rabochikh na fabrikakh i
zavodakh za trekhletie 1906–1908 gg.*, Spb., 1910, "Prilozheniia," pp. 67, 72; S. M. Dubrovskii,
Krest'ianskoe dvizhenie v revoliutsii 1905–1907 gg., M., 1956, p. 42.

These are the conventional figures and identify trends. However, the number of workers
who struck in all of 1905 was 80 percent higher than reported by the Factory Inspectorate,
which did not have jurisdiction over mines, railroads, and miscellaneous other industries.
The figures on peasant disorders were compiled by Dubrovskii and Grave in the mid-
1950s; since then, examination of local archives—still incomplete—has increased the
known peasant disorders for the years 1905–1907 by 150 percent. See A. S. Amalrik, "K
voprosu o chislennosti i geograficheskom razmeshchenii stachechnikov v Evropeiskoi
Rossii v 1905 godu," *IZ*, v. 52, 1955, pp. 142–85; and M. S. Simonova, "Krest'ianskoe
dvizhenie 1905–1907 gg. v sovetskoi istoriografii," *IZ*, v. 95, 1975, pp. 210–12. Figures for
political strikes are misleadingly high because the Factory Inspectorate classified as political all strikes with mixed motives, sympathy strikes, and strikes with no declared motives.
For the entire year, only 57% of workers counted as political strikers were involved in
strikes that were specifically and exclusively political. See Varzar, *Statistika . . . 1905*,
pp. 31–32, 35, 37, 43.

came into their hands the Tsar's command to seize land. Within a month
after Bloody Sunday there were rumors that the Tsar had authorized
land seizures, and peasants acted on these rumors at a quickening pace.[4]

The connection between urban and rural rebellion was thus mediated
by the peasant view of the social order. Peasants had a strong sense of
justice, and of themselves as victims of injustice, but they did not think
of themselves as capable of effecting change. Nor could they, since dependence on external forces—on nature, on local officials and the gentry—was the defining element of their social lives. However, peasants

were quite sensitive to fluctuations in the forces that controlled them, and when the power of gentry and officials appeared to have weakened, peasants did not hesitate to implement their own vision of a just society. But because they were dependent, they projected an external authority—a pretender, a golden charter, a genuine edict or newspaper article esoterically interpreted—to justify their acts.[5] The more prolonged and severe the urban disorders, the greater the peasants' propensity to conclude that justice could be attained and to create fictive authorization to do so.

Through much of 1905, the same psychology underlay the workers' movement: workers could not conceive of politics as a system of ends and means or of an alternative to the authority of the Tsar, but they had a strong urge to attain justice when they believed obstacles had been eliminated. Bloody Sunday set off a massive wave of strikes, but there was an enormous disparity between that causative event and the demands over wages and hours, decent treatment, and the right to choose representatives for negotiations that striking workers so often made. Even the many workers whose explicit motivation for striking was solidarity with victims of the massacre could not articulate what they wanted. Some of these "political" strikers beat up revolutionaries who attempted to impose explicit political goals, and for good measure beat up other members of educated society who passed by at the wrong moment.[6] Appropriately, Gapon's followers put in words the disorientation that such behavior reflected. When soldiers stopped shooting at Gapon's column, Gapon rose and muttered half to himself, "There is no God any longer. There is no Tsar," and the workers around him took up the refrain. This was more than a figure of speech. In the last few days before the march, Gapon in addressing the throngs of his followers had inserted into his litany of question and response, "What if the Tsar refuses to hear us out?" and the workers had chorused, "Then we have no Tsar."[7] In the Russian popular tradition of denying Tsars who too obviously failed in their function of ensuring justice, the Gaponovite workers concluded that there was a void at the center of their social universe. Not all workers leaped to such apocalyptic conclusions, or abjured the Tsar so vehemently, yet the psychology of the Gaponovites is evident in the massive and angry, but unfocused and inarticulate, strikes that followed January 9. There may no longer have been a Tsar, but neither was a pretender immediately at hand.

The rhythm of the post-January strikes reveals that workers, like peasants, were governed by forces outside their control, though by mid-year there were signs of a gathering purposefulness. After falling precipitously through March, strikes increased again in the summer. The am-plitude of the second strike wave was of course due to the surrounding turmoil (the powerful demonstration effect of their own strikes among other things), which gave workers a new conception of what was possible. But the timing of the summer strikes had little to do with politics: May, June, and July had always been the strike season in Russian industry.[8] However, the revolution did extend the strike season somewhat. Because their expectations were high, revolutionaries concluded that the May Day strikes and demonstrations had failed. In fact, the surge of strikes in April was due largely to the May Day events in Poland (where May Day arrived, via the Gregorian calendar, on April 18). Though May Day was not impressive elsewhere, political strikes were nevertheless the leading edge of the movement, and lasted into August. Moreover, summer brought particularly impressive examples of working class radicalism and capacity to organize—a general strike led by a city-wide strike council in Ivanovo-Voznesensk in May and June, insurrection in Lodz in June.[9] Still, through September the seasonal cycle rather than politics determined the modulations of worker activism.

In contrast to peasants and workers, European Russians—revolutionaries, liberals, moderates, even conservatives—knew what they wanted and not only responded to opportunity but also sought to overcome obstacles. They had, in other words, programs and tactics. Despite their differences, their goals were located on a common spectrum and were explicitly political: they wished to replace autocracy with a constitutional monarchy or a democratic republic and to reorder relationships among social groups. If statistics on the political activities of educated Russians (petitions and resolutions, meetings secret and public) were available, they would probably reveal either little month-to-month variation, or a steady ascending trend; measures of liberal and radical activism would certainly not reveal the wild oscillation characteristic of worker and peasant activism. In short, Europeanized liberals and revolutionaries engaged in a different kind of politics and a different sort of revolution than workers and peasants. Revolutions so different in character did not easily meld. The disjunction at the heart of the revolution was a major problem for the revolutionaries, who were not fully aware that they had more in common with liberals than with the lower orders. Revolutionaries engaged in a modern political calculus, but they did not always calculate correctly.

The most important feature of the revolutionary movement was its growth: revolutionaries became for the first time a major presence in the cities. From something on the order of 5,000 members on the eve of 1905, the combined strength of Bolsheviks, Mensheviks, and Socialist Revolutionaries reached approximately 25,000 during the course of the year. Counting the non-Russian parties—the Bund, the Polish Social Democrats (SDKPiL) and Polish Socialists (PPS), the Latvian Social Democrats, and the many other small parties—the total number of organized revolutionaries may have hit 70,000 by the end of the year.[10] Revolutionaries spoke to countless meetings and flooded the cities with handbills. They helped to organize, or at least assisted, unions and factory committees that, born during the strikes, provided a working class leadership. So far as their audience was concerned, the practical differences among the revolutionary parties were minor. Though Bolsheviks and Mensheviks insisted that Socialist Revolutionaries should confine their activity to peasants, SRs were quite active in the cities; though Mensheviks were more interested in unions than were Bolsheviks, Bolsheviks too found unions to be convenient bodies for mobilizing working class support. Together, the parties reinforced revolutionary sentiment in the factories and villages, and they provided some organizational stiffening to the mass movement. They did not, however, direct the masses; worker and peasant activism fluctuated independently of the revolutionaries.

The messages the revolutionary parties broadcast were equally undifferentiated, at least from the point of view of the recipients. All revolutionaries agreed that Bloody Sunday signalled the beginning of revolution, all asserted that revolution must logically culminate in an insurrection that would topple the autocratic regime, all believed a general strike was an appropriate prelude to insurrection. The competing doctrinal nuances—and there were many—were of interest only to the revolutionaries themselves, and at that chiefly to the emigré leaderships. SRs considered technical planning for an insurrection a matter of course, while Bolsheviks harped on the need for planning, because Mensheviks insisted that the insurrection could not be planned in advance and that revolutionaries should concentrate on intermediate tasks that would foster revolutionary consciousness. As a practical matter, Bolsheviks, Mensheviks, and SRs all realized that insurrection could not be scheduled in advance or its outcome foreseen, all (at least at the local level) made some preparations for insurrection, though the plans they laid were wholly irrelevant.[11] Nevertheless, the revolutionaries' common insistence on the need for insurrection and the utility of a general strike did have a cumulative impact on the working class.

Through October, liberals did more than revolutionaries to shape the revolution: liberal organizations had a larger membership than did the revolutionary parties, they came close to saturating polite society, and so they influenced the regime itself. Leadership of the liberal movement shifted in 1905 from the Union of Liberation to unions of professionals—

doctors, lawyers, journalists, professors, bookkeepers, engineers, statisticians, and the like, and (the one professional union to include workers and to be led by SRs as well as liberals) "railway workers and employees." The first of these political unions emerged from the banquet campaign of November and December 1904; in May 1905 fourteen of them formed the Union of Unions, which (not counting the railway union) by August had 50,000 and by October 100,000 members. In late April the railway and engineers' unions concluded that a general political strike was the best means to attain their goals—an end to the war, a constituent assembly—and in June the Central Bureau of the Union of Unions began discussing the organization of a general strike. Even moderates outside the professional unions became better organized and, following the lead of the Union of Unions, moved steadily to the left. A series of congresses of the Union of Liberation and the zemstvos mobilized the liberal and moderate nobility behind a demand for a parliamentary regime, and in July a zemstvo-city council congress met in defiance of a government ban and called on local zemstvos to hold mass political meetings. Local zemstvos defied orders to disperse and helped peasants draw up petitions of grievances. By midsummer, of course, zemstvo liberals were not only drawing strength from the mass movement, they were also increasingly wary of peasant rebellion and were seeking to direct peasant discontent into nonviolent political channels.[12]

The explosion of social and political animosity shook the regime's morale, which had been none too firm even before Bloody Sunday, and the resulting irresolution in official circles provided space for the opposition to organize. The government deployed troops against workers and peasants and declared martial law in one city and province after another, but that was an involuntary reflex, not policy. The government groped desperately for measures that would reconcile Russians to autocracy, but every gesture of Imperial benevolence produced results opposite to those intended. On February 18 the Tsar, yielding to the counsel of well-intentioned advisors, promised to convene an elected assembly for "preliminary discussion of legislation," but insisted that "the fundamental laws of the Empire" (i.e., autocracy) were inviolable. On the same day, the Tsar permitted individuals and institutions to submit petitions to the government (this provided semi-legal cover for the work of the white-collar unions, the various opposition congresses, and the presentation of petitions by peasants) but blamed the disorders on evil people bent on imposing alien institutions on Russia and called on Russians to "stand firm around Our Throne . . . and support autocracy." The initiatives of February 18 having no salutory effect, the regime abandoned the effort to fashion a policy to deal with the crisis. Over the next few months, opposition congresses were tolerated but not heeded, liberal leaders arrested and then released. The government was reduced to hoping that at some point the storm would subside. For his part, the Tsar received both liberal and reactionary deputations and gave every appearance of assenting to the suggestions of them all.[13] As always, the irresolution of the regime and the boldness of its enemies intertwined with and reinforced each other.

The one firm decision that civil disorder compelled the government to take was to seek peace with the Japanese. The immediate spur to negotiations was the destruction of the Russian fleet at Tsushima on May 14; until then, Nicholas had rejected all suggestions of a negotiated settlement. Loss of the fleet necessitated a reassessment of the strategic situation, but when the Tsar conferred with his military advisors on May 24, they stressed not just the military but also the domestic imperatives for peace: it was politically dangerous to attempt to mobilize more reserves; it was in fact advisable to call up more cossack regiments to combat domestic disorders; the conclusion of peace might restore calm to the empire. The Tsar decided to seek peace not on those grounds, but in order to forestall Japanese encroachment on Russian territory. He professed not to be alarmed by the extent of the disorders, but his was the equanimity of a dull mind. His military advisors understood that the measures that might bring the war to a successful conclusion would aggravate the domestic crisis, that the war was therefore unwinnable, and that the regime's principal task was to quell civil disorders.[14]

Soldiers under Pressure

Shortly after Bloody Sunday, Minister of Agriculture Aleksei Ermolov put bluntly the crucial question for the survival of the Tsarist regime. He was the first, on January 17, to urge the Tsar to convene an assembly of elected representatives. The troops had held firm on January 9, observed Ermolov, but would their numbers be sufficient when disorders spread from the cities to the villages? And, he asked, would discipline hold against the imprecations of the victims? After all, soldiers were being asked to shoot their own people. Responded Nicholas: "I understand that the position of the government is impossible if it relies only on the army."[15] Within weeks, it was evident that the regime could rely on nothing else and that, Ermolov's fears not withstanding, soldiers were most reliable when shooting civilians.

By 1905, the army had a well-practiced routine for dealing with civil disorders. As soon as the scope of the unrest became clear, garrison commanders issued or updated their directives on the disposition and proper use of troops to contain civil unrest. In cities, units secured specified factories, public utilities, and private and public institutions. One or two companies per battalion reinforced local police on a revolving basis, while troops not otherwise engaged were kept on stand-by alert. Rural areas were more difficult to police. Since there were not enough troops to maintain more than a token presence in any one district, mobile columns of infantry and cavalry periodically showed the colors and hastened *post factum* to the scene of agrarian disturbances. If landlords could bring enough pressure to bear, small detachments— often no more than ten men—might be left to prevent attacks on an estate, but this immobilized a part of the government's already overburdened forces.[16]

If the routine was familiar, the scale of operations against civilians was not, and severely strained available manpower. The Ministry of War reported that between January and the end of October troops assisted civil authorities 2,699 times, the units so deployed adding up to 15,297½ companies (the equivalent of almost 1,000 regiments) and 3,665½ cavalry and cossack squadrons (roughly 700 regiments), or on the order of 2 million men.[17] In fact, as of September 1905 there were only about 700,000 soldiers (many of them noncombatants) in European Russia; that included twenty-six second-line cossack regiments* mobilized between March and August specifically for use against civilians.[18] What the Ministry of War figures tell us is that men and units shifted repeatedly from one assignment to another. The experience of the 24th Lubensk dragoons, quartered in Kishinev, was typical. The regiment was permanently at the disposal of the city's police, but it also sent detachments outside the city. On February 18, one squadron went to Elizavetgrad, returning to Kishinev on March 21. Another squadron spent March 27 to May 3 in Akkerman. From March 31 to April 5, half a squadron operated against peasants around Kishinev. From April 24 to April 27, two squadrons took to the field against a peasant disturbance. Two more squadrons rode against the peasants between July 19 and August 25. To carry the story to the end of the year: one squadron went to Elizavetgrad on November 27 and did not return until the following summer, while on December 8 another squadron began operations in the countryside that continued into the spring.[19] Elements of this one regiment assisted civil

---

*After four years of active duty, cossacks spent eight years on call in their villages, four each in the second and third lines. When they were called back into service, second- and third-line cossacks formed new regiments.

authorities outside Kishinev nine times during 1905, while within the city patrols and crowd control were a permanent assignment.

Soldiers did not attack civilians every time they left the barracks. Ordinarily, in fact, they arrived on the scene too late to be of use, or were required to do no more than stand ready for action. The Main Staff of the Ministry of War complained, for instance, that from January 1 through June 11 troops were sent out at civilian request 1,390 times, but took action against disorders only 240 times. Generals claimed to believe that civilian officials were reacting hysterically to imagined dangers. The generals complained, too, that governors filed requests for military assistance through improper channels—through the Ministry of Interior, for instance, which applied pressure directly on the Ministry of War, rather than through the military district command—and that troops were being handed over to civilian officials of inferior rank.[20] These plaints echoed the military resentments of earlier years; even in the midst of revolution, Tsarist generals were reluctant to admit that a well-advertised readiness to use troops was all that preserved the regime, and that 240 engagements in half a year was evidence of an unprecedented civilian willingness to take on even the army. Yet if civilian officials were more in touch with political reality, the generals' grumbling was understandable. There were certainly times when troops marched to no purpose, and whether needed or not soldiers were under tremendous pressure. In September, Assistant Minister of Interior D. F. Trepov, in charge of the empire's police and not at all hesitant to employ troops for punitive purposes, admonished the governors:

> It is apparent from the reports coming into the military that units placed at the disposal of civil authorities are at times called out without real need and are often employed in ways other than those for which they are intended.
>
> Considering that such use of military units will lead to the complete exhaustion of the latter, and that forcing continuous replacement of the units dispatched makes it impossible for the military to ensure proper training and indoctrination of the troops, I request that you resort to the use of troops placed at your disposal only in cases of genuine necessity.[21]

Repeated forays not only exhausted the men, they also jeopardized unit cohesion. Soldiers from a single unit were parcelled out among different factories, or strung out over miles of rural roads. Grateful gentry and factory managers occasionally provided for the men (more frequently, for the officers) guarding their property, but that was not the rule. Even civil authorities often made no provision for quartering and feeding the troops, who were left to sleep in factory corridors or open fields and were reduced to eating the worst of gruel (inadequate money for supplies became even less adequate when divided among small detachments). The command system broke down as NCOs became the commanders on the spot; NCOs were utterly unable to squeeze provisions from civil authorities.[22] Missed training was the least of the army's problems. The real question was whether units so overburdened and so fragmented could continue to function.

How the soldiers reacted to events around them and to their duties as an occupying force in their own land depended principally upon the level of violence in their vicinity. So long as soldiers were not themselves in physical danger, the never-ending details in aid of civil authorities progressively weakened military discipline and breached the barrier between soldiers and civilians. An ex-soldier recalled later that standing guard at factories at first simply bored the men, but that they gradually became interested in what was going on around them—who was striking, for instance, and why. Some officers noticed the change. The commander of the 116th Maloiaroslavl infantry in Riga, for instance, observed that

> enlisted men guarding factories and other institutions are not maintaining the strict order of military service, do not have a military bearing, make friends and converse with the workers. . . . [Soldiers] stroll about in the factory yards as if at home. . . .[23]

What was true in Riga was true in other cities, and in the countryside as well. To take but one example: in Chernigov Province, a company of soldiers (reserves, as it happened) posted on an estate became friendly with the peasants against whom they were supposed to be offering protection, so the landlord requested that the unit be withdrawn. Fraternization with the peasantry was indeed a problem, since, as Teprov pointed out to Minister of War Rediger in June, reserves often served in their native provinces and "are called upon to act against their fellow villagers."[24]

The reasonableness of the soldiers' behavior should not mislead us: there was more to the erosion of discipline than the fact that soldiers had both an opportunity for and an interest in fraternization. Their hearts may have been on the side of workers and peasants, but there were serious obstacles to any display of sympathy. As a revolutionary working in the army reported at mid-year, soldiers believed that justice was on the side of the workers, but "barracks discipline makes itself felt—everyone fears that he will stand alone, that no one will support him."[25] Furthermore, soldiers resisted drawing political conclusions from the events they witnessed. Should a soldier be disciplined for expressing political convictions, he was shunned as an odd duck with whom association could only lead to trouble. Soldiers listened attentively to criticism of the barracks regime, but when talk turned to civilian affairs they clung to the belief that the good Tsar would eventually right the wrongs done by his ministers.[26]

It was the persistence of established military routine, even in the midst of war and revolution, that made indiscipline and fraternization possible. The need for close supervision of soldiers was greater than ever—there were fewer officers per unit, units were widely dispersed, soldiers were exposed to subversion—yet officers remained as distant from their men as in languid years past. The regimental economy, too, functioned as it always had. In the summer and fall of 1905, regimental commanders sent their men off to earn money harvesting (leading Trepov to complain that Kharkov had been stripped of soldiers). Railroad troops' found work year round in the depots, even in those to which they had been sent to prevent strikes. The men of the 249th Maikop reserve battalion in Stavropol continued through the summer to produce goods for civilians in the battalion shops, their commander hired them out to unload freight, and they set off on their own if they could find work that allowed them to turn over at least five rubles to the battalion.[27] Difficult as it is to credit that commanders sent their men out to work alongside the very workers and peasants whose disorders the army was hard pressed to contain, that is what happened. The officers' habit of treating soldiers as a labor resource was unshakeable, their incomprehension of their men profound.

Exposed so carelessly to the agitation in civilian society, soldiers gradually shed their fears and inhibitions. Indiscipline reached a minor peak in the middle of the year. Fraternization with workers and peasants was reported with special frequency in June and July, and in a few cities (Smolensk, for instance), soldiers joined in large public meetings. Talk of impending mutinies was heard at some of the summer encampments (outside Moscow, for one), and many soldiers slipped out of camp at night for meetings in forests and ravines. The Main Staff of the Ministry of War had to order—so slow were officers to understand what was happening—that camp commanders mount special patrols to keep the soldiers in camp.[28] Regimental chaplains reported that soldiers were losing religion—if discipline rested on religious sentiments, indiscipline necessarily meant irreligion—and that soldiers no longer heeded sermons on current events.[29]

June and July saw, too, the first significant cluster of mutinies. The most famous mutiny of the year, on the battleship *Potemkin*, began on

June 14, and within the next month and a half there were at least ten others. Mutinies by sailors in Libava and soldiers at the Ust-Dvinsk fortress (near Riga) were serious affairs lasting several days. The rest were in themselves of little consequence, and were scattered all over the map: sappers in Kiev presented a list of demands, an infantry regiment in Sukhum prevented the arrest of a soldier, a rifle company in Samarkand refused to go to the firing range until a soldier was released from the lockup, and so forth.[30] But by midsummer, soldiers in noticeable if not yet threatening numbers were beginning to defy their officers.

Yet if discipline had frayed, it did not snap. Into autumn, soldiers overwhelmingly obeyed direct orders to stand watch over factories and estates and to disperse mobs, for they had as yet no reason to believe they could escape punishment if they disobeyed. Moreover, indiscipline was most likely when soldiers were not in a stressful situation. Under stress, they were far more likely to release tension through violence against civilians than by bucking discipline. In May and June, as several hundred thousand soldiers entrained for Manchuria, the strain of garrison duty, anger over continuation of the war, and the soldiers' latent anti-Semitism issued in a series of pogroms. In Minsk, soldiers about to leave for the front attacked Jews in a two-day rampage, and there were similar pogroms in Narva, Brest-Litovsk, Siedlce, and Bialystok. Before soldiers climbed on troop trains in Kiev, they beat to death two Jews distributing revolutionary handbills at the station.[31]

The pogroms had a specific catalyst, imminent entrainment for the front; though they involved regulars as well as reserves, they were in effect the culmination of the mobilization disorders of 1904. Other situations constantly provoked soldier violence against civilians. As an order of September 2 to the Warsaw military district put it, too frequent use of troops, often without clear purpose,

> leads only to their being jeered by the mob and is in itself enough to embitter both sides. Once troops have been called out, they must act . . . energetically, so that the mob respect the troops as a force. Acting resolutely in every instance will, perhaps, produce excessive casualties, but this is inevitable.[32]

The order not only pinpointed the source of the emotional pressure on soldiers, it sanctioned the discharge of tension against civilians.

Soldiers suffered from more than taunts, of course. Especially in the borderlands, where national hatred of the Russian interlopers amplified social antagonisms, soldiers came under repeated attack for no other reason (albeit, not necessarily a bad one) than that they served the

Tsarist government. In the Baltic provinces, in Poland, in the Caucasus, civilians threw bombs at patrols and ambushed lone soldiers. Soldiers naturally responded in kind. In Lodz, spiraling civilian ambushes and unprovoked military assaults on civilians culminated on June 10 in a workers' insurrection and vicious reprisals by soldiers, who cornered and gunned down civilians in their apartments; between 250 and 300 civilians died, another 700 were wounded.[33] In Tiflis, following a series of demonstrations at the city council, cossacks were called on August 29 to clear the building. Responding to verbal abuse alone, they opened fire on the crowd sitting in the council chambers, killing (according to a semiofficial account) 39 and wounding up to 70. The cossacks sustained a few injuries because they were caught in their own crossfire.[34]

Massacres akin to those in Lodz and Tiflis were generally confined to the borderlands, at least between Bloody Sunday and October. Everywhere, however, there was a persistent undertone of barely suppressed rage. The principal perpetrators of violence were the cavalry—the cossacks above all—who had most frequently to face angry mobs of peasants, workers, and students. The behavior of the cossacks was such that they were despised even by the public whom they were ostensibly protecting. In Saratov Province, where cossacks took the field against particularly severe agrarian disturbances in June and July, the provincial zemstvo (representing those most threatened by peasant rebellion) attempted to file a complaint against the cossacks with the Ministry of War. In August, the Smolensk city council pronounced the quartering of cossacks on civilians illegal, suspended the payment of money to provision the cossacks, appealed to soldiers to be less violent, and discussed organizing a city militia for the defense of the public.[35] From all over Russia there were reports of unprovoked cossack assaults on civilians—sometimes against demonstrators, but almost as often against civilians whose only offense was to be on the streets when cossacks were about.

The soldiers' violent reaction to civilian taunts and assaults is understandable, it served the government's purposes, but it, too, was a species of demoralization. The excess of zeal that soldiers displayed in Lodz on June 10 may have gratified officers, but the fact that when the firing was over soldiers turned to looting, and that two nights later overwrought soldiers, mistaking shadows for insurgents, tore down the wall around their barracks and loosed a volley into the dark, ought to have caused concern.[36] The behavior of the cossacks at the Tiflis Duma was not a model of discipline, either. And even cossacks occasionally complained about being sent against every disorder and every demonstration—not out of sympathy with workers and peasants, but because they were overworked. Both the manner and frequency with which soldiers were deployed against civilians strained the army's cohesion. Nevertheless, the soldiers did their job: cossacks put a temporary end to peasant disorders in Saratov Province, soldiers broke the back of the workers' movement in Lodz and in so doing may have forestalled similar explosions in other Polish cities. Yet the endless patrols, the posts at factories and on estates, the cossacks, even the occasional bloodbaths, did not check the revolution.

The Potemkin *and the Revolutionaries: Mutiny Misunderstood*

The onset of revolution awakened the revolutionaries' interest in the army, but occasioned no reexamination of earlier assumptions. For instance, both Socialist Revolutionaries and Social Democrats continued to look for support first in the officer corps. Georgii Plekhanov for the Mensheviks and Aleksandr Bogdanov for the Bolsheviks urged that officers be recruited as the revolution's technicians. Sergei Mstislavskii, the librarian of the General Staff Academy and an SR, made contact with a group of liberal officers in the higher military schools in Petersburg early in 1905, and the SRs put the most radical of them to work on the technical planning for an insurrection in the capital. The insurrection that revolutionaries anticipated was civilian rather than military, but they hoped that sympathetic officers would provide leverage over large bodies of soldiers. As Mstislavskii wrote later, "There was no great zeal for work with soldiers. . . . The question was framed as follows: if we have the officers behind us, we will *thereby* get the soldiers, too—officers will be able to bring them out for the people's cause 'on command'."[37] Plekhanov subscribed fully to this view, arguing in February that the outcome of an uprising depended upon the behavior of the army, and that soldiers would follow the lead of their officers.[38]

Revolutionaries frankly doubted their ability to sway soldiers. When Bogdanov at the Bolshevik Third Congress in April 1905 urged that an all-out effort be made to win over selected units, a certain Rybkin, delegate from Baku, responded: "I think it is almost impossible to put propaganda among soldiers on a proper footing. It will hardly be possible to effect the transfer of a unit to our side, as comrade Bogdanov suggests."[39] To judge from the absence even of the words "army" and "soldiers" from the resolutions of the Third Congress, Rybkin expressed the Bolshevik consensus. Likewise, the Menshevik Conference of Party Workers, also meeting in April, declined for "lack of time" to discuss a resolution on agitation in the army.[40] Social Democratic publicists did urge that, even though peasant conscripts might be unreceptive to revolutionary propaganda, some attention be paid to soldiers, if only because the army could thwart the revolution. And revolutionaries did crank out many leaflets for soldiers. As a Bolshevik observed of these leaflets in June, however, "one gets the impression that they were written because it would be sinful not to, but the authors themselves do not believe very strongly in their utility or expedience."[41]

The activities of local revolutionary organizations reflected the prevailing scepticism about winning support in the army. A few SD organizations set up military organizations (as they were known generically) specifically to work in the garrisons, but their distribution suggests the low priority revolutionaries assigned to recruiting soldiers. Of the seventeen SD military organizations known to have existed as of June 1905, thirteen were in the Caucasus, the Baltic provinces, or in Poland and the adjacent areas of the Jewish Pale. The Bund and Latvian SDs were especially active in the barracks because they had proportionately larger followings among their peoples than did Russian SDs, and because Latvian and Jewish reserves were mobilized early and in large numbers in 1904. In Poland and the Caucasus, soldiers were the only sizeable Russian element to which Russian revolutionaries could devote their energies, while the mobilization of native reserves provided native revolutionaries an ideal entree to the barracks.[42] Through the middle of 1905, the Russian parties—SRs as well as SDs—had scarcely any contact with soldiers in the empire's heartland, except by way of leafletting. Only the special conditions of the borderlands induced revolutionaries to attend seriously to the barracks.

Though revolutionaries did not trust agitation to neutralize the army, they were not on that account prepared to foreswear revolution. They hoped instead to overcome the regular army with a "revolutionary army." "Revolutionary army" was a term vague enough to cover all elements of the population that opposed the regime, but ordinarily it connoted urban and rural guerrilla groups (in the training and leadership of which radical officers might prove of use). All the revolutionary parties, Mensheviks most definitely included, exhibited a lively interest in the technique and tactics of street and barricade fighting, but few believed that urban guerrillas could achieve a conventional military victory. They expected, rather, that hard fighting would demoralize the troops. As Lenin argued in January, if the army encountered armed resistance from the proletariat, soldiers would understand that they were being used criminally against their own brothers, would begin to waver, and would eventually come over to the revolution.[43] This vision was not unique to Lenin, but its broad currency did not make it any more accurate.

The revolutionaries' scepticism about their ability to foment revolution in the armed forces was legitimate, but as the *Potemkin* mutiny demonstrated, they did not know what to make of military rebellion even when it was thrust upon them.[44] During the winter of 1904–1905, the SD and SR sailor circles in the Black Sea Fleet merged into a single organization independent of the civilian revolutionary parties. Autonomy resulted from arrests that wiped out the civilian organizations in Sevastopol, the SDs until spring, the SRs until late 1905. In the absence of civilians, sailors established a "sailors' central" *(matrosskaia tsentral'ka)* of representatives from the circles of both parties. By the time sailors reestablished contact with the SDs in the spring, there were groups of revolutionary sailors on every ship in the fleet, the sailors' organization was far larger than the civilians', and it was running off its own proclamations. The sailors were also plotting insurrection. The idea of a fleet-wide mutiny began to take shape after Bloody Sunday and the widely (but falsely) rumored hanging of forty sailors for mutiny in the fleet sailing toward disaster at Tsushima. By May, the "sailors' central" had formulated a plan that was widely discussed in the barracks and approved by consensus: when the fleet put to sea for summer exercises, sailors would seize the ships and sail either to Odessa or the Caucasus to promote revolution. As sailors from the battleship *Potemkin* wrote the Sevastopol SDs in May,

> the limits of patience have, at last, been crossed, and the Russian people has at long last understood all the injustice of Tsarism and is trying with all its might to untangle and cast off the fetters that have ensnared it. But it will probably not soon succeed; given the unfavorable conditions in which the people presently finds itself, much blood will be shed, and there will be many innocent victims, if no aid is forthcoming.
>
> Seeing the lamentable state of our people, we sailors shudder with horror and indignation . . . and many of us are prepared to go all the way for the common weal. . . .[45]

The Sevastopol SDs were less than enthusiastic about the sailors' plans. The resolutions that civilians offered at meetings with sailors called for ending the war, overthrowing autocracy, and establishing a democratic republic, but these goals were somewhat distant: in their speeches, civilians stressed that while the revolution was developing rapidly in the cities, much remained to be done before an insurrection could be contemplated. Only after the people (meaning civilians) had taken up arms against autocracy, and after the army had joined the people, should the sailors mutiny. The sailors' point of view was put succinctly by one of their leaders: isolated civilian risings were doomed to defeat, whereas the Black Sea Fleet could be taken over in its entirety and could serve as the nucleus for insurrection around the entire Black Sea littoral.[46]

Civilian and sailor revolutionaries had very different views of the part that the Black Sea Fleet should play in the revolution, and the sailors refused to heed civilian admonitions. Sometime in early summer they asked that Petersburg and Warsaw be informed of their plans so that those cities could second the fleet's initiative. The sailors not only vastly overestimated the influence that revolutionary organizations could exert, they greatly underestimated the Sevastopol Social Democrats' disregard for the sailors' plans. Sevastopol informed the SD emigré leadership (both Menshevik and Bolshevik) that the mood in the fleet was quite revolutionary—the sailors' request that Petersburg and Warsaw be forewarned was used to illustrate the point—but did not bother to inform any other SD committees in the south that the fleet might mutiny. Evidently, because they did not believe a midsummer mutiny wise, they did not believe there would be a mutiny. Meanwhile, shortly before the *Potemkin* sailed, the "sailors' central" put the finishing touches to its plan.

The events immediately preceding the *Potemkin* mutiny, and the mutiny itself, are well enough known. The *Potemkin*, newly commissioned, sailed alone on June 12 to test its guns before the summer exercises proper got under way. No mutiny was scheduled before the rest of the fleet put to sea. On June 14, sailors on the *Potemkin* protested against wormy meat. Both the worms and the protest being common occurrences in the fleet, it came as something of a shock when the captain and first officer threatened to shoot the instigators. That overreaction provoked a mutiny—the fact that so many sailors knew a mutiny was in the works must have been decisive—that cost seven officers their lives. Having mutinied, the crew of the *Potemkin* were confident that the rest of the fleet would support them. The *Potemkin* steamed for Odessa in order to contact civilian revolutionaries and through them inform the rest of the fleet of what had happened.

The Odessa SDs—Bolsheviks, Mensheviks, Bundists—decided that with a battleship on their side they could safely urge continuation of a general strike and street demonstrations that had begun spontaneously a week earlier. They asked the crew of the *Potemkin* to put 300 or so sailors on shore to seize the city's arsenals and public institutions and to call on the Odessa garrison to side with the people. The committee running the ship explained that sailors on land were not the military force they were at sea, and that if the most revolutionary went ashore, those left on board might begin to waver. They preferred to defer action until the entire fleet joined the mutiny. After this rebuff, the SDs lost contact with the *Potemkin*, while the crew became spectators to events in the city. On the night of the 15th they watched much of the harbor district burn (by official count, 1,260 people died in the fire that police set and at the hands of soldiers who blocked egress from the port). On the 16th, a burial party went ashore to inter a sailor killed during the mutiny, and the ship fired three blanks and two live rounds into the city when some members of the party were shot. On the 17th, the *Potemkin* sailed alone against the fleet, was joined by the battleship *St. George* and cheered by the crews on the other ships (suspected sailor radicals, and the most revolutionary battleship, had been left behind in Sevastopol), fled in panic from Odessa after a countercoup on the *St. George* the next day, and terrified officials all around the Black Sea littoral as it shuttled aimlessly to Romania and back. Low on fuel and water and demoralized, the crew finally accepted internment in Romania on June 25, the twelfth day of the mutiny.

The *Potemkin* mutiny was of course unique, not least in its long gestation. Revolutionary sailors demonstrated a stunning capacity for large-scale and sustained illegal organization, and they operated for years without detection (the Tsarist secret police knew so little about the background to the mutiny that they appealed to the French Sûreté Générale for information).[47] The sailors had both the resolve and the political vision required to organize insurrection. These conditions would not in their totality be replicated elsewhere. On the other hand, the inability even of so politicized a crew as that of the *Potemkin* to expand mutiny beyond their military enclave proved to be a persistent feature of military rebellion. Civilians claimed for themselves the function of supplying the larger political leadership, but their experience with the Black Sea Fleet put their ability to do so in question. Sailors and civilians had developed incompatible views of revolution, the Sevastopol SDs had persistently underestimated the sailors, the Odessa SDs had been unable to second the mutiny. There were, of course, extenuating circumstances: there was no precedent for the mutiny of a battleship, or for the planning and organization that preceded it, and civilian revolutionaries were harrassed by the police and confronted with numerous competing demands on their limited resources. Yet the dominant note in civilian-sailor relationships was the civilian revolutionaries' fundamental misapprehension of sailors. It remained to be seen whether revolutionaries had learned anything from the mutiny.

Revolutionary leaders responded to news of the *Potemkin* mutiny with alacrity. The Bolshevik and Menshevik centers in Geneva dispatched emissaries to make contact with the ship and sent instructions to Social Democratic organizations in Russia urging that every possible advantage be taken of the opportunity that had presented itself. Articles in the

Social Democratic and Socialist Revolutionary press offered tactical advice and stated the immediate objectives: with unwonted unanimity, Bolshevik, Menshevik, and SR leaders called on workers and Black Sea sailors to seize power in Odessa, form a local revolutionary government, and use the city as a bridgehead from which to extend the revolution.[48] The *Potemkin* mutiny was over before advice or emissaries arrived, but the emigré leaderships—alerted now to the revolutionary potential of the armed forces—issued a flood of appeals to soldiers and sailors to emulate the *Potemkin* and bid local organizations to step up their work in the army. The circular instructions sent out by the Geneva Bolsheviks called on Bolshevik organizations in Russia to apply themselves to work among soldiers and officers, upon whom the mutiny "should produce a stupendous impression"; a mid-July Bolshevik Conference of Northern Committees called for the formation of special groups for work in the army. In late summer, a Bund Congress called for intensive work in the army and the establishment of non-party soldiers' organizations. The Menshevik leadership, too, appealed for increased work in the army. Local organizations issued numerous appeals of their own to soldiers, and in late June and July the number of local SD military organizations more than doubled—at least twenty-one were formed in that brief period, as against only seventeen before the *Potemkin* mutiny.[49] Revolutionaries on the scene in Russia grasped the import of the mutiny quite as well as their leaders in emigration.

It was one thing to understand that sailors, and maybe soldiers, too, could under certain circumstances mutiny, it was another to understand what those circumstances were—and revolutionaries got them wrong. Without exception, they continued to believe that the pressure exerted by the civilian revolution caused the armed forces to waver in their defense of, and then to revolt against, the Tsarist regime. Leaflets repeatedly appealed to soldiers to heed their consciences and cease shooting unarmed civilians, and revolutionaries sincerely believed that involvement in armed conflict with civilians would bring soldiers to their moral senses. A Bolshevik writing in *Rabochii*, the Central Committee's paper inside Russia, in late summer made that point in articles addressed to a proletarian audience. Martov, the principal Menshevik commentator on military matters, counted on clashes between civilians and soldiers not just to activate the soldiers' innate morality, but also to shake their morale. Barricades, he asserted, were more effective than a thousand proclamations: every time workers were able even temporarily to check Tsarist troops, the soldiers' belief in the ultimate victory of the revolution—and their own willingness to revolt—increased. An SR writer made the same point: the principal obstacle to the army's changing sides, or even remaining neutral, was the apparent weakness of the revolution. Hence, the best way to revolutionize the army was to step up the pace of civilian revolution.[50]

It is worth stressing that revolutionaries made no distinction between a generalized revolutionary atmosphere—which certainly was a cause, though far from immediate, of the *Potemkin* mutiny, and which did contribute to the slackening of discipline in army units—and local pressure in the form of military involvement in suppressing or containing major demonstrations. Emigré writers treated the *Potemkin* mutiny not as an exception to but as an illustration of the general rule—despite the fact that they were well-informed on the background to the mutiny, and despite the fact that at almost the same time that the *Potemkin* mutinied, soldiers in Lodz responded to demonstrations and barricades by massacring civilians. The revolutionaries' assumptions, initially plausible (and shared by Minister of Agriculture Ermolov), survived events that falsified them because they conformed to the prevailing sense of revolutionary propriety: in the early twentieth century, Russian revolutionaries could not conceive that developments not originating in the civilian masses could be genuinely revolutionary (SR terrorism was only a partial exception).

If the *Potemkin* mutiny did not alter the revolutionaries' preconceptions, it did allow them, at least temporarily, to recognize that the army was a barrier to successful revolution—because it now seemed that the barrier could be surmounted. As Plekhanov wrote shortly after the mutiny, "The further the Russian revolution proceeds, the more obvious is the truth that for the revolution to triumph over the old order a part of the army must come over to the people's side."[51] Other writers—Lenin, Martov, and lesser luminaries—said much the same thing, so long as there seemed to be a real possibility that regular units might change sides.

When it became clear that the army was not emulating the *Potemkin*, revolutionaries forgot the need for military support and lost interest in the army. The flood of commentary on the *Potemkin* and the army ended abruptly in August, while the number of SD military organizations formed in August and September fell to between three and five, as against the twenty-one set up in the preceding month and a half.[52] Lenin's changing use of the term "revolutionary army" illustrates the revolutionaries' penchant for suppressing the unpleasant. Immediately after the *Potemkin* mutiny, and for the first time, Lenin included within the "revolutionary army" regular units that sided with the revolution, and until the end of July he continued to include soldiers in the revolutionary army. In August and September, however, Lenin gave the term an exclusively civilian context—usually proletarian partisan groups.

Only in October, when soldiers began to mutiny in large numbers, did he again specifically include soldiers in the revolutionary army.[53]

October: Did the Army Fail the Regime?

Revolutionaries misunderstood the *Potemkin* mutiny, but it did contribute to their midyear euphoria. June also brought the insurrection in Lodz, the prolonged textile strike (which had begun in May) in Ivanovo-Voznesensk, and a great burst of peasant disorders. Local committees reported that revolutionary sentiment among workers and peasants was growing faster than the revolutionaries' ability to organize it. That was the context in which the SR leader Mikhail Gots, writing in the same issue of *Revoliutsionnaia Rossiia* that contained two enthusiastic articles on the *Potemkin* mutiny, suggested that the revolution might be "permanent," pushing beyond bourgeois reforms in Russia, spreading to Europe, and doubling back to fortify the Russian revolution.[54] Gots was not the only revolutionary to offer that entrancing vision. It appeared to many that it was time to join the separate strands of revolution into a full-scale assault on the autocracy.

In June and July, revolutionaries did begin to translate their aspirations into specific plans. SRs resolved in June to organize a post-harvest peasant rebellion as a prelude to an urban general strike, with a railroad strike paralyzing the government's ability to move troops. The general strike, SRs believed, would provide an atmosphere propitious for insurrection. SDs tied their strategy not to the harvest, but to the elections for the consultative Duma, plans for which were officially announced on August 6. In early September, representatives of the Bolsheviks, Bund, and various national SD organizations resolved to disrupt electoral meetings and organize a general strike during the elections (set for mid-December); the strike, it was hoped, might turn into an insurrection, which the SDs affirmed to be the only means to overthrow autocracy. The Menshevik leadership favored participation in the elections in order to seize control of electoral meetings and elect a workers' parliament, but many Menshevik committees in Russia preferred the more straightforward strategy of disruption and general strike.[55] The Union of Unions, too, decided to boycott the elections and press ahead with its plan for a general strike, but liberals outside the white collar unions took a different tack. The Union of Liberation, increasingly worried about anarchy, called for participation in the Duma as a means of turning it into a genuine parliament, and a congress of representatives of the zemstvos and city councils adopted an identical resolution.[56]

Yet even as revolutionaries laid plans for a general strike and insurrection, even as the most cautious liberals continued to demand constitutional monarchy, revolution was slipping away. The number of striking
workers counted by the factory inspectorate declined from over 150,000
in both June and July to 38,000 in September, while the number of
peasant disorders in Grave's and Dubrovskii's count fell from 492 in
June to 71 in September. That these conventional figures are low by a
factor of two does not alter their implications: by September the worker
and peasant movements were at their lowest ebb since the beginning of
the year (see Table III-1). The Tsarist empire was far from calm, there
were pockets of severe turbulence, but it appeared that the regime was
well on the way to restoring order. That, at any rate, was the view of the
diplomatic community. As the British ambassador reported on September 25 (St. Petersburg date), "Most of my colleagues have already left,
and as I do not foresee any urgent questions arising that would require
my presence here, I should be glad of a rest."[57]

Why disorders should have fallen so precipitously after July, and then
so sharply reversed course in October, is a question that the literature on
the 1905 Revolution has not addressed. Thousands of workers listened
to revolutionary speeches in the universities in late September, but they
did not always approve of what they heard, and in Moscow at least the
workers were absent from the university halls until they began to go out
on strike.[58] A conference of railway employees convened by the Ministry
of Transportation on September 20 to discuss pensions heightened the
expectations of railway workers, but the railway union issued its call for
a general strike only after the strike movement was under way. The
opening of the universities and the railway pension congress contributed, fortuitously, to the onset of the October general strike, but of
course they had no bearing on the earlier decline of worker activism.
The most likely explanation for the ebb and flow of the strike movement
is the employment cycle. There was a normal summer lull and fall revival in some industries, and in the printing and baking industries, the
first to go on strike in Moscow in September, strikes were linked directly
to the resumption of hiring. The war-related industrial recession and the
industrial upturn in the third quarter of the year exaggerated the am-
plitude of the seasonal hiring cycle.[59] The number of workers returning
to industry in late summer and early fall 1905 was thus larger than
normal, while recession and recovery exacerbated labor-management
relations.

Workers who struck in late September and early October were, after
nine months of revolution, far more determined to expand, organize,
and politicize their strikes than they had been earlier in the year. This
became clear in the late-September strikes in Moscow, which lit the fuse

for the general strike. The initial strikes revolved around wages and hours, but other shops shut down out of sympathy; by early October, workers were setting up city-wide strike councils and demanding the right to choose representatives for collective bargaining and, more generally, basic civil liberties. Revolutionaries—Mensheviks in particular, though with Bolshevik and SR cooperation—helped to establish the strike councils, but the strikes were the workers' own doing, and they were eager to organize.[60]

By early October, too, the wave of strikes had rippled out to other cities. As in Moscow, even if they had specific economic grievances, the workers were at root acting in sympathy with or emulation of others already on strike, and had goals that were at least implicitly political. Sensing the momentum, the leaders of the All-Russian Railroad Union, supported by the Union of Unions, called for a general railway strike to begin on October 7 that was to achieve improvements in the lot of railroad workers, civil liberties, a political amnesty, and a constituent assembly. The workers' response was electrifying. By October 12 traffic had stopped on all central lines, and within a few days had stopped in Siberia, Poland, and the Caucasus as well. As local depots shut down, factories allowed suit.

No one planned for a general strike in October, no one organized it, no one led it. Though they had issued the call and were the principal sponsors, the leaders of the Railroad Union were put out of action by arrests on October 9. The revolutionary parties opposed the general strike until it was well under way—the Petersburg Mensheviks were the first to support it, but not until October 11, and their support for a general strike was not crucial to its spread. The revolutionaries had contemplated a general strike not in October but some months later; they believed the working class was as yet insufficiently organized and that a premature general strike would disrupt their own plans. SRs and Bolsheviks believed that a general strike was no more than a prelude to insurrection, which alone could topple the autocracy but for which they were hopelessly ill-armed; on October 13 the Petersburg Bolsheviks finally assented to the general strike, but only as a transition to insurrection. Neither for the first nor the last time, the revolutionaries' timetable and tactics proved irrelevant. Yet the revolutionaries, like the Railroad Union, had prepared the workers for a general strike by championing the idea for months and by helping to seed the empire with worker organizations that could build the strike from the bottom up.[61]

Impressed by the size and spontaneous organization of the strike, professionals joined in—not just the white collar unions in the Union of Unions, but also unaffiliated municipal employees. The Kadet (Constitutional Democratic) Party—heir to the Union of Liberation—which

had earlier favored participation in the advisory Duma announced its
support for the general strike on October 14. City councils gave tacit
support, and sometimes more, as in Siberia where a few authorized
committees of public safety. By the middle of the month, the strike had
penetrated to the heart of the governing apparatus in Petersburg, as the
staffs of the exchequer, the Senate, and all the ministries went out. On
October 15, the employees of the State Bank, by a vote of all against 8,
called for the immediate liquidation of the old regime and the establishment of a new regime by a constituent assembly.[62] Quite apart from the
effect of such declarations on government morale, the paralysis of the
machinery of government was enough to unnerve even the most autocratic of rulers.

The general strike shattered government morale less because of its
magnitude than because the army appeared helpless to deal with it.
Determined to concede no more than an advisory Duma, the Tsar and
his ministers yielded only when they concluded that the army could not
save autocracy.

The army's tasks in October were two, both familiar though both
more urgent than ever before: preserving public order, and keeping the
trains and other essential public services operating. To carry out these
missions, the army had as of early October 720,000 men in the garrisons
of European Russia, the total including 18,000 reserves mobilized beginning on October 1 to beef up infantry regiments in the Caucasus.[63] The
bulk of the army was stuck in the Far East. Even after Russia and Japan
signed the Peace of Portsmouth on August 25 (September 5), General
Palitsyn, Chief of the General Staff, feared that the Japanese might deceive Russia; it was better, he felt, not to move the troops back to Russia
with undue haste. In late September, now nervous about the renewed
unrest, Palitsyn finally ordered General Linevich, Commander in Chief
in Manchuria, to send back the sixteen regiments of XIII and I corps to
reinforce the Moscow and Petersburg military districts. Elements of XIII
corps pulled out of Harbin on October 14; they were at best weeks away
from Europe, and in fact the railway strike halted the movement of XIII
corps on October 15.[64] The regime had to deal with the October crisis
with the troops already at hand.

The army operated in October as it had throughout the year, and as
the strikes spread, clashes between soldiers and civilians mounted both
in frequency and intensity. Soldiers clubbed and shot workers and students in Moscow from late September well into October, and by early
October troops were dispersing mobs in Petersburg and a scattering of
other cities. By the second week in October, troops were engaged
everywhere. On the 11th, 12th, and 13th alone, troops broke up mobs in

Riazan, Iaroslavl, Samara, Petersburg, Kursk, Moscow, Ekaterinoslav, and Kharkov, in some cases inflicting significant casualties.[65] In Ekaterinoslav on October 11, for instance, cossacks and infantry shot workers at the railway station, and then fired three volleys almost point blank at high school students who had set up barricades outside their school. Barricades went up in the factory district, too, but workers did not try to defend them. Instead, on the 12th and 13th military patrols were harrassed by bombs and potshots. The official count of the civilian dead during the disorders was twenty-eight (against one officer and one soldier killed), with an indeterminate number wounded.[66]

The Tsar's October 12 instructions to Trepov (in the latter's capacity as Governor-General of St. Petersburg) to take more aggressive action to suppress public disorders signalled no change in government policy. Nor did Trepov's October 14 instruction to the Petersburg garrison not to use blanks and not to worry about casualties affect the behavior of the troops. Nor was it really necessary for Trepov (in his capacity as Assistant Minister of Interior) to telegraph the governors on October 12 and 13 to "take the most severe measures, and not hesitate to use armed force."[67] The authorities were already doing everything they could to control the streets. Whenever mobs formed—and as the general strike progressed, workers became increasingly aggressive—troops beat them back. If the mobs reformed, soldiers fired again.

Yet even as soldiers followed orders and fired on civilians, there were new signs of demoralization in the ranks. Demoralization was most obvious in small garrisons, where the physical and psychological strain was most acute. The behavior of the Revel garrison is a case in point. On October 13, half of the 3,000 soldiers in Revel left to reinforce the garrison in Petersburg. Of the 1,500 men remaining, 1,200 were either non-combatants or were tied up in guard details at public institutions, leaving only 300 to patrol the streets. Rumors that the entire garrison had left sparked mob violence on October 14. A few military patrols fired at looters, but most acquiesced in the looting, and some soldiers helped themselves to liquor that civilians overlooked. The guard post at the municipal gas works stood aside when civilians broke in to shut off the gas, and thus the city's lights. A company sent to put out a fire at a theater looted the buffet, repaired to the fire house, and shared the liquor with an officer. Convinced that he lacked the military force to restore order, the local governor on the 15th yielded to the insistent demand of revolutionaries and the city council that he free political prisoners. However, just when it seemed that revolutionaries would take over the city, on October 16 a company marched to the market and, though there was no disorder (as even official accounts of the incident recognized), fired repeatedly and without warning. The commander of the 23rd Infantry Division reported that soldiers had killed and wounded 350 persons.[68]

Even though an officer gave the initial order to fire in Revel, the soldiers willingly—even eagerly—perpetrated the massacre, and that reflected demoralization as surely as their earlier acquiescence in civilian disorders and their own looting and drunkenness. The Revel garrison was no longer under the control of its officers, and its behavior was no longer predictable. Elsewhere, demoralization appeared in the less obvious guise of an excess of zeal—as manifested, for instance, by the cossacks and infantry who slaughtered high school students in Ekaterinoslav. That was how soldiers responded to similar pressures throughout the year: when they were constantly on the street or on alert, when they were threatened with bodily harm by mobs or lone gunmen, they struck out at civilians. But the pressure was more intense in October than ever before, the demoralization correspondingly greater, and when the civilian pressure on soldiers eased, demoralization would be expressed in ways other than violence against civilians. The soldiers' October rage was a prelude to mutiny.

Yet if demoralization in the ranks—which is more apparent in retrospect than it was at the height of the October strikes—was an early warning of future difficulties, the immediate problem for the regime was that the wholesale application of military force had no visible effect on the course of the strike. Soldiers could not drive workers back to factories and depots, students back to school, or civil servants back to their offices. Soldiers could not even clear the streets permanently. And they could not by themselves operate the railways or public utilities, though they tried. The five railroad battalions in European Russia (one of them in the Caucasus) could work no more than a handful of trains. They did manage to run a few trains between Moscow and Petersburg, and operated a few more at other depots. Technical troops, meanwhile, operated a few utilities: the water works in Moscow, the electrical power plant in Petersburg. This did not diminish the impact of the strike in the least.[69]

The army's ability to restore order was the principal topic for the Committee of Ministers—chaired by Sergei Witte, back from negotiating peace with the Japanese and the man to whom most in authority now looked to rescue the regime from its domestic crisis as well—when it met on October 12 to consider how to deal with the railway strike. Minister of War Rediger was far from reassuring. Rediger and Trepov reported that there were sufficient troops in the capital to suppress an insurrection (approximately a division of infantry was in the process of moving from Revel and Pskov to Petersburg to reinforce the nine Guards infantry and six Guards cavalry regiments in the city), but that it would be

impossible to restore movement on the railroad, even between Petersburg and the imperial residence at Peterhof, where the Tsar was cur-
rently residing. Rediger further implied that the army was overextended
and might be no more capable of controlling the streets than running the
trains. He pointed out that most of the army was in the Far East, that the
garrisons in Europe were weak, that prolonged employment of the army
in a police capacity had disorganized the European regiments, and that
reserves were becoming restive because they expected to be demobilized
now that the war was over. The Ministers concluded—and reported to
the Tsar—that there were not enough troops available to place striking
railway lines under martial law, that is, not enough men even to guard
the lines. When on October 13 the military and civil authorities in Moscow proposed that soldiers guard the stations and abandoned trains at
least within the city limits, Trepov responded that there were not
enough troops even for that.[70]

The army's obvious incapacity to restore rail and public services, and
its apparent inability to put an end to urban disorders, profoundly disheartened the government and was a major—perhaps the crucial—
consideration in the decision to issue the Imperial Manifesto of October
17 granting Russia civil liberties and a legislative assembly. The Tsar may
have believed, as he wrote his mother, that he had two realistic options:
"to find an energetic soldier and crush the rebellion by sheer force," or
"to give the people their civil rights, freedom of speech and press, also
to have all laws confirmed by a State Duma."[71] That was not, however,
the assessment of his advisors, not even of Witte, who repeatedly urged
the Tsar to choose between dictatorship and reform: Witte also told the
Tsar that he did not believe military dictatorship was feasible. Trepov
and Rediger had convinced Witte that the army was too demoralized
and too weak.[72]

By October 15, most of those who had the ear of the Tsar doubted that
the army could do the job. Since August senior officials had been discussing how the government could achieve consistency in its policy and
present a united front to the forthcoming advisory Duma. The discussions betrayed at first no sense of urgency, and centered on the establishment of a cabinet subordinate to a prime minister and bound to a
single policy (rather than the existing system whereby ministers were
responsible only to the Tsar and did not coordinate their actions). As the
strikes spread in October, talk turned from cabinet government to con-
stitutionalism, the more rapidly as confidence in the army faltered. The
ministerial conference of October 12 that reported to the Tsar on the
inability of the army to cope with the railway strike stated bluntly that a
unitary government with a settled (but as yet unspecified) policy was
the only way to end the crisis, and the Tsar assented on October 13,

appointing Witte to head the government.[73] By this point, however, no one believed that reorganizing the government would restore order. Witte first broached to the Tsar the subject of constitutional reforms on October 9, and on October 13 the Tsar informed an official urging military repression that he was prepared to grant a constitution. On October 14, the Tsar asked Witte to draft an Imperial Manifesto announcing the constitutionalist reforms that Witte had been urging; on October 15 Witte and others presented the draft of what would become the October Manifesto, and many of the Tsar's most trusted and conservative advisors—"almost everybody I had the opportunity of consulting," wrote Nicholas—urged him to accede to the demands for a constitution.[74] By that date officials in the Imperial household were contemplating flight abroad, and the Tsar's uncle and choice for military dictator, the Grand Duke Nikolai Nikolaevich, asserted that lack of troops ruled out a military dictatorship.[75]

Hesitant to the end, Nicholas asked Trepov to look over the October 15 draft, and to determine whether it would be possible to quell the disorders without excessive bloodshed. On the 16th, Trepov assented to the Manifesto (adding by way of consolation that the Prussian constitution had not worked out so badly), and told the Tsar that the military alternative would inevitably involve loss of life. As Nicholas knew (because Trepov reported such things to him), the army had already killed a great many people. He certainly did not have in mind a specific threshold beyond which casualties were unacceptable. Rather, Nicholas seems to have hoped that Trepov would assuage his autocratic conscience, and he subsequently noted that Trepov's reply "significantly eased the burden of the final decision."[76] Yet whatever may have been in the Tsar's muddled mind, it is clear that the decision to grant a constitution was made by Witte, Trepov, the Grand Duke Nikolai Nikolaevich, and the others who were—or like the Grand Duke might be—charged with seeing the regime through the crisis. Collectively and individually, these men pushed, prodded, and cajoled the Tsar because they were frightened. Never had so momentous a change in the Russian political system been rushed through in such haste. It had taken months to achieve cabinet government, just over a week to arrive at a legislative assembly and civil liberties. The Tsar's advisors, like the Tsar himself, may have quailed at the thought of further carnage. But if Trepov, Rediger, Witte, and the rest believed that massive bloodshed was, even if unacceptable, nevertheless a possible alternative, they gave no hint of this in their discussions, and they certainly did not act as though they had confidence in the army. The failure of the army to cope with the October strike impressed upon them the futility rather than the feasibility of a military solution to the political crisis.

It does not follow from the ministers' fears that the army could not have restored order and that the Tsar had no choice but to issue the October Manifesto. Soldiers in October as earlier in the year shot civilians with little hesitation, and they would have continued to do so. Indeed, in December soldiers would crush insurrection even though there were fewer of them and many had in the meantime mutinied. The only practical obstacle to military repression in October was that, scattered barricades aside, there was no insurrection to crush: there was no clear target against which to loose the army. Ironically, the absence of barricades disoriented revolutionaries as well. On October 16 and 17 the first signs of demoralization appeared among striking workers in Petersburg and Moscow. The government had given no sign of yielding to a mere general strike, and revolutionaries could see no way to turn the general strike into an insurrection. On October 17 the Bolshevik Central Committee told party activists in the capital that the strike was lost and that they should prepare to flee.[77] Loss of elan among revolutionaries and workers did not mean that the strike was about to end, but it does suggest that the government could have outlasted the workers. However, the Tsar and his ministers were demoralized because the principal prop of autocracy, the army, appeared to have failed them. Given so unsettling a turn of events, yielding to the demands of workers, professionals, and high-ranking civil servants suddenly seemed the reasonable thing to do. On the evening of October 17, the Tsar signed the Manifesto. Before retiring for the night, he wrote in his diary, "Lord, help us, pacify Russia."[78]

IV. Revolution in the Army

The October Manifesto failed signally to pacify the Russian empire. Although liberals backed away, and industrialists and gentry fled, from revolution, their absence was scarcely noticed in the up-welling of rebellion after October 17. The number of workers on strike naturally declined after the October peak, but workers continued to down tools in very large numbers, and the workers' movement acquired far more coherence and organization than it had previously exhibited. There was a burst of union creation, and though most unions were small, there were suddenly hundreds of them. More significant still were the soviets, which gave institutional expression to the politiciza-tion of the workers' movement that had become evident in the October strike; seven soviets emerged in October, fourteen in November, another fourteen in December, and in many other cities and factory settlements standing strike committees functioned as soviets. The early soviets, such as that in Petersburg, grew directly out of the city-wide strike commit-tees formed in October. Revolutionaries organized other soviets, as in Moscow, to wean workers away from strike committees too closely tied to the radical professional unions, and others still were set up under the pressure of workers to whom the revolutionary parties yielded. Though many revolutionaries (including Mensheviks outside Petersburg) viewed the soviets as competitors to their party organizations, most soon realized that the soviets could give revolutionaries leverage over vast numbers of previously unorganized workers. Revolutionaries viewed the soviets as political institutions mobilizing workers for a new assault on the regime; workers looked to soviets to secure economic gains. For both these reasons the soviets were soon arbitrating disputes between management and labor and in many other ways acting as local shadow governments.[1]

Less organized and far more frightening was the jacquerie in the rural districts. Under the impact of the general strike, the October Manifesto, and the ensuing turbulence in the cities, the peasant movement surged to a peak in both the incidence and violence of disorders. Railway workers, migrants returning from the cities, and the occasional radical teacher and priest urged peasants to emulate workers and seize the land, and peasants began to apply working class terminology to their own rebellion, occasionally calling the looting of a gentry estate a "strike." But peasants had no need of direct stimulus from workers or radicals—the October Manifesto and the government's obvious loss of control over the cities were sufficient to convince peasants that they ought to seize the land. Peasants interpreted the October Manifesto as the Tsar's long-awaited signal to drive out the gentry: the rumors that had circulated in the villages early in the year were no more than a shadowy anticipation of the peasants' unshakable post-Manifesto conviction that they could now order rural society as they pleased.[2] Peasant rebellion was most ferocious in the non-Russian borderlands, particularly in the Caucasus, where armed peasant bands took control of entire provinces, and in the Baltic, where peasants drove the German barons to the cities in terror and in some counties destroyed half the baronial manors.[3]

Stunned by the enormous and unanticipated threat to the continued existence of the Tsarist regime—in the rural districts, to the continued existence of any governmental authority—the government required the services of the army as never before. After October 17, however, revolution convulsed the army, too; there were 211 mutinies between October 17 and December 31.* Not only did the mutinies severely erode the army's capacity to suppress worker, peasant, and national revolution, they made of the army itself a threat to the regime.

For the purpose of this study, only those incidents that meet the test for "manifest insurrection" (*iavnoe vosstanie*), the most serious crime in the Tsarist code of military discipline, have been counted as mutinies. (Tsarist regulations included three lesser crimes that met the contemporaneous Anglo-Saxon definition of mutiny.) Manifest insurrection was defined as collective resistance to orders by eight or more soldiers, and military courts applied this article only to incidents in which collective resistance to orders was "active," involving the use or threat of force to compel the officer in command to rescind or issue a particular order. That is the article under which charges were preferred against soldiers involved in many of the disturbances, and it is the criterion that I have applied retroactively when there is no record of the article under which charges were, or might have been, preferred.[4] As a practical matter,

---

*The mutinies are listed in Appendix I. Unless otherwise noted, sources for the mutinies mentioned in this chapter are listed in Appendix I by date, city, and unit.

TABLE IV-1. Strikes, Peasant Disorders, and Mutinies
October–December 1905

	Workers on Strikes, as Reported by the Factory Inspectorate	Peasant Disorders, as Recorded by the Department of Police and Central Newspapers	Mutinies
October	518,752	219	17 (15 after Oct. 17)
November	325,534	796	130
December	433,357	575	66

SOURCES: On workers and peasants, see Table III-1. On mutinies, see Appendix I.

every "insurrection" of which there is a record involved all or most of the soldiers in the unit. Yet statistics on mutiny so defined measure only one manifestation of military disaffection. The typical mutiny occurred in a unit in which discipline had already disintegrated, in which prior to mutiny soldiers had collectively ignored or insulted their officers, left the barracks at will, and held impromptu meetings. But indiscipline did not always culminate in mutiny. Outright mutiny—deliberate and collective defiance of orders by an entire unit—often began when officers attempted to restore discipline. If officers ignored the indiscipline of their men, there might be no act of mutiny. In short, the very high incidence of mutiny reflected disaffection in the army as a whole rather than in mutinous units alone.

If the figure of 211 mutinies in late 1905 is just one index, rather than an absolute measure, of rebellion in the armed forces, it is also somewhat arbitrary. Some disturbances can be counted as one, two, or more mutinies. That is the case, for example, when two or more regiments in the same garrison mutinied together or within a few days of each other, or when one unit can be said to have mutinied several times in quick succession. My procedure has been to count mutinous events: a single event could involve mutinies in a cluster of units, or a cluster of mutinies in a single unit. The total of 211 "mutinies" is thus conservative; a different but equally reasonable enumeration would increase the total substantially. In any case, the global total does not tell us much except that mutiny was widespread. The individual mutinies ranged in significance from mutinies by entire garrisons or major portions thereof (47 mutinies in late 1905 involved more than one unit), down to mutinies in hospital commands and penal escort detachments.

Grouping the mutinies by region and arms provides a better gauge of their intensity and impact. In the last two and one-half months of 1905, there were mutinies in seventy line and reserve infantry regiments and brigaded reserve battalions in European Russia (including the Caucasus)—more than one-third of the 203 such regiments and battalions then garrisoned in Europe. There were mutinies in only three of the sixteen Guards infantry and rifle regiments, but in eight of the sixteen Grenadier infantry regiments. If all line, reserve, Guards, Grenadier, rifle, and other infantry formations are counted, we still find that there were mutinies in one-third of the infantry units in European Russia.[5] That is an extraordinarily high incidence of mutiny, especially if it is kept in mind that there were what might be called passive mutinies— widespread indiscipline that did not issue in "manifest insurrection"— in many, possibly a majority, of the remaining infantry regiments.[6] The incidence of mutiny in the other arms in Europe varied from 75 percent in technical units, down to about 25 percent in artillery brigades, 20 percent in cossack regiments and battalions, and 15 percent in line and Guards cavalry regiments.[7] Sailors were so thoroughly mutinous that the Ministry of War considered discharging all but a handpicked few and, in effect, temporarily mothballing the navy.[8]

In Siberia, mutinous garrisons and railway committees in late November and through most of December controlled the railroad and the cities and stations along the line from Krasnoiarsk to Harbin and Vladivostok. However, the Siberian mutinies were significant chiefly because of the bearing they had on the availability for use in Europe of units from the army in the field. Because of the number of units in transit, and because so much of the traffic consisted of reserves who took trains in Harbin by storm and were not organized by unit, it is impossible to quantify the Siberian disorders, but their impact was to trap the field army in Manchuria. XIII corps, which began evacuation on October 14, was detained to restore order along the Transsiberian railway. However, the men of XIII corps were so unreliable, and had so demoralizing an influence on other units, that local authorities begged to be rid of them; seven of the eight regiments of XIII corps mutinied before they quit Siberia, and the eighth was thoroughly disaffected. By the middle of December, only a few companies from these mutinous regiments were straggling into central Russia.[9] Reserves aside, no units other than those of XIII corps left Manchuria for Europe before January. It is not true, as the conventional judgment has it, that by "the end of the year the return of loyal troops from the Far East after the conclusion of the Japanese war restored the upper hand to the government."[10]

Irrespective of their causes and goals, the volume of mutinies requires a reexamination of the army's place in the revolution, and of the situation of the Tsarist regime in late 1905. The established view is that mutinies were not a salient feature of the revolution, and that the soldiers' overall dependability determined the outcome of the 1905 Revolution. One of the few Western historians who has felt the mutinies worth a close look concludes that despite "some minor and occasionally troublesome mutinies in the army and navy . . . the soldiers and sailors as a whole never became a truly revolutionary force (though their superiors had some qualms on this score), and they proved a reliable instrument for suppressing the revolution in the winter of 1905–1906."[11] The nearly identical Soviet view is that while "Tsarism had reason to fear the possible loss of its military support," in the end "the overwhelming majority of the peasant army, because of its social composition, remained loyal to Tsarism, and this was one of the reasons for the defeat of the revolution."[12] In the end, soldiers did suppress revolution, but explanations couched in terms of the soldiers' reliability and loyalty to the regime do not accord with the fact that a massive military rebellion—in fact, revolution—came close to destroying the army. The soldiers who finally suppressed revolution were for the most part not loyal but mutinous.

Discipline Shattered

The mutinies grew out of rampant indiscipline, which was in turn a product of the events soldiers witnessed and in which they participated: the general strike, the Imperial capitulation of October 17, and the immediately ensuing collapse of constituted civil authority. News of the October Manifesto brought joyous people into the streets by the thousands in every city in the empire, and after impromptu celebrations and speeches they ordinarily set off to governors' mansions, police stations, and jails to demand the release of political prisoners. The authorities did not know how to respond: the appearance of the October Manifesto had stunned and disoriented them. When a mob besieged the Governor of Perm Province in his home and demanded that he read the October Manifesto, he complied. When the mob demanded that he free political prisoners, he rushed half-dressed to the jail to satisfy that demand, too. As the governor later reported by way of exculpation, "The Imperial Manifesto, appearing unexpectedly and received first privately via railway telegraph, took the local administration, which had received no forewarning, completely by surprise; the administration did not know what to do with the irrupting manifestations of insolent triumph of the revolutionaries and the disorders that arose in consequence."[13] He was not alone. In Ekaterinoslav, Vindava, and Nizhnii Novgorod as well, authorities in panic released political prisoners. In Ufa, the governor congratulated the triumphant citizens of his city on receiving the long-awaited freedoms, distributed copies of the Manifesto, and promised to fire some of the police. Even in Moscow the Governor-General promised a jubilant throng that he would free political prisoners, and a mob 10,000 strong marched to the jails and obtained the prisoners' immediate release.[14]

The dominant chord in the days immediately following publication of the October Manifesto was violence rather than celebration, but most of the violence, too, resulted from the collapse of civil authority. Not that officials were everywhere panic-stricken or complaisant. Troops in Sevastopol opened fire on the crowd at the city jail, killing six and wounding three. In Petersburg, the procession to the jail was turned back without bloodshed, but soldiers fired at demonstrators elsewhere in the city, as they did in Warsaw, Minsk, Riga, Kremenchug, Kiev, Libava, and other cities.[15] The officially inflicted casualties were probably higher in the few days after than in the days before the Manifesto, because so many people were on the streets celebrating what they thought was the dawning of a new era. Unofficially inflicted casualties were even higher, due to the pogroms—150 in all—that burst on cities and towns in the week after October 17. Upwards of 500 died in Odessa (October 18–21), roughly 4,000 died in all. Pogroms were the response of those who saw the apparent triumph of the revolutionaries as a mortal offense to values they cherished. They included peasants, who attacked Jewish property and gentry estates with equal violence, some workers, and above all tradesmen (butchers seem to have been involved in every urban pogrom) and day laborers. Urged on by priests and anti-Semitic rabble rousers, and by local officials who either incited or connived at pogroms, they indulged in any orgy of murder, looting, and blind destruction.[16] However, virulent anti-Semitism was only one of the causes of the pogroms, and Jews were not the only victims of the post-Manifesto bloodletting. Russians attacked nationalities other than Jews, and there was a rash of murders of and mob attacks on workers, "intelligentsia," "students," and others whose physical appearance identified them as likely revolutionaries.[17] This anti-revolutionary, anti-Jewish, anti-elite violence appeared to be in the interests of the authorities, but it represented the collapse of civil authority as much as did the panicky release of prisoners.

By the end of October, the joyful demonstrations and mob violence had swept away the edifice of rules and regulations on public behavior that had buttressed the old regime. Even the most reactionary officials appeared to be helpless to maintain Tsarist law and order, and they certainly did not know any longer what was permitted and what was forbidden. Nor could they have known, since the government in Petersburg was slow to issue new administrative guidelines and itself appeared to be yielding to revolutionary pressure, for example by informing censors on October 19 that they should continue to enforce the old rules on the press but be guided by the spirit of the Manifesto, and by announcing a political amnesty on October 21. As October came to a close, mass political meetings were proceeding without letup, newspapers were appearing uncensored, and the soviets were meeting with little hindrance. Police were demoralized, and in some cities themselves attended political meetings and talked of going on strike. Appropriately, the weeks after the publication of the October Manifesto were later thought of as "the days of freedom."[18]

The collapse of civil authority and the uncontrolled revolutionary demonstrations and anti-revolutionary violence devastated the cohesion and discipline of units already exhausted from their labors during the general strike. In some cities, soldiers shot at the post-Manifesto crowds not because they were ordered to do so but out of panic. In Minsk on October 18, soldiers inside the train station who had just been tossed into the air by a joyful mob of railway workers opened fire when they heard shots in the distance, then took cover and kept firing; more than fifty civilians were killed and roughly one hundred wounded, most of them—as an official report noted—in the back. On a smaller scale, the same happened in other cities: soldiers confronted by large numbers of excited civilians became nervous and opened fire.[19] Soldiers also took part in the pogroms, either as operational units supposedly assigned to restore order, or spontaneously; in Ekaterinoslav, entire regiments poured out of their barracks to beat Jews.[20] In Kurgan, soldiers rushed from their barracks to attack a revolutionary demonstration, while in Askhabad soldiers in a patriotic demonstration fought revolutionary demonstrators. In Tiflis, after a few days of exchanging salutes with the celebrating crowds, on October 22 groups of unarmed soldiers accompanying a patriotic demonstration beat up natives who refused to cheer, while other soldiers responded to what they claimed were shots from a newspaper office by killing forty-one civilians.[21] On October 20, in one of the most gruesome incidents of the post-Manifesto days, a raging mob in Tomsk trapped revolutionaries and unlucky bystanders in the railway offices, set fire to the building, and bludgeoned to death everyone trying to escape. Soldiers on the fringes watched impassively, then shot anyone crawling out on the roof or window ledges to escape the flames. The dead and wounded numbered in the hundreds.[22] These were the acts of enraged soldiers lashing out blindly at civilians who appeared to threaten them, not of patriotic defenders of the regime. The soldiers had degenerated into a uniformed mob.

In other garrisons in different circumstances, demoralization took forms less violent and more transparently threatening to the well-being of the regime. In Viazma, Chardzhui, Novyi Margelan, and Blagoveshchensk, soldiers took a leading part in the revolutionary demonstrations that greeted the October Manifesto.[23] In Baku, sailors in the naval barracks beat up a patriotic demonstration, while soldiers who had earlier accompanied patriotic demonstrations were soon looting stores, molesting Moslem women, and brawling with police. In Tiflis, too, soldiers after October 22 beat up both natives and police.[24] Everywhere—in cities shaken by civilian and military violence no less than in cities where the authorities had offered no resistance to revolutionary mobs—officers found within a few days of October 17 that they no longer had any control over the behavior of their men on or off the street. Soldiers wandered out of barracks at will, mingled with the crowds that congregated on city streets, attended mass political meetings, themselves met to discuss current events, drank on and off duty, and smoked demonstratively in the presence of and talked back to their officers.[25] An order to units in the Vilna military district in early November observed that "the incidence of outrageous behavior by enlisted men outside the barracks, and especially on city streets, has increased to an extreme. In Vilna, for example, in the course of three weeks there have been 20 more or less serious disorders."[26] "Outrageous behavior" seeped into the very heart of the military machine: in an order of 23 November, Minister of War Rediger called attention to the frequent public drunkenness, disrespect for officers, and sloppy dress on the part of enlisted men employed in his ministry.[27] These and other orders calling on officers to restore discipline had not the slightest effect, and the cancer of insubordination ate rapidly away at the Tsarist military machine.

Soldiers repeatedly and insistently cited the October Manifesto to justify their indiscipline (or as they themselves said, their freedom), despite the fact that the Manifesto contained not a word about the army. The commander of the 50th reserve infantry brigade in Petersburg noted that "from personally questioning the men in my brigade, and in the depot infantry battalions, I am persuaded that they have an incorrect understanding of the meaning of the Imperial Manifesto of 17 October," and he instructed officers to explain that "there have been no changes in the order of military service."[28] The regimental chaplain of the Ekaterinoslav Grenadiers in Moscow, asked by the men to explain the meaning of the Manifesto, "stated categorically that the Manifesto did not apply to soldiers. The soldiers protested, declaring to the priest that they were citizens like all the rest. One of the soldiers, carried away in the argument, threw a pillow at Father Orlov."[29] In Warsaw, Vladivostok, and Saratov, too, garrison and regimental commanders felt compelled to explain the October Manifesto to the troops, because soldiers believed that the contents of the Manifesto were being kept from them. In other garrisons—the Rembertow artillery camp outside Warsaw, in Askhabad, in Kars, in Krasnovodsk, on the cruiser *Rossiia* in Vladivostok—soldiers and sailors forced their officers to read the Manifesto to them and insisted that the liberties promised therein applied to soldiers.[30] Like the pillow-throwing soldier in Moscow, they refused to believe assurances to the contrary.

The soldiers' insistence that the October Manifesto legitimated indiscipline reveals the psychological underpinnings of their post-Manifesto behavior: they acted precisely like peasants, which they were by origin and had remained while in service. Soldiers did not simply misunderstand the terms of the Manifesto. While it is conceivable that they may at first have believed that the Manifesto gave them the right to attend and organize meetings, there was only a psychological link between the Manifesto and other aspects of their post-Manifesto behavior: drinking, irregular dress, disrespect for officers, even violence against civilians. Soldiers acted as though the totality of the old rules and regulations had been annulled. Like peasants, they concluded from the obvious fracture of civil authority—general strike, Manifesto, demonstrations, pogroms, "days of freedom"—that the fetters restraining them had also snapped, and that they could seize their own freedom. And like peasants they insisted that the Tsar himself had so ordered. The bonds of discipline were at root psychological, and the October Manifesto and surrounding events had shattered them. Soldiers no longer believed they would be punished for insubordination. Because indiscipline and insubordination were universal, there was nothing officers could do about it.

Indiscipline, no matter how widespread, was not yet mutiny, though the variety of indiscipline that debilitated the armed forces after October 17—refusal to believe that the old code of discipline still applied—led logically to mutiny. The mutiny, or riot, or even insurrection, at the Kronstadt naval base on October 26–27 exemplifies one path from indiscipline to mutiny.[31] The mutiny itself was atypically violent, yet violence was not uncharacteristic of the behavior of soldiers and sailors in the post-Manifesto days. What was unusual at Kronstadt was that indiscipline and mutiny begat violence rather than the other way around. In any case, the ferment that preceded the Kronstadt mutiny differed little from what was going on in other garrisons, and we can see in it the revolutionary implications of indiscipline. Moreover, because the violence ensured wide publicity, Kronstadt's mutiny, though not the first after October 17, was the symbolic beginning of the soldiers' revolution.

The October Manifesto produced the same reaction in Kronstadt as elsewhere, but the garrison, both navy (9,000 men) and army (4,000), was unsettled even before October 17. The dispatch of ships to the

Pacific had entailed the transfer of large numbers of naval personnel from port to port, while Kronstadt's fortress gunners had been sent to Vladivostok and replaced by 2,000 time-expired artillerists from the western borders kept in service until the end of the war. Kronstadt also served as a dumping ground for unruly sailors from other bases, including a contingent of several hundred who had mutinied at Libava in June. In midsummer, Kronstadt experienced in acute form the indiscipline observed in so many garrisons: there were food riots and the destruction of brothels located conveniently opposite the barracks, and fortress infantry had repeatedly to break up mobs of sailors on the streets. News of the October Manifesto precipitated both patriotic and revolutionary demonstrations, sailors and soldiers mingled in the crowds listening to anti-government speeches, and they accompanied the action in the streets with vociferous protests against conditions in the barracks. General Beliaev, the fortress commandant, believing that enlisted personnel had misunderstood the October Manifesto, explained the Manifesto to an assembly of officers and senior NCOs and ordered them to tell the men that the Manifesto did not apply to the armed forces. Beliaev also asked military and civilian clergy to help calm the garrison.

Neither officers, nor priests, nor revolutionaries were able to persuade the Kronstadt garrison to ignore the Manifesto. At an October 23 meeting attended by as many as one thousand sailors, some fortress soldiers, and several thousand civilians, revolutionaries denounced the Manifesto, pointed out that it did nothing to address the needs of enlisted men, and urged their audience to protest barracks abuses. The soldiers and sailors who spoke came prepared with lists of demands. These included a reduction in the length of military service, more pay, better food and uniforms, free disposal of off-duty time, unrestricted access to all public events, removal of notices forbidding soldiers and sailors to walk in parks and gardens (the signs were posted directly beneath notices banning dogs), and the right to consume alcoholic beverages, "since sailors are not children under the care of their parents."[32] The commander of the Baltic Fleet, Admiral Nikonov, who had hastened to the scene to persuade the sailors to disperse, observed in a report the same day that "enlisted men, with the proclamation of the Imperial Manifesto, wish to know whether the freedoms extend to them, too, and protest against the existing state of affairs."[33] In fact, sailors insisted that the Manifesto applied to them. A draft petition presented by some sailors on the 23rd included, in addition to service-related demands, the following:

> According to the Manifesto, sailors are Russian citizens. As such, they have the right to gather and discuss their affairs . . . Freedom of speech. After all, enlisted men are allowed to say only: "Just so, sir," "No, sir," "Yes, sir."

They should have the right to say openly, to their commanders and everywhere, what they want.[34]

They were already acting as though this demand were an accomplished fact.

On October 24 and 25, Admiral Nikonov toured the barracks to listen to the men's complaints, and he reported that their demands fell into three categories: those that were "economic," pertaining to food, uniforms, and barracks conditions; those that could not be satisfied because funds were lacking, e.g., the establishment of libraries for enlisted personnel; and those that touched on changes in the very nature of military service, such as free disposal of off-duty time, elected disciplinary courts, and the like. In one of the barracks a sailor speaking for his unit argued passionately that enlisted men must be allowed to hold meetings to review all existing military regulations. Though they were advancing their claims piecemeal, the sailors were clearly after revolutionary changes in the structure of authority in the Tsarist armed forces.

Almost any incident might have precipitated the riot, but the immediate spark was itself a microcosm of the seething discontent in Kronstadt. Even as Nikonov toured the barracks, sailors and soldiers burned brothels, milled about on the streets, and turned over soup cauldrons, and rumors that an uprising was planned for the 30th (when another mass meeting was scheduled) swept through the garrison. On the morning of the 26th, a fortress infantry company handed their commander a list of demands and set out in an unsuccessful quest for support from sailors. They returned to their barracks "confident," as a report filed the same day (before the riot commenced and overshadowed the incident) remarked, "that the Imperial Manifesto of October 17 applied, with respect to all the rights granted, to the troops, who thus have an unlimited right to express their desires and state their needs, gathering for this end in open assembly."[35] Since officers did not see things in that light, the entire company (50 men) was arrested and in mid-afternoon loaded on the fortress railway for shipment to one of the outlying forts. When a mob of 700 sailors and artillerists that had been breaking windows and burning drapery in brothels and attempting to loot liquor stores heard about this, they rushed to the railway to free the soldiers. When part of the convoy opened fire, one sailor died, another was seriously wounded, and the enraged sailors ran to their barracks and grabbed their rifles. Word of the clash quickly spread through the garrison, and mobs of sailors were soon storming through the city.

The rioters numbered, at a minimum, between three and four thousand—armed with rifles, more than enough to terrorize the city. Six of the twelve naval barracks remained largely passive through the rest of the afternoon and night, in part because officers locked the gates. Of the other naval units, the torpedo school and four naval barracks rioted almost to a man. Many of the artillerists were on the street, and those who were not obviously sympathized with the rioters. Only the infantry remained under control, but they were too few to do more than defend their own barracks. Though the more politically sophisticated sailors tried to impose some organization on the riot, by and large the mutineers vented elemental passions. Some groups attacked barracks that had not joined, but most pillaged and destroyed liquor and other stores. All through the night they fired their rifles into the air, attacked officers who crossed their path, and destroyed officers' quarters. On the morning of the 27th, officers (including 21 of the rank of colonel and naval captain or better) and ordinary citizens fled the city. In the afternoon, eight battalions of reinforcements arrived, and the weary rioters formed into columns and drifted back to their barracks. Casualties, sustained mostly during the attacks on neutral barracks, were high: 26 killed (most of them rioting sailors), 107 wounded (including 81 enlisted men). Eleven naval barracks were disarmed on the 28th, 2,000 soldiers and sailors placed under arrest between the 29th and 31st.

Though the sailors were convinced that revolution had triumphed in civilian society, and though they aspired to a radical restructuring of the Tsarist armed forces, indiscriminate violence overwhelmed the revolutionary substructure of the Kronstadt riot. The same was true at the other end of the empire on October 30–31, when soldiers and sailors burned down much of Vladivostok and many Chinese with it. Even so, it was clear that because of the events of mid-October spontaneous military violence no longer played into the hands of the regime. It is also true that there was a poor fit between revolution as sailors and soldiers saw it and revolution as conceived by civilians. Revolutionaries warned the garrison not to give credence to the false promises in the Tsar's Manifesto, but the Manifesto was the key to the soldiers' and sailors' behavior. Through the few conscripts with whom they were in contact, revolutionaries tried, and failed, to lend direction and organization to military discontent. Under interrogation, one politicized sailor wept in anguish that the riot had not at all been what was intended, but sailors who attempted to restrain their fellows on the 26th were cursed and threatened.

The actions of the revolutionary movement after the riot did affect the construction that soldiers throughout the empire put on the Kronstadt events. Despite the fact that peace had been concluded, military authorities first ordered that those arrested in Kronstadt be subject to wartime penalties, including the death penalty. The Petersburg Soviet, which had already shown an interest in extending its influence to the army, decided on November 1 to declare a general strike to prevent execution (and also to protest against reimposition of martial law in Poland). Simultaneously, the Soviet issued a proclamation pointing out that the workers were interceding for soldiers and sailors, and by its action the Soviet did win popularity in the armed forces. Under renewed popular pressure, the government retreated, announcing on November 5 that those arrested would be tried under the peacetime code.[36] From the government's point of view, the consequences were disastrous, for the Soviet's intervention and the government's retreat reinforced the impact of the October Manifesto on the army. A Guards officer interviewed by the Paris *Temps* reported that the events in Kronstadt, and especially the workers' subsequent intervention, had made a big impression on the soldiers and that all units in Petersburg were restive.[37] Indeed, soldiers across the empire began to threaten their officers with "another Kronstadt" should their demands not be met.

Mutiny

The passage from rampant indiscipline to mutiny was easy, and through November it was accomplished by an increasing number of units with every passing week: 15 mutinies from October 18 to the end of the month, 44 in the first half of November, 86 in the second half. The overarching cause of mutiny was the soldiers' post–October 17 conviction that the old military order had collapsed: soldiers mutinied to implement their own vision of a just military society. Nevertheless, the precise circumstances that precipitated mutiny were as diverse as the soldiers were unruly. There were also important regional variations, and mutiny underwent a significant change in character in mid-November.

The 500,000 reserves in Manchuria and the Far East gave the soldiers' revolution there a character and dimensions impossible to measure with statistics on discrete mutiny: in effect, all 500,000 of the Manchurian reserves mutinied en masse and for two months. The October strikes severed communication between Europe and the Far East, and when word of the October Manifesto finally arrived (in Vladivostok by private wire on October 20, at army headquarters in Harbin on October 22), it had an explosive impact. The generals who ran Vladivostok (with a garrison of 6,500 sailors and 65,000 soldiers, of whom almost 40,000 were reserves) were as bewildered by the Manifesto as civilian officials to the west, and only on October 26, after receiving elucidation from Petersburg, did they forbid enlisted personnel to attend civilian meetings. That order had no effect other than to anger the soldiers. Both in Vladivostok and in the field, officers generally decided not to read the

Manifesto to their men; when soldiers asked, officers told them the Manifesto did not apply to the army. Soldiers concluded that their officers were hiding the truth, and the truth of which they were most convinced was that they should be sent home. Reserves had expected to be demobilized ever since the conclusion of peace, and they were both angered and worried by news from home that the allowances their families had been receiving had been terminated at the end of the war. With little hard information available about events back in Europe, wild rumors circulated among the reserves; the rumor with the most powerful effect was that in their absence peasants were already parceling out the land. But far more important than anything they knew or suspected was the reserves' absolute conviction that they should now be allowed to return to Russia. They were ungovernable, they expressed their hatred of their officers openly and without fear of retribution, and on October 30–31 the reserves in Vladivostok vented their rage in an orgy of violence beside which even the Kronstadt mutiny seemed pacific.[38]

So frightening was the behavior of the reserves that they got what they wanted. The evacuation schedule adopted in early October had called for XIII corps to be followed by cossack and cavalry divisions (the better to deal with domestic disorder) and by IX corps; no special provisions were made for reserves, who were to return with their units. However, in view of the Vladivostok violence and the mounting chaos in Harbin, and after a flood of entreaties from civil and military authorities in the Far East that they be freed of the reserves, General Linevich telegraphed the War Ministry on November 3 that it was imperative to ship home reserves before cadre units. On November 5 and again on November 10 (two orders, to reassure the reserves while the staff revised the shipping schedule), Linevich announced that reserves would leave first, in the order in which they had been called up; their trains were to be interspersed with those of the remaining elements of XIII corps, now diverted from its return trip and detailed to maintain order along the line, and IV Siberian corps, which was being sent to maintain order in Siberian cities.[39]

That order merely sanctioned the reserves' elemental flight home. Ignoring the niceties of the schedule, they mobbed the terminals and took trains by storm, the most aggressive and closest to Harbin getting first claim. To ensure that no obstacles stood in the reserves' way, Linevich treated with the railroad strike committees that had control over the line running from Harbin to Siberia. Other generals condemned Linevich for consorting with revolutionaries and even tried to incite soldiers against railway workers by blaming delays in evacuation on the intermittent strikes. But railway personnel were fully aware of the mortal danger in which they would stand should they antagonize the reserves, and they gave troop trains top priority and sent the reserves through even during strikes. By December evacuation was proceeding smoothly, the mob at Harbin had thinned, and reserves farther afield were beginning to calm down, though bands of them occasionally marched under arms to the nearest siding and commandeered the first passing train. With the reserves gone, cadre units isolated in Manchurian villages remained calm: in the field armies only two mutinies did not involve reserves.[40]

Evacuation of the reserves spared Harbin, but exposed the Transsiberian Railway to a military pogrom. After they had exhausted the ration money given them when they left Harbin, the reserves plundered station buffets along the line. They refused to abide by the regulation prohibiting entry into first-class buffets, and beat officers who stood in their way. Officers assigned to ride with them fled to passenger trains, but the reserves forced their way onto passenger trains, too, and squeezed into first-class compartments with generals. They refused to let other trains pass, shot up stations, beat up stationmasters who could not provide locomotives, and seized locomotives from switching yards and other trains. In short, the reserves terrorized cities, stations, railway personnel and everyone else who crossed their path from Harbin and Vladivostok all the way across the Urals. General Linevich telegraphed stations along the line to send the rioting troop trains through as quickly as possible. When the reserves finally crossed over into Europe, cadre troops were drawn up at the terminals to maintain order and speed them along.[41] The Ministry of War, unable to communicate with Harbin from mid-November until the end of the year because of telegraph strikes in Siberia (contact was finally reestablished via Shanghai), had no direct information on conditions in the Manchurian armies and saw only, as Rediger recalled, "trainloads of disorderly reserves, drunk and destroying the railroad," pouring into Europe.[42] Arrival in Europe was, however, a tonic. Once across the Volga, the reserves joined in revolutionary disturbances in only a few instances, for example pausing briefly to free arrested railway personnel.[43] Their overwhelming urge was to get home, where they played a notable role in the peasant rebellion.

Not only did the reserves control Siberian rail traffic into December, their mutiny spread to all of XIII corps, elements of IV Siberian corps, and all the garrisons as far west as Krasnoiarsk. The units of XIII corps, which still had their reserves, were as much a threat to the stations they were supposed to protect as were the reserves rolling through; they demanded to be sent home, and after they mutinied, they were.[44] Mutiny began in Chita on November 15 when the 3rd reserve railway battalion demanded demobilization of the reserves and grew until it had engulfed two of the regiments of XIII corps (141st Mozhaisk, 144th

Kashira) and the entire local garrison. The Chita SDs (the only substantial group of revolutionaries in the city) organized a soviet of soldier and cossack deputies and the military governor, General Kholshchevnikov, with absolutely no forces at his command, was reduced to ratifying the actions of the soviet (for which he was subsequently courtmartialled and imprisoned). In Krasnoiarsk, formal mutiny began when elements of 2nd Sofia and 141st Mozhaisk regiments (XIII corps), detained on November 16 and 17 to overawe workers and an unruly (but as yet nonmutinous) garrison, refused to leave their trains. On November 24, the 2nd railroad battalion mutinied and was joined by the rest of the garrison, which paraded through town on December 9. Elements of 10th Omsk and 11th Semiplatinsk Siberian infantry regiments (IV Siberian corps) refused to act against the mutineers, and the 2nd railroad battalion refused to leave Krasnoiarsk (an exceptional occurrence) and was the mainstay of a local workers' and soldiers' soviet. In Irkutsk, SDs and SRs discovered in November that reserves were so angry about being kept in service that they were conspiring to slaughter their officers, plunder the military stores, and "seek the truth" (or "seek justice," *pravdu iskat'*, truth and justice being identical so far as soldiers and peasants were concerned; the expression was common in peasant disturbances) of their demobilization.[45] The reserves did mutiny on November 26 and were joined by the local cossacks; elements of 144th Kashira refused to suppress this mutiny, too.

The revolt of the Manchurian reserves obtained the demobilization of reserves in Europe as well as their own. The Ministry of War had initially planned to demobilize only the 100 depot battalions (which held fewer than 50,000 men at the end of the war) that had fed replacements to regiments at the front, and only the oldest classes of reserves, men between 36 and 40, in other units. The bulk of the reserves in Europe were to be kept under arms until the return of the Manchurian units, because they were needed to combat revolution. However, on November 12 Minister of War Rediger reacted to the reserves' discontent just as General Linevich had done out in Manchuria: he reported to the Tsar that "it is impossible to go on like this, because the army is falling apart; to bring the army to order it is necessary to demobilize the dissatisfied element—the reserves."[46] The Tsar assented, and Rediger sent out the orders. Military district commanders were given discretion as to the rapidity with which they sent reserves home; there was hope that conditions in some districts might permit the retention of reserves. Most district and local commanders rid themselves of reserves as rapidly as available transportation permitted, and some went beyond official instructions, demobilizing time-expired soldiers who were not covered by the War Ministry order. By mid-December, most reserves in European Russia were home or on their way, cutting the army's strength by 240,000 men.[47]

It was less the behavior of reserves in Europe than the impact of early-November reports from Vladivostok and Manchuria and, possibly, an exchange of telegrams between the War Ministry and the Caucasus military district, where the 30,000 reserves mobilized in October were causing special problems, that inspired the rush to demobilize.[48] Rediger had reported to the ministerial conference of October 12 that reserves expected to be demobilized; reserves in Europe did express extreme unhappiness about the termination of allowances to their families (to pacify his garrison, the governor of Kazan ordered the allowances restored); and there is no doubt that, like Rediger, most officers identified reserves as the most unreliable element in the army.[49] Yet outside Manchuria and Siberia, reserves did not drive the soldiers' revolution. Reserves inspired only two of the twelve mutinies in European Russia between October 18 and October 31, only nine of the thirty-eight mutinies in Europe in the first fifteen days of November. Certainly reserves were involved in more mutinies than that—perhaps in as many as a third of the 211 mutinies in the last two and one-half months of the year—simply because so many units had filled up with reserves during the war.[50] But in relatively few cases did reserves either initiate mutiny, or dominate mutiny with their demand for demobilization.

The soldiers' revolution had deeper roots than the reserves' desire to go home, which is of course why demobilization had no impact on the incidence of mutiny; indeed, there were far more mutinies after than before demobilization began. Furthermore, if the reserves' discontent was unique, they acted for the same reasons that cadre soldiers did. Peace had been signed on August 23, and it is unlikely that reserves grasped the distinction between signing and ratification. Even after ratification on October 1, reserves did not act to force demobilization—they did so only after October 17. For reserves as for cadre troops, the October Manifesto eliminated the psychological constraints that had held rebellion in check.

The revolt of the Manchurian reserves aside, through the middle of November the majority of mutinies—22 of the 41 whose origins can be determined*—grew out of incidents that soldiers considered provocations and that galvanized them into mutiny. Given the rampant indiscipline, almost any affront could produce a mutinous reaction. For

---

*Characteristics of the mutinies are identified in Appendix I.

example, altercations between soldiers and civilians triggered three mutinies, including the Vladivostok riot, which began with soldiers beating up Chinese tradesmen. In Tiflis on November 9, when a patrol brought in two men of the 15th Tiflis Grenadiers for forcing butchers to reduce the price of meat, the regiment grabbed weapons, accused officers of showing favoritism to natives, and demanded (among other things) demobilization of reserves. In Lagodekhi (Tiflis Province) on November 14, when officers attempted to stop the men of the 264th Loriisk reserve infantry from beating merchants at the bazaar, soldiers stoned their officers and handed in a set of demands for changes in the barracks regime. The latter two mutinies were compounded equally of hostility to natives—after October 17, no security against mutiny—and the operation of the regimental economy, which forced the company *artel'* to procure provisions on a market in which prices fluctuated wildly because of railroad strikes.

The most common cause of mutiny before November 15 (13 of the set of 41 mutinies) was an attempt by officers to restore discipline by arresting the presumed instigators of insubordination or by dispersing unauthorized soldier meetings. Arrests touched off the Kronstadt riot and mutinies in the 7th Merv reserve battalion in Merv on October 28, a fortress artillery company in Batum on November 2, and the 249th Maikop reserve infantry battalion in Stavropol on November 10. An attempt to arrest a civilian talking to sailors in the barracks triggered mutiny in the 14th naval *equipage* in Petersburg on November 5, and an attempt to break up a sailors' meeting in Sevastopol on November 11 touched off full-blown insurrection. Closely related to these were mutinies that began when soldiers disobeyed routine orders (6 of the 41). On November 8, the Aleksandrovskoe local command (Irkutsk Province) refused to clear snow; when an officer tried to arrest a soldier for disobedience, the unit shot up the post. In Kremenchug on November 9, the 272nd Korochansk infantry disobeyed the morning order to begin drill, and then presented demands.

What all of these incidents had in common was the soldiers' refusal to acknowledge that their officers had the authority to enforce discipline and the customary military routine. The same attitude underlay the insubordination that swept the army after publication of the October Manifesto, and when officers challenged the soldiers' perception of the new military dispensation, the men mutinied. Such conflicts were especially likely immediately after October 17, before officers understood how completely their authority had collapsed. But officers learned from experience. Of the 87 mutinies between November 16 and the end of the year the origins of which are known, in only nine (as against 13 of 41 through November 15) did attempts to reestablish proper discipline trigger mutiny. Soldiers were no more submissive than before, but officers had come to accept indiscipline as a fact of life.

Soldiers were so volatile after October 17 that in 18 (of the 41) cases indiscipline reached the flashpoint of mutiny even in the absence of provocation. Most of these self-initiated mutinies were spontaneous, rather than deliberated beforehand, as when the sailors of the 8th naval *equipage* in Petersburg on October 18 grabbed their rifles and attempted to break out of their barracks to join a passing demonstration (Guards infantry stopped them), or when the sailors of the Caspian flotilla in Baku drove a patriotic demonstration away on October 20. In a few instances, the reserves' overwhelming urge to go home led directly to mutiny. In the 81st Apsheronsk infantry in Vladikavkaz, appeals for demobilization escalated on October 28 into a strike in support of 45 demands. Reserves in the 160th depot infantry battalion in Gomel, having learned that they were to be transferred to a line regiment, told their commander on November 5 that they would go nowhere but home. Neither in these or in most other self-initiated mutinies did soldiers actually plot mutiny. Rather, indiscipline in excess became mutiny. With so many indisciplined units about, some mutinies of this sort were statistically inevitable.

One way or another, the stew of indiscipline was directly responsible for almost all the mutinies between October 18 and November 15. Nevertheless, there were at least two mutinies—at Sveaborg (October 29–30) and Batum (November 13–14)—that hatched from conspiracy and during the organization and implementation of which soldiers articulated the assumptions that elsewhere went unspoken. The mutiny at the Sveaborg fortress in Helsingfors harbor, engineered by a small group of soldiers who were not in contact with any revolutionary group, illuminates the mix of objective and subjective factors that engendered mutiny after October 17. Conditions in the barracks were bad and petty restrictions on the soldiers' movements numerous. Exploitation of soldiers as personal servants (up to four per officer) and through graft (soldiers were not issued even the inadequate equipment officially due them and were made to purchase boots through the senior artillery officer) was particularly severe. Many artillerists in the fortress were time-expired and believed they had a right to discharge now that the war was over. Finally, officers suppressed information about the October Manifesto. A group of soldiers in the artillery and engineering units decided to crystallize the soldiers' discontent by organizing a meeting to discuss demobilization. The summons they sent around on October 29 illustrates the change the Manifesto had wrought in the soldiers' perception of the social order:

I pray, comrades, that you gather, because the Tsar has granted freedom of speech for soldiers, too, which we must explain to our commanders, and [we have] a right to demand from them immediate satisfaction of our needs. . . . Brothers, comrades, let us unite in one thought, arm in arm and forward. We will show them that the soldier is a human being and that no one should despise him, we shall cast off this yoke and then, believe me, it will be well with those who remain, and they will send us home. We shouldn't fear them, there are more of us than of them, we have only to shout boldly, and they will make concessions.[51]

The fortress commandant attempted to cut the agitation short by promising to petition Petersburg for demobilization and by calling the artillerists to a special church service, at which the chaplain exhorted them to "fear God and honor the Tsar." (A soldier is reported to have interjected: "We fear God all right, but why do they give us rotten boots?"[52]) Afterwards, the artillerists were drawn up in front of the church and surrounded by armed infantry, but they boldly shouted their demands and threatened force to attain them. The infantry shouted encouragement. Fearing another Kronstadt, officers told their men to present their grievances. Among the soldiers' twenty demands (mostly on specific abuses in the barracks) was one that "all regulations compiled and signed by Generals, Colonels and Captains" be replaced by regulations drawn up by peasant deputies to the forthcoming Duma. In Sveaborg as elsewhere, local grievances were merely the point of departure for an assault on the entire structure of military authority. The final Sveaborg demand was: "Soldier meetings are indispensable because we must agree on our needs and express our opinions. *Forward*, brothers, with God."[53] On November 1, the commandant issued a 33-point order meeting all of the demands within his power to satisfy. For his pains, he was removed from his post.

More typical of the self-initiated mutinies was that of the Grodno artillerists: their mutiny was spontaneous, but it was a response to all of the pressures acting on soldiers inside and outside the barracks. After publication of the October Manifesto, discipline collapsed in Grodno as everywhere else, most rapidly in the artillery. The 12th artillery brigade, manned entirely by reserves, pressed for demobilization and (somewhat illogically) more pay. In the 26th artillery brigade, soldiers talked of better rations and uniforms and fewer beatings. The Kronstadt riot, which they read about in the local press, emboldened the artillerists, and incidents in which officers were threatened with bodily harm and forced to leave the barracks became frequent. On November 4, insubordination grew into mutiny. The reserves of the 12th brigade became so vociferous that they won a promise of demobilization, and the first battery of the 26th brigade refused to leave the barracks for drill and reiterated their complaints. On the 5th, officers attempted to arrest a pair of "instigators" in the 26th brigade, but the soldiers refused to surrender their comrades; when an officer fired two shots in the air, the artillerists drove him from the barracks. The corps commander hastened to the scene. The artillerists again demanded tea and sugar rations, the removal of a brutal Sergeant Major, decent uniforms, and "freedom." When the artillerists refused to disperse or hand over the soldiers who were to be arrested, two companies of the 102nd Viatka regiment were summoned. The two "instigators" were finally arrested, and the rest forced to return to their barracks.

That night, the men of the 26th brigade met to discuss the situation, with a representative from the local Bund organization in attendance (the Grodno Bundists had set up a military organization early in the year and had contacts in the 26th brigade).[54] The soldiers compiled a list of thirty-eight grievances, mostly of a local character but with the usual admixture of demands for fundamental change in the structure of authority. The Bund military organization published the demands in a special proclamation the next day. On the 6th, too, the military command, having learned of the meeting on the night of the 5th, surrounded the barracks of the 26th brigade with ten (or six; official accounts vary) companies of the 103rd Petrozavodsk regiment. Some of the artillerists were jailed, the rest were locked in the barracks of the 102nd Viatka regiment.

Repression was only temporarily successful, for in Grodno as in most other garrisons mutinies spread from unit to unit. Within a few days, the infantry was as mutinous as the artillery. On November 7, the Bund military organization distributed a proclamation and convened a meeting of 100 soldiers to protest the arrest of the artillerists. On November 14, the military organization arranged a meeting of representatives from all units in the garrison, excepting only the cossacks. The meeting condemned the arrest of the artillerists, expressed solidarity with their demands, and resolved to continue the struggle until the demands made by the artillerists were met.[55] Within a few days, nonmutinous disorders hit the 103rd Petrozavodsk regiment: there were protests against a brutal Sergeant Major, there was a food riot, and the commander promised concessions. On November 22 and 23, soldiers in the Petrozavodsk regiment (apparently without civilian assistance) organized meetings of representatives from other infantry units in the city; at one meeting, thirteen men from the Petrozavodsk, 102nd Viatka and 171st Kobrinsk regiments were arrested. On December 4, at a meeting so large and so defiantly in contravention of the military code that it amounted to mutiny, soldiers from the Viatka and 101st Perm infantry were addressed by Bundists, who urged them to influence the 103rd Petrozavodsk, the only regiment that in the Bund's estimation had not yet sided with the revolution. On December 12, a fortress infantry company refused to disperse civilians, and the 4th sapper battalion may—the information is soft—have struck in support of forty-two demands at about the same time.[56]

The chain of mutinies in Grodno exemplifies the process by which entire garrisons were lost to the government. The Grodno garrison did not rise in armed rebellion, but by early December it had mutinied almost in its entirety. The first mutiny, erupting from acute disaffection and indiscipline, provided grounds for mutinies in other units and—in Grodno, at any rate—afforded revolutionaries an opportunity to step in and organize the soldiers' discontent. Whether civilian revolutionaries were active in a garrison or not, mutiny in one unit crystallized discontent in others, just as the Kronstadt riot had accelerated the drift toward mutiny in Grodno in the first place.

Around the middle of November, the character of the soldiers' revolution began to change: as in Grodno, spontaneity gave way to purposefulness, and as soldiers made a conscious choice for mutiny, the number of mutinies nearly doubled, from forty-four in the first half of November to eighty-six in the second. Though incidents of all kinds, including altercations with civilians, continued to precipitate mutiny out of indiscipline, this was no longer the rule. Of the eighty-seven mutinies between November 16 and December 31 whose origins can be specified, fifty-six were self-initiated; only nine began when officers attempted to restore order, and only nine began when soldiers refused to obey a routine command. And soldiers began their mutinies far more deliberately than they had in late October and early November. Deliberate decisions to mutiny were taken for many reasons, but the pronounced tendency was for soldiers to emulate the action of their fellows. In eleven cases after November 15, news of mutiny elsewhere was the immediate stimulus. The penal escort detachment *(konvoinaia komanda)* in Samara mutinied on November 20 after reading about mutinies in the day's paper. The Bobruisk disciplinary battalion mutinied on November 22 after learning of the mutiny in the Voronezh disciplinary battalion (November 18). The 51st artillery brigade in Belgorod mutinied on November 28 after learning of a mutiny in the 36th artillery brigade in nearby Karachev on November 27. In Kazan on November 29 the men of the 229th Sviazhsk reserve infantry battalion (which had gunned down civilians on October 17) read in a local paper about another unit that had demanded the removal of all reenlistees (meaning senior NCOs), then themselves mutinized to obtain the removal of their own NCOs.[57]

Even when soldiers did not find such specific inspiration in another
mutiny, what they learned about or could see for themselves certainly
encouraged them to mutiny. The men of the 17th Turkestan rifles
(Chardzhui) were exceptionally calculating, and delayed mutiny until
they could see how other mutinies in the garrison turned out.[58] Most
soldiers simply noted the frequency of mutiny and decided that they
should mutiny, too. As they did so, they copied each others demands.
The demands of the Grodno artillerists, distributed as a leaflet by the
Grodno Bundists and picked up by newspapers all over Russia, were
copied either in part or with additions by soldiers in at least nineteen
other mutinies, some as late as December. The demands of the 2nd
Transcaspian railroad battalion in Samarkand provided a similar model
for mutinous units in Central Asia, and other sets of demands had an
impact on smaller regions.[59]

As soldiers began to deliberate their mutinies, civilians offered assistance, but to only modest effect. Their interest in the army galvanized by
the post-Manifesto mutinies, revolutionaries set up new military organizations (no fewer than 25 by SDs, for a total of 64 SD military organizations after October, and a minimum of 27—no doubt many more—SR
military organizations in the same period), and military organizations
that had lapsed into inactivity showed new signs of life.[60] By mid-
November the military organizations had penetrated some garrisons
and had begun to organize soldiers. While civilians can be given credit
for initiating only 1 mutiny (of the 41 whose origin is known) before
November 15, they initiated 5 (of 87) after November 15, including the
mutiny in Grodno on December 4. The SD military organization in Tiflis
organized a series of mass meetings that engulfed most of the Tiflis
garrison and led to the presentation of numerous petitions of demands
(November 20–26), while SRs organized a mutiny by the 7th reserve
cavalry regiment in Tambov on November 30. Revolutionaries were also
heavily involved in mutinies in Kiev (SDs, November 16–18), Samara
(SRs, November 25–December 3), and a few other garrisons. Other revolutionary military organizations, like that in Grodno in early November,
helped mutinous soldiers compile lists of demands once soldiers had
mutinied for their own reasons. Nevertheless, the civilian contribution
to the soldiers' revolution was marginal. The soldiers' willingness to
mutiny antedated civilian involvement and it was the collapse of discipline and the inspiration provided by other mutinies that created an
opening for civilian intrusion. Moreover, most mutinies did not involve
civilians in any capacity, and soldiers frequently rejected civilian offers
of assistance.

The mutinies were overwhelmingly nonviolent, and the absence of
violence was one of the defining characteristics of the soldiers' revolu-

tion: violence was incompatible with the psychology that was the mainspring of soldiers' behavior. True enough, soldiers did stone or beat a few officers who triggered mutinies by attempting to reimpose discipline, and in many more cases soldiers demonstratively grabbed their rifles, but in only twelve of the 211 mutinies were shots fired.[61] These included the riots in Kronstadt and Vladivostok in October, disorderly firing by mutineers in the Aleksandrovskoe local detachment in November, a brutal prison riot in the Voronezh disciplinary battalion on November 18, dispersal by force of a peaceful march of sappers in Kiev in November 18, and the armed resistance that mutineers in Krasnoiarsk offered to a punitive detachment that arrived in January (a month and a half after the mutiny had begun). In Europe, the only mutiny that can reasonably be described as an armed insurrection occurred in Sevastopol, where half the Black Sea fleet, some fortress units, and some infantry mutinied between November 11 and November 15, and where on November 15 there was an exchange of fire between mutinous and nonmutinous ships, while sailors on shore resisted the infantry attacking their barracks. However, the Sevastopol insurrection was unintentional. It began when officers ordered a shore patrol to fire on a sailor meeting and one of the sailors in the patrol shot the officers instead. Once mutiny had commenced, the Black Sea sailors had the organizational and political experience needed to risk resisting a determined government effort to subdue them. Sevastopol was the exception. In most cases violence was a product of disorganization rather than organization, and few mutinous units no matter how well organized were prepared to offer armed resistance to loyalist units—but then, mutinous soldiers were rarely put to that test.

Most mutinies—at least 135 of the 211 after October 17—revolved around the presentation of a set of demands and nonviolent action (meetings, refusal to perform duties, marches) in support of the demands. These petitions spelled out the soldiers' view of the new military dispensation, and will be discussed shortly. Irrespective of their content, there was a logical connection between the presentation of petitions and the lack of violence. The mutinies were nonviolent because after October 17 soldiers believed that the old military order had collapsed; hence, violence was unnecessary. When officers goaded them into mutiny by challenging their post-Manifesto perceptions, or when mutinies elsewhere inspired them, soldiers articulated their view of the just military order. Had soldiers believed that the old disciplinary code, with its severe sanctions against mutiny, still applied, had they believed force were required to overturn the old military order, they would not have mutinied in the first place. They had not mutinied before October 17, though every one of the conditions whose elimination they later demanded had been present. Mutinies occurred after, not before, officers lost control of their units—no force was needed to accomplish that—and after soldiers had concluded that their officers' customary authority had lapsed.

Once the psychological obstacles vanished, the principal requirement for mutiny was the establishment among soldiers of a consensus on the shape of a new military order. Consensus could crystallize instantaneously during an angry confrontation with officers, but even then indiscipline and the airing of grievances preceded and made possible the mutinous response. Elsewhere, indiscipline and angry talk gradually cohered into a set of demands that soldiers then presented to their officers. Almost without exception, the demands were presented collectively, not by a group of soldiers in a company, battalion, or regiment, but by the entire unit. Furthermore, leadership in the ordinary sense was virtually nonexistent: soldiers made up their minds to mutiny all together or not at all. Only rarely (in at most 15 percent of the mutinies, and probably in no more than 10 percent) is it possible to establish that any group of militant soldiers (affiliated with a revolutionary organization or, as at Sveaborg, not) or any individual revolutionary conscript played a key role in fomenting mutiny.[62] There were surely some soldiers more forward, or whose opinion carried more weight, than others in every unit that mutinied, but it required the common consent of all for mutiny. This consensus was achieved much as it was in peasant villages, through a mass meeting at which soldiers voiced their complaints and argued back and forth on the proper course of action, until holdouts had given in.[63]

The operation of community consensus made for quantum rather than incremental differences in unit behavior: any substantial dissent prevented mutiny. While some battalions or companies might mutiny to a man, other battalions or companies from the same regiment might, again to a man, sit on the sidelines. Who mutinied often depended upon the arrangement of barracks: individual barracks rarely split, but a regiment strung out over a city could easily fragment during a mutiny. On the other hand, elements of mutinous units occasionally marched considerable distances to join their comrades. Or a group of units quartered in close proximity might mutiny together, while elements of the same units elsewhere did not. Once mutinies were underway, soldiers immediately appealed to (or, as in Kronstadt, tried to force) other units to join them in common action. There was, of course, strength in numbers. But the deeper motivation was the need soldiers felt to establish universal affirmation—and thus the legitimacy—of their acts. Like the peasants they were, soldiers instinctively sought to present a united front to the world beyond their community.

Once consensus had been established, it was often reinforced by symbolic action, frequently a march. Units marched to a meeting, or to present their demands formally to the unit or garrison commander. In at least sixteen mutinies, soldiers marched through town, bands playing— sometime two or three bands playing. Soldiers marched under arms in proper military order, dressed by NCOs or by some other soldiers who enjoyed authority in the unit. (Marches required and brought to the surface soldier leadership, and though the evidence is far from volumi- nous, it appears from the marches and a few other mutinies that NCOs—either those Sergeants Major who were not odious to the men or conscript NCOs—functioned as leaders by virtue of their position and authority prior to mutiny.[64]) In Kiev on November 18, two companies from two pontoon battalions marched to nearby barracks and were joined by elements of three other sapper and pontoon battalions and two bands (one an infantry band compelled to join, the body of the infantry regiment being locked in its barracks), then set off for the center of town expecting to pick up more units; the testimony of one GSO on the scene is that had a loyal infantry regiment not dispersed the march with fire (this was the only march to end in bloodshed), the mutiny would have gathered in most of the garrison.[65] On November 23, an infantry regiment in Kharkov marched with its band from barracks to barracks, was joined by elements of three other regiments and another band (an artillery brigade refused to join), then headed for the center of the city, where the division commander humbly accepted a set of de- mands. These and other marches traumatized the authorities, because they bore dramatic and unambiguous witness to the officers' powerless- ness to control soldiers. But the marching soldiers did not have aggres- sive intent. Soldiers meant instead to demonstrate their unanimity and firmness of purpose, both to their commanders and to themselves.

The mutinous soldiers' perceptions—that their officers' authority had lapsed, that the establishment of consensus sufficed to effect change— were self-verifying, because so long as they were widely shared the authorities could not cope with mutiny. And, in mutiny after mutiny— in sixty of the 137 mutinies whose resolution can be determined— soldiers did win concessions, or promises thereof, whereas in only thirty-seven cases did force or the threat of force bring mutinies to an end. In most other mutinies, officers simply ignored what their men were doing, in the hope that mutiny would go away.* So long as soldiers had no reason to believe that the old military order, or the social order in

---

*Most of the 74 mutinies with an unknown termination probably ended with real or tacit concessions, or in a standoff. Officers were more likely to report mutinies they had re- pressed than those they could do nothing about, and mutinies that ended when reliable troops surrounded mutineers were likely to attract public notice, and be reported in the press.

which it was embedded, was legitimate, so long as events did not falsify their post-Manifesto belief that the old social and military order had collapsed, there was nothing officers could do to reestablish their authority, and each mutiny made the next easier.

Social Revolution

The most common feature of the post-Manifesto mutinies—135 of 211 cases—was the presentation of a set of demands, often running to twenty, thirty, forty or more points.* Soldiers presented demands most frequently, in seventy of eighty-six mutinies (81 percent) in the second half of November, when their revolution was most deliberated; elaboration of a set of demands was itself evidence of the greater purposefulness of mutinous soldiers after mid-November. However, there was little difference between the earlier and later demands. Whether mutiny resulted from officer provocation, or erupted from indiscipline, or was decided upon at a meeting, the soldiers' conception of a just military society was the same. The only difference was whether or not the circumstances of mutiny afforded the soldiers an opportunity to articulate their views.

Even when committed to paper, the soldiers' program was not stated systematically, but must be extracted from the jumble of specific points. The demands of the Grodno artillerists, which enjoyed so much resonance in the army, were typical. The artillerists demanded, in no coherent order, shorter service, more pay, and free mailing, travel, and newspaper subscriptions; they demanded, too, that their underwear be washed at army expense. They demanded that soldiers be addressed "as befits human beings" (i.e., in the polite rather than the familiar). They demanded that they be allowed to go to theaters and libraries, and that their mail not be opened. They demanded in great detail improvements in food, uniforms, and kit (including bedlinen, pillows, and blankets). They demanded unrestricted leave from the barracks, and freedom to meet and discuss their needs. They demanded that the officer who had fired shots in the air be removed, and the removal of all reenlisted NCOs. And they demanded an end to searches in the barracks, the elimination of severe punishments for disciplinary infractions, improved medical services, and the demobilization of reserves.[66] Although the Grodno demands were written down by a member of the Bund, the

---

*These demands were written down by soldiers, or by officers as soldiers shouted them out. The 135 cases do not include mutinies in which soldiers made only one or two demands. In some of these 135 mutinies, two or more sets of demands were presented, for instance by different units.

language and spirit were the soldiers' own, and they capture the atmosphere of the meeting at which they were compiled: a packed room of exuberant soldiers shouting out demands as they came to mind, each grievance reminding them of others, the civilian scribe struggling to keep pace and put the demands in some sort of order.

The Grodno demands and the many other sets of demands were revolutionary, but it was easy to miss that point because they were not obviously political and because they were not presented systematically. Revolutionaries of the time classified the soldiers' demands as either "economic" (i.e., having to do with life in the army) or "political." They considered political demands—for a Constituent Assembly, abolition of the standing army, institution of the eight-hour day, land redistribution—manifestations of a truly revolutionary spirit, economic demands as at best useful grounds for agitation. Few revolutionaries appreciated that the soldiers' demands, if met, would have overturned military society. Officers, though acutely aware of the decomposition of the army, were also inclined to minimize the significance of the soldiers' demands. One who did not was the liberal General Grulev, who observed:

> If in that time of chaos "economic" demands flared up, that was only because questions of a material character were more accessible to the understanding of the masses than the subtleties of legal relations; but dissatisfaction was rooted in the latter. That was why increasing the soldiers' rations [and similar reforms] missed the mark. . . .[67]

Lurking beneath the mass of bewildering and often trivial detail was the soldiers' determination to change the two features of military society that most affected them, the operation of the regimental economy and the web of controls over their movements and activity. Of the eighty-four sets of demands analyzed by the Soviet historian V. A. Petrov, seventy-three—the highest incidence of any category of demands—called for changes in the operation of the regimental economy: improvements in pay, food, uniforms, and kit, elimination of labor in the civilian economy, and so forth. These were directed not just against the material hardship soldiers suffered while in service, but also the requirement that soldiers provide for themselves, out of their own pocket or through contract labor, much of their own equipment. Forty-nine sets of demands (almost 60 percent of Petrov's sample, the second highest incidence) called for civil and political rights for soldiers: freedom to meet in the barracks and attend meetings outside the barracks, freedom to go to theaters and other public entertainments, inviolability of correspondence, and the like. These demands posed an even more fundamental challenge to the functioning of the army than did the economic demands, and they derived immediately from the revolutionary environment of late 1905: soldiers sought to transfer the new freedoms and the elimination of social restraints evident in civilian society to military society. Soldiers demanded demobilization of reserves or time-expired soldiers in forty-six petitions, the third highest incidence, but one indicating that pressure from the reserves was not the mainspring of the soldiers' revolution.[68]

Demands for improvements in kit and for freedom of movement implicitly challenged the structure of authority in the regiments, but soldiers also challenged that structure directly, counterposing the company *artel'* (or a vaguer regimental equivalent) to officers. A total of forty-one sets of demands (almost 50 percent of Petrov's sample) either called for the institution of the electoral principle in some area of military society (e.g., in 15 cases, or 18 percent, there was a demand that elected soldier committees supervise provision and supply) or specified that soldiers should have the right to initiate changes in military practices. In twenty-one (25 percent) of the petitions there was a point on the removal of NCOs, at times generalized to apply to all reenlistees. In five instances, soldiers demanded that NCOs be elected.[69] Soldiers sought in one way or another to invest the company *artel'* or the regimental soldier community with the power to control the unit economy and determine the rules governing soldier behavior, and to exclude from their community those, such as NCO lifers, who did not properly belong. Of course, every time soldiers handed over a petition of demands they were acting on the assumption that they had the right to determine the conditions of service, but they did not always make this an explicit part of their program.

Soldiers intended to prevent officers from intruding on soldier society by establishing soldier committees and by giving soldiers the right to initiate change, but their hostility toward officers derived less from the desire to restructure authority than from the polarization between peasant and European Russias. Soldiers did not seek to eliminate officers (and only three sets of demands called for elected officers) any more than they sought to abolish the standing army. When they thought about officers, soldiers focused on officers' social attitudes. The most frequent demand soldiers made of their officers (31 cases, 37 percent of the sample) was that officers address them as equals, in the polite rather than the familiar. In seventeen sets of demands (20 percent), soldiers called for the removal of specific officers, and in some cases generalized this to include the removal of "all rude commanders."[70] Officers were a part of the army, the existence of which soldiers did not question, but soldiers would no longer accept the inferior social status that officers and educated Russians in general assigned to them.

That the soldiers' antagonism was founded more on what officers represented than how officers behaved comes through clearly in the inability of liberal officers to achieve rapport with their men. Many officers—not a majority, but a perceptible minority—welcomed the October Manifesto and were caught up in the heady atmosphere of the post-Manifesto days of freedom. There were even officers who established "unions" to support political reform and press for military change as well. These liberal officer groups hoped to reestablish moral authority over their men, and were for that reason tolerated by some commanders. But soldiers would have nothing to do with officers, no matter how liberal they might be or how sincere their protestations of having the soldiers' interests at heart.[71] In Chita, soldiers maintained an aloof distance from an officers' union that seconded their mutiny. Members of the Samara Union of Officers who met with soldiers found the soldiers reluctant to speak and positively insulting once the ice was broken: the soldiers declared that officers' pay should be reduced and the money given to enlisted men, that officers did not need horses, that soldiers did not intend to bargain but to present demands, and that the only reason officers now deigned to talk with their men was fear. Deeply offended, some of the officers walked out of the meeting. Liberal and conservative officers everywhere were suddenly conscious of the depth of the soldiers' animosity, and were profoundly demoralized by the unexpected rejection of paternal solicitude.[72]

The sense of social distance that informed the soldiers' revolution, that militated against soldiers reaching an accommodation even with those officers willing to support their demands, also prevented soldiers from linking their revolution to the other revolutions around them. Soldiers understood that their actions had an important bearing on the revolution in civilian society, and their demand (30 cases, or 36 percent of Petrov's sample) that they not be used in a police capacity was at least partly motivated by political considerations, or at least by a sense of identity with peasants: the soldiers' most frequent explicit recognition of the revolution outside their barracks was their insistence that they not be deployed against peasants. The men of the 231st Kotelnich reserve infantry battalion in Viatka declared they would not act against hungry and impoverished peasants "who are no enemy of the soldier," and reserves in the 160th depot infantry battalion in Gomel stated their unwillingness "to defend the gentry from our peasant brother." Likewise, soldiers showed a great deal of interest in reports on peasant disorders and collected newspapers and leaflets to take home to their villages. But only in the most exceptional circumstances—as when prisoners broke out of the Voronezh disciplinary battalion—did they become involved in agrarian disturbances themselves.[73]

Beyond specific sympathy with peasants and a general interest in events around them soldiers did not go. In only eighteen cases (21 percent of the sample) did soldiers make demands touching on civilian society (redistribution of the land, the eight-hour day, a Constituent Assembly), and these were ordinarily included at the urging of civilian revolutionaries who helped print up the demands. When soldiers adopted political demands, it was more to humor civilians than because they felt such demands to be of immediate concern to themselves. It was not uncommon for soldiers to shout down proposed political demands, and civilian badgering of soldiers was likely to turn soldiers away from revolution. Moreover, when soldiers expelled officers from the barracks, they frequently also refused admission to civilians. During their demonstrations and meetings, soldiers as often as not refused to permit civilians to address them or march with them. Civilians were told that soldiers could take care of their own affairs. And in no more than six mutinies did soldiers hand over any weapons to civilians.[74] Soldiers were not opposed to civilian revolution, but civilian demands did not speak to their own desire to overturn the command and social hierarchies in the army. Yet soldiers were no less radical for having limited political vision.

The disjunction between the military and civilian revolutions corresponded to the differences between the psychology of peasant revolution and the psychology of the liberal and revolutionary movements in polite society—which was only natural, since soldiers were peasants. Civilian denunciation of abuses by officers and conditions in the barracks was fine, and civilian agitators might be permitted to attack "autocracy" as the root of all evil, but attacks on the Tsar merely angered soldiers. One of the Samara soldiers told the liberal Samara officers that he "had nothing against the Tsar, and that if the soldiers' complaints don't reach him that is because he is cut off by a thick wall of commanders."[75] Since in the soldiers' view it was the Tsar's Manifesto of October 17 that had authorized their revolution, this attitude is not surprising. Soldiers also occasionally protested their loyalty even as they mutinied. This was the case, for instance, in the 252nd Anapa reserve infantry battalion in Ekaterinodar, which mutinied on November 16, marched under arms to present demands to their commander, and while presenting their demands to the corps commander on the 18th insisted that they would not violate their oath. The 1st Don Cossack regiment in Moscow, as it handed in its demands on November 26, stressed repeatedly that this was not mutiny *(bunt)*.[76] The bands that accompanied mutinous soldiers as they marched invariably played "God Save the Tsar," and the Ekaterinogradskaia disciplinary battalion carried a portrait of the Tsar as it marched on December 4.[77] This, too, accorded with the soldiers' understanding of the situation in the army after October 17:

since the old military order was no longer legitimate, since the Tsar had authorized freedom for soldiers as well as civilians, then demanding fundamental alterations in military society was not mutiny. Of course, soldiers must also have hoped that by employing patriotic symbols they might deflect the ire of the authorities. Yet if, again, soldiers had believed their commanders had the authority to uphold the old order, they would not have mutinied.

Sentiments such as these suggest that the soldiers were engaged not in revolution but in rebellion against authorities—their officers—whose actions offended against what soldiers believed to be the legitimate and established order of things. They rebelled against officers in the name of the Tsar, as peasants rebelled against nobles and officials in the name of the Tsar. And the soldiers' social and political values were traditional, just as traditional values underpinned peasant rebellion. Yet the changes soldiers wished to make in the army had nothing to do with an idealized past. They aimed, in what Chalmers Johnson contends distinguishes revolution from rebellion, at "the recasting of the social division of labor according to a pattern which is self-consciously unprecedented in the context of a particular social system."[78] Mutinous soldiers did not claim that the new structure of authority they sought was really an old command structure freed of corruption, they understood that the "freedoms" they claimed were new. The soldiers were, perhaps, revolutionaries in spite of themselves, but they were revolutionaries—if only within military society—nonetheless.

Impact

Whether revolution or rebellion, the mutinies sweeping through the army gravely weakened the government. Indeed, by late November the soldiers' revolution posed the single greatest threat to the continued existence of the Tsarist regime. Not only was the army shot through with disaffection, the troops theoretically at the disposal of the government were far fewer than a month earlier. Demobilization had not stopped mutiny, but had reduced the garrisons in Europe by 240,000 men. After demobilization, company strength in the Baltic provinces fell from 100 to between twenty and forty men. The average strength of infantry companies in rebellious Chernigov, Poltava and Kursk provinces fell to thirty-five men. In the Caucasus, too, companies were reduced to twenty-five or thirty men. Everywhere garrisons experienced a sudden and severe loss of manpower. The garrison in Revel, a city of 90,000 in the troubled Baltic area, had but 300 effectives. Revolutionaries seized de facto control of Pinsk, Gomel, and Sochi after demobilization cut garrison strength to a few hundred men.[79] The authorities in many other small and medium cities were almost as helpless, and the situation in the rural districts was even more desperate. Even before demobilization, over half the troops outside Manchuria and Siberia had been concentrated in the Warsaw, Vilna, and Causasus military districts, leaving the vast interior of the empire virtually uncovered.[80] As the Governor of Tambov Province, the scene of some of the most serious agrarian disorders in Russia, reported:

> In view of the order on the demobilization of the reserves of the Bobrov and Pronsk regiments, an order that came out of the clear blue sky, my basic forces are significantly weaker, and the four infantry companies that have come from Moscow make it possible only to ‚cover the loss; this long-awaited, indispensable reinforcement has lost all significance, and with it all hope of the possibility of a more rapid cessation of the insurrection has collapsed.[81]

At that, the governor was lucky to get reinforcements. Despairing appeals for troops poured into the ministries in Petersburg, but as Minister of War Rediger later recalled, "I could only forward them to district commanders, knowing in advance that they would scarcely be able to help."[82] Units that could be sent as reinforcements were so small that they were sometimes not recognized for what they were. Prime Minister Witte recalled that a company sent to one city numbered twelve soldiers, and that local authorities failed to realize that this was the unit they had been waiting for. Desperate officials hijacked soldiers passing through their bailiwicks: officials in Poltava detained without authorization half of a relief force on its way to Kharkov.[83]

Short of men, the government had no choice but to yield territory to the revolution. Units scattered about the rural districts were, after demobilization, so small that they could not defend themselves, and in late November and early December insurgents captured a number of them.[84] General Rediger had recognized that demobilizing the reserves would make isolated units vulnerable, had so informed both the Tsar and Minister of Interior Durnovo on November 12, and had added that he would have to order small units to fall back on the cities. On November 23, the Ministry of War did order the military district staffs to pull back to the cities and regroup "the detachments and units dispersed in various places," and explained: "the service of the army in aid of civil authorities for the purpose of maintaining order in the empire cannot continue at the same level of intensity as has been the case up to now."[85] In the most volatile regions, the Caucasus and the Baltic, soldiers had to fight their way back to their bases. Guerrillas repeatedly ambushed a column of infantry and cossacks during its four-day retreat to the Latvian city of Venden. Those and other retreating units in the Baltic suffered casualties, though partisans permitted some units to withdraw without incident under locally arranged cease-fires.[86] In the Baltic, in the Caucasus, and in the Russian heartland, the army had by early December surrendered the rural districts to the peasants.

Urban garrisons offered security against peasants but not against mutiny, and in late November and early December, mutinies effectively deprived civil authorities of control over ten of the nineteen cities in the Russian empire with a population over 100,000. In Moscow, between November 25 and December 2, four Grenadier infantry regiments, one line infantry regiment, two sapper battalions, and a cossack regiment mutinied. In Ekaterinoslav, there were mutinies in all three infantry regiments and in a cossack regiment. In Kharkov, two mutinous regiments and elements of two others marched triumphantly through the center of the city on November 23. In Tiflis, two Grenadier infantry regiments, one rifle battalion, one cavalry regiment, two sapper battalions, one railroad battalion, and assorted smaller units (including the bodyguard of the Viceroy) mutinied, and in late November soldiers from all units met several thousand at a time with complete impunity. In Baku, three infantry regiments, a cossack regiment, and an artillery brigade mutinied. Mutinies struck two infantry regiments in Riga, an infantry regiment in Lodz, an infantry battalion in Kazan, and an infantry regiment in Saratov; in these cities, there were nonmutinous disorders—protests over food, meetings, expressions of hostility to the "black hundreds"—in almost all other units. The one infantry regiment in Rostov-on-Don was judged so sympathetic to the workers that in late November it was withdrawn from the city; the cossacks and artillery that remained refused to parade on December 6, the Tsar's name day.[87]

Elsewhere, the authorities remained in control but had reason to be uneasy. In Vilna, for instance, one infantry regiment mutinied and there was widespread indiscipline in other units. In Kiev, five sapper and pontoon battalions had marched on November 18, an artillery division had mutinied in sympathy, and an infantry regiment had been ready to join. The Odessa garrison was somewhat more stable, though a depot infantry battalion and part of an artillery brigade mutinied, and soldiers from various units met at the university. The government was likewise in command in Tashkent, where the suppression of a mid-November insurrection by the fortress infantry battalion had sobered restive soldiers in other units. Soldiers posed no threat to civil authority in Astrakhan and Tula because there were only a handful of soldiers in those cities. In Warsaw and Petersburg, the few mutinous regiments were outweighed by large concentrations of relatively disciplined troops (though two Guards regiments and a Guards artillery brigade mutinied in Warsaw in late November).[88] Of the large cities with sizeable garrisons, only Kishinev appears to have been wholly free of mutiny.

Not only was the number of mutinies in late November large and increasing, the soldiers' revolution had a cumulative impact: once they had mutinied, regiments remained unreliable even after mutiny had formally ended. Most mutinies were brought to an end, after all, by allowing soldiers to have their own way, and in the aftermath of mutiny soldiers in effect determined how their units would be employed. Nor, given the momentum of the soldiers' revolution in late November, was it likely that units that had not mutinied would long refrain from doing so; several score were so indisciplined that it could not be long before they, too, reached a consensus for mutiny. Even those units that had proved relatively immune to disaffection, the Guards and the cavalry, could not be expected to hold out much longer. In the Petersburg Guards regiments, where psychological bonds to the throne were especially strong, there was considerable ferment in late November and early December.[89] Of this the most difficult period in his tenure as Minister of War, General Rediger recalled without the slightest hyperbole: "Dozens of reports on disorders in various units were received daily! It was obvious that the time was approaching when it would prove impossible to rely even on the army, and desolation would set in!"[90]

V. December 1905: Mutineers Save the Regime

As November turned into December, the regime's situation was truly desperate: it had lost control over the peasantry, it was losing control over the urban garrisons and therefore over the cities, and the soviets were operating with near impunity. Mutinous reserves clogged the line through Siberia, many of the Siberian garrisons had mutinied and given revolutionaries the opportunity to seize effective power, and the field army was trapped in Manchuria.

As always in an emergency, the regime called on the cossacks. The Ministry of War had been activating cossack reserve regiments* for internal service since late 1904, and by October 1905 seventy-odd cossack regiments, thirty of them manned entirely by reserves, were in action in Europe. On November 1 the Ministry activated ten more cossack reserve regiments. As infantry reserves left the army these extra regiments fell far short of requirements, so a succession of additional mobilization orders went out. By the end of February 1906, twenty-nine reserve regiments and six reserve cossack foot battalions had joined the thirty reserve regiments activated before October.[1] This was, however, considerably fewer regiments than the Ministry had hoped to mobilize, and the cossack reserves called up in November and December were as disaffected and as prone to mutiny as the infantry.

Most cossack regulars and most reserves mobilized early in 1905 were locked into a cycle of violence that impeded the drift toward mutiny, but by October revolution had penetrated cossack villages, and mutinies followed hard on the November mobilization.[2] Between October 17 and the end of the year, eleven Kuban cossack units, nine Siberian units, five Don units, and one Terek unit mutinied. The Siberian cossack mutinies,

---

*That is, regiments of the second and third lines. Formally, these were not reserves but units of cossacks on extended leave.

a byproduct of the mutinies of the Manchurian reserves and the Siberian garrisons, were in themselves of no special significance. Far more ominous was Don cossack disaffection, which is not adequately reflected by the low incidence of mutiny (two in first-line regiments, one in a second-line regiment mobilized in March 1905, one in a second-line regiment mobilized in November, one in an unidentified unit).[3] The behavior of the five (and last available) second-line Don regiments activated after November 1 was so alarming—one regiment stopped the train on which it was being shipped north and plundered the surrounding countryside for two days—and resistance to mobilization in the Don cossack villages so fierce, that the Ministry of War decided not to activate the seventeen third-line regiments (three were finally called up in February 1906).[4]

Worse even than the absence of additional Don regiments was the presence of the Kuban regiments. The Kuban mutinies, involving one of the seven first-line mounted regiments in Europe, one of the first-line plastoon (foot) battalions, six of the nine second-line mounted regiments mobilized before November, and three of the six third-line plastoon battalions mobilized in November (a fourth which did not quite mutiny promised to emulate the sailors of the *Potemkin* if its needs were not addressed), were especially threatening because they all occurred in the Caucasus.[5] The stated grievances of the Kuban mutineers centered on the peculiar burdens of their service. Cossacks bore the expense of providing military-grade horses, saddles, uniforms, and other accouterment, and two units demanded the cancellation of all debts incurred during mobilization. However, as the commander of the mutinous 2nd Caucasus Kuban regiment observed, such demands provided no more than the pretext for mutiny:

> Their principal demand is to be sent home, because they have no desire to protect the interests of landowners and the rich in general at a time when the cossacks' own farms are falling into decay and they and their families are enduring hardship.[6]

And in fact, five of the mutinies involved self-demobilization, a type of mutiny unique to the Kuban cossacks: they boarded trains and, with the cooperation of striking railroad workers, set off for home.[7] Their departure immediately shifted the local balance of power. When two of the three squadrons of the 2nd Urup regiment and then the 17th plastoon battalion pulled out of Novorossiisk in December, they cleared the way for the short-lived "Novorossiisk Republic." When the three squadrons of the 2nd Urup in Ekaterinodar joined their comrades from Novorossiisk, and when the 15th plastoon battalion left Ekaterinodar as well, they very nearly precipitated the formation of an "Ekaterinodar Republic."[8] And as the Kuban cossacks disappeared, there were suddenly no units available to send against the Georgian, Ossetian, and multitudinous other natives who had thrown off the Russian yoke.

By late December, the government had managed to mobilize only fourteen additional cossack regiments and battalions, and of these at least four had mutinied and others were so badly disaffected as to be unusable. By late February another twenty-one cossack regiments had taken the field but in December, the month of greatest need, the regime was bereft of reinforcements. That is not to deny that cossacks were crucial to the regime's survival: without the 60,000 cossacks in Europe as of October, the regime might well have collapsed. Able to bring substantial numbers of soldiers into battle against workers and peasants only under exceptional circumstances, local authorities discovered, sometimes to their surprise, that a handful of cossacks thrown into the breach could scatter peasants and even flush workers out from behind their barricades. But 60,000 cossacks were too few to turn the tide by themselves.

With the Manchurian army unavailable and reserve cossacks mutinous, the regime's survival hinged on the behavior of the mutinous garrison army in Europe. At the last possible moment, the European garrisons turned. Mutiny subsided in December as suddenly as it had spread in October and November: from fifteen mutinies in late October, to forty-four in the first half of November, peaking at eighty-six in the second half of November, down to fifty in the first half of December, only sixteen in the last half of that month. The national totals, in fact, understate the abruptness with which the soldiers' revolution collapsed. Of the fifty mutinies in the first half of December, fifteen were in Manchuria and along the Siberian route of the reserves' flight to Europe, eleven were in the Caucasus, and most of those in central Russia occurred in the first week of the month. By mid-December, the soldiers' revolution was over except on the fringes of the empire, and hitherto mutinous units were busily repressing civilians.

There is no simple and elegant explanation for the soldiers' abrupt about-face, but some possible explanations may be discarded. The soldiers' revolution did not end, for instance, because mutinies were forcibly suppressed. Force was effectively applied against mutinies in Kronstadt in late October, and in Tashkent, Sevastopol, and Kiev in mid-November. Repression generally served as a local deterrent to further mutiny, but despite extensive publicity provided no object lesson for soldiers elsewhere. Indeed, mutiny was far more widespread after the shooting in Sevastopol and Kiev than it had been before. There was no instance of armed repression of mutiny in late November or early December that might have inspired fear in soldiers. By that point, of course, it was difficult to find units that could be relied upon to suppress mutiny.

The end of the soldiers' revolution did coincide with the enactment of reforms intended to alleviate many of the hardships of military service. Since the middle of the year the Ministry of War had been planning to reduce the length and change the conditions of service as part of an effort to repair deficiencies disclosed during the Russo-Japanese War, but as the mutinies began in late October the reforms acquired political urgency. The Ministry issued periodic reminders that reforms were in the offing, and they were officially announced to the soldiers on the Tsar's name day, December 6. Effective immediately, the daily meat ration rose from ¼ to ¾ pound, a tea and sugar ration was added, and pay for enlisted personnel rose 2½- to 3-fold (varying by rank). The issue of underwear and boots was to be increased as of January 1, 1906, at which time, too, blankets, bedlinen, field shirts, towels, and handkerchiefs were to be issued for the first time. (The practice of hiring out soldiers for civilian work was proscribed in January 1906, while reduction in the length of service—from 4 to 3 years in the infantry, from 5 to 4 years in cavalry and engineering units, from 7 to 5 years in the navy—was made official in Imperial rescripts issued in March 1906.) These reforms amounted to a complete capitulation to the strictly economic demands advanced by mutinous soldiers. Minister of War Rediger admitted as much, noting that he included handkerchiefs among the items newly issued "in order to show that soldiers were given not only what they demanded, but even a luxury that had not occurred to them."[9]

Nevertheless, despite the chronological association between the announcement of the reforms and the decline of mutiny, satisfaction of the mutineers' demands played at best a marginal role in restoring order in the armed forces. In some units, the announcement persuaded soldiers to revert from mutiny to chronic indiscipline of the sort that had preceded mutiny; in others officers nullified the potentially tranquilizing effect of the reforms by attempting to root out sedition.[10] While mutiny and indiscipline receded rapidly after December 6, capitulation by the Ministry of War was unlikely to convince soldiers that they had anything to fear from mutiny, still less that they must unfailingly obey their officers. If anything, the reverse held: just as the success of one mutiny encouraged other units to mutiny, soldiers might have concluded after December 6 that since they had forced the government to demobilize the reserves and augment pay, kit, and rations, they should continue to press their other demands.

The soldiers' revolution came to an end not because of anything that occurred within the army—either the suppression of or concessions to mutiny—but because of events in civilian society. The regime in late November and early December undertook actions that on the one hand triggered worker insurgency and placed soldiers' lives in jeopardy, and on the other caused soldiers to reevaluate their post-Manifesto assumptions about the structure of authority in society and army. In all but a few cases, it is impossible to specify which of the many events outside the barracks was the decisive influence on soldier thinking and behavior in December. What is clear is that had mutinous and disaffected soldiers not concluded in December that they must submit to the old disciplinary norms, the Tsarist regime, for all its determination to survive, would have fallen.

Punitive Expeditions on the Periphery

Prime Minister Witte had hoped that the October Manifesto and the related conciliatory gestures that he had urged on the Tsar during the October crisis would restore domestic tranquility. He had anticipated that the October Manifesto would touch off demonstrations, and had not wished to undercut the effect of the promises of civil liberties and a legislative assembly by taking a hard line against public disorders. By the end of November, however, Witte and his cabinet had concluded that the revolution must be brought to an end whatever the cost to the regime's image.[11] This necessarily entailed military repression. Yet if the policy requirement was clear, the government could not plan a systematic campaign against the revolution. For one thing, at the end of November the soldiers' revolution was at peak strength, reserves were being sent home, and units were being recalled from the villages; there were not enough reliable troops available to put an ambitious policy of repression into effect. For another, the revolution was still metastasizing, and in December the government had to contend with a new set of crises, some the direct result of its changed political tack.

The government ultimately hit upon punitive expeditions as its weapon of last resort, but the policy of official terror that the punitive expeditions embodied was arrived at incrementally. On October 27, acting Minister of Interior Durnovo suggested to the Tsar that a member of the Imperial suite be sent to take charge of the restoration of order in Chernigov Province, where peasant disorders threatened the complete destruction of gentry estates. The Imperial chancery enlarged on this idea, and informed Witte on October 30 that three members of the Tsar's suite were being sent to chastise the Russian peasantry: Admiral Dubasov to Chernigov, Kursk, and Poltava Provinces; General Sakharov to Saratov and Penza Provinces; and General Strukov to Tambov and (at

Strukov's request) Voronezh Provinces. The Tsar later dispatched two other plenipotentiaries to deal with the peasants of Kherson and Stavropol Provinces.[12]

The generals did not lead punitive expeditions in the proper sense; they were, rather, just what they were purported to be, imperial plenipotentiaries vested with extensive powers and instructed to "restore order and tranquillity." They immediately confronted three major obstacles to the accomplishment of their mission: peasant rebellion flared up in an apparently random pattern and so presented no fixed target for repression; the troops available were too few to persuade peasants to desist; and mutiny rendered many of the units at hand unusable. By the time Admiral Dubasov arrived in Chernigov, for instance, the first wave of agrarian violence had subsided. Accompanied by a half squadron of cossacks, some infantry, and local officials, Dubasov went on tour, threatening in the name of the Tsar to level the villages should there be any further incidents and compelling village assemblies to select undesirable elements for resettlement in Siberia. The Admiral then moved on to Kursk Province, still in the grip of peasant disorders. Dubasov had only local units—1,350 infantry and 850 cossacks—to combat the peasants. However, the infantry could not be used because so many of them were reserves from the local population, and because they were on the verge of mutiny; Dubasov's first act in Kursk was to tour infantry barracks and demobilize reserves. Dubasov was at that point recalled to deal with the crisis in Moscow. When his replacement, General Panteleev, arrived in Kursk he had to contend with a mutiny in an artillery brigade. Meanwhile, a new round of disturbances had broken out in Chernigov Province, where demobilization had reduced the infantry to 400 men. Panteleev concluded, as had Dubasov before him, that the only way to halt peasant rebellion was to shoot peasants. He consolidated his few remaining troops into operational detachments and sent them out to suppress disorders by force of arms. By late November the other plenipotentiaries were doing the same, though to no immediate effect.[13]

The obvious lesson of the operations of the generals in the agricultural center was that no amount of persuasion would bring peasants to heel, and the government in Petersburg took heed. Of course, by early December the crises in the Baltic, the Caucasus, Siberia, and the cities had also come to a head, so forceful action of some sort was mandatory. Nevertheless, the Imperial plenipotentiaries had shown the way. Early in December, the State Council began discussion of new rules for the use of troops against civil disorders that would virtually require soldiers to shoot whenever they faced civilians, on December 13 the Council of

Ministers called on the military to give no quarter to revolutionaries, and on December 15 the Ministry of War sent a circular to the military districts outlining the government's new policy.[14]

Though they scarcely needed encouragement, the government communicated its new policy to the plenipotentiaries. Durnovo telegraphed Panteleev on December 19 that "only the most severe measures and merciless treatment of the insurgents, reprisals without trial, can suppress the rebellion," and he followed that with other telegrams demanding the destruction of villages.[15] Yet even officially sanctioned ferocity did not produce immediate results. A brief hiatus in the disturbances in Chernigov and Kursk Provinces in mid-December was followed by a new outburst at the end of the month. Nevertheless, by late December reinforcements were arriving (from the 42nd division, originally intended for the Far East but not sent because of the termination of the war), and mobile columns of cossacks, dragoons, and some infantry were cutting back and forth across Chernigov, Kursk, and Poltava Provinces (and other provinces not within Panteleev's purview), beating, whipping, and burning as they went. Even government functionaries admitted that the cossacks acted with unwarranted brutality. Peasants, convinced that unanimity and sheer numbers could overcome the soldiers' superior firepower, at times attempted to resist. They were massacred (e.g., in the village of Sorochintsy in Poltava Province, an incident made famous by Korolenko) for their innocence. By the end of January, General Panteleev was able to report that order was being restored, at least temporarily, but that it would be necessary to increase the troop presence if the lid were to be kept on peasant discontent.[16] Victory over the Russian and Ukrainian peasantry did not come easily, but during the campaign the regime in its desperation hit upon the only effective tactics, terror pure and simple.

The first punitive expedition—as opposed to punitive general—was sent into the Baltic provinces of Courland, Lifland, and Estland (present-day Latvia and Estonia), where the revolution was more fierce even than in the empire's heartland. In November, Latvian peasants deposed constituted village and county authorities and elected their own local governments. At the end of the month, insurgents drove a small garrison from the city of Tukkum (in Courland) and beat back the first counterattack, inflicting heavy casualties on the troops. The German barons fled to the larger cities, often convoyed by retreating soldiers, or were murdered. Durnovo, requesting the Tsar to declare martial law in the Baltic, reported that on November 21 rebels had disarmed the soldiers guarding an estate in Lifland and had dragged two barons from the manor and shot them. Martial law was proclaimed, and on November 24 the Tsar established a Provisional Baltic Governor Generalcy, to which General Sollogub was soon appointed.[17]

It was one thing to proclaim martial law, quite another to provide the troops to enforce it. Units in the Baltic region were under strength and falling back on the cities, and local authorities, who were inundating Petersburg with requests for reinforcements, complained that the staff of the Vilna military district (which included Courland and Lifland) was pulling units out of the provinces. The district commander reported that he was so short of troops that he had authorized the arming of Old Believers and gentry-financed militias. The Riga garrison was small, wracked by mutiny, and unable to do more than maintain a presence on the streets barely sufficient to keep bands of armed workers from seizing control.[18] Durnovo, taking the initiative on Baltic as on other problems, repeatedly demanded that the Ministry of War send additional units to the Baltic. Petersburg was extremely reluctant to let go of its troops— quite naturally, given the tense situation in the capital. General Raukh, Quartermaster General for the district, noted in his diary on November 30 that he simply had no troops to spare for the Baltic. Nevertheless, on November 30 General Sollogub met with ranking officers in Petersburg to plan the dispatch of punitive expeditions.[19]

The punitive expedition to the Baltic provinces was far and away the largest military operation the regime undertook against the revolution. The Warsaw military district, which had been kept near peacetime strength during the war against the hypothetical threat of attack from the west, sent two infantry regiments, six squadrons of cavalry and two artillery batteries into Courland. The Petersburg district provided four infantry battalions, eight cavalry squadrons, and some sappers for Lifland and, no other units being available, four battalions of sailors for Estland. The sailors, under barracks arrest in Kronstadt, were promised remission of punishment for exemplary service; to ensure reliability, there was one officer or petty officer for every four ordinary sailors.[20] That the government had to resort to this expedient is a good indication of how tautly its forces were drawn. The troops from Petersburg, on the other hand, were among the best the government had: elite Ulan cavalry, Imperial Kirasirsk cavalry, Guards infantry, even Guards sappers. Finally, companies and squadrons from a number of units in the Vilna district were sent back into the area. In all, three to four infantry regiments, twenty-two artillery pieces and, most importantly, four or five cavalry and cossack regiments were involved.[21] But the territory they had to cover was large, and the situation required at least that many men.

Once outfitted, the detachments had to fight their way to their assigned areas. Revolutionaries turned back a unit sent by rail to relieve Riga. Other detachments compelled engineers to proceed at gunpoint; to avoid sabotage, the trains moved slowly and with extreme caution. Governor General Sollogub himself arrived in Riga, very circuitously, only on December 14. By the middle of December, too, the railway strike broken, troops began to arrive.[22]

This being the period of greatest official ferocity, Tsar Nicholas, Witte, and Durnovo sent one telegram after another demanding ruthlessness. Witte informed Sollogub on December 22 that harsh measures were required because of the paucity of troops at the government's disposal. At about the same time, Petersburg military headquarters telegraphed General Orlov, commander of the principal detachment in Lifland: "You will not be condemned for excessive severity; sooner the reverse."[23] Petersburg had no cause for concern on this score. On December 19 General Sollogub informed the commanders of the detachments that in the event villagers were reluctant to hand over or reveal the identities of "instigators" they should destroy houses, using explosives "for greater moral effect." General Orlov ordered that those who incited disobedience, the overthrow of the government, attacks on property, and so on be shot forthwith. Commanders of the sailor battalions were told that they would not be held accountable for the consequences of their action, even if they made mistakes and shot innocent people. Other detachments operated under similar guidelines. Furthermore, all units were authorized to take what supplies they needed from the local population without payment.[24]

Given a completely free hand, the military set about terrorizing Latvians and Estonians into submission. Each of the major detachments sent out smaller groups (primarily cavalry and cossacks) to clean up the provinces section by section. The soldiers whipped, hanged, shot, and bombarded the local populace, and levied punitive fines at gunpoint. Typically, a squadron of Ulans from Orlov's group in the space of five days destroyed property for punitive purposes in four villages. Another detachment found occasion to whip peasants daily. That much officers coolly related in their after-action reports. The information supplied by victims and witnesses is more bloodcurdling. In one town, to take the most gruesome, though not an isolated, example, a cavalry officer, Captain von Sievers, informed that there were no positively identified political criminals available for execution, ordered that forty-two "generally suspect" persons be handed over. Twenty-two were collected from the jail, twenty more seized in their homes, and all were shot. Not surprisingly, this sort of activity utterly demoralized the troops involved. General Orlov reported in January that the cossacks with him were engaged solely in pillage, and the commander of a sailor battalion reported that his men had become excessively bloodthirsty and had to be held in check. By the end of January, the Baltic provinces were under control. Government figures had it that as of June 1906 the Baltic expeditions had executed eighteen persons by hanging and 621 by firing squad, and had killed 320 others in armed combat. A Kadet calculation based on censored press reports was that soldiers killed 749 people in January and February alone.[25] Precise totals are of course irrelevant. No one denied that the punitive detachments had acted ruthlessly and, what is to the point, effectively in suppressing national and social revolution in the Baltic.

Outside the Baltic, the only centrally planned punitive operation that was important to the restoration of order was in Siberia. On December 13, Nicholas sent Commander-in-Chief Linevich a telegram ordering that General Rennenkampf, who had earned a reputation for heroism and decisiveness during the Russian intervention against the Boxers in 1900, and who was one of the few Russian commanders to emerge from the Russo-Japanese War with his reputation intact, be empowered to restore order on the Transbaikal and Siberian railroads. By the time the telegram finally reached Linevich on December 25, the Ministry of War had at Witte's urging decided on December 20 to send as well a punitive detachment under the command of General Meller-Zakomelskii (who had won favor by suppressing the Sevastopol mutiny in mid-November) to open the line from the west. Rennenkampf, who could draw on the entire Manchurian army, had no difficulty manning two trains with three infantry companies, some cavalry, some technical troops, two guns, and four machine guns, and he left Harbin on January 9. Rennenkampf also had at his disposal the 5th East Siberian rifle division, which was moving ahead of him. Finding troops for Meller's expedition was more difficult: when he left Moscow on January 1 he had a total of 184 men (including 130 Guards infantry from Warsaw), thirteen officers, two guns, and two machine guns, and it was with this force that he crossed the Urals into Siberia on January 5.[26]

By the time Meller's and Rennenkampf's trains were rolling, the situation in Siberia had stabilized. Meller discovered that the farther east he moved the less disorderly the trains of reserves; he credited this to the fact that cadre troops of IV Siberian corps had restored order on the line. At the Harbin end, the field army had disgorged sufficient numbers of reserves to relieve the pressure from that quarter, trainloads of reserves were being alternated with cadre units, and evacuation was proceeding in good order.[27] The arrival of 5th Irkutsk and 6th Enisei Siberian infantry (IV Siberian corps) in Irkutsk in the first week of December had broken the back of the Irkutsk mutiny, while the mutinous 2nd railroad battalion in Krasnoiarsk had surrendered on January 3rd after a day-long battle at the railway depot with 7th Krasnoiarsk Siberian infantry (IV Siberian corps) and some other small units gathered from passing troop trains.[28] Of the major cities, only Chita remained in the hands of mutineers and revolutionaries, though strike committees continued to control most of the stations and settlements along the line. Rennen-kampf proceeded slowly toward Chita, while Meller, who had much the farther to go, raced to beat Rennenkampf to that goal and reap for himself the glory of reducing it. As they moved toward their goal, both arrested the members of station strike committees and any other sus-pected revolutionaries who fell into their hands (no one was so foolhardy as to offer resistance) and shot many of them, while Meller perpetrated one unprovoked massacre (approximately fifty died) at Ilansk station when depot workers requested that their comrades be freed. Despite his best efforts, Meller reached Chita only after Rennen-kampf had compelled mutineers and revolutionaries to capitulate (Jan-uary 19–21). Meller thereupon withdrew in a sulk without establishing contact with Rennenkampf, and complained that his rival had shown undue leniency to the rebels.[29]

The punitive expeditions, and their commanders, achieved great notoriety, but can scarcely be credited with saving the regime. Opera-tions in the Baltic and Siberia were literally peripheral to the outcome of the revolution in 1905. It was in the center that the issue was deter-mined, and a mid-December punitive run by a battalion of the 170th Molodechno infantry did more to preserve the Tsarist order than any-thing that Rennenkampf or Meller-Zakomelskii accomplished.[30] The punitive expeditions also came late: operations in the Baltic and Siberia got underway only toward the end of December and early January. The Baltic campaign became possible only after the regime had broken the back of urban revolution and the railway strike, and the ease with which Meller and Rennenkampf restored order was due in large part to the fact that by January revolutionaries and mutineers in Siberia understood that the tide was running against them. The other punitive operation of note, by the Semenovsk Guards regiment in Moscow, was also, as we shall see, mounted late: the Semenovtsy arrived after the local garrison had confined the insurrection to a single district of the city. Except in the Baltic, the centrally directed punitive expeditions amounted to no more than mopping up operations. Furthermore, even counting the Baltic expedition, the number of men involved was small, because few reliable units could be found, and fewer still spared. Picked units and cossack regulars together could cover only a small part of the vast territory engulfed by revolution.

As military operations the punitive expeditions contributed little to the survival of the regime, but as expressions of policy they were crucial. They reconquered the Baltic provinces and helped consolidate Tsarist authority in Siberia, but those victories would have been insignificant had the regime not been able to hold the Russian center. The Imperial plenipotentiaries achieved success against the peasants in the central agrarian provinces, but only after the regime had already crushed revolution in the cities, and peasant rebellion receded as much because of the collapse of urban revolution as because of cossack attacks. The heart of the revolution was in the Russian cities, and they fell neither to plenipotentiaries nor to punitive expeditions, but to units that had mutinied or were in the process of doing so; there were no other units around. Most of the locally mounted punitive detachments that took the field in late December and early January were also filled out with units that had earlier mutinied. The small size, peripheral location, and belatedness of the punitive operations underscores the fact that the regime's survival depended upon its regaining control over the mutinous European garrisons. But if they were not important militarily, the punitive operations were quite significant politically. Even before they actually took the field, the policy of violent and merciless repression of which they were a part communicated to soldiers and civilians alike that the regime would do whatever was necessary to survive. That resolve, together with the civilian revolutionaries' response to it, were the principal reasons for the soldiers' volte-face. Had the minds of soldiers not been changed—had disaffected units not ceased to mutiny and mutinous units not turned against revolution—the Tsarist regime could not have held on to power in the center or reconquered the borderlands.

Mutineers against Revolution: The Response to Insurrection

In early December, two forces—government measures to restore regime authority, and civilian insurrection—pressed upon the great mass of disaffected soldiers on whose behavior the survival of the regime depended. In broadcasting its resolve to continue to define the social and political rules (more prosaically, to suppress revolution), the regime undercut the soldiers' post-Manifesto conviction that the old order and their officers' authority had lapsed. These signals, coming at the peak of the soldiers' revolution, did not penetrate the barracks immediately, but as they became stronger the soldiers' perception of the regime's authority gradually changed. Revolutionaries unwittingly amplified the government's message by resisting suppression; their decision to defend the freedom of action acquired de facto after October 17 produced a new round of violence and thus placed soldiers in precisely the circumstances that turned them against civilians.

The government's turn toward repression in late November and early December was embodied not just in the command that generals wreak vengeance upon rebellious peasants, or the decision to dispatch a punitive expedition into the Baltic provinces, but also in measures to suppress public-sector unions, the soviets, and other organizations seeking to direct the rebellions welling up from the depths of Russian society. The leaders of the All-Russian Peasant Union were arrested in Moscow on November 15. Also on November 15, the government ordered the dispersal of a congress of the Union of Postal and Telegraph Employees; the government had previously declared that public employees did not have the right to form unions. When postal and telegraph employees went on strike, the government on November 20 arrested the union leadership, arrested the new leadership on November 25, and then fired striking personnel. On November 26 the chairman of the Petersburg Soviet was arrested. On December 2 the Council of Ministers declared illegal all strikes "in enterprises of importance to society or state" (on November 25, the Council had determined that "in extreme cases" armed force should be used to suppress strikes). On December 3, the Executive Committee of the Petersburg Soviet (260-odd persons, including guests) was arrested. In the meantime, Minister of Interior Durnovo had ordered governors to arrest the leaders of all anti-government organizations, and in late November and early December the government placed the Baltic provinces, Poland, most of the Caucasus, and many other cities and provinces under martial law.[31]

Even moderates took this turn in government policy to represent the abrogation of the promises contained in the October Manifesto, and Miliukov, the Kadet leader, suspected that the government was bent on provoking insurrection, the better to scourge the cities.[32] That does not appear to have been conscious government design. The real question, of course, was whether the regime had the force to implement its policy, be it provocative or not. Arrests were made in Petersburg and Moscow, but in most other cities officials simply ignored Durnovo's instructions. Unlike the Ministers in Petersburg, they had only mutinous garrisons with which to combat revolution.

The regime's determination to roll back the revolution forced a decision on revolutionaries at a moment they considered inopportune for insurrection, which they believed to be the only means to topple the regime and thereby secure the freedom promised in the October Manifesto. Workers, the revolutionaries feared, were as yet insufficiently armed and organized. In early November Trotsky, in the name of the Petersburg Soviet's Executive Committee, urged that a final confrontation be delayed a few months, in mid-November Lenin urged that the workers not give in to provocation, while the SRs insisted throughout that insurrection be postponed until spring, when peasants would be prepared to rise and workers would thus not risk defeat in isolation. As the SR leader Viktor Chernov put it: "The peasantry will be able to move into the fire *en masse* only in the spring, when work gets under way, and in no case during the autumn quagmire, and not even during the winter dead season."[33] (In the meantime peasants were rebelling on an unprecedented scale, following the lead of the cities rather than the cycle of the seasons.) According to Chernov, Bolsheviks shared the SRs' concern about worker isolation, but were carried along by the pressure of the workers and by the radical example of the Menshevik leaders of the Petersburg Soviet.[34] Indeed, worker demands for an eight-hour day did impel the leaders of the Petersburg Soviet to support strikes; the revolutionaries feared that failure to act would debilitate the workers' movement. By the end of November, however, the collapse of the campaign for an eight-hour day had led to a recession of worker radicalism in the capital. On the other hand, the increasing links between the Petersburg Soviet and soviets and revolutionary organizations elsewhere persuaded the Petersburg revolutionaries that, nationally, the revolution was still gathering momentum.[35]

The great burst of mutinies in late November contributed measurably to the revolutionaries' conviction that momentum favored them. They had not at first understood the nature or extent of the revolution in the army: they saw in Kronstadt a destructive riot that subsided as rapidly as it had flared up, while the economic demands that mutinous soldiers presented did not seem to bespeak commitment to revolution.[36] The Sevastopol and Kiev mutinies in mid-November, and the others that followed in quick succession, convinced revolutionaries that the unrest in the armed forces was substantial and enduring, and their pronouncements on the army became increasingly confident. Only the cossacks and a handful of aristocratic infantry units remained loyal, observed the SRs' *Syn otechestva*, and the paper warned that cossacks were liable to be exterminated by soldiers whose villages were suffering from cossack depredations. Though the Guards units in Petersburg remained worrisome, by the end of November revolutionaries were convinced that they could count on the army's support in the country at large.[37]

However, if the mutinies gave revolutionaries confidence, their analysis of the relationship between military and civilian revolutions rested on the same inappropriate assumptions as earlier in the year: it was the pressure of civilian revolution that turned soldiers against the regime; the role of military revolution was to support civilian initiatives; if the timing of the mutinies could be subordinated to the pace of civilian revolution, victory was assured for soldiers and civilians alike.[38] On December 2, a few days before the Moscow insurrection, a Menshevik restated the revolutionaries' theory of military revolution in an article entitled "The Soldiers' and Sailors' General Strike." Revolutionaries, this writer asserted, should do their best to restrain soldiers, who risked isolating themselves because their mutinies were running ahead of the workers' preparedness to support them (many of the military organizations in this period did in fact attempt to restrain soldiers). The decisive showdown with the government would begin with a workers' general strike, which would trigger a general strike by soldiers and sailors as well.[39] This writer ignored, and may not have been aware of, the discrepancy between fact and forecast—on the one hand, the soldiers' revolution running out of control, on the other revolutionary soldiers waiting patiently for workers to give them their cue. His forecast accurately reflected the collective revolutionary wisdom.

Moscow

Urban revolution culminated in the Moscow insurrection, and in retrospect it appears that the workers' movement had since January been building toward that sanguinary denouement. Yet what seems from a national perspective a logical progression from demonstrations and strikes, to general strike, to soviets, to insurrection, involved in Moscow itself a sudden, explosive, and largely unanticipated transmutation. Until the end of November, revolutionary leaders were impressed by the weakness and disorganization of the workers' movement in Moscow as compared to Petersburg and other industrialized cities. Revolutionaries set up the Moscow Soviet only on November 21, when strikes were on the decline locally and the regime had already taken the offensive. The Soviet met infrequently, and its leaders steered it away from confrontation with the authorities: they urged workers to organize rather than strike, and though they expressed sympathy for the telegraph strike (directed from Moscow), they did not suggest that factory workers strike in sympathy.[40] Revolutionaries spoke frequently of a new general strike and insurrection, but they were not eager to turn words into deed. The behavior of the garrison certainly did not offer a great deal of hope to revolutionaries: discipline had eroded after October 17, but soldiers in Moscow appeared less prone actually to mutiny even than soldiers in Petersburg. After mid-November, revolutionaries in Moscow as elsewhere wrote approving commentary on mutinies, but were noticeably reticent about the Moscow garrison.[41]

Between November 25 and December 2, mutinies swept through the garrison and thereby transformed revolutionary politics in Moscow. There is no evident reason why the mutinies should have occurred just when they did. Bolsheviks, Mensheviks, and SRs all had active military organizations that distributed leaflets, convened meetings of soldiers, and otherwise sought to attract support for revolution, but (with one exception) there is no evidence that revolutionaries themselves had any direct role in provoking mutiny.[42] Rather, it was the cumulative impact of news of mutiny elsewhere that finally galvanized soldiers in Moscow. That, at least, was the opinion of the city governor, who reported to the military district staff on November 25 that disorders in other garrisons were beginning to have an effect in Moscow.[43] Indeed, on November 25 two squadrons of the 1st Don cossack regiment refused to mount patrols and submitted a list of demands. On the 26th, the cossacks demanded to be sent home; they claimed that they were not really disobeying orders, it was just that they were utterly exhausted from their police duties and needed an extended rest. On the 26th, the men of the 3rd and 5th reserve sapper battalions, joined by a neighboring battalion of the 221st Troitse-Sergiev reserve infantry regiment, held a meeting and decided to present demands. The immediate spur to the mutiny was the arrest of a sapper who had made revolutionary speeches; the sappers demanded that their comrade be freed immediately, and took the occasion to make other demands as well. By the 27th the atmosphere in the sapper battalions was charged, and the sappers threatened to strike if their demands were not met within a week. On the 27th the police reported that the mood in the rest of the garrison was alarming and that other units might support the sappers' demands, and on the 28th the military district staff learned that increasing numbers of soldiers were fraternizing with workers and attending worker meetings, to which they reported that their units sympathized with "the people."[44]

Other units did not make the sappers' demands their own, but they took up the sappers' example. Between November 29 and December 2, mutinies commenced in the Nesvizh, Pernov, Ekaterinoslav, and Rostov Grenadier regiments, and perhaps in the Tauride Grenadier regiment and an artillery brigade as well. All of the mutinies involved the presentation of demands, but neither grenadiers nor sappers were inclined to push their mutinies much beyond that (indeed, the sappers rejected an appeal by the politicized volunteers in the battalions to expel officers and seize control). On the other hand, mutinous soldiers did not believe they had to do more than threaten to strike to obtain what they wanted, because their officers promised to take the soldiers' case to higher authorities. As they handed in their demands on December 1, the Nesvizh Grenadiers promised that they would postpone a strike until December

6, the date when, their commander promised them, the Tsar would meet their demands. It appeared to the soldiers that they had wrung concessions from their officers. While they waited for formal ratification of their victory, they attempted to spread their mutinies to other units: the Nesvizh and part of the Pernov Grenadier regiments marched with a band to the barracks of the 3rd Sumy dragoons (but failed to persuade the dragoons to join in a meeting), the Ekaterinoslav Grenadiers announced when they handed in their service-related demands that they would have some political demands when the entire garrison had agreed on them.[45]

The abrupt disintegration of the garrison heartened revolutionaries, but they were divided over how to take advantage of it. The initial reaction of Moscow's SD leaders conformed to the prevailing revolutionary opinion that confrontation with the regime should be delayed and that soldiers should subordinate mutiny to the pace of the workers' movement. The Bolsheviks and Mensheviks on the Executive Committee of the Moscow Soviet (apparently without informing the SR members) told a sapper delegation, which on the night of the 27th offered to seize the arsenal and begin an uprising, that the sappers should bide their time. A speaker from the Menshevik military organization set forth the SD position at a meeting of the Presnia-Khamovniki district soviet on December 2: work in the garrison was expanding rapidly, but "despite the efforts of the SD military organization to restrain separate outbursts" until there was greater organizational contact between soldiers and the workers' movement, "we must reckon with the possibility of an unexpected uprising." All present at the meeting agreed that the transfer of the army to the people's side would guarantee victory, and that they did not have long to wait for this outcome.[46]

The SR military organization, on the other hand, sought to foment further disorders with a view toward engaging the garrison in insurrection in mid-December. It is not clear that the SR military organization was acting with the knowledge of the Moscow SR leaders, but the SRs in Moscow emphatically did not share their party leadership's view that insurrection should await spring. Both the core of future SR Maximalists in the Moscow organization and the more orthodox local leaders were eager for a confrontation with the regime. In any case, on December 1, a meeting of SR soldiers decided that it was time for another regiment to mutiny, and the representative from the Rostov Grenadier regiment volunteered his unit. The Bolshevik military organization, learning what the SRs were up to, attempted to forestall the mutiny.[47]

Conditions in the Rostov regiment were indeed conducive to mutiny. Besides being influenced by the other disturbances, the Rostov soldiers had numerous grievances. In November, they had been angered when their commander withheld money due them from their labor in the civilian economy. There had in addition been considerable discontent when one company from the Rostov regiment had been called out on November 27 for possible action against the sappers; after standing for hours in the cold and becoming increasingly irritated by the lack of hot food, the men were returned to their barracks—which in no way eased their discontent. On December 1, there was a dispute when rations were reduced (because, explained the officers, soldiers were no longer performing extra guard duty). Finally, revolutionary circles had been operating in the regiment since early November (the SRs had the largest following).[48]

The mutiny of the Rostov Grenadiers was by far the most serious in Moscow, for the soldiers unexpectedly found themselves suddenly in complete control, while the local military command was unable to do anything to suppress them.[49] On the morning of December 2, the SR leader in the Rostov regiment distributed handbills calling soldiers to a 1:00 P.M. meeting. When the commander had him and some other politically suspect soldiers arrested, the regiment mutinied spontaneously. Soldiers drove officers from the barracks (two were temporarily held hostage), elected a committee to run the regiment (with an SD chairman and an SR secretary, though most of the members were conscript NCOs, the soldiers' natural leaders, rather than conscious revolutionaries), and posted guards to keep out officers from the garrison staff. The committee immediately set to work compiling the regiment's demands, using the Grodno demands as a model. On this first day of the mutiny, the soldiers were enthusiastic; they expected, and received assurances of, support from other regiments. In the evening, the ranking officers of the Moscow garrison met to discuss the situation; no regimental commander would vouch that his men could be used to suppress the Rostov regiment, and many feared that the attempt would produce more mutinies. They decided to temporize and sent urgent telegrams to Petersburg begging for reinforcements.

Events on December 3 unfolded along two sharply diverging lines. Presenting their petition to the regimental commander, the committee running the Rostov regiment said that demands that went beyond the unit's own immediate grievances would be officially communicated (they had already been published) in consort with the rest of the garrison. The Rostov committee issued an appeal to other units to remove their commanders and elect deputies for a common decision on the soldiers' needs. On the night of the 3rd, a soldiers' soviet, with representatives from four Grenadier regiments, three sapper battalions, a cossack regiment and all three civilian military organizations, met for the first and only time. Unit delegates reported that the garrison was in a very revolutionary mood, that it might possibly support a civilian uprising and would certainly not allow itself to be used to repress civilians.

Even as the soldiers' soviet met, however, sentiment in the Rostov regiment turned sharply against continuation of the mutiny. News of the mutiny had brought a massive influx of civilians hailing the soldiers' action. The civilian presence first made the soldiers nervous, then provoked hostility. The chairman of the regimental committee had to cut short some of the civilians' speeches; soldiers rejected outright requests by the striking telegraph workers for assistance in driving telegraph officials from their offices and by worker combat squads for weapons. On the evening of the 3rd, the regimental committee promised that no more civilians would be allowed into the barracks, but the damage had been done, and a consensus developed overnight that the mutiny should be ended. The soldiers had been impressed by the promise of forthcoming reforms (the Tsar's December 6 concessions) and by a rumor that time-expired soldiers would be demobilized as soon as the mutiny was over (this particularly affected conscript NCOs, the most influential group in the regiment). On the morning of December 4, the regimental committee tried to rally the men, but was met with shouts of "We promised not to fire at the people, why are you demanding that we go openly against the Tsar?" Thereupon, the soldiers arrested their own committee.

The mutiny of the Rostov Grenadiers was of critical importance not because it was in any major way unusual—its origins and demands, the soldiers' animosity toward civilians and belief that they had won concessions, were quite typical—but because it came at a critical juncture: it was during the Rostov mutiny that revolutionary leaders in Moscow were deciding how (indeed, whether) to respond to government repression, in particular the arrest of the Executive Committee of the Petersburg Soviet on December 3. The Bolsheviks and Mensheviks who controlled the Moscow Soviet hesitated to call for a general strike, because they were not confident that the strike would be supported in Petersburg. Indeed, because of the evident demoralization of workers in the capital, the Executive Committee of the Petersburg Soviet itself, at its last session on December 3, had decided only to make contact with revolutionary organizations elsewhere to devise a plan and appoint a date for a new general strike; this was really a decision to continue to delay confrontation by shifting responsibility, but the Petersburg SRs opposed even that. A Bolshevik emissary from Petersburg was unable on December 4 to convince the Moscow Bolsheviks that Petersburg would support a strike, and the delegates to a conference of the railway union meeting in Moscow on December 5 doubted that a new political strike would succeed. Moscow's Bolsheviks and Mensheviks did finally conclude that they had no choice except to assume the responsibility that had fallen to them, and so called for a strike; in Moscow, only the SRs were genuinely eager to begin a general strike and insurrection (while the SR leader, Viktor Chernov, rushed to Moscow to attempt to persuade the railway union not to approve a strike). With the exception of the SRs, the Moscow revolutionaries found themselves pushed toward action they would rather have avoided.[50]

Revolutionaries resolved on a strike and insurrection not just because they felt they had to do something, but also because of the Moscow mutinies and because of the militancy of the Moscow workers, which was itself fueled by the mutinies. Workers all over the city reported that soldiers were promising support (though one such promise was qualified by the request that workers please not throw any bombs). The mood of the workers was reflected in a November 30 resolution by the printers' union: we have been reading with joy the daily accounts of regiments joining the people, and this gives the government no hope of suppressing insurrection. Other things than mutiny contributed to the workers' determination to strike, but mutiny did indeed inspire them, and revolutionary leaders felt that they could not at this point defy the sentiments of their constituency.[51]

Revolutionaries were not so optimistic as workers, but they, too, believed a rising would obtain military support. As one Bolshevik later recalled, the revolutionaries convinced each other that soldiers really would join in a rising, because that was what they all hoped for.[52] Even the collapse of the Rostov mutiny did not occasion reconsideration: civilians blamed the failure on mistakes committed by soldier revolutionaries, not on a lack of congruence between military and civilian revolutions, and they did not believe that the outcome of the Rostov mutiny had altered the garrison's revolutionary mood. On December 4, the Moscow Soviet asserted that many units in the city were ready to join the people, and called on soldiers to take over their regiments but to wait for the workers to rise before taking to the streets. The Menshevik and Bolshevik military organizations reported to their respective party conferences on December 4 and 5 (these conferences prepared the way for the rising) that though it was not certain how much active support soldiers would provide, the infantry regiments would certainly not oppose a rising. And Viktor Chernov recalled that at the December 5 meeting of the railway union, SR, Bolshevik, and Menshevik representatives all spoke of continued support from the garrison. With all revolutionary organizations in the city agreed, and with the consent of the railway union, the Moscow Soviet on December 6 called for a general strike-cum-uprising (the emphasis varied confusingly from one moment to the next) to commence on the 7th, and on the 7th the railway union proclaimed a national strike.[53]

The apparent collapse of the Moscow garrison was not only of paramount importance in the revolutionaries' decision to act, it also colored their thinking on the nature of an uprising. The Soviet on the 6th called, as it had on the 4th, for the soldiers to elect their own leaders, but this time asked them to join the people at once. There is every indication that this is what the revolutionaries expected to happen, and that they took this to be the culmination of the uprising; in the first few days of the strike they certainly had no plans for taking the offensive themselves. They subscribed, in short, to the view expounded in "The Soldiers' and Sailors' General Strike": a strike vaster than that in October would trigger a military strike, and this would bring down the government. The revolutionaries' inactivity gives the impression, as one Soviet historian has observed, that the revolutionaries had temporarily forgotten their call for insurrection.[54] In fact, they simply used the term loosely.

Faced with a proclaimed though strangely passive insurrection, the authorities in Moscow had to rely on the same garrison that gave the revolutionaries so much hope. It is not entirely clear how large the garrison was on December 7. There had been 17,000 men in the garrison as of November 13, but 11,000 had been in nine infantry regiments, and demobilization had reduced the strength of these regiments dramatically. A Menshevik estimate (probably that of their military organizer) was that the infantry averaged 500 to 600 men per regiment (one-third normal strength) or about 5,000 men in all, but even that may have been high. The garrison commander reported he had only 1,850 infantry to guard barracks, hold government institutions, and operate on the streets. There were probably 2,600 men in other units (principally cavalry and artillery), and 1,800 armed police, but except for the police the rest of the garrison looked to be almost as unreliable as the infantry.[55] The local command, and Admiral Dubasov after he assumed his new duties as Governor-General of Moscow on December 4, repeatedly appealed to Petersburg for reinforcements, an infantry brigade (two regiments) if possible. Petersburg, reluctant to weaken its own garrison, at first responded that it had no troops to spare and tried to placate Moscow with half of the 16th Ladoga infantry from Poland. But when the railway strike held up the Ladoga regiment, Petersburg finally gave Moscow the Semenovsk Guards infantry, one guards artillery battery, and one troop (a quarter-squadron) of Guards cavalry.[56]

Until December 15, however, the Moscow garrison was on its own. Of the infantry, the authorities could rely completely only on the Astrakhan

Grenadiers, whose honorary commander was the Tsar himself and who periodically received presents from members of the imperial family; men from the Astrakhan regiment provided the backbone for mixed companies formed from picked men of all units. Money, much of it donated by private citizens, was quickly found to buy the soldiers' loyalty (the Astrakhan regiment, according to an official account, was given 500 rubles plus various payments in kind, and it was not alone) and rations (spiked liberally with vodka) were increased. Officers worked overtime spreading rumors of civilian attacks on soldiers.[57]

The troops were at first sympathetic to the strike. On the 7th and 8th they talked with civilian demonstrators and even the cavalry only went through the motions of breaking up crowds; a holiday atmosphere prevailed. On the 8th the Executive Committee of the Soviet instructed workers to talk to soldiers and to avoid clashes if at all possible. (Similar instructions were delivered to partisan squads on the 11th, and one group of partisans threatened instant execution for anyone who violated this rule.) But no regiment was willing to commit itself to the revolution. The men of one regiment, "with tears in their eyes," told a revolutionary agitator that they just could not come out openly in support of the workers, though as soon as the workers had won soldiers would join them. On December 9, the Menshevik leaders discussed holding a mass march to the barracks to bring the soldiers out; the Executive Committee of the Soviet adopted a resolution to this effect on the 10th, but the plan was abandoned on the 11th.[58] By then it was clear that soldiers were not to be won over by moral suasion.

The Menshevik military organizer reported a change in the mood of the garrison as early as the 9th, the day the first shots were exchanged between civilians and soldiers. By the 10th, barricades were going up, and artillery was being used to clear the streets in the center of the city. The nature of the rising had changed completely. On December 11, the Soviet editorialized in its *Izvestiia* that the fighting would so appall the soldiers that they would at last come over. In the familiar pattern, just the reverse was happening: as the first casualties were recorded among the troops (and momentarily exaggerated), soldiers performed an increasing number of bestialities upon civilians. Yet hope died hard; rumors of disturbances in the barracks (one had it that a regiment emerged playing the *Marseillaise*) greatly influenced the Bolsheviks' December 12 decision to continue with the uprising.[59]

On the 14th, on the other hand, a Menshevik conference decided to end the uprising because the army had not risen as expected, and the Bolshevik partisan leader called for an end to the uprising for the same reason. A rump session of the Soviet on the 15th would not hear of such defeatism (this obstinacy was fueled by new rumors of disturbances in the barracks), and even the Mensheviks would not openly opppose the apparent will of the masses. But on the night of the 15th, the Mensheviks decided to end the rising even if the Bolsheviks were opposed; the Bolsheviks came to the same decision some hours later, about the same time the SRs decided the game was lost. On the 16th, the Executive Committee of the Soviet proclaimed that the uprising would end as of the 19th.[60]

The behavior of the Moscow garrison had determined the outcome of the insurrection even before the Semenovsk Guards regiment arrived on the 15th. The Semenovsk regiment did not even take the offensive until the 17th, when the rising was already over. At that point, half the regiment, after an artillery barrage, broke through the undefended barricades of the Presnia district and wreaked bloody vengeance there, the other half shot its way up and down the Moscow end of the Moscow-Kazan railway, killing approximately 150 civilians. (In Moscow itself, civilian casualties totalled approximately 700 dead and 2,000 wounded, as against 10 dead and 54 wounded among the troops.)[61] But the punitive expedition was, again, largely irrelevant to the defeat of the insurrection.

That defeat was prefigured in the termination of the Rostov Grenadiers' mutiny. The Grenadiers had refused outright to involve themselves in civilian revolution, and when civilians became too importunate had ended their mutiny. The greater pressure of insurrection—with the inevitable threat to the soldiers' lives—turned a mutinous garrison into accomplices in repression. One may presume that the soldiers' contradictory impulses caused them considerable psychic pain, and that many gladly took the vodka their officers proffered them precisely to stupify the demons within. Whatever their feelings, soldiers who had been thoroughly mutinous on December 2 were shooting civilians a week later. Even as they went down to defeat, revolutionaries continued to misunderstand what had occurred. In a proclamation explaining why the strike and insurrection were being brought to an end, the Executive Committee of the Moscow Soviet observed that defeat (not labelled as such) had resulted from the failure of the troops to join the rising, but that soldiers would not have the stomach for repression much longer. Therefore, concluded the proclamation, the armed struggle had contributed to the revolutionizing of the troops, had accelerated the indispensable and inevitable transfer of the soldiers' allegiance.[62]

The Provinces

Moscow was at the center of the revolution in December, not just because it experienced the heaviest fighting, but also because the appeal of the Moscow Soviet and the railway conference in Moscow for a general strike was taken up in many other cities. The factory inspectorate reported somewhat fewer workers on strike in December (over 430,000) than in October (almost 520,000), but larger numbers engaged in political strikes (about 385,000) than in any other month of 1905.[63] Railway workers played the premier role in December as they had in October. They were especially militant in the south, where they pushed for insurrection in the cities and themselves took control of many of the stations along the railway lines. Worker partisan groups fought soldiers in many places—December was the most violent month of the year—and the effect was everywhere the same as in Moscow: hitherto mutinous soldiers submitted to discipline and suppressed revolution.[64]

The most prolonged conflict between workers and troops in European cities occurred in Rostov-on-Don.[65] The battle was lengthy because government forces were exceptionally weak. On the eve of insurrection, the Rostov garrison had disintegrated. The 196th Zaslavl infantry and the local reserve artillery battery were (as the secret police reported) "so obviously demoralized (enlisted men gathered on the streets near the barracks around revolutionary speakers)" that they were withdrawn from the city and additional cossacks brought in. Cossacks had set off a two-day pogrom in October and had employed arms against workers since, but by December even they were wavering. On December 4 a delegation of six cossacks expressed solidarity with the workers' soviet, on the 5th the cossack delegates were arrested, and on the 6th the largely cossack garrison in protest refused to march in honor of the Tsar and the reforms officially announced that day. When the general strike began, then, local authorities had at their disposal one artillery battery, one company of infantry, and four cossack squadrons, but none of these units could be trusted. For their part, revolutionaries had a militia of 300 to 400 workers armed mostly with revolvers.

On December 7, the Rostov soviet and the local branch of the railroad union declared a strike in support of Moscow. Local authorities panicked, arresting twelve revolutionary leaders then releasing them on the soviet's demand. The two highest civilian officials in the city reported sick and fled. Colonel Makeev, commander of the garrison and the only prominent official remaining, proclaimed martial law and began recruiting volunteers at 40 rubles a month from nearby cossack villages. Military operations began on December 10, when troops made a half-hearted and unsuccessful attempt to break up a public meeting. During the next few days, workers mounted patrols at intersections and soldiers left them alone. On the 13th, the workers attacked the train station—that is, they marched in in such numbers that the infantry on duty were overwhelmed. Standing shoulder to shoulder with the workers, the soldiers disobeyed an order to fire and were withdrawn. Colonel Makeev ordered the station retaken, and for the next six days the fighting centered on the station and nearby barricades. On the 13th and 14th the station was subjected to artillery bombardment and retaken. On the 14th, cossacks and infantry attacked the barricades but were driven back. On the 15th, the workers' militia recaptured the station, driving out a company of infantry and a squadron of cossacks, and the artillery bombardment resumed. As of December 16, hospitals reported 113 wounded and twenty-eight killed, though casualties were certainly much higher. One officer and six enlisted men had been wounded.

In the course of the fighting, the mood of the garrison turned dramatically. Driven from the station on the 13th more by moral suasion than by force of arms, the soldiers were embittered by the few casualties they had subsequently sustained at civilian hands. The secret police reported that "the troops, police, and especially the cossacks are terribly enraged against the revolutionaries." Cossacks were particularly outraged by bombs (which killed one of their number), and though they shied away from barricades they beat and robbed passers-by and fired at will on open streets. Military operations, suspended on the 17th and 18th because of dense fog, resumed on the 19th. On the 20th, artillery (just reinforced) again shelled the station, railway shops, and barricades; infantry and cossacks then advanced in proper military fashion, recaptured the station and broke through the barricades. As in Moscow, liberal use of artillery and a few squadrons of formerly mutinous but now enraged cossacks had crushed the insurrection.

In a number of other cities—Nizhnii Novgorod, Perm, Novorossiisk— worker uprisings followed much the same pattern as in Rostov. In Nizhnii Novgorod, after the demobilization of reserves from the mutinous 307th Arzamas infantry and the 1st reserve artillery brigade, the garrison amounted to only 100 cossacks and about thirty infantry in excess of those guarding public buildings. The local governor quite naturally panicked, even providing arms for a voluntary right-wing militia (which workers forthwith dispersed). Nevertheless, the 100 cossacks, once given artillery support, broke up the workers' barricades and put down the rising.[66] In Novorossiisk, the garrison had literally vanished when the 16th Kuban plastoon battalion and the 2nd Urup Kuban cossack regiment set off homeward. The local commander, with a little more than one cossack squadron left at his command, took refuge in the railway station until a punitive expedition of cossacks and artillery and a battleship appeared simultaneously on December 25. With artillery trained on the city from the surrounding hills, and knowing that the risings elsewhere were over, the workers gave in without a fight.[67]

Garrisons were not everywhere so minuscule, but more units meant more mutinies, and local commanders generally feared to bring their soldiers into action. In Ekaterinoslav, where soldiers had taken enthusiastic part in the October pogrom, mutinies in three infantry regiments and a cossack squadron so shook the confidence of the authorities that they feared to move against the workers (who had set up barricades in their district but did not attempt to extend their control over the rest of the city); indeed, unrest continued in the infantry until mid-December. By the time reinforcements arrived from Sevastopol on December 18, the workers had learned that the Moscow rising had been defeated and had ended the strike on their own.[68] In Kharkov, elements of four infantry regiments had mutinied and marched through the city on November 23. At a conference of unit commanders following that shattering event, only commanders of the cossacks and of one infantry regiment (which had arrived in town on November 23, making it the fifth) could vouch that their men would fire if the workers rose. Apprised of the revolutionaries' plans by an informer, the command decided to test the garrison by surrounding the lesser of two groups of worker militia. On December 12, that worker band was trapped in a factory by elements of three infantry and one cossack regiment and subjected to desultory artillery fire. When the larger workers' militia rushed to their comrades' aid and charged firing across an open square, the soldiers turned withering fire on the workers, inflicting well over 150 casualties.[69]

The Caucasus

The situation in the Caucasus was comparable to that in the Baltic provinces, with the difference that reliable troops did not pour into the region at the end of the year; the local command had to contend with revolution with the units already at hand—and those among the most mutinous anywhere in the empire. Georgian peasants and mountaineers of many nationalities had been fighting a partisan war against the army since late 1904, and counterinsurgency sweeps organized from Tiflis had failed dismally to pacify the country. After publication of the October Manifesto, the authorities lost control over most of the rural districts. Additionally, twenty-eight of the forty-six infantry regiments and battalions in the Caucasus military district mutinied, as did three of the six cavalry regiments and twelve of the twenty-nine cossack regiments and battalions. The mutineers included three of the four regiments of the 33rd infantry division, originally mobilized for service in the Far East but sent instead to the Caucasus after the end of the war (the 33rd division had arrived by September), and three of the six plastoon battalions called up after the October Manifesto.[70] In late October and early November, General Vorontsov-Dashkov, Imperial Viceroy for the Caucasus, sent telegram after telegram begging for yet more reinforcements, to which the Ministry of War responded that uncommitted units were not to be had. Indeed, the Ministry ordered Vorontsov-Dashkov to send some of his troops outside the district (Vorontsov refused, pleading mutiny). During the weeks of the Viceroy's travail (twice he begged to be allowed to resign), the Tsar and his ministers informed him that they expected decisive and ruthless action against revolutionaries.[71]

At the end of the year, national and racial passions, which lent the revolution in the Caucasus anarchic fury, had very nearly swept away the imperial administration and thereby created the setting for mutiny, consumed the revolution itself. Native attacks on military patrols had enraged soldiers before October 17, and the soldiers' animosity toward the native population continued to mount thereafter; even mutinous units would as soon do violence to civilians as not. The liberal governor of Kutais Province reported that the men "burned with impatience to carry out the order" to wreak vengeance upon rebellious natives. Often, in fact, the men did not await orders: between November 27 and 30, small cossack units attacked civilians in four separate incidents in Kutais Province. Men from the unhappy 33rd division, used in the eastern Caucasus principally to restore movement on the railway, were involved in constant, often violent, clashes with passengers and local officials; when quartered in cities, they took whatever they wanted without paying.[72]

Throughout the Caucasus, garrisons shifted loyalties abruptly. The garrison in Batum mutinied in the middle of November, but on November 28 civilians disarmed a cossack and men from his regiment rushed to the local bazaar and whipped and bayoneted everyone who fell into their hands. Within fifteen minutes, seven civilians were dead, and four subsequently died of their wounds. Civilians thereupon erected barricades, a bomb was tossed at some infantry, and the latter, too, joined the fray, shooting indiscriminately. Civilians dismantled the barricades under threat of bombardment from the fortress, and over the next several days soldiers broke into houses and executed on the spot those found with guns.[73] In the city of Kutais, also the scene of a mid-November mutiny, cossacks issued from their barracks at night for plunder and pillage. Such incidents goaded natives into erecting barricades on November 27 and 28, and that together with native attacks on small units in the surrounding districts in early December inflamed the entire garrison.[74] In Tiflis, where most units (including cavalry) had taken part in mass revolutionary meetings and a mob march in late November, military authorities by playing on racial animosities and natives by attacking isolated soldiers turned the garrison around. Large numbers of troops reconquered the city's native working class districts in the third week of December.[75]

By the end of the year, most units in the Caucasus were acting as voluntary, if ill-disciplined, counterinsurgency forces, terrorizing civilians in the vicinity of their garrisons. The numerous special punitive expeditions put into operation in the rural districts in late December and early January were no less eager for blood, and they were all authorized to destroy villages at the slightest hint of resistance. Artillery was employed as a matter of course to announce the arrival of a detachment, levies were extracted from villages under threat of bombardment, and cossacks were given free rein for pillage, arson, and rape. Most of these punitive expeditions defy precise description because they were little more than bands of heavily armed men gone officially berserk. The fact that many of the units involved had recently mutinied merely contributed to the fury.[76]

The one exception to this pattern was the well-managed expedition led by Colonel Liakhov in early January against the Ossetians, who in the middle of December had plundered the estates of intruding Russian and Georgian gentry and had destroyed some factories for good measure. Liakhov's force included two artillery batteries, two companies of the 84th Shirvansk infantry (another part of the regiment had mutinied), three companies of the 18th Kuban plastoons, three companies of the 250th Akhulginsk infantry (which had mutinied), and one squadron each from three Terek cossack regiments (one of which had mutinied). Since all but the cossack units were under strength, the expedition probably totalled 300 infantry, 300 plastoons, and 300 mounted cossacks, plus the artillery. The detachment followed a set ritual: artillery was trained on a village; Liakhov then demanded that arms, stolen property, and brigands be handed over and that an agreement for the immediate payment of fines (of up to 36,000 rubles) be signed; when these demands were not instantly met, a few rounds of artillery induced hysteria and abject capitulation. Official reports claimed that the artillery was not fired directly at the villages, but at Magometanskoe shrapnel wounded sixteen Ossetians, some fatally. There may well have been other such cases; shrapnel was certainly meant to do more than inspire fear. In two weeks, the expedition extorted agreements for the payment by thirteen villages of 234,750 rubles in fines, destroyed dozens of houses, burned one school, formally executed three natives, slaughtered a great many cattle, and arrested up to 1,500 persons (most of whom were soon released because there was no place to detain them). In addition, the detachment collected 1,112 rubles per day in maintenance from the villages along its line of march. An official order congratulated the soldiers for suppressing the Ossetians "practically without bloodshed."[77]

As a matter of fact, only prolonged bloodletting maintained Russian hegemony in the Caucasus. One can do no more than guess at total casualties, but the punitive expeditions alone must have produced in the range of three or more thousand. Mopping up operations lasted well into 1906 (punitive forces were still being sent into the hinterland of Kutais Province in March) because of the rugged terrain. As in the Baltic, the forces involved were sizeable, though drawn mostly from the large permanent garrisons and not nearly so well coordinated as in the northwest. For insurance, the 33rd division was held in the Caucasus until the end of 1906.[78]

What one learns from the lengthy chronicle of violence in December 1905 is that the perpetration of violence on a very large scale was the sole reason for the survival of the Tsarist regime: military repression alone preserved Tsarist rule in the Caucasus, in Moscow, Rostov, Kharkov and other Russian cities, as well as in the Baltic provinces, Siberia, and the central agricultural region. The more significant implication of the December events is that escalation of the level of violence delivered to the regime the armed force necessary to make a policy of repression effective. Suppressing ill-armed civilian insurgents required relatively few men: a few thousand in Moscow, a few hundred in Rostov and Nizhnii Novgorod, a thousand or so against the entire Ossetian nation. However, in early December the regime did not have that small force. By late November, the regime, if it were to survive, had no choice except to demand of its servitors the application of brute force. Yet if the ministers in Petersburg were confident, or at least refused to allow themselves to doubt, that repression would work, officials on the spot were very uncertain, as were Dubasov in Moscow and Vorontsov-Dashkov in Tiflis, who reported the utter unreliability of their troops and begged for reinforcements, the commanders in Kharkov and Ekaterinoslav, so shaken that they hesitated to take action against insurgents, and the officials who fled Rostov. It was, indeed, the obvious disintegration of the Tsarist armed forces that gave revolutionaries confidence, or at least hope, that they could turn the regime's counteroffensive to their own advantage. Revolutionaries—in the Russian heartland, at any rate—understood the need not to provoke soldiers, but once barricades went up casualties were inevitable and the soldiers' response predictable.

Soldiers themselves were aware of the way in which civilian violence acted on them, and so—as in Moscow—asked workers not to throw bombs. What they were incapable of doing was making allowances for the pressure that drove civilians to do them injury. The men of the 165th Lutsk infantry, which had mutinied twice in Kharkov and, according to an official report, on December 12 fired at workers at the railway shops only with great reluctance (apparently they at first refused), sent a message to the Kharkov Social Democratic Federative Council after the shooting:

> Is it true that the workers burned the trunks of the men of the Lutsk regiment at the station, and that they were incited to do this? Was this really an act of revenge? If so, let them know that they have gained in the person of the soldiers the fiercest enemies, and that the soldiers' vengeance will know no limits. Let the workers absolve themselves, and the soldiers will stand on their side with all their heart.[79]

The mutinous Lutsk regiment did not shun contact with revolutionaries and at least held out the possibility of friendship with workers once the violence had abated. Other mutinous regiments whose behavior conformed more closely to the determined self-isolation of the soldiers' revolution must have been less reluctant to engage civilians once the first shot had been fired. And it was the psychology and behavior of the 165th and scores of other mutinous and nearly mutinous regiments that determined the fate of the regime: they, and not the few handpicked units in the punitive expeditions operating on the periphery of the empire, suppressed revolution when and where it mattered.

Collapse of the Soldiers' Revolution: Perceptions of Authority

The December violence, as important as it was in cutting short mutiny and mutinous inclinations, was only a part of the changing environment that brought the soldiers' revolution to an end. The regime's determination to repress civilians did not, for instance, ensure that soldiers would leave their barracks and expose themselves to civilian anger. One of the more frequent demands that mutinous units made was that they not be deployed against civilians, and mutineers sought to isolate themselves in their barracks. The 165th Lutsk, when mutinying in November, had refused to send patrols into the city, yet on December 12 it left the barracks, even if with reluctance and even if its companies were interspersed with units in which the authorities placed more trust.[80] By the time they left the barracks, the men of the 165th Lutsk had ceased to be mutinous, though it was as yet uncertain that they would obey an order to fire. Between November 23, when they had marched with three other regiments through the center of Kharkov, and December 12, something had led them to concede some authority to their officers. There were, moreover, many cities, such as Ekaterinoslav, in which mutinous units were not involved in gunplay at all and nevertheless returned to discipline. Even absent the tonic of violence, in other words, soldiers in December concluded that they must cease to mutiny and must obey their officers.

Cities in which soldiers were not influenced even by a potential of violence were not numerous, but Piatigorsk in the Caucasus was one, and the behavior of the 250th Akhulginsk reserve battalion presents as pure a case as can be found of how soldiers reacted to information that bore on the authority of the regime and of their officers. The Akhulginsk battalion, which provided the bulk of the Piatigorsk garrison (there were also two artillery batteries and a half squadron of cossacks in the city), mutinied on November 17, apparently under the influence of mutinies in other garrisons in the region and in response to civilian invitation to attend a mass meeting. The battalion marched twice through Piatigorsk, elected two sergeants as battalion and garrison commanders, freed some soldiers from the guardhouse, presented a petition of thirty-two demands, refused to have any contact with officers until their demands were met, and drew up a "Provisional Disciplinary Code" for the duration of the mutiny. Except for the code, the mutiny of the Akhulginsk battalion, which spread to the local artillerists, was typical of mutinies in the second half of November. Typically, too, on November 28 the corps commander met a number of the Akhulginsk demands.[81]

By early December, the Akhulginsk battalion was no longer formally in a state of mutiny; soldiers had resumed drill and had returned to their posts at the local bank. But the battalion was of no use to the authorities. In December, telegraph and railroad strikes isolated Piatigorsk from the outside world, and local authorities lost control of the city to a revolutionary Committee of Self-Defense. The soldiers kept to themselves, assisting neither revolutionaries nor the authorities. The only good word that the regional gendarme chief had for the Akhulgintsy in a report written on December 21 was that they had not yet handed over any weapons to civilians. On December 22, cossack villagers recruited by officials for a counterinsurgency detachment went to the Akhulginsk barracks to obtain weapons, but the soldiers refused to provide any, and fired on the cossacks when it appeared that they were about to attack. At that point the Akhulginsk battalion considered providing weapons to the Committee of Self-Defense, but in the end decided not to. Throughout the weeks of Piatigorsk's isolation, the Akhulgintsy behaved as though through mutiny they had acquired the right to make the key decisions affecting the disposition of the unit. Again, this was typical of soldier behavior in the aftermath of mutiny, as was the battalion's disinclination to become directly involved in civil conflict. What was unusual was the duration of Akhulginsk self-rule, and that was a result of Piatigorsk's isolation and the absence of information that could undercut the soldiers' belief in their right to order their own affairs. The soldiers' self-assurance collapsed only when the first newspapers from the outside arrived on December 24 and they learned that the government was everywhere mopping up the revolution. Acting under no local compulsion but anticipating that the old order would eventually be restored in Piatigorsk as well, on December 26 the Akhulgintsy confiscated weapons from civilians. On December 28, they marched with a band to greet a cossack detachment arriving at the train station. Within a few days, the Akhulginsk battalion was taking part in Colonel Liakhov's march through Ossetia.[82]

In Piatigorsk, the soldiers' revolution ended abruptly on December 24 because its basic premise had been invalidated. The soldiers' assumption that the old social and military fabric had been rent irreparably on October 17, an assumption apparently confirmed by the success of the November mutiny and acted on through most of December, was shown to be badly in error. Of course, for soldiers in Piatigorsk to end their revolution on December 24 was a matter of prudence and common sense. Nevertheless, the behavior of the Akhulginsk battalion establishes how soldiers responded to clear evidence of government authority when no other factors were involved. Had government action not convinced the 250th Akhulginsk and other mutinous regiments of the continued vitality of the Tsarist regime, the soldiers' revolution might have persisted indefinitely.

Outside of Piatigorsk, it is difficult to identify precisely what information was decisive in influencing soldier behavior, or to disentangle the impact on soldiers of signals about government authority on the one hand from the threat of civilian violence on the other, especially because the reassertion of regime authority prompted civilian insurrection. Nevertheless, it can be said that the decline of mutiny—from eighty-six instances in the second half of November to fifty in the first half of December to a mere sixteen in the second half of December—coincided with the development of the regime's counteroffensive: from the suppression of public sector unions, to the arrest of the chairman and then the executive committee of the Petersburg Soviet, to the proclamation of martial law, to the demand that rebellious peasants and insurgent work-

TABLE V-1. Biweekly Totals of Mutinies,
October 18–December 31, 1905, by Region

	Oct. 18–31	Nov. 1–15	Nov. 16–30	Dec. 1–15	Dec. 16–31
Central Asia	3	5	1	0	1
Petersburg region	4	5	6	3	0
Poland	0	1	11	2	1
Central Russia	1	3	24	6	0
Baltic provinces	1	4	5	1	2
Belorussia	0	4	3	5	2
Ukraine	0	4	12	7	2
Siberia and Manchuria	3	7	8	15	4
Caucasus	3	11	18	11	4
Total	15	44	86	50	16

ers be destroyed, to the destruction itself. The accumulating evidence of regime authority, to the extent that soldiers were aware of it, must cumulatively have had the same effect that the news arriving in Piatigorsk on December 24 had on the 250th Akhulginsk. Not just violence, but the regime's commitment to violence sobered mutinous and indisciplined units. As the regime regained control over more units, commitment turned to deed, and news of repression accelerated the restoration of discipline.

One gets a clearer view of the impact on soldiers of signals about regime authority by tracing the decline of the soldiers' revolution regionally, because the harder regime policy did not become effective everywhere at the same time. The virtual absence of mutinies in Central Asia after mid-November was a preview of the effect that unambiguous determination to suppress revolution had on the soldiers' behavior. A mutiny at the Tashkent fortress in mid-November was repressed by force, and after that the Turkestan military district command used the troops at hand to send small punitive detachments to restore order in cities whose garrisons were mutinous or otherwise unusable.[83] In and around Petersburg, in the Russian heartland, in Poland, and in the Baltic provinces, the soldiers' revolution was over by the first week in December. These were all areas in which the government's policy of repression had by then been put into effect or where its intent was well known. The precipitous decline of mutinies around the capital and in central Russia coincided with the well-advertised events in Petersburg and with operations against the Russian peasantry. In Poland, where martial law was in effect between October 29 and November 17, and where the very large body of troops was freely (if not successfully) deployed to maintain order, there was only one mutiny through November 15. When martial law was lifted and troops kept a lower profile, there was a surge of civilian disorders and, simultaneously, of disaffection in the Polish garrisons. Renewed application of military force at the very end of November cut short the soldiers' revolution in Poland.[84] In the Baltic, where martial law was also proclaimed in late November, reconquest of the provinces had to await the arrival of reinforcements from Petersburg. While soldiers may have been impressed by the authorities' stern proclamations, their passivity in early December is more likely attributable to the fact that by then they were effectively under siege.

The soldiers' revolution persisted precisely where the least information about government policy was available and where local authorities were themselves unable to take any action to restore civil order. In the Ukraine and Belorussia, the authorities were generally indecisive because they were unable to mount punitive operations—the number of reliable troops was quite small—while the December railroad and telegraph strikes prevented soldiers from obtaining a clear view of what was happening elsewhere; judging from what they could see around themselves in the first half of December, soldiers had good reason to conclude that civil authority was still in a state of disarray, and so their revolution continued unabated. By the middle of December, reports arriving from the rest of Russia produced the usual effect on soldiers.[85] In Siberia, the soldiers' revolution spread from the large to the small garrisons in early December, but began to end after mid-month because communications had been partially restored and the evacuation of the field army from Manchuria was at last proceeding smoothly. In the Caucasus, the number of new mutinies fell somewhat in the first half of December, but as in Piatigorsk many units that had mutinied in late November remained indisciplined into December, and the complete isolation of much of the Caucasus until late December meant that many soldiers had no reason to conclude that the authority of the regime had been restored. In the Caucasus, those units that reverted to discipline before late December generally did so because of the conflicts with natives.

The overarching reason for the end of the soldiers' revolution was that the government's determination to restore civil order altered the soldiers' perception of the regime's authority. The message got through at different times in different places, but when it did the soldiers' reaction was everywhere the same: mutinies ceased abruptly, and soldiers joined in the extirpation of civilian revolution. Armed conflict between soldiers and civilians had in some garrisons a more immediate impact than did the signals the regime was broadcasting, but the fighting itself became one more piece of information for soldiers to consider. As the annual report of the Petersburg military district for 1905 observed complacently, "Resolute action was reflected well in the morale and spirit of the troops—it destroyed all hesitation among them and eliminated any thought that it was possible to violate their oath and not do their duty."[86]

If the behavior of any one regiment is considered in isolation, it does not seem particularly remarkable that evidence of the regime's continuing authority should have brought soldiers to heel. Soldiers risked their lives if they miscalculated the power their officers had over them. It had taken evidence of an extraordinary collapse of the social order to free soldiers from their fear of punishment. It only required uncertainty about the extent of their officers' authority for soldiers to conclude that they must submit to discipline, at least until the outcome of the revolution was clear. No doubt it was that uncertainty that carried the men of the 165th Lutsk infantry onto the streets of Kharkov on December 12, as it was trepidation that kept the previously mutinous Grenadier regiments in their barracks during the first days of the Moscow insurrection.

But mutinous regiments were not acting alone: they knew about other mutinies in their own garrisons and in garrisons across the empire, and they knew that soldiers everywhere had the same vision of an equitable military order as they. Soldiers did not conclude from this knowledge, as they could have, that they had the power to get what they wanted. They had mutinied in the first place when they convinced themselves they had authorization to implement their own conception of a just military society; they ceased to mutiny when they saw a resurgence of traditional authority. In both cases, their behavior betrayed their dependence upon external authority. Had soldiers not been so sensitive to what government action implied about the structure of authority in society and army, had they continued mutinous in the face of the regime's commitment to repression, the Tsarist regime could not have survived.

The psychological underpinning of mutiny was thus extraordinarily fragile, but the eruption of indiscipline and mutiny after October 17 was evidence of a gross and enduring disparity between what soldiers had normally to endure and their notion of justice. By the same token, so sweeping a rejection of the structure of military society indicates how deeply repressed were the soldiers' instinctive desires under ordinary circumstances. The thoroughness with which the soldiers' desires were repressed—by those who controlled them, of course, but more importantly by themselves—accounts for the explosive collapse of discipline once the psychological constraints on mutiny had been removed. So long as the tension between reality and desire (even unconscious desire) was not relieved, there was potential for another explosion. The collapse of the soldiers' revolution in December 1905 was no guarantee that if circumstances once again gave soldiers the psychological space for mutiny they might not once more threaten the existence of the Tsarist regime.

VI. Preparations for the Second Round

Historians of Russia have not been kind to the year 1906, relegating it to the rank of anonymous, lower-case years falling between the aggressively Upper-Case Years 1905 and 1917. In the Western view, the Revolution of 1905 ground to a halt in the rubble of Moscow's Presnia district, and no ranting of revolutionaries could restart it. Workers, battered and exhausted from their labors of 1905, had neither the capacity nor the mind to undertake a new insurrection. The workers' movement (as measured by strikes) trailed off, and isolated peasant disorders posed no threat to the regime. The Duma was radical enough, but when in July it became too obstreperous, the government dispersed it, and the deputies' appeal for support from the people caused scarcely a ripple in the calm that was settling over the Tsarist empire.[1] Soviet historians do allot the revolution a "second phase," from January 1906 to June 1907, and point to periodic (if progressively weaker) surges in strikes, a scattering of mutinies, and a second round of peasant rebellion in mid-1906, and the connection between the Duma's proposals for redistribution of the land and peasant disorders. However, because of their preoccupation with workers and antipathy to the Duma, Soviet historians do not see the events of mid-1906 as constituting a serious crisis akin to the October and December crises of 1905: they conceive of the second phase of the revolution as a slow but steady retreat from the line of farthest advance reached in December 1905. Indeed, a glance at any Soviet monograph on the "Revolution of 1905–1907" reveals that Soviet and Western historians are in fact if not theory at one as to the termination of the revolution in December 1905: the "second phase" is ordinarily compressed into a brief epilogue. Soviet historical convention attaches the honorific "revolution" to this period largely because Lenin insisted until 1907 that the revolution was not over and that another insurrection loomed just over the horizon. Implicit in Soviet treatment of the revolution is that Lenin's judgment was wrong.[2]

Not Lenin alone, but most revolutionaries expected the revolution to continue after December 1905. While it is easy to dismiss their prognostications as so much wishful thinking, all the elements that together had made up revolution in 1905 persisted through the first half of 1906. The mood of the workers in 1906 is indeed problematical, but the workers' movement did not collapse, and it is difficult to find any but ambiguous hints of its impending disintegration. Peasant rebellion was as intense in the summer of 1906 as it had been in late 1905. The army at mid-year was almost as mutinous and just as disaffected as it had been in November 1905, and revolutionaries were in a far better position to exploit mutiny than they had been in 1905. In fact, the revolutionary parties as organizations were far stronger in 1906 than before. Liberals, though more suspicious of revolutionaries than in 1905, were as unreconciled to the regime as ever and challenged the legitimacy of the government from the rostrum of the Duma. For its part, the regime was uncertain how to respond to the challenge. Many of these strands of revolution came together in the summer of 1906 to produce a serious threat to the regime's continued existence. Given the behavior of the soldiers, there is no obvious reason why nothing came of the crisis. What is certain is that soldiers were at its center.

Anticipating Upheaval

In the immediate aftermath of the Moscow insurrection, revolutionaries of all persuasions, taking their cue from the Executive Committee of the Moscow Soviet, maintained with near unanimity that the fighting had not been in vain. If the workers of Moscow seemed to have gone down to defeat, the defeat was one of appearance only. Like the "defeat" of the workers who had marched on Bloody Sunday, the suppression of the Moscow insurrection had won new allies for the revolution because of the regime's indiscriminate use of artillery and summary executions. Some revolutionaries even contended that armed workers in Moscow had shown they could successfully take on a modern army. And at least through January, most revolutionaries believed that the army was becoming progressively more revolutionary, that the wave of mutinies that had begun in October, far from receding, was now reaching into the regime's supposed mainstay, the cossacks (late reports from the Caucasus and other outlying areas contributed to that belief). There were a few dissonant voices (Plekhanov's was one) but as the smoke lifted, most revolutionaries detected no essential alteration of the political landscape.[3]

Such optimistic projections were in part the result of nervous excitement induced by the December fighting, and some revolutionary lead-

ers soon had second thoughts. Many others, however, believed that
there was solid reason to expect a quick recurrence of insurrection—the
seasonal cycle of peasant labors and therefore, they supposed, of peasant rebellion. Socialist Revolutionaries had argued since October that
spring was the best time for insurrection, because the sowing season
would provide peasants a natural opportunity to rebel. Thus, the failure
of insurrection in December in no way demonstrated that workers seconded by peasants could not overthrow Tsarism. When the SRs held
their first party congress (December 29–January 4), the conclusion of the
congress' commission on tactics, as reported out by Viktor Chernov, was
that it was "quite possible that a broad, spontaneous [peasant] movement will begin in the spring. . . . The disagreement among the members of the commission is only whether the decision should be made in
advance, whether to exhort the peasants to rise."[4] Chernov argued that
because of the repression following the untimely December insurrections peasant rebellion in the spring was no longer an absolute certainty;
SRs should prepare, but they should not themselves incite peasant disorders. On the other hand, some of the most influential delegates (party
stalwarts Natanson and Rakitnikov, Rudnev fresh from Moscow) urged
that since a spring upheaval was virtually foreordained, SRs must seize
the initiative in order to lend peasant rebellion maximum organization
and impact. Caution prevailed in the end, as the congress by a vote of 32
to 19 decided not to commit itself to spring insurrection, but the congress did resolve that all party organizations should ready themselves
for the likelihood of spring agrarian disorders.[5]

Expectations of spring peasant rebellion remained strong in February
and March, and not just among SRs (one of whom wrote in February
that the intelligentsia and "laboring people" were in an "ecstacy of anticipation"[6]). Lenin, too, posited a link between spring sowing and insurrection, though like Chernov he was by February no longer certain
peasants were about to rebel. Martov, the Menshevik leader, was more
optimistic, and warned in February that Social Democrats must prepare
for the imminent explosion among peasants and should lay plans for a
national proletarian and peasant insurrection.[7] In February, a conference
of SR organizations in the south resolved to prepare for the inevitable
spring peasant rising, which would likely set off urban insurrection as
well, and in March, Chernov suggested that the government might
suppress the Duma shortly after it convened and thereby spark substantial disorders.[8] In late March, the agent of the Sûreté Générale keeping
track of Russian revolutionaries in London reported that recent arrivals
were convinced that, because the elections had been rigged, the opening
of the Duma would set off an upheaval greater than Russia had ever
before experienced, and that this insurrection would have a far greater

chance of success than the last because famine was driving peasants to rebellion and intensive revolutionary agitation in the armed forces was winning the support of soldiers and sailors.[9] Wherever they looked, revolutionaries saw the makings of conflagration.

Revolutionaries were not alone in anticipating a new revolutionary crisis, or in thinking that peasant rebellion would set it off. The governor of Perm Province warned in December that "one must expect major clashes when field work begins in spring"; in January gentry in the south asked Minister of War Rediger to send more troops because peasants "are preparing to seize and plow proprietary land" as soon as the sowing season began; and Prime Minister Witte warned Tsar Nicholas on December 25 and January 10 that peasant disorders surpassing those of late 1905 could be anticipated in the spring.[10] Consequently, the government began preparations for the next campaign even while mopping up the last pockets of resistance in midwinter.

The first step was to codify the tactics employed in the punitive operations. The thinking of commanders in the field was reflected in a memorandum of December 21 from General Kryzhanovskii, whose 2nd cavalry division was fighting peasants in five provinces. Kryzhanovskii maintained that "pseudo-humanitarian half-measures" not only failed to check peasant unrest, they also undermined both the army's moral authority and military discipline, since soldiers merely standing around became objects of scorn and themselves lost confidence in their mission. Troops should not be used for routine police functions, asserted Kryzhanovskii, they should be called out only as a last resort, in large units, and should without fail act ruthlessly (e.g., bombarding and burning villages). The Council of Ministers discussed the memorandum on January 10 and endorsed its recommendations.[11] Only Minister of War Rediger disapproved. He felt that even the procedures Kryzhanovskii recommended smacked too much of police operations, were bound to demoralize soldiers, and were no way to restore public support for the army after the debacle of the Russo-Japanese War (and with the Duma in the offing, this was one of Rediger's principal concerns).[12] In a related development, on February 7 new rules on the use of troops to assist civil authorities, under discussion in the State Council since December, were officially announced. Among the provisions was one that, a verbal warning having been given, soldiers were under no circumstances to fire blanks or aim a first volley over the heads of a mob. It was hoped that publication of the new rules would of itself deter antigovernment demonstrations.[13]

Next, impressed by the effectiveness of the punitive expeditions operating along the Transsiberian railway (and other lines), the government institutionalized the punitive train. In January, the Ministry of War ordered the military districts in European Russia to prepare special trains, manned by infantry, cavalry and artillery, to restore movement on the railways in the event of new strikes. Punitive trains were also held in readiness in the Caucasus and Siberia. Though these trains were never used, they were put together just in case; by June they were tying down more than 200 locomotives and 500 pieces of rolling stock.[14]

Operational procedures were adjusted without controversy. Not so easily resolved was the question of the army's overall redeployment, which had been a matter of contention between military and civil authorities since December. In reports to the Tsar on December 17 and 21, Prime Minister Witte complained that neither he nor the Minister of Interior knew where troops were located or what units were available, and argued that "the question of the disposition of troops must be governed by political considerations, as must the relations between the Ministries of Interior and War." Witte requested, and the Tsar appointed, a special conference to clear up the matter.[15]

Meanwhile, generals in command of operations against the peasants were submitting their own recommendations. Both Generals Panteleev and Strukov called for the army to be redeployed to deal with the civilian insurgency; Panteleev suggested that an infantry division and a cavalry brigade be quartered in every restive province. But the Ministry of War, despite the recommendations of its field commanders, was reluctant thus to formalize the army's role as a domestic police force. By way of an alternative, the Ministry of War in December submitted to the Council of Ministers a proposal for the formation of a territorial militia. Witte at first supported the proposal, but on the representations of the Ministers of Interior and Justice, the Tsar and the Council of Ministers ultimately rejected the plan: it was deemed unwise to trust a militia to take action against fellow villagers. On the other hand, everyone agreed on the desirability of increasing the strength of the rural—especially mounted—police; but development of a strong rural police force was proceeding slowly.[16] There was in fact no alternative to using the army to maintain order within the empire.

Reluctantly, then, Generals Rediger (Minister of War), Polivanov (Chief of the Main Staff), and Palitsyn (Chief of the General Staff) sat down with Witte and Minister of Interior Durnovo on January 28 to consider how the army could best be used against revolution. (Grand Duke Nikolai Nikolaevich, in his capacity as Chairman of the Council of State Defense, sat in as an observer.) Discussion centered on the deployment of units and on proper lines of authority when the army was called out. The latter question was easily resolved: when in action, the military would be in charge. The question of deployment was not so amicably settled. Durnovo, supported by Witte, came to the meeting with a list of provinces where spring agrarian disorders were most likely to occur. Durnovo proposed that additional units be brought into these provinces, and that they be distributed uniformly over the territory in question in garrisons "no smaller" than an infantry battalion, cavalry squadron, or artillery battery so that troops would always be at hand. The generals objected that the proposed redeployment would seriously weaken the empire's western defenses, and that subdividing units, never desirable, would be especially dangerous under present circumstances, when discipline had to be carefully monitored and draftees trained, neither of which was possible in fractional units. At any rate, the generals insisted, redeployment could not get under way before March, when appreciable numbers of units would be returning from Manchuria. Witte immediately countered that, surely, the most important task facing the government at that moment was the prevention of agrarian disorders. The generals reluctantly agreed.

By the time the conference met again on March 1, a compromise had been reached. Still protesting against weakening the western defenses, the Ministry of War agreed to the principle of redeployment; however, units would be maintained in their integrity, not fragmented. The generals stated that under the best of circumstances they would be short 119 battalions of the number required to be in place by spring; the most volatile provinces would have to be served first. The generals also won the point that, considering the state of the troops returning from the Far East, it would be best to allow units to proceed to their permanent quarters for resupply and reorganization before they headed for their new bases. As a matter of fact, the understanding was not adhered to. On March 12, the Tsar approved orders authorizing the deployment of the soldiers in units as small as battalions and individual cavalry squadrons, and parcellization of units and uncertainty about who controlled them remained sources of friction between the Ministries of War and Interior.[17]

Peasants did not rebel in the spring of 1906, and by April the sense of imminent crisis had given way to sullen malaise—distemper, really—in all elements of society. Abatement of tension produced within the regime a resumption of the customary feuding among ministers, and between ministers and the Tsar's intimates. Prime Minister Witte's authority declined precipitously; the Tsar kept him on only so that negotiations for a badly needed loan from French banks could be brought to completion. Witte busied himself preparing a program of legislation that could be presented to the Duma and thereby involve at least the moderate opposition in the work of government, but at the same time, Witte ensured that the Duma would in no way be able to obstruct the regime: the Duma was given no control over ministers or bureaucracy, it had only a very limited right actually to initiate legislation, the Tsar had an absolute veto, and the Tsar could dismiss the Duma whenever he wished. The Tsar, seconded by most of his advisors, was himself unwilling to entrust substantive decisions to the Duma and simply waited to see how the Duma would behave. Goremykin, who replaced Witte as Prime Minister just before the Duma opened in late April, intended to have as little to do with the Duma as possible and ignored the legislative program that Witte's ministry had put together.[18]

Rifts appeared among the revolutionaries, too, as the prospects for immediate insurrection faded and they had to reassess their assumptions and strategy. SRs and Bolsheviks maintained that peasant rebellion had merely been delayed until after the fall harvest, and so insisted that insurrection was still on the agenda.[19] Meanwhile, however, revolutionaries had to decide what attitude to adopt toward the Duma. In the revolutionary euphoria of late 1905 Bolsheviks and Mensheviks had buried their differences and moved toward reunification, but by the time the IV Congress of the RSDRP met in April to put the seal on unity, the debate over the Duma had divided the two factions as badly as ever. Alone of the revolutionary groups, Mensheviks favored participation in the elections, because they believed that—despite limitations on workers' voting rights, despite the martial law conditions that obstructed a free electoral campaign, despite the Duma's limited mandate—the Duma would be hostile to the government. To denounce the Duma, they argued, would be to aid the regime; SDs ought instead to use the Duma for revolutionary purposes by seconding conflicts between the Duma liberals and the regime and thus demonstrating that freedom could not be obtained until the Tsarist regime had fallen. All other revolutionary parties—not just Bolsheviks, but also Bundists and Zionist Socialists, Polish Social Democrats and Polish Socialists, Latvian Social Democrats, Ukrainian SDs, and SRs, in fact even some Mensheviks for a while—demanded a boycott or even disruption of elections, because the electoral laws and the conditions under which elections were being held ensured that the Duma would not be truly representative, it could achieve nothing anyway, yet its existence might create the illusion of a constitutional system and thereby distract the masses from the goals of insurrection and constituent assembly. After the bitter struggle over the Duma, the Menshevik-dominated SD Central Committee and the Bolshevik-controlled Petersburg Committee were in a virtual state of war; whatever one did, the other opposed.[20]

Social Democrats were no more fractious than any other revolutionary party. The SRs, too, split early in 1906. Disputes within the SR Party that had threatened to lead to a schism in the middle of 1905 had been shelved late in the year, but after the December insurrections a Maximalist wing broke away from the body of the party. SR-Maximalists denounced what they thought to be the dictatorial control exercised by the SR Central Committee, rejected the orthodox SR goal of establishing a bourgeois democratic republic after insurrection and called instead for the immediate establishment of a socialist workers' republic, and rejected the party's decision to suspend terror while the Duma was in session. The Maximalists made significant inroads into the regular SR organizations, especially in Moscow, where the split virtually paralyzed the party.[21] When revolution stalled, tactical and ideological differences came to the surface among SDs and SRs both. Unity was easy when revolutionaries rode the crest of popular disorders, difficult to sustain when hard decisions had to be made.

Disputes among the revolutionaries had as their counterpart a perceptible disorientation among workers. The factional bickering of the intelligentsia disgusted workers, who were already dispirited by the failure of the December general strike and insurrections. However, the widely reported apathy of workers early in the year had as much to do with the changing conditions of revolutionary activity as with any loss of commitment to revolution. After 1905, it was impossible to return to meetings in small propaganda circles, but there seemed to be no task to which the thousands of workers who had joined the revolutionary parties in 1905 could be set. Certainly after massive strikes and soviets, anything less seemed pale and unexciting. Yet even as it marked time, the workers' movement was consolidating: the membership of the Social Democratic and Socialist Revolutionaries Parties rose from around 25,000 in late 1905 to well over 100,000 by October 1906, and there was by that time probably an equally large membership in the Bund, the SDKPiL, the Latvian SDP, the PPS, and the host of revolutionary parties among the other national minorities. Most of these new members must have been workers (and, in far smaller numbers, peasants) who had made contact with revolutionary organizations in late 1905 and signed on formally during 1906. Moreover, if workers in the big mills who had been most militant in 1905 appeared to be apathetic in early 1906, workers from small shops who before had stood on the sidelines were noticeably more aggressive in organizing unions and demanding concessions from their employers. And the political strikes on May 1 were a stunning success in large mills and small.[22] Nothing in the behavior of the revolutionary parties' mass support, or in the behavior of the working class as a whole, indicated that workers were no longer capable of challenging the regime. It is likely, in fact, that while workers were less volatile in early 1906 they were better organized politically, and that the workers' movement was in terms of organization expanding rather than contracting. Of course, if organization had replaced spontaneity, the behavior of the working class depended far more on decisions made by revolutionaries than had been the case in 1905, and the divided counsels of the revolutionary leadership did not bode well for the future.

Only the liberals had a relatively clear vision of what they wanted and how to go about getting it. Liberals had distanced themselves from the revolutionary movement in late 1905, and the December violence had appalled them, but they blamed the regime more than revolutionaries. They denounced the flagrant violation even of Tsarist law by the punitive expeditions, the imposition of martial and siege law in two-thirds of the empire's provinces, the arrest of thousands of persons on the flimsiest of excuses in early 1906, the reimposition of press censorship and regulations on meetings, and the evisceration of the Duma. The Kadets (with 100,000 members at the opening of the year) arrived in the Duma—in which they held about 35 percent of the seats, by far the largest organized bloc, because parties to the left had boycotted the elections and because Kadets favored redistribution of land to benefit peasants and thus obtained considerable peasant support at electoral meetings—determined to convert the Duma into a genuine legislature and to overhaul Russia's social and political institutions. They did not, however, have any clear view of what would happen if the regime refused to acquiesce in their plans. They were torn between confidence that the regime would have to bow to the clearly expressed will of the people, and willingness to contemplate continued revolution should the regime prove obdurate. In any case, Kadets no less than SDs and SRs assumed in early 1906 that the revolution was still incomplete.[23]

In fact, by the time the Duma met even revolutionaries who had urged a boycott of the elections were having second thoughts, because it was clear that the goals of the Duma and the government were irreconcilable. Peasants had sent their deputies to the Duma with instructions to obtain land, and were certain that the Duma would do as they commanded. If that belief indicated that peasants were indeed under the illusion that the Duma was a legislature that could express and implement the will of the people, it was also evident that conflict between Duma and government over land redistribution would dispel those illusions, and might persuade peasants to support the overthrow of the regime. Such, at least, was the hope of Bolsheviks and SRs. There was every reason to expect that the sessions of the Duma would stir rather than dampen political emotions. If spring had failed to deliver peasant rebellion, summer had provided in the Duma a wonderful tool for educating the Russian people in the need for insurrection.[24]

Organizing for Military Revolution

The conviction that upheaval loomed just ahead gave a powerful boost to the revolutionary military organizations. In 1905, they had been inconsequential, little more than a barometer of the revolutionaries' awareness of disaffection in the armed forces. They had emerged in response to mutiny, and revolutionaries involved in them had for the most part shared the prevailing assumption that rebellious soldiers should come to the support of civilian revolution at a moment civilians deemed appropriate. Even had revolutionaries had a better understanding of what caused soldiers to mutiny, the soldiers' revolution would have overwhelmed them. In the course of the year, a few of the military organizations had concluded that mutinies were sufficiently important to the success of the revolution to warrant keying insurrection to regionally or nationally coordinated mutinies at a time dictated by the pace of revolution in the army itself, but that notion had made no impression whatsoever on revolutionary leaders, and the fledgling military organizations had themselves been unable to control soldiers in their own garrisons, let alone implement ambitious national schemes.[25] It was that thinking, however, that inspired the military organizations in 1906. Those who threw themselves into revolutionizing the army in early 1906 were certain that a new revolutionary crisis impended, and they believed the army could deliver victory to the revolution. Persuaded by the December fighting that urban guerrillas alone could not provide the armed force needed to topple the regime, and by the November mutinies that mutinous soldiers properly handled could, the military organizations set about preparing to use soldiers and sailors as the shock troops of revolution.

Confidence in the potential of military revolution produced a sustained, widespread effort to win support in the army even after mutinies had ceased: military organizers did not intend to be caught unprepared, as they had been in 1905, when soldiers once again rebelled. In late December and January most military organizations were badly disrupted by arrests (or the threat thereof, which drove many revolutionaries underground in distant cities), or collapsed as garrisons were demobilized into temporary nonexistence. But they recovered in strength: no fewer than eighty SD military organizations were active in the first half of 1906, and at least forty-seven (certainly more) SR military organizations operated in the same period. These were without question serious enterprises, involving by mid-year on the order of 1,100 to 1,300 civilians on a full-time basis, an indeterminate but large number of others part-time or temporarily. They churned out a flood of revolutionary leaflets (the SD military organization in Riga ran off 11,000 pieces of literature in the month of May, and that was not atypical of military organization productivity), and in the first half of the year twenty-one SD and nine SR organizations published newspapers for soldiers.[26]

Appealing to soldiers was not, however, the chief concern of the military organizations in early 1906. They were certain they had a receptive audience. Their principal goal was instead to position themselves to take advantage of the soldiers' rebellion when it came, and to do this they held conferences to fashion regional and—eventually—national military organizations. In January, a conference of SR military organizations in the Caucasus resolved to initiate an All-Russian Military Union and even set up an organizational bureau to convene a national conference in March. Nothing came of this, though all the SR military organizations in the Caucasus did relabel themselves local branches of the All-Russian Military Union. Early in 1906 the SD military organization in Kharkov (formally Menshevik) attempted to convene a conference of the SD military organizations in the south, and there was a conference of the SD military organizations in Lithuania. An SR-Maximalist Military Union that emerged in Moscow in February relabelled itself "All-Russian" in May; no national organization resulted from this titular inflation, though the Moscow Maximalists may have been in contact with a Maximalist military organization in Vilna.[27] Whatever their factional and ideological differences, Bolshevik, Menshevik, SR, and SR-Maximalist military organizations all aspired to fashion national organizations. They took the prospect of insurrection seriously, believed that soldiers would play the crucial role, and insisted that mutinies would have maximum impact if a mechanism for coordinating them were in place when they occurred.

Within the Social Democratic Party, the impetus for creating a national directorate for military revolution came from Moscow, and from the beginning the SD military organizations there—Bolsheviks and Mensheviks each had their own—planned to draw in proletarian combat organizations as equal partners in a military campaign against the regime. SD military organizations in Sevastopol, Rostov, Kiev (all three Menshevik), Kaluga, Riga, and probably elsewhere, also worked in tandem with combat organizations, either through mutual representation in their respective committees, or with a joint leadership group. In Perm SD combat activists initiated work in the garrison.[28] This association betrayed the military organizations' preoccupation with insurrection, for the combat organizations' sole purpose was to train a "revolutionary army" to do battle with the regime. Many of the SD military organizations' problems with the rest of the party stemmed from their alliance with the combat organizations, which Menshevik leaders soon repudiated and Bolshevik leaders treated warily. In January the Moscow Bolsheviks set up a Military Technical Bureau (headed by a Menshevik, A. A. Vanovskii, who had led the Kiev military organization in 1905) to assist Social Democrats throughout central Russia in preparing proletarian and military insurrection; activities included training proletarian combatants, manufacturing bombs, reconnaissance, and so on. The local Bolshevik and Menshevik military organizations, both of which anticipated insurrection in the spring, had representatives on the Bureau, and the Bureau sent a questionnaire to SD military organizations in central Russia in order to ascertain the size of garrisons, deployment of units, the soldiers' principal interests and grievances, and their general mood. The Moscow Bolshevik military organization, led by Emelian Iaroslavskii, used the Technical Bureau to establish contact with other SD military organizations, and in March convened a conference on work in the region's garrisons. The Bolshevik military organization then dispatched organizers to found or reinforce military organizations in other cities, and it thereafter served as a clearing house for SD military organizations in central Russia, passing on the names of contacts when units transferred from one garrison to another.[29]

In March, too, the Moscow Bolshevik Military Organization (presumably with the cooperation of the local Menshevik military organization; they were on the verge of complete merger) convened a rump national SD military organization conference. The Muscovites clearly felt a need for haste, because, as they told the Petersburg military organization (then led by the Mensheviks Antonov-Ovseenko and Mikhail Pavlovich), they expected a rising at about the time the Duma convened, i.e., at the end of April. Though such major military organizations as those in Finland, Warsaw, and Sevastopol apparently agreed to send delegates, when the conference opened on March 27 only Moscow, Petersburg, Vilna, and Dvinsk were represented. Additionally, representatives of the battle-hardened Latvian combat organization and the Central Committee (a Bolshevik, Sammer) were present.

The most significant item on the agenda was the proper relationship between the military organizations and the rest of the party. The Moscow Bolshevik military organization offered for consideration its own statutes, which stated that the immediate task was to form military-combat organizations from all revolutionary elements in the army "for a decisive, nationwide insurrection against the autocratic government." Military organizations were to be autonomous in their own affairs and, during the insurrection, autonomous in their dealings with non-SD military organizations (though they would be guided by the Central Committee's political directives). The conference took no decision on this or any other matter because all the participants were arrested at the first session (most escaped from jail within a few days), but—also on March 27—the Military Technical Bureau issued a draft resolution on insurrection, for consideration at the party's upcoming Fourth Congress, that spelled out the implications of the military organizations' conception of their role during an insurrection: "leadership of the insurrection should pass into the hands of combat councils, appointed in advance and consisting of representatives of the proletarian, military, and combat organizations, with the latter two predominating."[30] That plank would henceforth be at the center of the SD military organizations' program, and it was supported by both Bolshevik and Menshevik military organizers. To the military organizations, such combat councils were merely an instrument for implementing the party's goal of overthrowing the regime. To party leaders, they were a major challenge to the existing party structure, and when they became aware of what the military organizations were driving at both Bolshevik and Menshevik leaders categorically rejected the idea. Bolshevik hierarchs were no more willing than Menshevik to abdicate leadership of any sort to military and combat organizers.[31]

More than the dispute over lines of authority bedeviled relations between the Social Democratic Party and its military organizations: party leaders did not believe that organizing soldiers for insurrection was crucial to the outcome of revolution. This became clear at the Fourth Congress of the RSDRP (April 1906), where the army figured frequently in the debates but only to buttress the Bolsheviks' and Mensheviks' opposing views on the Duma, liberals, and peasants, and planning for insurrection.[32] Mensheviks, now arguing that the Moscow uprising had ended in a decisive defeat, asserted that "victory for the popular uprising is conceivable only in the event that the armed forces are disorganized and that at least a part switch to the people's side."[33] They did not conclude that the party must therefore devote more attention to the army: because soldiers were peasants, they would not follow the socialists' lead. Soldiers would support revolution only if they saw that the peasantry and the bourgeoisie, too, were fighting the government—which in the Menshevik paradigm was an argument for supporting the Duma. Bolsheviks, who as late as March had been confident of the prospects for military revolution but by April were impressed by a dearth of mutinies, countered that the Moscow insurrection had shown that one could not count on the troops switching sides; the most one could hope for was that some units might come over when civilians were on the verge of triumph anyway. Insurrection therefore must be carefully prepared, and Moscow had demonstrated that worker insurgents could take on the army. Recognizing that they were on weak ground, the Bolsheviks equivocated (Moscow had "not disproved" their contention) and cited Kautsky's positive assessment ("which does mean something") of the success of urban insurgency.[34] Neither Bolsheviks nor Mensheviks viewed military revolution as anything more than a by-product of civilian revolution.

The military organizations themselves scarcely received a hearing at the congress. A few Bolshevik and Menshevik delegates, either associated with or on instructions from local military organizations, attempted to place work in the army on the agenda. The attitude of the congress was summed up by the Menshevik Ramishvili: "In my opinion, there is no need to put this question to the Congress for discussion. The Congress, which must deal with many serious and complex matters, cannot concern itself with such trifles."[35] Iaroslavskii rejoined that "a mass of revolutionary energy in the army is going unused," and he and a dozen or so others (roughly half of them Mensheviks) who had connections with military work offered a resolution calling for the training of urban guerrillas and the establishment of a council under the Central Committee to centralize the work of combat and military organizations. That resolution was overwhelmingly defeated—by Bolshevik as well as Menshevik votes—though the congress did make one concession to the military organizers. At Iaroslavskii's urging, the congress instructed the Central Committee to convene a conference of military organizations. The Central Committee, controlled by Mensheviks after the Fourth Congress, ignored the resolution.[36]

The rapid expansion and increased assertiveness of the military organizations occasioned much less tension within the Socialist Revolutionary Party. In early January, the SR party congress itself called for stepped-up agitation and organization in the armed forces, and, apparently with the encouragement of the leadership, SR activists shifted perceptibly away from preoccupation with urban combat groups and towards military work.[37] There were a number of reasons for the SR leadership's receptiveness to work in the army. The SRs thought of themselves as the heirs to the revolutionaries of the 1870s and 1880s who had run a centralized military organization, they were unselfconsciously committed to planning for insurrection, and they had years of experience with a centralized terrorist operation. The key consideration in early 1906, however, was their reading of the political situation. As one party official recalled a year and a half later,

> the political balance—autocracy on the one hand, the masses, gripped by excitement, on the other—was deemed to be so unstable that it seemed as

though it would be enough to throw "the sword of Bren" onto the scales, to revolutionize the army, in order with a free hand to bring the revolution to culmination.[38]

In consequence, the SR Central Committee made major financial contributions to military work, tolerated a large measure of military organization autonomy, and no later than May established an ambitious central directorate for military work.[39]

Nevertheless, differences did emerge between the SR party hierarchy and the military organizations. The SR's national military coordinator, S. F. Makhalevich, better known as Jan, was a veteran of the revolutionary movement of the 1880s. He believed that revolutionary soldiers by themselves could destroy the Tsarist regime: in late 1905, he had witnessed first-hand the prolonged mutiny of the Krasnoiarsk garrison that had permitted revolutionaries to hold power in the city for over a month, and the experience had convinced him that soldiers were the key to successful insurrection. Personally supervising the work of the SR military organizations in and around Petersburg, Jan came to share the point of view of the SR military organization in Krondstadt: the Baltic Fleet was destined to play the central role in the revolution, forcing the government to its knees by training the ships' guns on the capital (this was an idea that went all the way back to the late 1870s, though there is no evidence that the Krondstadt SRs were aware of the link). Jan was impatient to get the insurrection under way, and was certain that once Krondstadt rose all the other pieces would fall into place. The SR Central Committee, on the other hand, did not believe insurrection was an exclusively military enterprise, or that soldiers and sailors should dictate the pace of revolution. The Central Committee maintained that insurrection should be delayed until peasant rebellion was underway, in the fall.[40] Unlike the Social Democratic leaders, who either questioned the importance or denied the very possibility of winning support in the army, the SR Central Committee wished merely to ensure that mutinous soldiers would not be defeated in isolation. But even differences over the timing of insurrection could have a bearing on revolutionary strategy.

The implications of the dispute between the SR leadership and the military organizations became apparent during a discussion of tactics at a conference of SR military organizations that Jan and the Central Committee convened in late June. Fifteen military organizations were represented, and a large number of civilians from the party's central institutions also attended (itself a good indication of the importance the SR leadership attached to work in the army).[41] The immediate context for the discussion was provided by mutinies that—to anticipate—were by June once more sweeping through the army. The military organizations did not explicitly challenge the SR axiom that fall was the appropriate time for insurrection, but they claimed they could not long hold their soldier following on a short leash: unless the moment were seized, support for revolution in the army would evaporate. Soldiers were so important to the outcome of insurrection, asserted the military organizers, that if they could not be restrained they should be allowed to initiate insurrection. Indeed, the conference resolved that if a major military insurrection should occur spontaneously SR military organizations would have to assume leadership of it—and that, of course, would force the hand of the Central Committee.

The logic of their insistence on the crucial importance of revolution in the army for the success of the revolution as a whole led the SR military organizations, no less than their SD counterparts, into conflict with their party leaders. The difference, of course, was that the SR leadership was far more willing to concede the importance of military revolution than were the Bolshevik and Menshevik leaderships. Yet military organizations of all revolutionary factions were in far more agreement with each other than with their respective party leaders. All believed that soldiers would support revolution and that the behavior of the army would determine the outcome of revolution. They all believed, by extension, that should revolution break out in the army civilians must follow the soldiers' lead, and that national coordination of military organization activity, and of mutinies, was essential preparation for that eventuality. Indeed, the number of assumptions that military organizations of all parties and factions held in common was so great that military organizers were able to cooperate with each other far more closely than could the revolutionary leaders. Of course, the harmony among the military organizations, and the disagreements among party leaders, would have been utterly irrelevant had not soldiers been as mutinous in 1906 as in 1905, and had the military organizations not in fact had considerable success mobilizing support for revolution in the army.

Bidding for the Soldiers' Loyalty

The Ministry of War was aware of the designs that revolutionaries had on the army and—properly impressed by the extent of the soldiers' disaffection in late 1905—feared that soldiers might respond to the revolutionaries' blandishments. The generals understood that revolutionary agitation could not be deflected simply by increasing pay and rations and by reducing the length of service; it was equally important to deny revolutionaries a monopoly in dealing with issues that exercised soldiers. A "Directive to the Commanders of Units in the Warsaw District," dated 15 November 1905, addressed that problem squarely. Despite pious talk of the moral underpinnings of discipline, observed the "Directive," fear alone had sustained discipline hitherto; soldiers were not, therefore, innately reliable. Officers had failed miserably to isolate soldiers from revolutionary propaganda, and revolutionaries spoke to issues of vital interest to soldiers. Moreover, soldiers read newspapers eagerly to find out what was going on in the country. If soldiers were to perform reliably in the midst of the tumult around them, officers must win moral influence over their men, and must therefore explain events to them, even if that meant talking frankly about mutinies. The major difficulty, concluded the "Directive," was that officers were incapable of discussing political questions. But they must learn. In December, the Ministry of War recommended the Warsaw district's "Directive" to all officers, and in January an article in the official military paper, *Russkii invalid*, again called on officers to discuss current events, even to discuss (and refute) the demands of the extreme parties.[42]

Not content with broad hints, the Ministry of War ordered the military districts to see that officers conducted discussions in their units, and the navy set up "Lecture Commissions" in Kronstadt, Libava, and Sevastopol for the same purpose. The Moscow military district periodically issued guidelines for officers. One in January instructed them:

> It is necessary to explain the true sense of events, to indicate the role of the leaders of the disorders and to stress with especial insistence the exalted significance of the army and its valorous participation in the cause of pacifying the country, especially in the suppression of the Moscow insurrection. This is one of the clearest proofs of just how honorable and exalted is the soldier's calling.[43]

Officers were soon speechifying to their men at the drop of a hat, lecturing on current events and even reading from and responding to revolutionary proclamations being distributed in the army. Though some officers reported that these discussions went well, the reverse was the rule. It was normal, for instance, for officers to lecture soldiers on the evils of the "Jewish press," which printed false information for profit, or to call on soldiers simply to "extirpate the Jews" and other "domestic enemies." Though Russian soldiers certainly had a soft spot in their hearts for anti-Semitism, crude right-wing diatribes could not create bonds of trust between officers and men.[44] The Ministry of War was aware of the political illiteracy of its officers, and in June 1906 ordered the establishment of political courses in officer schools. A commission of generals and social scientists (including such luminaries as Professors

Platonov and Sergeevich) was appointed to draw up the curriculum and to recommend likely candidates for teaching positions. The program was to familiarize future officers with the historical and ideological bases of the existing order and with the main points of socialist doctrine, and these lessons were to provide the material for the officers' subsequent talks with their men.[45]

Talk was complemented by a literary campaign. Until the end of 1905, the only reading matter generally available to soldiers in their barracks were two long-standing literary journals for enlisted men and a series of stories published by the Berezovskii military publishing house. This literature aimed at instilling a few simple lessons: the sanctity of the soldiers' oath, the good prospects for obtaining decorations for valorous service, the superiority of military to civilian society, and (of course) anti-Semitism. The stories had little to do with the army as soldiers experienced it, and they went unread. After October 17, a few pamphlets explaining the October Manifesto and the forthcoming Duma were published especially for soldiers, but these do not seem to have been widely circulated.[46]

This situation changed dramatically in 1906: conservative and monarchist literature inundated the barracks. The Main Staff at the Ministry of War, and then a newly established "Committee on Military Education," issued lists of recommended pamphlets, and some divisions and army corps established committees of their own to select proper reading matter for soldiers.[47] The Berezovskii publishing house attached free pamphlets for soldiers to its officers' journal, *Razvedchik*, and a cavalry journal, *Vestnik russkoi konnitsy*, began to append supplements for enlisted men. The output of short unit histories and memorial brochures was stepped up, and the emphasis was now often on the exploits of the unit's enlisted men in the fight against revolutionaries (some of the brochures were conveniently divided into "discussions"). Units took out subscriptions to right-wing papers, and the Petersburg military district provided subsidies to *Zor'ka*, a paper for peasants published by the Octobrist Party beginning in February 1906, on condition that the paper include articles for soldiers.[48] Regimental staffs even began to issue their own proclamations—universally anti-Semitic. The proclamation by the command of the 42nd Yakutsk regiment (Zhitomir), for instance, attributed revolutionary propaganda to "Jews and ill-educated young people. Jews hate Christians, they want to destroy Orthodoxy and introduce their own Jewish empire."[49] Nor was the army left to its own devices. Right-wing organizations distributed large amounts of free literature in the barracks.[50]

The most ambitious undertaking was the publication of military-political periodicals for enlisted men by the staffs of the military districts.

These began to appear, either in weekly or twice-weekly form, in February. They dealt with topics of current interest, especially the Duma and the land question, both of which were treated from a very conservative and (one scarcely needs add) often anti-Semitic point of view. The military chaplaincy chipped in with its own soldiers' weekly, *Dobroe slovo*, which emphasized the terrible sacrilege of all revolutionary acts and the sanctity of the soldiers' oath, while the chaplains' own journal, *Vestnik voennogo dukhovenstva*, printed model anti-revolutionary sermons.[51]

The volume of counter-revolutionary propaganda the military churned out—a measure of the generals' honest fear—was truly impressive, yet its impact was minimal. Even some officers noted that the new policy of officer-led discussions did not remove the basic obstacle to a healthy army: soldiers still had no way to seek redress of grievances (collective complaints were still construed as mutiny), soldiers were still treated as second-class citizens by their officers and in law, and officers were still immured in caste traditions (for example, in May the Ministry of War felt it necessary to order officers to avoid public drunkenness, which undermined their moral authority over soldiers).[52] Given these circumstances, there could be no common ground between officers and men. Many of the pamphlets written for enlisted men were frankly insulting; one informed soldiers that they did not have the right to attend meetings because they might, unbeknownst to themselves, be seduced into mutiny. At any rate, as one officer noted, "The content of the brochures and leaflets on social and political questions . . . is pale and uninteresting, and people don't willingly take up this sort of reading."[53]

Even assuming that the Ministry of War could have won a war of ideas with revolutionaries, problems in implementing the reforms that had been introduced in December badly undermined ideological indoctrination. For instance, the text of the order announcing the reforms was contradictory: at one point it indicated that blankets and bedlinen were to be issued to all soldiers, at another that these were to be issued only to current conscripts. When it turned out at the annual issue of equipment that only draftees obtained the full benefits, the older soldiers muttered angrily about this new injustice. Not until July 1906 did a new order extend the benefits to all soldiers.[54] Even the provisions of the order that were not in question were often—perhaps in most cases—honored in the breach. In many units equipment was issued in pre-December quantities either because the necessary stocks were not available or because commanders preferred to lay supplies away for a rainy day. Since soldiers knew what they were entitled to, the supply problems were more than ordinarily aggravating. Even the reduction in length of service was handled badly. The army simply could not discharge immediately all those who had completed three years of service—to do so would have eliminated almost all noncommissioned officers. Instead, the reduction was spread over three years, and did not begin until the fall of 1906. Again, of course, soldiers felt they had been taken in by the authorities.[55] The soldiers of the 1903 draft (who had served three years) in the 49th Brest infantry—which had led the attack on the rebellious naval barracks in Sevastopol in November—petitioned the Minister of War "as loyal sons and servants of the Tsar father" for assistance in securing discharge. They also requested that they be issued all the equipment that was due them under the December 6 order, and concluded: "If these two demands are not met, we will be compelled to go another route, and then everyone will be behind us, of which we inform your excellency."[56]

The supply problems, at least, were not entirely a matter of the authorities' clumsiness and ill will. Because of the cost of the Russo-Japanese War, the army was in dire financial straits just when it had to make good an immense shortage of boots, uniforms, and other supplies (stocks were so far depleted that the Ministry of War feared the army could not be mobilized if need arose). Since the government as a whole lacked money, the army could expect little succor. In fact, the government demanded that the army hand over to the treasury monies that units in the Far East had saved from provisions allowances. (Twenty million rubles were involved; Minister of War Rediger disobeyed a cabinet order and saved twelve million for resupply needs.) The units in the worst condition were those returning, often in rags, from Manchuria. It was difficult enough to bring these units back to their prewar supply levels, simply impossible to supply them according to letter of the December 6 order. The soldiers' resentment on this score was amplified by the fact that returning units were often immediately deployed against workers and peasants. And the soldiers who had been through the war were the most recalcitrant to discipline and the most likely to demand satisfaction. Indeed, soldiers in many units seem to have organized on the return trek, and immediately upon establishment in their quarters they sought out contact with revolutionary parties for the purpose of planning action to win what they felt was due them. The consensus of both generals and revolutionaries was that units back from the war were extremely fertile soil for revolutionary agitation.[57]

The military organizations found it easy to take advantage of conditions in the army, since even officers admitted that revolutionary agitators could play to the soldiers' genuine grievances. Reasonably typical of the thrust of the military organizations' appeal is a series of twenty-four hectographed leaflets that the SD (Bundist) military organization in Mariampol distributed, mostly to the 111th Don infantry, between February and June 1906.[58] They were written in the first person ("our blood-sucking commander is exploiting us"), and though civilians probably composed them they reveal an intimate knowledge of the life of the regiment. A number of the leaflets pointed out that officers were holding back money due the soldiers, that food was bad, that shirts were rotten, and that soldiers had not received the goods due them under the terms of the December 6 reform. These grievances were then cumulated into a petition of demands submitted (anonymously) to the regimental commander and printed up as a leaflet. Another leaflet complained about the work soldiers performed in the regimental garden, the vegetables from which went only to the officers' mess, and urged soldier gardeners to uproot the cabbage. When soldiers were marched to the rifle range in the rain, that, too, was worth a leaflet.

The Mariampol military organization (like all military organizations) also sought to raise the soldiers' political consciousness. One leaflet pointed out that the Ministry of War had reduced the term of service to three years only because it had been forced to, and drew the obvious conclusion that if soldiers exerted enough pressure they could get what they wanted. Other leaflets called on soldiers being discharged to spread their revolutionary ideas in their home villages, promised departing soldiers that the work they had begun in the 111th Don would be continued by younger soldiers, and appealed to the 112th Urals to follow the revolutionary example of the 111th Don. The transfer of the 2nd battalion of the 111th Don to Vitebsk elicited a series of leaflets: after appealing to the soldiers to try to resist, and reminding them that part of the 111th had refused to go to Kovna in late 1905, the military organization then begged the 2nd battalion as it was departing not to shame the rest of the regiment by suppressing workers and peasants. Later, the Mariampol military organization exploited the conflict between the regime and the Duma to remind the soldiers of the needs of the peasantry, and to drive home the lesson that the government was the enemy of the people.

There is no reason to doubt that these leaflets made a strong impression on the soldiers. The Mariampol Bundists could not have chronicled the life of the 111th Don so well had soldiers not been willing to provide information. (By the same token, the lack of information on the 112th Urals infantry indicates that the military organization did not carry the entire garrison with it.) Military organizations in the larger garrisons could not trace the life of individual regiments so closely in their leaflets, but they did address specific incidents in specific units. But of course interest in what the military organizations were saying did not mean that soldiers heeded the advice offered. The soldiers of the 2nd battalion of the 111th Don did, after all, proceed to Vitebsk.

A more potent means of agitation than leaflets were the military organization newspapers, which provided soldiers with a forum for expressing their own grievances. Some of the papers devoted a great deal
of space to articles explaining the history of the revolutionary movement
and outlining in detail the revolutionaries' position on current political
issues; these could not have been particularly popular (the newspapers
published by the SD military organizations in Moscow were among the
most boring). However, even the papers with the greatest theoretical
pretensions did give over considerable space to garrison life and to
soldiers' letters. Some papers amounted to little more than letters from
soldiers attacking what they believed to be the brutality and chicanery of
individual officers and NCOs. It is difficult to gauge precisely the impact
these papers had, but they appear to have been extremely popular
among the soldiers, providing them a greater sense than did mere
leaflets that a strong organization was speaking for them. Even officers
took the papers seriously. Two papers in particular stand out, the Social
Democrats' *Soldat* (Sevastopol) and the Socialist Revolutionaries' *Voennyi
listok* (Simferopol, then Sevastopol). The charges that soldiers made in
these papers stung officers into defending themselves—officers drew up
their men and entered into public debate with the anonymous soldiers
who were writing to the paper. The soldiers who in turn reported the
officers' responses understandably gloated over their commanders'
discomfiture, and the military organizations' prestige rose accordingly.[59]

With prestige went membership. By the middle of 1906, SD and SR
military organizations together had in excess of 25,000, probably around
35,000, soldier and sailor members.[60] These were members, not merely
"sympathizers": the military organizations reported that they had "influence" over or enjoyed the "sympathy" of even larger numbers of
soldiers. Total membership was of course small when measured against
the million men in the army, and small in most garrisons (though a
number of military organizations claimed 500 or more members). But
given the risks that membership entailed for soldiers, and given the fact
that soldiers lived in barracks isolated from civilians, the figures were
impressive. Indeed, proportionately as many soldiers as workers were
members of revolutionary organizations, and if worker revoutionaries in
some sense stood for the much greater number of politically unorganized workers, the same was true of soldier revolutionaries. The military organizations' assumption that they could mobilize soldiers for
revolution had proved correct.

Rank and file membership was sufficiently large to shape the military
organizations to the soldiers' ideas and interests. Civilian military organizers discovered that soldiers—even those in the military organizations—adamantly rejected party labels and factional polemics. Civilians

were willing to disavow explicitly party-line propaganda in the armed forces. As a draft statute drawn up by a conference of SD military organizations in Latvia stated, the military organizations' purpose was "to organize soldiers for a nationwide armed insurrection," so membership in the SD military organizations was open to "any revolutionary and politically conscious soldier"—i.e., to any soldier willing to join, whether he professed social democratic beliefs or not.[61] Similarly, the January conference of SR military organizations in the Caucasus opted for avowedly non-party military organizations so as not to fragment the "revolutionary barracks."[62] Quite exceptionally, the SR military organizations in the Caucasus required that civilians withdraw from their party positions and become civilian personnel of the non-party military union. No other military organization took factional neutrality so far as that. However, even the commitment not to advocate among soldiers a program that would accentuate differences in revolutionary ideologies elicited reprimands from party leaders, especially SR party leaders. At the June SR military organization conference the SR Central Committee insisted that the military organizations must include in their programs the specifically SR position on land redistribution. When the military organizations passed a resolution for a more general statement on the land question, the Central Committee unilaterally annulled the resolution. The SR leadership continued thereafter to insist on a larger dose of SR ideology than the military organizations were willing to accept. Social Democratic military organizations had fewer problems with their party leaders on this score, because they concealed the extent to which they ignored party doctrine in their work with soldiers.[63] Nevertheless, civilians insisted on counting the military organizations as constituent elements in their parties and attempted to maintain at least a nominally party identity for their soldier following.

The travails of the SR military organization in Moscow demonstrate the peril of bringing a party spirit into the barracks. Early in 1906 the Bolshevik military organization approached the SR military organization with a proposal for a joint SR-SD platform for propaganda among officers and enlisted men. The SR's were agreeable to non-party propaganda among officers, but rejected a common platform for enlisted men. Unfortunately for the regular SR's, early in 1906 SR-Maximalists in Moscow set up a military union with an adamantly non-party program; all the soldiers in the SR military organization deserted to the Maximalists, whereupon most of the SR military organizers followed suit and the regular SR military organization disappeared. The Moscow Bolsheviks maintained a soldiers' organization (capped, as was the Maximalists' military union, by a garrison soviet) of their own but had an observer in the military union. Needless to say, the Bolshevik military organization carefully avoided propaganda in a party spirit.[64] The soldiers' determination that *partiinost'* be left at the barracks gates was not something to be trifled with, even if they enrolled in a military organization that bore an SD or SR label.

Not only did soldiers in the military organizations shape the revolutionary program they supported, they also occasionally seized control of the military organizations from civilians. The structure of the military organizations ensured that soldiers would have a major voice in decisions. Almost all military organizations consisted of a hierarchy of unit committees, capped by a garrison soviet; the only important exceptions were organizations in very large garrisons where a full-fledged soviet of unit representatives was virtually ruled out by security considerations.[65] This organizational structure was dictated by the structure of the army itself and by the physical barriers between civilians and soldiers, but the fact that the majority of garrison bodies labelled themselves soviets—and not, say, committees—indicates the impact the workers' soviets of 1905 had on the Russian political imagination; at the time, soviets were by definition non-party institutions. Given the fact that both SDs and SRs had military organizations in most of the larger garrisons, it seemed to the soldiers to make sense to merge the parallel committees and soviets. SD and SR military organizers were in fact anxious to coordinate their activities in the garrisons; in most cities they had some sort of regular contact, often institutionalized (as in Moscow). By and large, however, civilians opposed the complete merger of their military organizations, but could not always resist rank-and-file pressure.

In Kronstadt, for example, by April both SDs and SRs had smoothly functioning military organizations with large followings that longed for the day when they could rise against their officers and autocracy. Soldiers and sailors took this goal so seriously that they decided to unite for better planning, so they arranged a meeting of military and civilian representatives of the two organizations. All of the civilians with the exception of one SD opposed a merger, but at a meeting on April 23 sailor and soldier unit representatives decided to set up a provisional technical bureau, of three enlisted men from each organization, to draw up plans for insurrection and to devise methods for joint SD-SR work in the garrison. A few days later, a meeting of the rank and file decided— again in opposition to the civilians—to make this arrangement permanent, with a bureau of six elected military representatives and four civilians (two delegated from each party) answerable to a garrison council; to eliminate even the potential of civilian domination, the civilian members were to be changed frequently. SD civilians insisted on treating this as no more than a contact commission, but the soldiers and sailors henceforth considered themselves members of a single organization.[66]

Much the same thing occurred in Sevastopol, though with SR connivance (the Sevastopol SRs were late in gaining a foothold in the garrison and believed that a merger would increase their influence), and that was logical enough—the Sevastopol and Kronstadt garrisons had long traditions of revolutionary organization, and revolutionary soldiers and sailors there thus had the self-confidence required to assert themselves organizationally.[67] But if Kronstadt and Sevastopol were extreme cases, the potential for conflict was built into all military organizations: soldiers could desert to an organization more to their liking, as in Moscow, or they could assert their will through the garrison soviets. The civilians in the military organizations had to respond to their military constituency if they wished to retain influence in the garrisons—which was, after all, the military organizations' *raison d'etre.*

However, civilians were answerable to more than soldiers; they were responsible as well to their larger party organizations. Soldiers and sailors in Kronstadt engineered the merger of the SD and SR organizations partly because they wished to do more than just talk about insurrection. This sentiment gratified civilian military organizers, but it was precisely decisions such as those involved in setting dates and coordinating plans for insurrection that civilians were reluctant to permit soldiers to make. SDs in Kronstadt complained that the garrison council had in effect arrogated to itself the right to make decisions that properly belonged to the revolutionary parties (surely one of the few times a Social Democrat defended, even by implication, the prerogatives of the SR Central Committee). To which some sailors replied in disgust: "We want to lay down our lives for the people and our country, and we're forbidden to have an opinion on the matter."[68]

Tensions within the military organizations were a mark of their success: only because civilians had enlisted large numbers of soldiers and sailors in support of revolution was the issue of control so touchy. Tension arose, however, less from the allocation of authority between civilians and soldiers than from the uneasy juncture that the military organizations had effected between the two societies that coexisted in Russia. Soldiers and sailors were hostile to the ideological disputes that were so important to revolutionaries from polite society, and they resented the pretensions of civilian revolutionaries to guide them. The attitude of the Kronstadt militants resembled that of the revolutionary sailors on the *Potemkin*, who had also wished "to go all the way for the common weal," had ignored the analysis of the revolutionary process offered by their civilian mentors, and had planned and executed mutiny

on their own. Even those civilian revolutionaries who were most enthusiastic about the prospects for military revolution considered soldiers' insurrections to be only a part of a larger revolutionary equation.
To soldiers and sailors, revolution was far more immediate: like the
mutineers of late 1905, revolutionary soldiers believed that once they
had achieved unity of purpose, they should act.

The military organizations worked hard to summon forth this revolutionary spirit in the armed forces, but it was the construction that soldiers and sailors put on their efforts rather than the substance of their
message that drew most soldiers to them. By early summer of 1906, a
legend was circulating among the sailors in the Baltic Fleet that there
was an all-powerful secret committee bent on avenging the abuses
heaped upon the people. According to a sailor who was well aware that
it was naive, the legend of the revolutionary committee had replaced
faith in the Tsar, even in God.[69] Given the manner in which revolutionaries operated in Kronstadt and elsewhere, the legend was in some respects congruent with reality, but the mythical secret committee was
larger than life—it was an authority that legitimated rebellion. To soldiers and sailors, precisely what the military organizations said was
irrelevant, though of course the military organizations were saying what
soldiers wanted to hear. Such myths did not arise in a vacuum. It was
the conflict between Duma and regime that provided an opening for the
myth of the revolutionary committee, gave the military organizations
the opportunity to win adherents, and inspired soldiers to mutiny once
again.

VII. "These Words Pleased Us Very Much": Soldiers and Politics

Mutinies recurred in the army in the summer of 1906 on about the same scale as in late 1905. The available documentation, however, is too heavily dependent on military sources and provides an incomplete picture of the upheaval. In 1906 as in 1905, commanders shirked reporting mutinies because they were subject to court-martial and possible dismissal from service if their units mutinied.[1] They sought to minimize the extent of disorders and as in 1905 acquiesced in the demands of mutineers or to the best of their ability ignored mutiny in the hope that it would go away or could be depicted as a trivial misunderstanding. Reports from unit commanders forwarded to the Ministry of War yield information on only ninety or so mutinies between October 17 and the end of 1905; it is from reports filed by gendarmes (a principal source) and civilian officials, and from carefully sifted newspaper accounts, that we can establish that there were at least 211 mutinies in those two and one-half months. In 1906, reports of 104 mutinies reached the Ministry of War through military channels.[2] Police sources again provide information on additional mutinies, but in 1906 most mutinies occurred in the summer, when many units were in rural encampments far from the eyes of the watchful gendarmes, and serving under conditions that made it especially easy for commanders to cover up mutiny. Nor was newspaper coverage adequate in 1906: while some papers managed to report on events in local garrisons, there were provinces, particularly in the important Vilna, Warsaw, and Kiev military districts, where censorship kept almost all information on the army out of the press. Newspapers in Petersburg and Moscow carried reports from the provinces, but are poor compensation for the dearth of local sources on the garrisons in the west. There are authoritative if vague references to disturbances in the garrisons in these districts, but only in a few cases has there been enough information to be certain that the disturbances were genuine mutinies and to identify the units involved.[3]

Still, there is adequate documentation, mostly from official sources, of 202 mutinies (of which forty involved more than one unit) in 1906.* Judging from official reports that list, without date or detail, units in which there were "disturbances," and about which no other information is available, the number of mutinies in 1906 was probably on the order of 240 to 250.[4] The figure of 202 mutinies that will be used here is based on the same conservative enumeration of "mutinous events" as was applied to the mutinies of late 1905, and on a reasonably conservative evaluation of the sources. There were, for instance, frequent reports that small detachments had refused to fire at or otherwise disperse worker and peasant mobs. Such incidents are difficult to confirm (newspapers being a particularly suspect source in this case), but twenty-three mutinies of that type can be verified from official sources. Given the volume of newspaper accounts, there were probably twice that many.

Even the set of 202 mutinies yields remarkable rates of incidence. Most mutinies—153 of the 202 (thirty-seven of the forty involving more than one unit)—occurred during the Duma months, April through July. There were mutinies in at least sixty-six (but probably as many as eighty) of the 271 line and reserve infantry regiments (which were garrisoned in Europe), and in eleven of the forty-four Siberian infantry and East Siberian rifle regiments. When all types of infantry are counted (Guards, Grenadier, Finland rifles, and so forth), about 22 percent of all units mutinied. There were mutinies in almost 60 percent of the technical units, better than 25 percent of the cossack regiments, 15 percent of all artillery brigades, and 6 percent of line and Guards cavalry regiments.[5] Overall, the incidence of mutiny in 1906 was somewhat lower than in late 1905, but still quite high for a year in which revolution is supposed to have been over. And of course, these are not only conservative figures, just as for 1905 they do not measure the full extent of military disaffection. There were at least as many units in 1906 as in 1905 in which discipline disintegrated without formal mutiny occurring, and in contradistinction to 1905 these indisciplined units included the Guards. In 1906, it was more difficult to find a reliable core within the disaffected mass.

The association of the second round of the soldiers' revolution with the meeting of the Duma is clear. The twelve mutinies in January were

---

*Statistics on mutiny in this chapter are based on the data in Appendix II.

TABLE VII-1. Strikes, Peasant Disorders, and Mutinies, 1906

	Workers on Strike, as Reported by the Factory Inspectorate	Peasant Disorders, as Recorded by the Department of Police and Central Newspapers	Mutinies
January	190,188	179	12
February	27,418	27	6
March	51,697	33	5
April	221,280	47	4
May	157,143	160	24
June	101,166	739	84
July	168,728	682	41
August	39,637	224	8
September	88,329	198	7
October	31,824	117	8
November	13,109	106	1
December	17,887	88	2

SOURCES: For peasant and worker disorders, Dubrovskii, *Krest'ianskoe dvizhenie* p. 42; for mutinies, Appendix II.

the last gasp of the Year 1905, as were the strikes and manor-burnings of that month. Mutinies then trailed off to virtually nothing, though it is only because of the high standards for disorder set in 1905 that fifteen mutinies in three months appear insignificant. Full-scale military rebellion resumed in May and continued through July. The cycle of mutinies corresponded exactly to the cycle of peasant rebellion, as had been true in 1905 as well. What was very different from 1905 was that peasant and soldier rebellion did not rise and fall in the trail of strikes: in 1906, urban disorders did not prompt peasants and soldiers to rebel (nor could that be the explanation, since urban disorders were minimal). It was, rather, the Duma itself that was the focal point of peasant and soldier rebellion, both because of the extended debates on land redistribution, and because of the way the Duma altered soldiers' and peasants' perceptions of authority.

Soldiers and the Duma

No sooner had the Tsar delivered a noncommittal salutation to the assembled deputies to the Duma on April 27—with several thousand courtiers, generals, and officials in full regalia gawking at the bearded peasant deputies—than Duma and regime were deadlocked. The Duma adopted overwhelmingly an address to the Tsar setting forth the Kadet program: political amnesty, an end to political persecution, civil liberties, universal suffrage, expropriation of land for distribution to peasants, and a ministry responsible to the Duma. Prime Minister Goremykin delivered the cabinet's response in person: private property was inviolable, the other elements in the Duma's address concerned the fundamental laws of the empire and were thus outside the Duma's purview, and the government would oppose all measures that threatened society and state. The Duma thereupon called for the cabinet's resignation and replacement by ministers who enjoyed the Duma's confidence.

After some consideration, the regime decided not to dismiss the Duma but, as Foreign Minister Izvolskii observed, to boycott it.[6] Though the Duma could adopt legislation only if the government failed for thirty days to respond to a request for a bill, the government presented very few bills, and those trivial: the first submitted, on May 15, concerned the authorization of private schools and appropriations for a laundry and greenhouse at Dorpat University. Goremykin not only refused to have anything to do with the Duma, he did not permit even the Council of Ministers to have a program; he convened the council only three times in May and five in June, and he informed the ministers that whatever their opinions might be he would do nothing without the Tsar's express command. The Duma filled the void with interpellations (391 in all during its brief life) accusing the regime of lawless acts, and defiantly framed legislation that the regime was pledged to reject. The government's obvious disdain for the Duma infuriated even those moderates who had hoped to cooperate with the regime, and ministers who appeared before the Duma were met with cries of "Resign! Resign!"[7]

There may have been, as Roberta Manning has recently suggested and as many revolutionaries suspected at the time, hope for compromise on most issues—the Kadets who set the tone in the Duma in its first weeks blunted some of their demands, Goremykin indicated a willingness to consider some secondary reforms—but there could be no agreement on land reform, the principal topic on the Duma's agenda.[8] The government repeatedly stated its refusal to countenance expropriation, and recommended instead the conversion of communal into private holdings and measures to facilitate peasant land purchases; Prime Minister Goremykin had said before his appointment that if the Duma advocated expropriation it should be dismissed. Yet the sentiment of the Duma was clear: private land must be expropriated. The Kadets called for the expropriation of state and church land and of as much gentry land as required to satisfy peasant needs (basically, the land peasants already rented), with peasants paying for the land they used. Kadets understood that they could not count on popular support for the Duma unless they promised peasants land, but the modesty of their offering cost them the support of the large bloc of peasant deputies, 20 to 25 percent of the Duma, who formed the Trudovik Group (80 percent of whom actually were peasants by origin). Willing to follow the Kadets' lead on most issues, the Trudoviks denounced the Kadet land program as a poor imitation of the Emancipation, and 104 of them called for the expropriation of all private land above that which a household could farm on its own (the "labor [*trudovaia*] norm"), with perhaps minimal compensation to be paid by the government; peasants themselves would determine locally the size of allotments and the amount (if any) of compensation gentry were to receive. A minority of thirty-three Trudoviks offered the SR program: abolition of all private property in land and its distribution on an egalitarian basis. To Kadet objections that the complete elimination of gentry estates would destroy the source of culture and civilization in the villages, a peasant deputy responded: "This culture is needed only by gentlemen, who use it to get money from the labor of the poor."[9] Messages poured in from the villages reminding the deputies what peasants had sent them to obtain. Kadets could not carry the Duma on the land question, yet the Kadet program was itself unacceptable to the government.[10]

Though it would not yield, the regime nevertheless hesitated to take action against the Duma, and indecision provided an opening for revolution. The extended debate on land reform was published, summarized, and commented upon at length in the press, and followed eagerly by peasants. Peasants sent messages and delegations to express support for expropriation, chiefly in the Trudovik version, and Trudovik deputies dispatched letters to their constituents explaining the conflict with the regime; a few Trudoviks even toured the provinces. Peasants asked their deputies to intercede in disputes with gentry, and took action themselves—declaring strikes, forcing their own terms on landlords, using gentry land as their own—in the firm belief that they were doing what the Duma would wish them to do. Given the sentiment in the Duma, peasants scarcely needed to fabricate fictive authorization for land seizures; in the months the Duma met, peasant disorders—especially impressive because they were orderly—reached the same volume as in the frightening fall of 1905 (see Tables IV-1 and VII-1).[11]

Short of dissolving the Duma, the government did not know how to bring the disorders to an end, and fear of an even greater explosion should the Duma be dismissed was one major reason for the government's irresolution. The Ministry of Interior ordered police to prevent the public reading of letters from Duma deputies, to intercept peasant

telegrams to the Duma, and to stamp out agrarian rebellion at its inception, but to no avail. And it was not just peasants whom the Duma
aroused. The anger of the deputies spilled over into the cities, too, and
governors informed Minister of Interior Stolypin that the debates in the
Duma were regenerating the revolutionary excitement that the December fighting had almost extinguished, and that even provincial officials
were becoming rebellious. The regime, reported the governors, was
being discredited, everyone looked to the Duma for direction, while the
government's passivity in the face of the onslaught from the Duma
paralyzed local authorities.[12] Once again, irresolution had spread from
the capital to the provinces.

Like peasants, soldiers invested enormous hope in the Duma, and
had done so long before the Duma met. In late October 1905 the mutinous Sveaborg artillerists demanded that peasant deputies to the Duma
draw up new military regulations to replace those "compiled and signed
by Generals, Colonels, and Captains," in November the mutinous 1st
Transcaspian railway battalion pledged to support the demands of the
Duma, and during the November insurrection in Sevastopol the crew of
the battleship *Panteleimon* (née *Potemkin*) decided not to press their demands but to wait until the Duma met before requiring satisfaction.[13]
Once the Duma gathered, the impatient anticipation that swept the
villages mounted in the army, too. As Vorontsov-Dashkov, Imperial
Viceroy for the Caucasus, reported, "interest in the historic events
transpiring in the empire is so great and has so strong a grip" on the
nation that it was impossible to "isolate the troops from the influence of
the mood and dominant tendencies" of the civilian population.[14]

The Duma debates on land reform transfixed the soldiers, and they
followed the debates closely. The secret police reported from Voronezh
in June that soldiers

> are beginning to reason that they are all peasants and shouldn't go against
> their own, they are talking about the possibility of disobeying orders, about
> refusing to fire.
>   Moreover, the enlisted men are deeply interested in the debates in the
> Duma and throw themselves upon newspapers that come into their hands,
> especially newspapers of an extreme tendency.[15]

Vorontsov-Dashkov, too, noted the impact of newspaper reports on soldiers, and commanders everywhere reported that the debates in the
Duma were having an "extremely pernicious" effect on their men. A
corps commander observed that soldiers in Vladikavkaz were not only
fully informed about the programs of the parties in the Duma, they were

able to quote "entire tirades by Trudovik speakers, as well as statements by the ministers."[16]

Speeches from the rostrum of the Duma posed a special problem for the authorities, because no matter how subversive they could not be censored. In at least one unit the commander forbade soldiers to read any newspaper other than the government's *Pravitel'skii vestnik,* and in another furious officers burned newspapers containing speeches by Duma deputies.[17] These angry gestures eliminated neither the Duma nor the flow of information into the barracks and could only have demonstrated to the soldiers how fearful their officers were. Yet the high command's more reasoned response—to attempt to refute the arguments for expropriation—was equally futile. Officers were ordered to hold special discussions on the Duma, and officers and the new official newspapers for soldiers explained carefully that the government could not afford to divest itself of all state lands and that the sanctity of private property must be respected. Soldiers were no more impressed by such arguments than were the peasant deputies in the Duma.[18]

Far more persuasive than anything their officers had to say were the letters that soldiers received from home. Peasants wrote of the threat of hunger and crop failure, the depredations of cossacks and rural police, and the need to support the Duma. The men of the Preobrazhensk Guards regiment received letters commanding them (as an officer summarized the message) not to go against the people's "emissaries": "We have sent them to get land, so you defend them."[19] The number of reports of soldiers in garrisons all over the empire receiving these instructions is sufficient to warrant the conclusion that the phenomenon was well-nigh universal. Peasants, who had good reason to understand the army's role in maintaining the existing social order, appear to have rushed spontaneously to protect the Duma by subverting the army. All reports agree that these letters caused a tremendous stir among the soldiers. If they had for any reason forgotten their peasant origins, their parents reminded them of it, and of the duty of solidarity with kith and kin.

The intensity of the soldiers' support for the Duma not only overwhelmed officers, it had as well a marked impact on the revolutionary military organizations. The military organizations initially sought to dispel the illusions soldiers had about the Duma. Bolshevik and SR military organizations followed the party line in their hostility to the Duma, but Menshevik military organizations were equally hostile and attempted—as did the Menshevik Moscow military organization, with reasoning identical to that of the Bolshevik military organization in Moscow—to persuade soldiers that the Duma was meant only to help the government obtain a loan from European bankers and to assist the regime in repressing the people.[20] Denunciations persisted even after the Duma opened. As the SD military organization in Riga observed in mid-May, the Duma had met for three weeks, yet everything remained as before; nothing could be expected of it; soldiers must instead prepare for insurrection.[21]

The military organizations soon discovered that they could not argue away the soldiers' conviction that the Duma would give peasants land, but that they could exploit the conflict between Duma and regime. The Grodno SD (Bundist) military organization, which was uncompromising in its antagonism to the Duma and devoted an entire meeting (300 soldiers participated) in late June to arguing that the existence of the Duma did not alter the political situation one iota, and that only a constituent assembly could express the will of the people, grudgingly conceded that the government's attitude toward the Duma was of some use in educating the most backward elements of the population.[22] Most military organizations had by late May or early June rather more completely revised their pronouncements on the Duma. The SR military organization in Simferopol, for instance, continued to call for insurrection and a constituent assembly, but pointedly observed that "the Tsar wants to disperse the Duma, only he fears the people: he scorns the people's elect."[23] The Bolshevik military organization in Moscow, reversing its earlier position, declared: "If the Duma defends the people's cause, works to get land and liberty and an improvement in the soldiers' lot, we will not only not attack it, we will as one man defend it from the traitorous Tsar."[24] That was a major departure from the official Bolshevik position, which did not contemplate defense of the Duma under any circumstances. Though they still maintained that only insurrection would win land for the peasants, the military organizations had gone a long way toward accommodating the sentiment of soldiers and sailors. They had no choice if they were to retain influence in the garrisons, but in linking the fate of the revolution to the Duma, Bolshevik and SR military organizations had strayed from the path marked out by their party leaders.

By late May, soldiers were sending the Duma instructions (*nakazy*) and pledges of support. Representative of the spirit of the soldiers' missives was one from the Vladikavkaz garrison: "Do your work, for which you were sent by our fathers, obtain everything that our fathers bid you— may Providence aid you in this—and we, their sons, will endeavor here not to allow into our weak heads the shameful thoughts the government is developing."[25] All the *nakazy* demanded that peasants receive all the land, most went to Trudovik deputies (or the small SD group that separated from the Trudoviks in mid-June), most asserted the soldiers' ardent faith in the deputies. These, clearly, were the work of the soldiers themselves, though some military organizations encouraged soldiers to draw up *nakazy* and forwarded them to the Duma.[26] Soldiers also asked the Duma to intercede on their behalf. Eight soldiers of the 1st Transcaspian railway battalion in Kushka, who had been arrested after their unit sent a telegram of congratulations to the President of the Duma, asked the Georgian Menshevik deputy Zhordania to take up their case. Eight hundred soldiers in Tiflis asked Zhordania to see to it that twenty-seven soldiers of the 16th Mingrelian Grenadiers were not executed for their part in a mutiny in March. Soldiers of the 226th Bobruisk reserve regiment who had been arrested after a November mutiny asked for help from the Trudovik Teslia, and soldiers on trial for mutiny in Vilna asked the Trudovik Aladin to get permission for a civilian lawyer to represent them. Soldiers of the 3rd Siberian division who had lost their belongings at Port Arthur asked assistance from a non-party peasant deputy from Mogilev Province (which must have been home to some of the soldiers).[27] When their commanders threatened them with death, violated their rights, or merely failed to appreciate the soldiers' sense of fairness, soldiers appealed to the Duma and believed it would stand by them.

The fervor that the Duma elicited in the army as a whole approached ecstasy in the garrisons in and around Petersburg, because soldiers there had a chance to meet the deputies personally. The Trudoviks saw to that. When they realized that the regime would never agree to the expropriation of gentry estates, Trudoviks, like their peasant supporters in the villages, set out to win the soldiers' support. The series of newspapers that they began publishing in the middle of May devoted considerable attention to the injustices that soldiers suffered, for, as a Trudovik "Soldiers' Well-Wisher" pointed out in an article bluntly entitled "The Duma Should Show Concern for the Troops," while the government possessed the guns, guns did not shoot of themselves; if soldiers sided with the Duma, the "situation in the country" (such circumlocutions were needed to avert confiscation) would change fundamentally. Furthermore, wrote the well-wisher, many soldiers (i.e., many Trudoviks) wished to change the induction oath so that soldiers swore allegiance to the Duma as well as to the Tsar.[28] Trudoviks also contacted soldiers directly, using the services of the SR military organizations. The Trudovik deputies Aladin, Anikin, and Onipko spoke at conspiratorial meetings in the military camps outside the capital. In Kronstadt, they met with small groups of sailors and soldiers whom they asked to compile a list of abuses they suffered, and used the material as the basis for an interpellation to the Minister of War.[29] Soldiers sent messages of thanks, and one delegation of sixteen soldiers, at considerable risk to themselves, went personally to the Duma to thank the Trudoviks for watching out for the soldiers' interests.[30]

After listening to a Trudovik deputy, an unidentified regiment dispatched a *nakaz* to the Trudoviks that epitomizes the soldiers' hopes and expectations in mid-1906:

> We soldier peasants salute the Trudovik group for its determined action. We will support it in the moment of need if necessary, if it demands all land in communal tenure without redemption, and all liberty. In our view, the land is God's, the land should be free, no one should have the right to buy, sell or mortgage it; the right to buy is fine for the rich, but for the poor it is a very, very bad right. . . . We soldiers are poor, we have no money to buy land when we return home from service, and every peasant needs land desperately. . . . The land is God's, the land is no one's, the land is free— and on this, God's free land, should toil God's free workers, not hired laborers for the gentry and kulaks. These words pleased us very much, we soldiers even learned them by heart. Deputies, if you will demand this then we, for our part, will lay down our lives to support these demands. Further, we most humbly ask your excellencies, respected deputies, immediately to demand of the authorities that they no longer persecute us for reading newspapers—are we really not men, are we little children that they won't let us know anything. . . . But this is all in vain—we read and will read. Your excellencies, peasant deputies, don't forget about us, and demand that they give us freedom to read what we want.[31]

Pledges of support were easier to make than to act upon, but there can be no doubt that the soldiers' desire was to assist the Duma in any way possible, and the pledges themselves were significant enough. The expectations that soldiers had of the Duma were not unique—aside from the massive outpouring of peasant sympathy, everyone's gaze was fixed on the Duma, and many besides peasants turned to it for assistance— but they powerfully subverted military discipline. In dispatching their *nakazy* and appeals for help, soldiers not only defied their officers, they acted on the assumption that the Duma really did have the authority to right wrongs and supersede their officers. From their assumption that they had an authority to which to appeal against their officers, it was but a short step to mutiny.

Mutinies Deliberate and Political

The mutinies of 1906 were comparable in number but quite different in origin and character from those of 1905. They were, for one thing, far less conditioned by the disintegration of discipline, far more the result of deliberate choice. In 1905, discipline collapsed catastrophically throughout the army prior to the onset of mutiny, and between October 17 and the middle of November mutiny in individual units most frequently began spontaneously when soldiers resisted their officers' efforts to enforce their customary prerogatives. Soldiers themselves initiated over half of the mutinies after mid-November, but the choice to mutiny was often nearly spontaneous, as when news of mutiny in one unit immediately prompted mutiny in another. By contrast, soldiers deliberated upon mutiny throughout the second round of their revolution. Of the 114 mutinies from April through July 1906 whose origins can be determined, soldiers began sixty-five after due consideration: in all three mutinies of known origin in April, eleven of twenty in May, thirty-eight of sixty-one in June, fourteen of thirty in July. So far as the available evidence reveals, not one of these mutinies was prompted by news of mutiny elsewhere, though of course by late May soldiers were aware of other mutinies. In some units severe indiscipline did precede a decision to mutiny, but in many others that was not the case at all; shattered discipline was not in 1906 a prerequisite for mutiny. Indiscipline itself was as widespread and presented the same challenge to the integrity of the army in mid-1906 as in late 1905, but was more a parallel to than a precursor of mutiny. Indeed, many units appear to have deliberately chosen not to turn indiscipline into mutiny.

The very first mutiny that is an identifiable part of the wave of mutinies that crested in June and July, by the 145th Novocherkassk infantry regiment in Petersburg, was a model of deliberation. On April 11, the 5th and 6th companies, before setting off to guard two factories, informed their officers that while they would take up their posts they would if need be join with rather than act against workers (a "threat of force" that qualified the declaration as mutiny had officers wished, or been able, to treat it as such). The next day the command replaced the 5th and 6th with the 7th and 8th companies, but these adopted an identical resolution. By the middle of May, the men of the 145th still stubbornly adhering to their principles, part of the regiment had been sent to outlying suburbs and to Finland, while the remainder had been confined to barracks with a squadron of Guards Dragoons to watch over them.* Just as deliberate was the mutiny of the 10th Novo-Ingermanland infantry in its camp outside Tule on June 5–8. After a regimental meeting, the soldiers presented their commander a list of demands for changes in the regimental economy, and the commander promised satis-

---

*Unless otherwise noted, sources for this and other mutinies will be found in Appendix II, which lists the mutinies of 1906 by order of commencement.

faction. Mutinies virtually identical to that occurred in the 138th Bolkhov infantry outside Riazan, June 6–8, and the 137th Nezhin infantry in Moscow, June 22. The Turkestan and Transcaspian sapper battalions encamped outside Tashkent decided to march to the train station in the city to liberate soldiers being shipped to Siberia for their part in a November mutiny, and did so on July 3; they were ambushed as they approached the station and fled back to camp after an exchange of gunfire.

Perhaps most deliberate of all were mutinies that began when soldiers refused to fire at or take other action against workers and peasants. In seventeen cases (April–July) there is no direct evidence that the soldiers had agreed beforehand that they would not shoot, evidence only that— as was the case with the 12th company of the 82nd Dagestan regiment in Grozny on June 15—soldiers brought to the scene of a disturbance refused to shoot; the secret police reported that before being withdrawn the Dagestanis four times disobeyed the order to ready their rifles. These, surely, were mutinies planned in advance. Prior decisions not to shoot were widely reported, though soldiers did not always have to act on them (as the 145th Novocherkassk did not). The men of the 87th Neishlot infantry, sent from Novgorod to Petersburg, made no secret of the fact that they would refuse to shoot at workers, though they apparently did not announce this formally to their commander and so did not, formally, mutiny (though additional evidence might disclose that their action constituted mutiny); they were nevertheless confined to barracks.[32] The secret police reported that the men of the 9th company of the 133rd Simferopol infantry, in camp outside Ekaterinoslav, had decided among themselves that they would not shoot if sent against civilians; the company apparently never had to act on its resolution, and the 113th, though completely indisciplined, did not mutiny.[33] On the other hand, on June 21 the 1st squadron of the 41st Don cossacks refused to leave Taganrog because it did not wish to suppress peasants (this was a decision acted upon before the squadron actually confronted peasants), and the cossacks on the same day informed a workers' meeting that they would not harm workers, either. Not all units were able to reach such agreements. Before leaving their barracks to break up a demonstration by unemployed workers in Simferopol, a company of the 51st Litovsk infantry met to talk over what they would do. Though they agreed that justice was on the side of the unemployed, the soldiers did not trust each other to act in consort, so they carried out orders and dispersed the demonstration.[34] Indeed, had soldiers not been able to agree in advance, the likelihood that a unit would refuse to disperse workers or peasants was quite small, because each soldier would fear that he would stand alone. There must have been units in which some soldiers fired and others did not, but there is no clear trace of them in the record. The degree of planning exhibited by units that decided in advance the circumstances under which they would mutiny, and then unanimously followed through on the decision, has no parallel in the mutinies of 1905.

Other mutinies, too, must have been deliberated beforehand—some of the twelve mutinies (April–July) that began when soldiers refused to execute routine orders, for instance—but many mutinies were spontaneous responses to provocation. The incident that most often triggered mutiny was an attempt to arrest soldiers (twenty-one mutinies began that way), followed by conflicts over food and supplies (eight cases; food riots have not been classified as mutiny unless they developed into more serious disturbances), the imposition of new restrictions on the soldiers' movements (four), and physical assaults by officers on soldiers (three). As in 1905, such incidents precipitated mutiny out of indiscipline because soldiers had concluded that they could challenge what in the past had been their officers' normal prerogatives. Almost every mutiny, of course, indicated that soldiers no longer conceded their officers much authority. What is significant is that in 1906 sudden and acute conflicts between officers and men were only a secondary cause of mutiny. Soldiers were quite capable of organizing mutiny themselves, even of preparing contingency plans for mutiny.

During the summer, units not keeping watch over factories and villages removed to rural training camps. Indiscipline immediately assumed ominous proportions as soldiers took advantage of the greater freedom of movement the camps provided to slip away from their officers. In early June, for instance, the men of the 133rd Simferopol and 134th Feodosii infantry encamped outside Ekaterinoslav met "secretly" in groups of up to eighty at a time and discussed presenting formal demands. These meetings could not have gone unnoted by officers, and there were in fact daily altercations between officers and men in these regiments, and in the 278th Berdiansk infantry battalion in the same camp.[35] Discipline was so poor and meetings so frequent in the 52nd Vilna infantry on the outskirts of Warsaw that the military district commander called in the 184th Warsaw infantry from Lodz to keep the 52nd Vilna in line. However, in late June the soldiers of the 184th Warsaw declared that they would not serve in Warsaw because they had no intention of suppressing the 52nd Vilna, and that they would not leave camp at all except to return to Lodz. (The 184th thus mutinied, while the 52nd Vilna—judging by the military district commander's laconic telegram on its behavior—did not.[36]) In the sapper encampment (1st, 18th, and Guards sapper battalions) near Petersburg, soldiers held meetings, sang revolutionary songs, protested bad food (and destroyed crates of wormy cabbage), and met with workers from a nearby factory. The command placed infantry and cavalry between the sappers and workers, and then in late June transferred the sappers to camps in Novgorod and Vladimir provinces.[37] Officers tried desperately to keep their men occupied, provided special entertainments (concerts, slide shows, games) during off-duty hours, and mounted round-the-clock patrols to keep soldiers in camp and civilians out. These measures rarely obstructed gatherings in camp, and soldiers often used the distraction provided by evening entertainments to slip out of camp for meetings.[38] In the odd case, restrictions on the soldiers' movements triggered genuine mutiny, as when the 213th Orovaisk and 216th Insar infantry mutinied outside Penza on June 13 after the camp commandant announced that no one would be allowed more than fifty paces beyond the camp perimeter.

Even as they tried to eliminate the opportunity for indiscipline, officers ignored the infractions they witnessed. That was true in the infantry camps outside Ekaterinoslav and Warsaw, in the sapper camp near Petersburg, and in cities as well. In Sevastopol, for instance, soldiers and sailors in June gathered in massive meetings on shore, and officers appear to have made no effort to disperse them.[39] Officers ignored indiscipline because they feared their men. As one officer is reported to have said, "Discipline has collapsed completely. Even our own soldiers don't salute us. And we're afraid to impose even mild disciplinary penalties, we try any way we can not to notice. Our lives are dearer."[40] Indeed, officers bent over backwards to mollify their men. For example, on July 18 one company of the 228th Khvalynsk infantry (Saratov) complained to their captain about the bad meat they had been served. When the captain swore at them, the soldiers threw the meat on the floor. Hastening to the scene, the regimental commander reprimanded the captain and ordered that the soldiers be given money for food.[41]

Officers who had spent late 1905 in Europe had learned from bitter experience the danger of attempting to repair discipline that had collapsed; officers who had spent the winter in Manchuria had not. Of the 187 line infantry units that had been in Europe in 1905, only thirty-five (19 percent) are known to have mutinied in 1906. The incidence of mutiny in line infantry that had fought in Manchuria was almost twice as high: thirty-one of eighty-four (37 percent, slightly higher than the incidence of mutiny in the infantry in Europe in late 1905).[42] The field army had wintered in Manchuria without incident, officers had not there experienced the uncontrollable indiscipline that swept the units in Europe, and they were unprepared to deal with—that is, to ignore or placate—their men when indiscipline struck. There is no reason at all to suppose that the collapse of the soldiers' revolution in late 1905 had chastened soldiers who had spent the year in Europe. The 133rd Simferopol, 134th Feodosii, 228th Khvalynsk, and 278th Berdiansk had all spent 1905 in Europe, did not mutiny in 1906, but did not fear to defy their officers. It was, rather, officers who had been chastened. Their disinclination to enforce regulations was one reason why officers provoked so few mutinies in 1906, and so a reason as well for the lower incidence of mutiny in 1906. But soldiers who did not mutiny merely because their officers let them do as they pleased were no more likely to prove a reliable force for suppressing civilians than soldiers who did mutiny.

Conditions in the camps often made the borderline between indiscipline and mutiny hazy, and when the unspoken compact by which officers tolerated indiscipline and soldiers refrained from outright mutiny broke down mutiny was likely to go on for some time. The 1st and 3rd artillery brigades from Rostov (Iaroslavskii), thoroughly indisciplined even before they left their winter quarters in late April, began holding small meetings in camp and large meetings in nearby villages as soon as they arrived. Commanders abstained from countermeasures (such as searching the soldiers' belongings for revolutionary literature) for fear of provoking mutiny. On the night of June 18, however, the artillerists themselves achieved a state of mutiny when they defiantly held a mass meeting in the middle of camp, opposite camp headquarters, to formulate their grievances. They held another meeting there on June 20, and repeatedly ignored orders to disperse. A few companies of infantry were quickly brought in, but they immediately displayed their sympathy for the artillerists. Officers continued thereafter to make only a pretence of enforcing discipline (so the secret police reported), and the governor of Iaroslavl Province complained that the brigade commanders were doing nothing to restore order. In a camp outside Odessa, the 12th sapper battalion approached mutiny on June 12, the day it arrived from the Far East. The sappers held a battalion meeting that day, and at a joint meeting with the 11th sapper battalion on the next resolved not to slaughter their officers but to push for the gradual implementation of their economic demands, to refuse to suppress workers, and to send a message of support to the Trudoviks. These meetings continued for at least another two weeks, the sappers did formally present demands for changes in the regimental economy, and at one meeting with over a thousand participants forced officers to sign up to speak just like everyone else. The three railway battalions encamped outside Baranovichi were in a state of mutiny from May 25, when the brigade commander attempted to use one company to force another to eat supper and the designated punitive detachment ran away, to the end of July. Soldiers won the right to sit on a food commission, marched under arms to Baranovichi to prevent a rumored pogrom, won the release of two arrested soldiers (a battalion commander decided that the soldiers had been arrested by mistake), went to nearby villages to urge peasants not to pay taxes and to seize gentry land, and of course regularly held meetings in and out of camp. At the artillery, sapper, and railway camps, officers could not prevent soldiers from crossing the line that separated endemic indiscipline from mutiny, and mutiny continued until soldiers themselves decided to grant their officers a minimal degree of authority.

While these mutinies were the work of soldiers, a civilian presence can be detected in all of them. The secret police reported that soldiers from the railway battalions met with "Jewish youths" near Baranovichi, that soldiers met with civilians outside the Rostov artillery camp, and that civilians—a woman among them—addressed the large meetings in the sapper camp outside Odessa.[43] Civilians hovered in the background of a great many mutinies in 1906, and certainly played a much larger role than they had in late 1905. The summer encampments facilitated not just indiscipline, but the work of the revolutionary military organizations as well. It was almost as easy for civilians to don stolen uniforms, slip into camp, and move about undetected as it was for soldiers to slip out for meetings, because officers could not know the men from all the different units in camp. Other than camps far from major settlements and distant from railway lines (as for instance the sapper camp in Kaluga Province), it is difficult to find any that revolutionaries did not penetrate. Given access to large numbers of soldiers already inclined to ignore their officers and deeply interested in the proceedings of the Duma and the Duma's conflict with the regime, the military organizations swelled to their greatest size. Revolutionaries—after some hesitation—helped soldiers articulate their political interests, and many of the military organizations encouraged soldiers to present demands to their officers. They did not, however, encourage action more aggressive than that, because they wished to avoid insurrection until workers and peasants were ready.[44] Soldiers were of course quite capable of mutinying on their own, but the military organizations did contribute to the ferment in the camps.

The mutiny of the Kursk encampment—123rd Kozlov, 203rd Graivoron, and 204th Oboian infantry, and the 68th artillery brigade—exhibited all of the characteristics of the soldiers' revolution in 1906: soldiers planned and executed the mutiny, mutiny was prolonged, and revolutionaries were involved.[45] As of early May indiscipline in the 68th artillery was so bad that the brigade commander was planning to transfer 300 artillerists to another camp, and in the city of Kursk itself the behavior of the contingent of Don cossacks was so worrisome that their barracks were searched on the night of May 19. The most disaffected unit was the 123rd Kozlov, which had arrived from Manchuria in January. What upset the Kozlovtsy most was the fact that they had not been given the equipment due them under the terms of the December 6 order, and the retention of the conscripts of the class of 1903. By early May they were muttering angrily that something would happen soon, and on May 20 a group of forty soldiers agreed that they would no longer use their weapons against civilians. On the evening of May 21, between 600 and 800 soldiers of the Kozlov regiment decided that as of the morning of the 22nd they would not perform guard duty until they obtained satisfaction.

On the morning of the 22nd, the entire Kozlov regiment gathered near the camp lock-up to work out and present demands for the discharge of the 1903 draft, money to purchase gear due them, and an end to guard duty in the city. An SR spoke to the meeting and distributed large quantities of SR literature, and the soldiers roughed up an officer who attempted to arrest the civilian. While it seems likely that the SR military organization had a hand in organizing the mutiny, on May 22 the principal SR contribution was, with the aid of soldiers in their organization, to dissuade the regiment from storming the lock-up and freeing all the soldiers within. Officers could find no troops to employ against the mutineers. According to different accounts, either the cossacks (angry because their barracks had been searched), the 203rd Graivoron, or the artillerists, or all of them, refused to move against the Kozlov regiment. The authorities sent for some Kuban cossacks from another city.

The 123rd Kozlov achieved a quick victory and then retreated. On the 23rd there were more meetings and soldiers again prevented the arrest of civilians, and the commander of the regiment began to capitulate: new blankets and shirts were distributed. The division commander arrived from Kharkov on the 23rd, and on the 24th he began interviewing soldiers from the regiment. He rejected their principal demand, for money to equip themselves according to the terms of the December 6 reform (he claimed that the money simply was not available), but he did add to the concessions already granted. With that, mutiny receded. There are conflicting reports as to whether or not soldiers resumed guard duty on the 24th, but on the 24th and over the next few days officers did manage to arrest some Kozlov soldiers, perhaps because cossack reinforcements had arrived, perhaps because the soldiers were overawed by the gold braid, perhaps simply because the division commander had charisma.

Yet if indiscipline had sunk below the critical level it did not go away, and began to spread to other units. Officers of the Graivoron and Oboian regiments attempted to isolate their men from the Kozlov regiment, but pickets posted around the Kozlov camp permitted soldiers to come and go unhindered. Officers patrolled the road into town, but civilians—SDs as well as SRs—continued to visit the camp at the soldiers' invitation. When officers tried to break up meetings, soldiers threatened unpleasantness, and by early June officers were permitting meetings in camp on condition that politics not be discussed. Politics—expressions of support for the Duma above all—were by now a principal topic of the meetings, and the soldiers also stated categorically that they would not take any action against peasants. The men of the Graivoron regiment demanded, apparently in this interval, the removal of their commander, the artillerists met in large numbers, and the Kuban cossacks in the city sent the Ministry of War a telegram asking to be demobilized because their farms were going to ruin.

The second peak of this long-running mutiny came on June 18, when a mob of civilians and soldiers held a political meeting outside Kursk. Civilians called on soldiers to stand by the people, soldiers rose to say that they now understood who their friends were and that they would not shoot civilians. Cossacks sent to break up the meeting instead declared their complete sympathy, announced they would not disperse the crowd or allow the police to do so, and cursed the police for sending them on a pointless mission. On June 26, a meeting in camp adopted a resolution, to be sent to the SD group in the Duma, calling for changes in military service (487 voted in favor, 16 against, and 2 abstained.) By this point, every unit in camp and city except the 204th Oboian infantry had mutinied (and the men of the 204th freely attended meetings), and political concerns overshadowed the economic issues that had provided the original grounds for mutiny.

Utterly unable to control the Kursk camp, the military district command decided as a last resort to shift regiments around, transferring the Kozlov regiment to Kharkov (where the garrison was already unstable) and bringing in two new regiments. In late June and early July, too, officers distributed large numbers of reactionary proclamations. After the Kozlov regiment left, indiscipline sank below the critical level, reverting from mutiny to mere widespread discontent and grumbling. There was no assurance, however, that soldiers would not again regroup for mutiny.

Mutinous soldiers in 1906 rarely engaged in violence and frequently presented lists of demands, and as was the case in late 1905 those two facets of the soldiers' behavior were closely connected. From April through the dissolution of the Duma on July 9, mutineers exchanged fire with other troops only two times, shot off artillery once, and fired their rifles in the air twice. Four times they did violence to officers or officer quarters, once they beat up police, and four times they burned or wrecked their own barracks or equipment. Officers feared violence, mutineers frequently threatened violence, and it is possible, given the sketchiness of the evidence on many mutinies, that the lesser forms of violence occurred more frequently than presently appears to have been the case. But only after the dissolution of the Duma—within two weeks of which there were five military insurrections—did violence become a characteristic of mutiny.

When soldiers believed mutiny did not entail violence, they confidently presented their demands: in at least fifty-three of 151 mutinies (35 percent) between April and July 8, in only five of thirty-two mutinies (16 percent) between July 9 and the end of the month. The contents of one set of demands are unknown, but forty-six others touched only on the life of the unit and ordinarily included implementation of the December 6 reforms, the discharge of soldiers who had served three years, freedom to meet, election of food commissions by soldiers, and removal of abusive NCOs and officers. (Details are so often lacking that it is impossible to order the demands by frequency.) In short, the demands were of the same sort soldiers had made in 1905, and if implemented would have altered the regimental economy and the structure of military authority. During eleven mutinies soldiers presented political demands as well. That is a somewhat higher proportion than in 1905, and there is no evidence that soldiers in 1906 adopted political demands to humor civilians. Nevertheless, when soldiers presented demands they preferred to stick to grievances their commanders could satisfy.

Yet if the demands were comparable to those of 1905, soldiers made them much less frequently. No doubt soldiers presented more than fifty-eight sets of demands between April and July, but it is most unlikely that any amount of additional evidence would bring the ratio of demands to mutinies close to the two out of three achieved in late 1905. Evidently, many soldiers chose not to make demands as they mutinied. For instance, the mutinies in which soldiers at the instant of contact with workers and peasants refused to act were never (so far as the evidence reveals) accompanied by demands. Soldiers who mutinied when already drawn up on the street certainly had the capacity to make demands, but they did not have the interest.

It was, it appears, the soldiers' enormously increased interest in political questions that depressed the incidence of demands. Certainly soldiers exhibited far more interest in political issues than they had in 1905. Only eleven sets of demands touched on politics, but in other cases soldiers accompanied their demands with separate political statements. The Odessa sappers, for instance, handed in a set of military demands and also dispatched a message to the Trudoviks in the Duma, while the 9th Tobolsk Siberian infantry (which mutinied in camp outside Tiumen, June 21–26), after formulating military demands, declared: "We present these demands, hoping that the State Duma will support them."[46] The Duma itself figured in five sets of demands, one of which was accompanied by a *nakaz* to the Duma, and *nakazy* were sent to the Duma during at least seven other mutinies (most *nakazy* were not sent in the context of mutiny). In all, the Duma figured in at least twenty-nine mutinies, either in demands, *nakazy*, expressions of support during meetings, or as the immediate cause of mutiny or insurrection. At least fourteen other mutinies featured political statements or political demonstrations (some of which probably involved the Duma, though that is not clear from the available evidence). Thus, soldiers articulated their political sentiments during at least forty-three of 153 mutinies between April and July.

Other mutinies had unmistakable political motives that the soldiers did not—again, judging from the evidence at hand—articulate. The formal declaration by the men of the 145th Novocherkassk infantry that they would join with rather than act against workers was a statement of political preference, and the sixteen mutinies in which soldiers did nothing more than disobey orders to disperse workers or peasants were equally political. Likewise, the four mutinies in which soldiers took part in workers' strikes or refused to replace striking workers were political gestures. In all, from April through July there were at least twenty-six mutinies that had clear political overtones without known articulation of political motive, for a total of seventy of 153 mutinies (46 percent) that were at least in part politically motivated. The proportion of mutinies with a known political element held relatively constant: one of four in April, ten of twenty-four in May, thirty-nine of eighty-four in June, nineteen of forty-one in July.

The high proportion of politically engaged mutinies accords completely with the soldiers' intense interest in the Duma, and with the growth of the revolutionary military organizations. But soldiers who mutinied with politics in mind knew that their officers could not give them satisfaction. Soldiers who refused to replace striking workers, or to disperse worker demonstrations, did not feel impelled to present demands. Indeed, they did not feel it necessary to prolong their mutinies: there is no known case in which a unit that had refused to fire did not then resume its customary duties. In the summer of 1906, a great many soldiers were prepared to wait for the Duma to act, and refused to perform only those duties that violated their sense of political propriety.

The mutinies of 1906 were more deliberate, more organized, and far more political than they had been in 1905. They also tended to last longer, as soldiers sometimes fluctuated between mutiny and severe indiscipline for a month or more. Above all other differences, however, one looms largest: there was no general strike, no Imperial Manifesto, no shattering collapse of the civil order from which soldiers could conclude that the old military order, too, had lapsed and that they had the opportunity—even Imperial authorization—to refashion the army to their liking. The principal source of instability in mid-1906 was the Duma, to which soldiers looked to transform Russian society and to cover their aspirations for the army with its own authority. But soldiers also knew that the Duma's authority was not secure, and so they pledged their support for its struggle against the regime. Soldiers eager to bring nearer the day of social revolution initiated mutiny, and they expressed their political will either during their mutinies or in the very form the mutinies took. Soldiers in 1906 mutinied in anticipation of social transformation, not on the assumption that the transformation had already been accomplished. The regime's determination to survive, no matter how well advertised, could not in 1906 deter soldiers from mutiny. If the mutinies were to end, soldiers would have to lose all hope that the authority of the Duma could triumph over the authority of the regime.

Impact

The soldiers' revolution did not pose so immediate a threat to the survival of the regime in mid-1906 as it had in late 1905, because as it reached its peak workers and revolutionaries were not threatening to seize power in the cities. Furthermore, because many of the mutinies occurred in the summer encampments, they did not so dramatically undercut the credibility of the regime's military deterrent to insurrection. Nevertheless, the mutinies severely impaired the regime's ability to contain peasant rebellion. And though their reverberations in the cities were muted, they did begin to clear the way for successful revolutionary action—especially because the soldiers' revolution itself was highly politicized.

The mutinies increased geometrically in the first six weeks after the Duma convened, just as they had in the first six weeks after the publication of the October Manifesto: seven mutinies in the first half of May, seventeen in the second half of the month, forty-two in the first half of June. Each new mutiny must have encouraged others, and the soldiers' political sensitivity must also have increased as the sessions of the Duma continued. The incidence of mutiny held steady at forty-two in the second half of June, though at least nine mutinies that had begun earlier were still under way, including one that had begun in the first half, and two that had begun in the second half, of May.

Moreover, the mutinies were cumulative. Units that had once mutinied were of doubtful reliability even after mutiny ended, because mutineers were only rarely punished. Of the seventy-three mutinies from April through June whose outcomes are known, ten ended when the units involved were transferred (which could scarcely have been interpreted as punishment; in one other case mutiny continued even after transfer). Seventeen ended with outright concessions to the mutineers. For instance, when on May 27 the commander of a company of the 2nd Transcaspian railway battalion in Novy Margelan ignored his men's demand that their Sergeant Major be removed, the company declared a strike; the garrison commander court-martialled the Sergeant Major and locked the captain up for three days. Five other mutinies ended with promises of concessions followed some time later by arrests. Twenty mutinies subsided on their own, with commanders ignoring the illegal actions of their men (in two of these cases, soldiers were arrested some time after the mutiny ended). In all, mutinies ended on the soldiers' terms or without immediate incident to them in fifty of seventy-three mutinies through June. The rest were brought to an end by arrests (in nine cases reliable units were drawn up against the mutineers). Through the first half of June, in fact, soldiers did even better, mutinying with impunity in thirty-nine of fifty cases whose outcome is known. Officers suffered mutineers to go unpunished because they feared to provoke their men, and because with mutiny and indiscipline so widespread it was often impossible to find reliable troops with which to suppress mutiny. Given the impunity with which they mutinied, soldiers had no reason to conclude that mutiny held great peril for them.

Nevertheless, the level of mutinies did stabilize in late June. It is possible, though not likely, that the greater resolve that officers then exhibited had an impact. In the last two weeks of June, arrests terminated twelve of the twenty-three mutinies whose endings are known (and in July, when the situation in the country was rather different, arrests or repression terminated fifteen of the twenty-eight mutinies with a known outcome). Yet there was in late June no well-publicized repression of a major mutiny, and it is unlikely that word about arrests spread fast enough to dissuade other soldiers from mutinying. Quite likely, the arrests had little impact on the course of the soldiers' revolution in June and soldiers were for their own reasons—to be taken up in the next chapter—choosing not to mutiny.

In any case, the mutinies were sufficiently high in the second half of

June—at least forty-two in two weeks—to constitute a continuation if not an escalation of the soldiers' revolution, and they ate away at the regime's ability to deal with agrarian rebellion. In early June the governor of Kaluga Province requested reinforcements because he anticipated civil disorders; by the time he was told he would get no more troops, all five of the infantry battalions and both cossack squadrons in the province had mutinied.[47] On June 13, the governor of Tambov Province asked for more cavalry, because an infantry company had refused to disperse a peasant mob and in general "the mood of the infantry in the province is unreliable."[48] On June 18, the governor learned that no additional cavalry was available; on the same day, one of the two cavalry regiments in the province mutinied. A few weeks later, one of the two infantry regiments mutinied.[49] In Penza Province, half of the six cossack squadrons were on leave, and there were mutinies in all three of the infantry regiments in June and July.[50] The situation was no better in Kursk Province, or for that matter anywhere else in central Russia.

Not only were line units fast deserting the regime, but those units that had proved most reliable in 1905—the Guards and cossacks (other than those mobilized at the end of the year)—threatened to do so as well. The Guards encampment at Krasnoe Selo resembled all the other encampments of 1906. The soldiers held meetings in and out of camp, listened eagerly to revolutionaries and Trudoviks, and dispatched *nakazy* to the Duma. When no speakers were at hand, the Guards read the revolutionary leaflets that circulated in camp and met in groups outside the camp perimeter. Rumors circulated in May that the entire Krasnoe Selo camp would rise, and Minister of War Rediger admitted that there was a certain amount of ferment in all the Guards regiments.[51]

Rather ominously for the regime, discontent in the Guards peaked at the Imperial residence at Peterhof, in the 1st battalion of the Preobrazhensk infantry, a battalion of which the Tsar himself was nominal commander.[52] Like the other Guards regiments, the Preobrazhensk had in 1905 faithfully dispersed revolutionary demonstrations, but in 1906 the mood in the regiment was no different than in the humble line infantry. As an NCO related during the investigation of the mutiny, soldiers in the Preobrazhensk regiment "constantly get letters from the villages on the land question; they are reproached for the fact that soldiers fire at the people during disturbances, which ends them and prevents the peasants from getting land."[53] The Preobrazhentsy shared the general enthusiasm for the Trudoviks and eagerly read the revolutionary leaflets that came their way. In May, searches of their belongings and the arrest of some soldiers for possession of subversive literature pushed the regiment close to mutiny.

The incident that finally impelled the 1st battalion to mutiny was trivial, but the mutiny was not. Angered because they had had to march—rather than take the train—from Krasnoe Selo to Peterhof for their tour of guard duty at the palace, the men of the 1st battalion met on June 9 to discuss their grievances. On the 10th, they presented their demands: they wanted the full issue of bedlinen, money to buy gear, the release of the soldiers who had been arrested, freedom to discuss their needs, and so forth. And they added: "We express our solidarity (agreement) with the demands of the Duma deputies on allotting land to the peasants." The commander of the 1st Guards division, shaken by the mutiny and worried about the consequences for his own career, accepted the demands, promised the soldiers they would not be punished, and instructed the regiment's officers to act as though nothing had happened. However, higher authorities (including Grand Duke Nikolai Nikolaevich, Commander of the Guards corps and the Petersburg military district) ruled otherwise. On the 12th, two soldiers suspected of instigating the mutiny were arrested, the mutiny collapsed, the 1st battalion was deprived of its Guards status, and it was shipped under guard to a camp in Novgorod Province that had formerly held Japanese POWs.

Minister of War Rediger later wrote that the Preobrazhensk mutiny brought the Guards to their senses, but that was not at all the case. Hearing of the Preobrazhensk mutiny, the Semenov Guards, scourge of revolution in December 1905, expressed their support (but did not mutiny), while the Guards sapper batallion did mutiny by adopting the Preobrazhensk demands as its own. In the second half of June there were minor mutinies in both the Horse Guards and the Guards Cuirassiers, and openly expressed discontent in other Guards regiments. The SR military organization in Petersburg reported in late June that the revolutionary mood at Krasnoe Selo was fading, but the gendarmes reported that 4,000 Guards met in camp on July 4th.[54] The Guards were almost as restive after the Preobrazhensk mutiny as they had been before.

As for the cossacks, while the press continued to chronicle their brutality there were in midsummer an equal number of reports on mutinies and other signs of cossack dissaffection. Many of the reports cannot be verified, but cossacks were involved in at least twenty mutinies from May through July, five more in August, and two later in the year. Unidentified Don, Kuban, and Orenburg cossacks were involved in three mutinies. Of the identifiable mutinous units, eleven were Don cossack regiments (two of eighteen first-line regiments, nine of nineteen second- and third-line regiments), and four were second-line Kuban regiments (out of eighteen first- and second-line regiments). Among Orenburg and Urals cossacks, unswervingly faithful to the regime in

1905, four of fifteen regiments are known to have mutinied.[55] At least seven of the mutinous regiments sent *nakazy* to the Duma (not always during mutiny) demanding the demobilization of the second and third lines, and so did at least nine cossack regiments that did not mutiny; the 7th Urals regiment sent two, one from the squadrons in Penza, the other from the squadrons in Kazan. There were likely many more *nakazy*, since one of the cossack deputies reported to the Duma that he received letters and telegrams from cossack regiments every day begging the Duma for demobilization.[56] The serving cossacks merely reflected the sentiment in their villages: more than fifty Don cossack villages dispatched delegations to appeal directly to the Duma for demobilization.[57]

Cossacks complained both about the hardship they suffered and the shame of their role as police. Money promised to cossack reserves to meet the expenses of equipping themselves for service and supporting their families was either not delivered at all or proved insufficient (for which reason the wives of cossacks submitted hardship petitions and even demonstratively set out to accompany their men), and when the cossack deputies in the Duma demanded an interpellation to the Minister of War questioning the legality of the mobilization of the second and third lines they painted a bleak picture of the collapse of the cossack farms and the desperate longing of wives and parents for the return of their men. As one *nakaz* from a cossack unit put it:

> Esteemed electors from the whole of Christ's world, we beg of you as of our fathers. We cossacks have abandoned our fathers and mothers in their declining years, and our wives with young children, and our households have crumbled into dust, and the Lord did not give us sinners a harvest, so that our families will die of hunger.[58]

The same cossack *nakaz* also instructed the Duma: "You must satisfy our Russian people. This is what we demand—give the peasants land." It was not at all uncommon for cossacks to mingle, and identify their own interests, with the peasants they were supposed to suppress. In Tambov province, an official reported, the cossacks were "sluggish" and told peasants to go ahead and cart grain away from gentry estates. Indeed, many of the cossack mutinies and cossack *nakazy* centered on the refusal to suppress peasants. As one of the *nakazy* from the 7th Urals cossacks said, "We won't protect the gentry any more."[59] The government attempted to have village atamans organize loyal petitions to the Duma to counteract all the others, but to no effect: when pressed, Orenburg and Don cossack villages instead passed resolutions of support for the cossack deputies and their demands. Reports in June that the Ministry of War planned to mobilize three additional Don regiments triggered angry protests, demonstrations, and resolutions expressing vehement opposition. The Ministry hastily denied that it had any such plans.[60] The regime did need reinforcements, but they were not to be had from the Don, or from any other cossack territory. Cossacks in their villages were as restive as any peasants, cossacks in the regiments as mutinous as the infantry.

There was little the Ministry of War could do to check the disintegration of the army. Orders that officers be polite, avoid drunkenness, and see that their men got what was coming to them obviously failed to do the trick.[61] Once again, then, the generals' thoughts turned toward appeasement. By the second half of May military district commanders were under orders to visit the scene of the disturbances and report on their causes, in June a conference of senior army and navy commanders met to consider the evidence, and a commission was established within the Ministry of War for the same purpose. The commission, to its credit, rejected the easy explanation that the mutinies were the product of criminal agitation and concluded instead that the soldiers' material deprivation was largely responsible. That was a superficial judgment but the soldiers' demands did point in that direction and the Ministry at least had the power to eliminate material sources of discontent. Military sources reported in early July that the government was leaning toward new concessions to soldiers on the pattern of the December 6 reforms: another increase in pay, further augmentation of the gear issued.[62]

The Ministry of War understood, of course, that soldiers were also affected by the revolutionary sentiment around them, and so attempted to quarantine the troops. On June 20, Minister of War Rediger ordered his military district commanders to reduce to the absolute minimum the number of troops used to aid civil authority, because otherwise there was danger of "the total disintegration of the army and the loss of it as an organized military force."[63] On June 23, the Ministry of War, over the heated objections of the Ministry of Transportation, ordered the gradual reduction of the detachments posted at major railway stations, and on June 28 ordered units bivouacked in areas swept by agrarian disorders to return to their urban barracks. Units in Saratov, Samara, Chernigov, and Kharkov Provinces were to decamp immediately.[64] These were precisely the provinces most in need of troops. As peasant disorders and mutinies crested simultaneously in late June, the Ministry of War reenacted the retreat of November 1905.

Official statistics on the number of units sent to aid civil authorities reveal how complete the retreat was. The number of infantry companies deployed against civilians dropped from 25,283 in 1905 to 3,142 in 1906, cavalry and cossack squadrons from 5,354 to 1,058. This represented a reduction from approximately 2,800,000 men in 1905 to about 400,000 in

1906. While the need for troops may not have been so great in 1906 as in 1905, it had not declined so dramatically as that. Indeed, the number of troops used to aid civil authorities in 1907, when revolution had passed, was about the same as in 1906.[65] Fear for the reliability of the army was not the only reason the generals resisted placing units at the disposal of civil authorities. They had always resented the use of the army for police purposes, and never more than in 1906, when the army badly needed to regroup after its defeat in Manchuria.[66] Yet it is clear that in the summer of 1906 the generals feared—and had ample reason to fear—that military rebellion threatened the integrity of the army and that the only way to forestall complete collapse was to prevent any sort of contact between soldiers and civilians, and to let civil authorities fend for themselves. Their calculations were shortsighted at best. If the army could be saved only by withdrawing from the fight against revolution, the Tsarist order would collapse. And in any case soldiers could not be isolated from the influence of the Duma, which was in 1906 the mainspring of their revolution.

VIII. July 1906: The Revolution That Might Have Been

In early July, V.D. Kuzmin-Karavaev, formerly professor at the Military Juridicial Academy and now a moderate deputy in the Duma, observed that the "situation in the country" bore all the marks of a gathering storm—not the quiet, but the thunderheads themselves. There was no insurrection, but everywhere revolver shots and the explosion of bombs. Gentry estates were not being consumed by fire, but here and there they were burning, and peasants were carting away gentry grain. There was no general strike, but strikes took place in every city. Troops were not openly mutinous, but soldiers everywhere were in ferment (an inaccurate but not unreasonable characterization given the behavior of mutineers). "Everyone's nerves are drawn to the last degree of tension. Everyone is on edge, waiting, trying to guess what will come tomorrow, in a month, in a year."[1] The atmosphere was so highly charged, he concluded, that even a liberal ministry would have great difficulty riding out the anarchy.

Kuzmin-Karavaev worried about the dangers facing a liberal government because by June the rumors of impending dissolution of the Duma that had been circulating since May had been joined by rumors that the regime would invite the Kadets to take over the government. The competing rumors accurately reflected the irresolution of the regime, which was paralyzed by its antipathy to the Duma and its fear that dissolution would unleash the storm. The cabinet resolved on June 1 and again (with the Tsar in attendance) on June 7–8 that the Duma must be dissolved, but neither Prime Minister Goremykin nor the Tsar did anything to implement these resolutions. Within the cabinet, the liberal Minister of Foreign Affairs, Alexander Izvolskii, without informing his colleagues, contacted Duma liberals and then presented to the Tsar a memorial they had composed urging that only the inclusion of public figures in the cabinet could restore confidence in the government. At the court, unbeknownst to Izvolskii or anyone else in the cabinet, General Trepov (now Palace Commandant) sought out the leaders of the Kadet Party and in the middle of June actually met with Miliukov and expressed his willingness to accept a Kadet cabinet and limited expropriation of gentry land as proposed by the Kadets. Trepov's motives were clear: he feared for the survival of Tsarism. To his brother's objections to a compromise with the Duma, Trepov responded: "All is lost, and we must save the Emperor and the dynasty from an inevitable catastrophe."[2] The Tsar followed up Trepov's initiative by authorizing Izvolskii and Minister of Interior Stolypin to sound out the Kadets. Stolypin apparently favored inclusion of a few Kadets in the cabinet only if that would make the inevitable dissolution of the Duma more palatable to at least a part of the public, but the Tsar's uncles and a few liberal officials were prepared to accept a liberal ministry for its own sake. All of this intriguing behind the scenes galvanized conservatives in and out of the cabinet, and they pressed for speedy dissolution. The cabinet on June 20 issued another declaration on the unacceptability of expropriation. Trepov retreated but did not yield: in a famous interview with Reuters on June 23 he maintained that expropriation was impossible, but asserted that a Kadet ministry offered the best hope of restoring order, though if that failed another course would have to be chosen. The Tsar himself on June 28 deigned to hear out the moderate leader Shipov's plea for a liberal cabinet.[3] While it is difficult to conceive of the Tsar actually appointing Kadets to high office, at the end of June the regime was still unable to decide what to do. And every passing day brought more agrarian disorders, more strikes, and more mutinies.

The crisis generated by the Duma divided revolutionaries no less than the regime. Because they believed the public supported the Duma as an institution, Mensheviks favored revolutionary mass action in the summer. They supported the demand for a ministry responsible to the Duma, urged the Duma to appeal to the public for support, and themselves organized meetings between the SD deputies and the Petersburg workers. As of mid-June, Menshevik leaders held that it was not yet time to force a confrontation with the government because the public was not psychologically prepared for the demise of Tsarism, and the proletariat was as yet inadequately organized. In early July, however, Menshevik strategists urged the Duma to force expropriation by appealing directly to the people, and believed that such an appeal would be the first step on the way to making the Duma a genuine "organ of power." The latter euphemism was necessary in the legal press, but Mensheviks exploited it for its vagueness; precisely what they envisioned as the end product of revolutionary action was unclear. Alone of the important revolutionary groups, however, Mensheviks in early

July contemplated a midsummer assault on the regime. While the Duma could not openly call on the people to take "immediate action," read a Menshevik editorial of July 5, the Duma must know that if the people waited for events to unfold the Duma would never pass a law and would be dissolved.[4] Only revolution could save the Duma, and in the Menshevik view only the Duma could provide a rallying point for successful revolution.

Bolsheviks and Socialist Revolutionaries denied that the Duma could serve as an "organ of power"—for them, the revolution must not stop short of a constituent assembly—and they were utterly unwilling to link revolutionary action to the Duma. They continued to key their plans, instead, to the peasantry, who would be ready for insurrection only after the harvest. Bolsheviks denounced any proposal for a "responsible ministry"—a Kadet ministry—as betrayal of the revolution. Instead of fostering a revolutionary confrontation between the regime and the Duma as a whole, they hoped to persuade the Trudoviks, and through them the peasants, that their belief in the Duma's capacity to obtain justice was misplaced and that only insurrection could provide land and liberty. Mensheviks and Bolsheviks carried their dispute into workers meetings, where Bolsheviks played on worker antipathy to polite society and made effective use of the Kadets' apparent willingness to compromise with the regime. Even Mensheviks felt obliged to denounce the Kadets for avoiding any action that would provide the regime a pretext for dissolving the Duma.[5] Conflict over how best to turn the Duma to the advantage of revolution thus produced not only disarray among revolutionaries, but confused and contradictory messages to their working class following.

Reining in Revolutionary Soldiers

The mutinies in the army had no impact on revolutionary strategy, though by May they were drawing appreciative comment. As a Bolshevik wrote in early July, "Unfolding your newspaper, you automatically look for reports from the army. This is completely understandable now, given the prospect that the army will play an enormous role in liberating the country."[6] A Poltava Menshevik, writing shortly after a mutiny in the Poltava garrison, expressed the common view that the disturbances in the army were not especially threatening "in an active sense" since the regiments that had gone on strike had principally economic demands. Nevertheless, the mutinies did reflect "the spirit of the times" and raised doubts as to whether the army, the pillar of the "bureaucracy," would take action against the people.[7] Revolutionaries might have been more enthusiastic if their hopes for the army had not been disappointed in 1905. The SR leader Viktor Chernov wrote in June that "In general, our mutinies, as experience has shown, proceed in an extremely disorderly fashion and the soldiers show no capacity to resist or to take the initiative themselves." There was always, too, potential for an outburst of random violence, a consequence of the suppression of the soldiers' individuality. But, Chernov concluded hopefully, the government's policy of arresting instigators only increased the number of disturbances.[8] (That, of course, was why officers generally feared to arrest instigators.) All revolutionaries saw the connection between mutinies and the Duma, but that did not influence their views on proper revolutionary strategy.[9]

The military organizations themselves attempted to restrain soldiers and sailors from rising until the time appointed by revolutionary leaders. A resolution adopted in April by the SD (Menshevik) military organization in Sevastopol, where pressure for insurrection came to a head first, set forth the thinking of all the military organizations.

Taking into account:
1) that a military insurrection on any scale at all is unthinkable without a popular insurrection,
2) that premature attempts to begin a military insurrection will lead only to the more or less complete destruction of the forces of revolution,
3) that more or less extensive disorder in any one unit could at present lead to the same result,
—Taking all of this into account, the Sevastopol Committee of the Military Organization of the RSDRP has resolved:
a) immediately to explain to sailors and soldiers that a military insurrection depends on a national insurrection;
b) given disorder in any unit, to make every effort to prevent this disorder from turning into a premature, hence doomed, insurrection;
c) to point out to sailors and soldiers the recklessness of those who are adventuristically attempting to call them to such an insurrection.[10]

Similar resolutions were common. In May, the SD (Menshevik) and SR military organizations in Kiev jointly agreed not to respond to repressive actions for at least two months, and in the meantime to prepare for insurrection at harvest time. In early June, the SD (Bolshevik) military organization in Finland called on soldiers not to respond to the provocative actions of their officers, these being designed to deprive soldiers of their leaders, and argued that despite the many midsummer peasant disorders, the most politically conscious peasants understood that the best time for agrarian revolution was autumn. At the same time, the SR Maximalists in Moscow urged soldiers to do nothing, at least until the regime dissolved the Duma or took some other extreme step. In late June, the Petersburg SR military organization persuaded its soldier members to pass a resolution against reacting to arrests and even against presenting demands. In June and early July, SD and SR military organizations in Ekaterinoslav, Kazan, Kronstadt, Nizhnii Novgorod, Penza, Tiflis—almost everywhere, in fact—faced strong pressure for action from their soldier members but urged upon them resolutions calling for delay until the rest of the country was ready.[11]

The surge of mutinies through May and June would seem to indicate that these resolutions were offered in vain, but that is not an entirely accurate impression. A common pattern seems (the evidence is suggestive rather than conclusive) to have been that soldiers who were not in the military organizations but had some contact with them started mutinies; once begun, military organization soldiers exercised a moderating influence. Where military organization soldiers were involved in presenting petitions of grievances, they attempted to prevent incidents that might lead to all-or-nothing confrontations with the military command (as in Kursk, where SR soldiers managed to prevent other soldiers from storming the camp jail). In Abo (Finland), soldiers in the SD military organization talked their fellows out of a further confrontation after demands had been presented. In Samara, the arrest of some soldiers triggered a mutiny that the SR military organization had been trying to head off, but SR soldiers were able to prevent the mutiny from getting out of control. In Nizhnii Novgorod, the SD military organization in early June dissuaded the 32nd Don cossacks from mutiny when the cossacks were told to hand in their weapons, but arrest of some cossacks did produce mutiny on June 18.[12]

While in many garrisons the military organizations had at best tenuous control over the soldiers' behavior, in the garrisons that were best organized they were able despite intense pressure to prevent the outbreak of mutinies altogether. In Petersburg, the SR military organization succeeded repeatedly in May and June in preventing units from mutinying. In late May the sappers encamped at Kolpino outside Petersburg were ready to blow up their officers' club, seize the local arsenal, and march on Petersburg; they could be talked out of this only by a representative of the SR Central Committee, Andrei Argunov. By June, the leading soldiers in the SR Petersburg organization no longer even subscribed to the view that they should wait for civilians to prepare before themselves beginning the uprising.[13] In Sevastopol, too, despite the increasing displeasure of the soldiers and sailors (and their threats to begin without civilian authorization) the SD and SR military organizations were able to avert a garrison-wide mutiny that threatened to explode at any moment.[14]

The situation in Kronstadt in May and June was summed up in a secret police report, which noted that half of the garrison as well as 80 percent of the fleet was untrustworthy.

> Meetings are for the most part organized in the barracks, with revolutionary speakers admitted to the meetings almost daily. . . . In the naval barracks, announcements are posted on the day of the meetings. . . . At every meeting, the government's policy with respect to the Duma is criticized and the need to support the demands of the latter is asserted. . . . According to the politically conscious sailors, the revolutionary mood is at such a pitch that they will not wait for the moment of conflict between Duma and government. . . . The outbursts among sailors on economic grounds that have occurred lately have been restrained by the revolutionaries so as to conserve strength for when it will be needed.[15]

In late May, sailors were talking of shelling the Tsar's residence at Peterhof. In May, too, the sailing of the ships for summer exercises almost triggered a rising because the ships' guns were activated and the sailors temporarily had access to rifles. In June, a rumor that the artillerists were to be transferred led to a tense two-day discussion by SD and SR military organizations of the pros and cons of an uprising. The SR military organization sent to Petersburg for Jan, the SR national military organizer and very popular in the Kronstadt garrison, who brought along a Trudovik deputy (because of the Trudoviks' immense moral authority among the sailors) and Argunov of the SR Central Committee. The soldiers and sailors were finally persuaded not to rise—no mean accomplishment given the mood in the garrison.[16]

The mutiny of the 6th sapper brigade illustrates the military organizations' ability to control revolutionary soldiers, and the conditions under which control broke down.[17] In May, the sappers, back from the war and permanently quartered in Moscow, encamped in Kaluga Province. Tension at the camp was high from the start, as soldiers met openly and in large numbers (up to 700 at a time). Sappers connected with the SD military organization in Moscow set up a complete hierarchy of committees from company to brigade level, though they apparently maintained for themselves an inner, "secret organization" (according to the secret police report). The committees discussed how to prepare the sappers for mutiny and the demands that should be presented. In anticipation of a mutiny, the sappers wrote the Moscow SD military organization requesting that it ascertain the number and mood of the troops in Kaluga ("because we will soon have dealings with them") and to send a civilian organizer on receipt of a coded telegram. The brigade committee then dispatched one soldier to talk things over with the military organization in Moscow, another to look into the situation in nearby cities (the latter reported that soldiers in Kaluga and Tula were "reliable and will not fire at the sappers"). However, the sapper sent to Moscow returned with the directive that "no demands be presented before receipt of a signal from Moscow, since not everything is ready [there]."

The sapper organization attempted to comply, but eventually lost control over the camp. On June 22 a sapper informed his battalion that he had been sentenced to two years in a disciplinary battalion and asked, "Will you let me be sent there or not?" The sapper organization was powerless to check the spontaneous, angry reaction. The sappers demanded the release of their arrested comrade, then presented other demands. For about a week, the soldiers met almost continuously, with intermittent breaks for drill. The sapper organization wished to take the mutiny further, but its messages were not received in Moscow (the police had discovered one letter drop); the organization seems in consequence to have exercised a restraining influence. On June 29, two infantry regiments (one the Astrakhan Grenadiers) arrived from Moscow. On the 30th, thirty-nine sapper leaders were summoned to camp headquarters, which had been secretly surrounded by two companies of Astrakhan infantry. The thirty-nine were arrested; the camp reacted with outrage; a mob formed (and threatened the officers who fell in their path), but without leaders the sappers were uncertain how to proceed. Over the next few days another 100 sappers were arrested. Nevertheless, on July 4 a report on the incident to the Ministry of War noted that the sappers were still "very agitated" and that there was a "persistent rumor that the 9th Ingermanland regiment would come from Kaluga" to help liberate the arrested sappers. Though the mutiny as such was over, the sappers were not cowed.

Despite the rush of mutinies in late May and June, the military organization did use their considerable influence to prevent mutiny, or failing that to keep mutiny within moderate limits. That the number of mutinies did not rise in the second half of June must be attributed in part to the efforts of the military organizations. Not surprisingly, they were uncomfortable with the role they were playing. By June many SD and SR military organizations were laying plans for insurrection even if for the time being they felt constrained not to put them into effect. By the end of June the SR military organization in Kronstadt had decided that when it became impossible to restrain the soldiers and sailors any longer it would lead the uprising. The civilian SR military organizers in Petersburg voted in June to begin a military insurrection but were overruled by the SR Central Committee. In June, too, the Tiflis Menshevik military organization urged soldiers to rise if the Duma should be dispersed, the Bolshevik military organization in Nizhnii Novgorod drew up plans for a summer rising, and the Menshevik military organization in Simbirsk sought agreement from its sister organizations for coordinated mutinies in all the garrisons of the middle Volga.[18]

The SR military organizations had the opportunity, at their national conference in late June, to press their party leadership for insurrection as the soldiers were pressing them. The military organizations informed the party leaders present that they could not hold the soldiers in check indefinitely and that in some garrisons the limit had already been reached. A report on tactics delivered by a representative of the Petersburg military organization attributed this to a psychology specific to the armed forces: unlike workers and peasants, once soldiers had been set in motion they had to be allowed to move forward, they could not for long sustain a high level of tension. But, he went on, this was not necessarily a drawback. While soldiers might be subsidiary with respect to the revolution as a whole, they could certainly initiate insurrection. Soldiers themselves did not wish to wait on peasants and workers, while peasants and workers would certainly hasten to the soldiers' assistance. In the final analysis, it was not up to revolutionaries to dictate the timing of insurrection, which certainly could not be scheduled in advance for the autumn. A member of the SR Central Committee objected that the party was not yet ready for insurrection, workers were not ready, the railway union was not ready, and the Trudoviks—valued allies—were not ready; and he reaffirmed that the next uprising should be timed to coincide with the autumnal peak of peasant unrest. On the other hand, he promised that if the government were to dissolve the Duma, the party would call for insurrection. As events would prove, the SR leadership did not mean by that term what the military organizers had in mind.

The SR military organizations did not explicitly challenge their Central Committee's right to determine party strategy, but their restiveness came through during the discussion of the proper response to spontaneous mutiny. The principal proponents of military organization independence in this matter, spokesmen for the Sevastopol and Petersburg organizations, admitted that ideally the Central Comittee should orchestrate a nation-wide military insurrection, but argued that if a serious mutiny were in the offing the local military organization must take the initiative and lend mutiny a maximum degree of organization. Since there was general agreement that the military organizations had a moral responsibility to assume leadership of mutinous soldiers, the conference adopted a resolution incorporating that proposition. That gave the military organizations considerable leeway, but at least the resolution paid verbal obeisance to the canon that the military, peasant, and worker revolutions ought preferably to begin together. The delegate from Sevastopol, on the other hand, coolly informed the conference that should the Black Sea Fleet sail (this would involve activating the ships' guns and so would put immense firepower in the hands of revolutionary sailors), his organization would begin insurrection on its own initiative.[19]

So matters stood as the regime prepared at last to dissolve the Duma: the army engulfed by mutiny; revolutionary soldiers and sailors pressing for insurrection; the military organizations gradually yielding to the pressure; the leaders of the revolutionary parties demanding restraint. The upheaval in the army was only a part of the larger crisis that the Duma had touched off: at midsummer, agrarian disorders mounted as rapidly as mutiny, and strikes—though not on the ascendant—were numerous. The revolutionaries' appeal to soldiers to postpone mutiny derived in large part from their refusal to concede that the conflict between Duma and regime stood at the center of the crisis. It remained to be seen whether the soldiers' willingness to rebel would survive the regime's reassertion of its absolute authority, and whether revolutionaries would be able, or at least willing, to make something of the soldiers' revolution should it continue.

The Duma Dissolved, Revolutionaries Divided

The decisions leading up to the dissolution are shrouded in mystification stemming from the Tsar's habit of masking indecision with reticence, and intentionally fostered by the ministers most directly involved. Prime Minister Goremykin, Minister of Interior Stolypin, and Minister of War Rediger made an apparently firm decision on July 2 to dissolve the Duma on Sunday, July 9, and thereupon ordered that troops be brought to the capital by the evening of the 8th to ensure public order. Neither Goremykin nor Stolypin would have committed himself without the assent of the Tsar (Rediger was brought in only as a technical consultant, not as policy maker), so we must presume that the Tsar had as of that date made up his mind. Yet there is no evidence about who or what swayed him. The most likely candidate is Stolypin, who, bypassing Goremykin, had been urging firm decisions on the Tsar and presumably reported that negotiations with the Kadets were fruitless, using as a compelling argument for dissolution the Duma's decision to issue an appeal to the people not to consider the government's June 20 denunciation of expropriation the last word on the land question. Shortly the Tsar would reward Stolypin for his decisiveness by appointing him Prime Minister. Yet the Tsar and the three ministers who were making arrangements carefully concealed the decision from the rest of the cabinet. The Tsar informed State Controller Schwanebach on July 5, but on July 7 Goremykin announced to the cabinet that because of the Duma's appeal to the people on the land issue he would recommend to the Tsar immediate dissolution. On the 8th Goremykin presented the cabinet the signed manifesto on dissolution, and news that Stolypin would replace him.[20] The sequence of events suggests that Goremykin and Stolypin were unsure even after July 2 that the Tsar would go through with his decision.

Even as the cabinet as a whole remained uninformed, Stolypin's Ministry of Interior made preparations to deal with the consequences of dissolution. In the week preceding July 9 the secret police offices were polled on how the public would react, and on the likelihood that the revolutionaries would be able to agree on a common response. The secret police unanimously reported that the public (presumably urban) would remain calm and revolutionaries as disunited as ever. The Ministry of Interior was not worried about the peasants, because it did not believe that agrarian disorders could pose any immediate peril to the regime. According to the secret police official Bakai (whose testimony is indirectly supported by Foreign Minister Izvolskii), only the mutinies in the army caused the government concern—and grave concern—but the government was confident nonetheless that mutinies could be suppressed one way or another.[21] Beginning on July 6, the cabinet still unaware, Guards units moved into the capital from the Krasnoe Selo camp (by the 10th a total of 22,000 troops occupied Petersburg). Secret police officials in the provinces were warned to prepare for disorders on July 9, and orders went out to round up revolutionaries working on the railroads, in guerrilla organizations, and in the army, and to keep an especially close watch on units infected by revolutionary propaganda. In Petersburg, the police on the 7th and 8th arrested most of the SD Petersburg Committee and a part of the SR Central Committee (Chernov and Argunov escaped through a window of the newspaper office where they had been trapped.)[22]

The regime's preparation for the dissolution was thus as complete as possible, but the decision remained in doubt even after the announcement to the cabinet on July 8. When they learned that the Tsar had signed the manifesto, Trepov and his equally conservative and equally fearful cohort, Minister of Court Baron Friederichs, implored the Tsar not to go through with the dissolution. Late at night on July 8 a messenger arrived from the Tsar to tell Goremykin to hold back the manifesto. Goremykin, foreseeing that Nicholas might lose his nerve, had already handed the manifesto to the printers with instructions for immediate publication, and had locked himself in his room with orders that he not be disturbed under any circumstances.[23] As in October 1905, Nicholas' advisors had made the key decisions for him.

In the event, the dissolution provoked not upheaval but a great silence—whether ominous or stunned was not immediately apparent. Dissolution, because it was carried out on a Sunday when the Duma was not meeting, involved no more than sealing the Duma chambers and posting police and soldiers to turn away any deputies who might appear. The streets of Petersburg were abnormally and eerily quiet, and calm prevailed in Moscow and most other cities as well. Maurice Baring, travelling third class between Petersburg and Moscow on four successive nights to ascertain the public reaction, found his fellow passengers absorbed in talk of politics and popular disorders, but detected no inclination on their part to rebel despite their evident sympathy for the Duma.[24] In the countryside, on the other hand, where rebellion was already under way, Bernard Pares found that "for the first time within my knowledge voices were freely raised on the village green in criticism even of the dynasty itself," and when a village priest read the manifesto on dissolution the peasants refused to hear him out and left the church when he continued to read it over their objections.[25] Peasants were indeed angry. Those who believed the Tsar had dispersed the Duma did not therefore abandon their intention of seizing land. Many peasants simply refused to believe that the Tsar had betrayed them, and converted the Duma into a mythical source of authority. Maurice Baring heard peasants in a village outside Moscow assert that "the authorities" had signed the manifesto on dissolution but the Tsar had not. After the manifesto was read to some peasants in Orel Province, they shouted: "There is no such Manifesto and there could not be. . . . We have to do as we see fit, to get what we need and what the Duma demanded."[26]

How the peoples of the Russian Empire would react after July 9 depended in part, obviously, on the reaction of the Duma itself. No group in the Duma had made plans for dissolution. The Kadets had discussed the possibility of responding with a manifesto of some sort, but had made no decision; they had also talked about passively resisting expulsion from the Duma chamber, but only as a show of solidarity if the Trudoviks refused to leave (the manner of dissolution ruled out that possibility). Confronted with dissolution, the Kadets decided to do no more than make an angry gesture. On the 9th the Kadet Central Committee and 200-odd deputies (120 of them Kadets) repaired across the Finnish border to Vyborg, and there on the 10th 181 of them signed a Kadet-authored manifesto—inspired by the Kadet desire to keep their response within strictly constitutional limits—calling on the country to demand popular representation and to refuse to pay taxes or submit to military conscription until a new Duma provided legal authority for these functions of government. That feeble appeal satisfied no one but the Kadets, and was in fact too radical for many of them.[27]

The Trudoviks, especially, had expected dissolution to have far more serious consequences. Their leaders had concluded by late June that dissolution would trigger revolution, and some of the Trudovik deputies touring their constituencies publicly urged peasants to join in insurrection if it came to that. On July 9 and 10, the Trudovik deputies urged the Kadets to defy the government and resume the sessions of the Duma in Petersburg, to join in the establishment of a committee of the Duma to direct popular resistance to the regime, and to join the Trudoviks in an appeal for a political general strike. The Trudoviks themselves took the initiative in issuing, on July 12, an appeal to the army (which the SD deputies endorsed), the gist of which was that soldiers should not obey the orders of an illegal government. By then the Trudoviks were intimately involved in the consultations at which revolutionary parties and organizations sought to settle upon a common strategy. Meanwhile, a number of Trudovik deputies toured the villages to encourage peasants not to pay taxes or report to conscription boards and to seize land, and workers in factory settlements to set up soviets. Peasants responded enthusiastically to these appeals and defended their deputies from arrest.[28] Dissolution had turned the Trudoviks, at least temporarily, into a genuinely revolutionary party whose enormous appeal to peasants all over Russia more then compensated for its utter lack of local organizations.

The Trudoviks received as little support from the revolutionary parties as from the Kadets for their view that the Duma dissolved should spearhead revolution. Only the Menshevik leadership believed that dissolution would be understood by all classes as the occasion for overthrowing the regime. The Menshevik-controlled SD Central Committee called upon the Duma to refuse to accept dissolution and to assume the responsibility for convening a constituent assembly, and like the Trudoviks urged a general strike to force the regime to capitulate and reconvene the Duma. When on about July 14 a conference of all the revolutionary organizations turned down the Menshevik proposal, the SD Central Committee instructed SD committees to organize "local mass protest demonstrations" in the hope that these would precipitate a general strike.

Bolsheviks refused to submit to the Central Committee's instructions. The Duma was not worth defending, they asserted, and insurrection, the inevitable byproduct of a general strike, must be postponed until the expected post-harvest peasant disorders. Bolsheviks on the Central

Committee claimed that the government had dissolved the Duma precisely in order to provoke worker insurrection before peasants were ready, and Lenin's immediate reaction to the dissolution was to dash off a pamphlet explaining why the revolutionary parties should do nothing until the harvest. Bolsheviks urged that preparations be drawn up for action in the fall, but they had been calling for such preparations all along. The only immediate measure they recommended was that workers form soviets to prepare for insurrection; in the meantime, workers should refrain even from going on strike. Congenital antipathy to the Duma and instinctive suspicion of Menshevik recommendations of course played a part in the Bolsheviks' disinclination to respond to the dissolution, but they also raised serious practical objections to the Menshevik plans. They worried, for instance, that the proletariat simply was not prepared for the insurrection that would grow out of a general strike. And if the government should call the Duma back into session, would revolutionaries have to suspend the strike without forcing the conflict to its logical conclusion, the overthrow of the regime? It was in any case preposterous, they said, to defend the Duma when the Duma had been unwilling to act on its own behalf. Even the left-liberal lawyers' union asserted that the Duma's day had passed.[29]

Bolsheviks and Mensheviks carried their dispute over tactics to the Petersburg workers and into the provinces, and the Menshevik leadership failed signally to win support. Even solidly Menshevik committees such as those in Rostov-on-Don and Irkutsk urged workers not to respond to government provocation. The Bolshevik Central Region Committee and Bolshevik committees in Nizhnii Novgorod and Moscow urged peasants to rise and workers to wait. Some committees were uncertain how to react to the dissolution, and like the Bolshevik committees in Iaroslavl and Ekaterinburg called on workers to prepare for insurrection without indicating whether or not insurrection was about to commence. Yet if—understandably enough—some SDs lacked a clear view of tactics immediately after July 9, the great majority believed they should hold the workers back. The SD parties among the national minorities evinced no uncertainty at all: they adamantly opposed responding to the dissolution of the Duma with a general strike or insurrection. The Riga Federative Committee (Latvian SD, Bund, RSDRP) warned workers against government provocation, the Latvian and Polish SD Central Committees appealed to workers to do nothing, and the Bund stressed the untimeliness of any action in midsummer.[30]

SRs, too, argued against precipitate action, but they at least came up with a scheme that gave an appearance of movement. The SR leadership concluded that, even though the harvest was not in, the dissolution of the Duma had provided the spark for a peasant rising. The SRs first tried to persuade the members of the Duma to reconvene in the capital and oblige the regime to disperse them by force, as this would provide more compelling grounds for insurrection. That effort failing, and after consulting with the Trudoviks and the All-Russian Peasant and Railway Unions (both closely affiliated with the SRs), the SR Central Committee decided to implement a plan originally devised to take advantage of the expected fall surge in agrarian disorders and designed to protect workers from the isolation that SRs believed had doomed the insurrections in December. On July 12 the SRs issued an appeal for peasant insurrection, and followed that up on the 13th or 14th with appropriate instructions to local SR committees. Peasants were to replace local officials, seize land and turn it over to revolutionary committees, and, when a base had been established locally, expand their insurgency. SR military organizations were to instruct revolutionary troops to cease obeying their officers immediately (and the SR leadership authorized military organizers to draw up but not implement a plan for insurrection in the Baltic Fleet). Workers were to form soviets wherever possible, but they were not to undertake other action until the peasant movement was well underway (SRs joined Bolsheviks in agitating against an immediate political strike). As a member of the SR Central Committee explained two months later, peasants, no matter how agitated by government treachery, would not rise everywhere at the same time. If the response to the SR appeal demonstrated that peasants were ready for insurrection, and it would be some time before one could be certain, then soldiers would be unleashed, and following that a general strike would commence.[31] The SR plan, in other words, was to see what peasants would do, in the meantime plan for but not begin military insurrection, and hold the workers back until the last moment. Since this scheme did not commit them to anything definite, all the other revolutionary organizations could—and did—support it.[32]

As the Bolsheviks pointed out, every passing day made a general strike in the name of the Duma more absurd, though of course the Bolsheviks bore their share of responsibility for the delay. But the Bolsheviks were not alone; all the revolutionary parties and organizations rejected the Menshevik-Trudovik appeal for a general strike, and all issued appeals of their own to the workers to do nothing. The secret police prognosis that revolutionaries would be unable to agree on a common course of action proved overly pessimistic: while they remained divided on tactics and strategy, they agreed with near-unanimity that for the moment they need do nothing at all. They would have continued to do nothing had soldiers and sailors not forced action upon them.

Soldiers Rise Alone

Soldiers and sailors did not believe that the dissolution of the Duma had put an end to the revolution. In Petersburg itself, a deputation of soldiers sought out deputies to the Duma on July 9 and offered their support if the Duma would defy the government. Two cossack deputations, one of officers, the other of enlisted men, informed cossack deputies that the cossack regiments in the capital were at their disposal. Immediately upon receiving news of dissolution on July 9, eighty sailors on the light cruiser *Rus* at Libava resolved that they would rise at the first summons. Cossacks in Taganrog refused on July 9 to fire on a workers' protest demonstration (the streets were not everywhere quiet), and the local paper in Kostroma reported that on the 11th cossacks disobeyed orders to disperse a crowd of young workers singing revolutionary songs.[33] At the camp outside the Brest-Litovsk fortress, artillerists infuriated by the dissolution of the Duma formed a mob after evening roll call on July 9, threw dirt and rocks at their officers, and burned down the officers' mess. Shortly after July 9 the entire Askhabad garrison held a meeting to discuss the dissolution. When an officer disciplined two men of the 111th Don infantry in camp outside Mariampol on July 15, the soldiers mutinied, presented demands, voiced their anger over the dissolution of the Duma, and swore at the regimental chaplain when he tried to calm them.

Dissolution of the Duma did not discourage mutiny, whether undertaken for political or other reasons. So far as the available evidence reveals, in fact, the proportion of mutinies with manifest political content was no greater in the two weeks following dissolution than before: fourteen of thirty mutinies (47 percent) July 9–23, fifty-four of 121 mutinies (45 percent) April–July 8. Four sapper battalions mutinied in camp at Orany (near Vilna) on July 10 and presented demands without, apparently, expressing any political sentiments, while a company of the 4th Andizhan reserve battalion in Novy Margelan mutinied on July 15 to prevent two soldiers from being sent to a disciplinary battalion. These soldiers disclosed not their political views, but their reading of the political situation: they did not believe that dissolution had foreclosed the opportunity for mutiny. That was an assessment shared by many others. At no time in July did the incidence of mutiny quite reach the June level, but—though weekly numbers are small and subject to random fluctuation—soldiers appear to have been somewhat more prone to mutiny immediately after than immediately before July 9: nine mutinies July 1–8, fourteen mutinies July 9–16, sixteen mutinies July 17–23. So far as soldiers were concerned, the condition that had permitted mutiny before July 9—disbelief in the regime's ability to make good its claim to sole authority—continued to hold. As the secret police reported from Tikhoretsk, soldiers guarding the station had decided that they would not act against workers in the event of disorders, because "we don't know whom we have to serve, the government or the people."[34]

Many soldiers professed to know the answer to that question and claimed like the cossacks in Petersburg and sailors in Libava to be awaiting the signal for insurrection. Military organizers reported from Sevastopol and Nizhnii Novgorod that soldiers and sailors were eager to rise, and the prior mutinies and indiscipline in those garrisons lend the reports credence. The military organizations were under instructions to restrain soldiers and most did so, though with some difficulty. In Dvinsk, for instance, soldiers insisted that the SD military organization draw up plans for insurrection, but agreed to wait until either Riga or Petersburg had risen.[35] Soldiers did answer the call of the Poltava SR military organization, which decided to convert the soldiers' cointinuing urge to mutiny into regional military insurrection. On July 14, the training detail of the 34th Sevsk infantry decided to mutiny because two of their number had been arrested for possession of revolutionary literature. The Poltava SR military organization expanded upon that decision by calling on the entire Poltava garrison to rise, and sent word to the SR military organizations in Kharkov and Kremenchug to do likewise (there is no record of SR attempts to incite disturbances in those two garrisons). Because the dissolution of the Duma had angered the Poltava soldiers, they responded eagerly to the SR appeal. On July 15, the entire Sevsk regiment, joined by two batteries of the 9th artillery brigade with eight loaded guns, marched to the jail to free their comrades. However, when officers and cossacks opened fire with a machine gun, the mutineers fled back to their barracks.[36]

Soldiers did not always wait patiently for civilians to lead the way. The SD soldiers' organization in the 83rd Samur infantry planned to seize power in Deshlagar (Azerbaijan) after coordinating plans with other regiments in the region. When officers learned of the plot on July 16, the revolutionary soldiers decided to mutiny immediately in order to forestall arrests. On the 17th, all five of the companies of the 83rd Samur then in Deshlagar rose, and soldiers wired the three other regiments of the 21st infantry division that they had taken power. The soldiers then marched through town with their band and held a meeting at which the leader of the soldiers' organization explained that other regiments would follow their lead and that together they could overthrow the Tsarist regime. The soldiers began enthusiastically to dig trenches on the approaches to town. Most of them were badly frightened, however, when their officers resisted arrest (one took a shot at a soldier) and the arresting party killed the regimental commander, three other officers, and the regimental chaplain (one of whose anti-revolutionary sermons was subsequently published in the military chaplains' journal). Many of the soldiers thereupon ran off into the hills, and in the evening others arrested the sixty or so who wished to continue the mutiny.[37]

The insurrections in Poltava and Deshlagar reveal both the willingness of soldiers to rise against the regime and the propensity even of politically motivated mutineers to panic when they felt themselves standing alone and exposed to retribution. As the Sevastopol SD and other military organizations had warned, isolated military insurrections were doomed to defeat, not because the regime had so many reliable units to deploy against mutineers, but because most soldiers were psychologically incapable of sustaining their mutinies in isolation. Soldiers mutinied when they believed their action would be supported by others. What the continuation of the mutinies and the pledges of support for insurrection after July 9 indicate is that for two weeks after the dissolution of the Duma soldiers and sailors continued to believe support would be forthcoming. What the ignominious collapse of insurrection in Poltava and Deshlagar tells us is that soldiers could not make the revolution by themselves.

Revolutionary soldiers and sailors in Kronstadt thought they could. They were as eager for insurrection as any one in the empire—they had been looking forward to it since April—and they were numerous, well-organized, and determined to carry mutiny through even in the face of resistance. Anticipating trouble in Kronstadt, the police on the eve of the dissolution rounded up most of the civilians in the local SD military organization (most of the SRs remained at large), and also pulled in many soldiers and sailors who represented their units in the garrison assembly. Fearing mutiny on the ships that were at sea for summer exercises, the Naval Minister ordered that no ship be allowed to enter Kronstadt without his express authorization. The arrests almost triggered mutiny in the Kronstadt fortress mine company, but the soldiers decided to permit the arrests rather than disrupt plans for mutiny by the entire garrison; deputy representatives, previously selected for just this eventuality, took the place of the arrested men. The soldiers' and sailors' organization thus remained strong, and after July 9 waited expectantly for the signal to rise.[38]

Convinced that the dissolution of the Duma provided both the necessary motivation for soldiers who had thus far refused to commit themselves and the perfect occasion for an insurrection that would spread from Kronstadt to the rest of the empire, the Kronstadt SRs on July 9 began feverishly to make final preparations for seizing control of the base (the SR national military organizer, Jan, sat in on the round-the-clock conference of the planning committee), and on the same day sent a man to Helsingfors to work out a plan for mutiny by the entire Baltic Fleet. The SR military organization in Helsingfors was eager to begin, and even the solidly Bolshevik military organization there gave its assent. The Helsingfors Bolsheviks had begun to draft plans for a mutiny by the fleet even before July 9, and though they were aware of the Bolshevik leadership's opposition to a midsummer rising linked to the Duma, they took the Menshevik call for a general strike and the Bolshevik summons to "prepare" for the same thing to be sufficient justification for cooperating with the SRs. The three military organizations decided that the rising would begin in Helsingfors as soon as the capital ships returned. Helsingfors would inform Kronstadt (and Revel, summer base for the cruisers) when the battleships were ready to mutiny, Kronstadt would cable Helsingfors when the Kronstadt garrison was ready, then Helsingfors would cable Kronstadt when the ships had risen. The object of insurrection in Kronstadt was to ensure that the mutinous ships would not have to brave the guns of Kronstadt's ring of island forts, and from Kronstadt the fleet would move on Petersburg and compel the regime to convene a constituent assembly. The Helsingfors SD military organization later claimed that it had agreed to the plan only with the proviso that the sanction of the SD Central Committee be obtained, but it clearly was impatient to begin. The Revel SD military organization, on the other hand, informed of the plan by two SRs from Helsingfors, said that it could do nothing without instructions from the party Central Committee.[39]

The leaders of the revolutionary parties most certainly did not approve of what their military organizations were doing. Through Jan the SR Central Committee was aware that the SR military organizations in Kronstradt and Helsingfors were planning for an insurrection by the Baltic Fleet, and even authorized planning for military insurrection elsewhere as well. But it did not intend that these plans be executed immediately; the mood of the peasants had first to be ascertained. Through the Petersburg SD military organization, whom the Kronstadt SRs attempted to involve, the Bolshevik leadership, too, learned of the plans for insurrection and took determined steps to thwart them. On July 16, a group of Bolsheviks arrived in Kronstadt to talk sailors and soldiers out of rising. One member of the Bolshevik delegation was inclined to go along with the Kronstadt SRs, but the rest adamantly insisted that while insurrection should be prepared it must not be undertaken. The meeting of unit delegates before which the Bolsheviks and SRs thrashed out the issue—little better than a shouting match, which itself discouraged the soldiers—concluded that the uprising should be postponed. Bolshevik arguments swayed the infantry delegates, or at least gave them an excuse for backing away from a risky venture, and the lack of infantry support was reason enough to delay mutiny because the sailors in port were unarmed.[40]

The revolutionaries' inability to agree on a response to the dissolution of the Duma thus percolated down to the military organizations and disrupted plans for insurrection. SR and, in Helsingfors, Bolshevik military organizers were under rank and file pressure to authorize mutiny, and they took advantage of ambiguous instructions to forge ahead on their own. The SR military organizations acted as though their Central Committee's agreement to planning amounted to permission to undertake insurrection, while the Bolshevik military organization in Helsingfors interpreted the conflicting appeals by Menshevik and Bolshevik leaders to suit its own purposes. But the military organizations could not in the end prevail against their party leaderships. At one point the SR Jan appealed to the SD Central Committee to bring the Bolshevik military organization in Petersburg around, but given the relationship between the SD factions, Menshevik intervention would only have made the Bolsheviks more obdurate.[41] When the debilitating divisions within the revolutionary camp were thrust upon them, even the Kronstadt militants began to have second thoughts.

The Baltic insurrection began in Helsingfors, where there were no unseemly disputes among revolutionaries to discourage soldiers and sailors, and where the soldiers' eagerness to rebel outstripped the military organizations' ability to restrain them and made a hash of the plan for coordinated mutinies around the Baltic littoral.[42] The Helsingfors garrison consisted of three geographically distinct parts: infantry in the city itself; naval units based on Skatuden peninsula (in July, principally destroyer crews); and the garrison of Sveaborg fortress, the "Gibraltar of the North," on a chain of islands guarding the entrance to the harbor. Revolutionary sentiment was strongest among the sailors and the Sveaborg artillerists. The artillerists had mutinied in October and since May had routinely taunted the fortress's ranking officers during weekly reviews; both SD and SR military organizations had worked hard to keep them from mutinying. The artillerists' impatience for revolution mounted rapidly after the dissolution of the Duma, in part because Helsingfors was the scene of angry protest rallies addressed by Social Democratic and Trudovik deputies to the Duma and other radicals (the writer Leonid Andreev among them). The military organizations continued to discourage mutiny while they put the final touches on their plan—allotting a role to the large Finnish workers' Red Guard, for instance. Sveaborg fortress was not itself an important objective; the key to the success of insurrection lay with the big ships, still at sea.

The Helsingfors military organizations lost control over their follow-ing because of the soldiers' propensity to challenge their officers' author-ity and the difficulty of maintaining close contact with all of the scattered segments of the garrison. On July 15, artillerists, the fortress mine com-pany, and some other soldiers met on one of the fortress islands and discussed the plan for a fleet insurrection (officers soon heard about the meeting and the plan). This was probably the first time the artillerists learned the details, and presumably one of the purposes of the meeting was to explain the importance of restraint. On July 16, the mine com-pany after evening roll demanded the traditional "spirits money" that had recently been diverted into the mess budget. The fortress comman-dant came to calm the men, but they refused to disperse, cursed, and insisted that the money be returned. On the morning of the 17th they refused to drill, so infantry were called in to disarm and guard the mine company. However, the infantry were sympathetic and permitted con-tact between miners and artillerists, who promised their support and decided to begin an uprising at midnight.

The SD and SR military organizations in Helsingfors learned of the artillerists' decision late in the afternoon, and both attempted to prevent the rising. The SD military organization urged a messenger from the artillerists to persuade the others not to make a final decision until the battleships returned. The leader of the SR military organization, Captain Tsion, himself an artillerist and so able to gain access to the fortress, rushed to Sveaborg and by 9:00 P.M. had persuaded the artillerists to postpone their mutiny for at least five days, by which time, he prom-ised, Kronstadt would be ready and the Baltic Fleet could even expect support from the Black Sea Fleet. The SD military organization informed the SD Petersburg Committee (the effective Bolshevik leadership) that Sveaborg might blow at any moment. The Petersburg Committee hastily dispatched a delegation to head off the mutiny if that were possible without serious losses, or in the worst case to assist in leading the mutiny. The SD and SR military organizations in Helsingfors were impa-tient to get the rising under way, but there was nothing frivolous about their endeavor.

Though Captain Tsion had extracted a promise that nothing would happen on the 17th, artillerists on one of the outlying islands had not been informed. When about midnight they fired a shot signalling the beginning of the rising, the other artillerists concluded that the plan had been changed again and that the mutiny was on. Some immediately rushed to free miners and artillerists who were under arrest. Officers positioned infantry to block the raid, but the infantry ran away rather than fire. Nevertheless, a stray shot turned some of the infantry against the artillerists, and the artillerists withdrew without freeing the miners rather than shoot it out. Seven of the ten fortress artillery companies quickly took over the three islands with the big guns. The central, or Commandant's, island remained in the hands of officers, the fortress infantry regiment, and two companies of Finland rifles who arrived before boats from the mainland were subject to fire.

Presented with a mutiny in progress, the military organizations decided immediately to support it in Helsingfors and in the garrisons elsewhere in Finland. On the morning of the 18th, the SD military organization attempted to bring out the sailors in the barracks on Skatuden Peninsula and on the few ships in the harbor. The sailors on shore rose and arrested their officers; sailors on ship had been locked below deck, officers and petty officers fired the ships' guns at the barracks, and mutineers trapped on the peninsula by cossacks and infantry surrendered. At the same time, the Finnish Red Guard took to the streets, sending some detachments to join the artillerists and sailors, others to block railway bridges, destroy telegraph lines, and otherwise hamper the convergence on Helsingfors of a punitive force. The Red Guard attempted to call a general strike, but the leadership of the Finnish Social Democratic Party opposed it, maintaining that this was a wholly Russian affair that Russians should settle. By the afternoon of the 18th the insurrection was once again confined to the fortress, but the artillerists were not disheartened. They were well led—besides Captain Tsion, two Social Democratic artillery officers had joined them—and had raised a red flag inscribed on one side "Land and Liberty," on the other "Constituent Assembly." They began to bombard Commandant's Island and another held by infantry, and after renewed bombardment in the very early morning of the 19th (at that time of year it is never dark in Helsingfors, and there is full daylight for about twenty-one hours a day) the infantry surrendered. A general whom the artillerists captured wrote the fortress commandant that there was no recourse but capitulation, but the commandant refused to give in.

News of the mutiny at Sveaborg fell upon revolutionaries in Kronstadt without any forewarning; they learned of it from the papers on the 18th. It was all the more unexpected because they had agreed only two days earlier to postpone insurrection. Then in the early afternoon they received from Helsingfors a coded telegram that the fleet had risen and was sailing toward Kronstadt, which was stranger still—the coded telegram that was to have been sent prior to mutiny had not been received. Two interpretations were possible: either the fleet had in fact risen, or whoever sent the telegram had not known that information on the Sveaborg mutiny would appear in the press and, having established no code for a mutiny at Sveaborg alone, had sent the only message available to let Kronstadt know that a mutiny had begun. On the evening of the 18th, SR civilians and sailors met to discuss what to do. The sailors were impatient to begin, but the meeting concluded that not enough were present to make so fateful a decision. A meeting of the entire garrison assembly was set for the morning of the 19th, and an SR hurried off to Petersburg to find Jan and get instructions.[43]

By the time soldiers and sailors gathered on the 19th, the SR, Bolshevik, and Menshevik leaderships had all decided that the mutiny in Sveaborg must be supported. Chernov and Azef from the SR Central Committee—Azef from the secret police as well—led a party of SRs to Helsingfors to direct the rising there and to place revolutionaries on the capital ships when they arrived. Ilia Fundaminskii, another leading SR, set off to raise Revel, and the SR leadership instructed the Sevastopol SRs to begin military insurrection as well. Jan came with word that a meeting of the SD Central Committee he had attended on the 18th had agreed to insurrection. The SD Central Committee pulled out all the stops: messages went to SDs in Revel, Libava, Ust-Dvinsk (near Riga), and Sevastopol to bring out the soldiers and sailors. The Bolshevik Petersburg Committee and Petersburg military organization sent men to Kronstadt to help organize and lead insurrection, and a Trudovik Duma deputy, Fedot Onipko, also came to take part. The Kronstadt unit representatives and revolutionaries were thus assured that they had the full backing of the revolutionary parties. They were confident that sailors, miners, and artillerists would rise without hesitation, and that part of the infantry would join once the insurrection was under way. The major weakness was that sailors lacked rifles, so the first act—set for midnight—would be to capture the arsenal.[44]

No sooner had all revolutionaries finally agreed to support insurrection than the entire enterprise unravelled. During the afternoon of the 19th, careless handling of munitions at Sveaborg set off an explosion in a powder magazine that killed and injured sixty mutineers. The artillerists might still have been able to take the rest of the fortress by storm and were preparing to do so when the battleship *Tsesarevich* and the cruiser *Bogatyr* steamed up and began shelling the islands. Grand Duke Nikolai Nikolaevich, commander of the Petersburg military district, had feared the ships would mutiny and only the insistence of Quartermaster General Raukh had overcome his considerable reluctance to send them. Their guns manned by officers, cadets, and trusted sailors, the ships pounded the islands, and on the night of the 19th the Sveaborg artillerists decided to surrender the next day, as many as possible escaping in the meantime.[45] In Kronstadt, the authorities learned the details of the revolutionaries' plan a few hours before the insurrection began—not through Azef, apparently, but from local sources—and they positioned infantry to block the sailors as soon as they emerged from their barracks.

The sailors on shore rose (killing five officers), as did the miners (killing two officers) and sappers. Infantry drove the sailors back into their barracks with scarcely any gunfire, but the miners and sappers captured one of the outer forts. The artillerists did not rise, at least in part because they had thought insurrection postponed and were not fully aware or convinced of the wisdom of the change in plans. The crew of the one ship in port (the battleship *Alexander II*), also poorly informed, did not rise but refused to go ashore to help suppress the rising. When they learned they stood alone, the miners and sappers surrendered. By the morning of the 20th, execution of mutineers was already under way.[46] The SD military organization in Revel engineered mutiny on the cruiser *Pamiat' Azova* on the night of July 19–20. In taking over the ship, mutineers killed six officers and wounded others, and that frightened most of the crew. During the evening of the 20th the petty officers, fearing for their own lives, recaptured the ship. Ilia Fundaminskii was arrested when he came on board later that night.[47]

There was nothing revolutionaries could have done to salvage the Baltic insurrections, but they did provide a sorry epilogue. In approving the insurrection in Kronstadt, the Menshevik-controlled SD Central Committee had on July 19 attempted to convene a conference of all revolutionary groups to proclaim at last a general strike, and the Bolshevik-dominated SD Petersburg Committee had set about organizing a city-wide strike to support the Sveaborg and Kronstadt insurgents. Failing to gather representatives of the revolutionary parties, the SD Central Committee on its own issued an appeal for a general strike under the slogan, "Struggle for the Duma as an Organ of Power for Convening the Constituent Assembly" (as infelicitous in Russian as in English), and sent out emissaries to the major cities to give local committees similar instructions. Since Bolsheviks had opposed a strike to support the Duma ever since the dissolution, the Bolshevik members of the SD Central Committee issued a sharp protest, and the Bolsheviks' refusal to agitate for a strike linked in any way with the Duma badly disrupted preparations for a strike in Petersburg. Eventually the Petersburg Committee (or a part of it—the majority felt this amounted to a coup) and the Central Committee did agree to begin a strike on July 21, but the goal of the strike remained unclear.[48]

On the very eve of the strike, the night of July 20–21, the Mensheviks finally organized a conference of the principal revolutionary organizations (the Bolsheviks, not being a separate party, did not participate). At the outset only the Trudoviks and the Mensheviks themselves favored an immediate general strike. The Bund and the PPS agreed to the strike only because it appeared that the Russians were going to go ahead anyway. The SRs continued to oppose a strike, and proposed that the initiative should instead be left to the village, or that the Baltic insurgents be supported by other military insurrections. In the end the SRs gave in, conceding that it would be criminal to call on the army to revolt without providing maximum support. All parties involved in the negotiations had at last agreed to a strike—the soldiers and sailors of Sveaborg and Kronstadt had forced them to it—but most did so only against their better judgment.[49]

A strike called over so much opposition, preceded by almost two weeks of agitation against a strike and several days of wrangling over its purpose, and which began when everyone knew that the Baltic insurrections had already been suppressed, could not help but fail. Workers who had not previously been involved in strikes downed tools in Petersburg, street car drivers went out, and even the cabmen struck. By July 22 roughly 60,000 of Petersburg's workers, one-quarter of the total, were on strike. But the workers in some of the largest and most politicized plants—the Semiannikov, Obukhov, and Baltic works, the most important shops in the Putilov works—refused to take part. Since workers in the major plants had not gone out, by July 23 striking workers were returning to their jobs. They let it be known that they felt betrayed by the workers whom they had expected to show the way, and that they would not soon again take part in a political strike. Normally activist workers explained that they would strike only for the final showdown with the government, and that a precondition for this was a stronger peasant movement and, especially, participation by the railway union. Railway workers said they could join only during the final, most critical stage of the strike. A complete fiasco in Petersburg, the general strike never got off the ground anywhere else. The Moscow SD committee, after considerable resistance, agreed to call a strike; it got under way on July 24 and miscarried almost immediately. In Sevastopol and Odessa, Bolsheviks and Mensheviks together refused to call a strike, turned down as well their Central Committee's call for military insurrection, and forced the Sevastopol SRs to cancel a garrison insurrection at the last minute. SR committees in the provinces refused to foment peasant disorders that they believed to be poorly prepared and untimely.[50] Only in Petersburg had the Baltic insurrections persuaded revolutionaries even temporarily that July was a good month for revolution.

Revolutionary Theory versus the Psychology of Revolution

The attempt to overthrow the Tsarist regime in July 1906 failed so ignominiously that the failure has about it the aura of inevitability. Many of the circumstances contributing to the fiasco could not have been altered. Given that the military organizations had drawn in large numbers of soldiers and sailors, it was inevitable that the authorities would in some garrisons, as in Kronstadt, get wind of plans for insurrection. Revolutionary sentiment in the armed forces was so explosive that some mutinies, as at Sveaborg, naturally broke out ahead of schedule and disrupted the revolutionaries' plans. Given the ideological differences among them, and the gravity of a decision to call for a general strike or insurrection, the revolutionary parties were bound to differ over tactics and strategy. In warning against precipitate action, SRs and Bolsheviks displayed an admirable capacity for caution and responsibility: revolution was a dangerous business and lives ought not to be needlessly squandered. Yet the Bolsheviks' and SRs' persistent campaign to delay the assault on the regime derived from a wrongheaded analysis of peasant rebellion and deserves much of the credit for the failure of the general strike even to get off the ground.

The regime at midsummer was in an unenviable situation. By late June the army was of such doubtful reliability that the government in effect conceded rural Russia to peasant rebellion, and agrarian disorders achieved the same level as in November 1905. From the regime's point of view, the only saving feature of agrarian rebellion in the summer of 1906 was that peasants were withholding labor and rent rather than burning and looting. That reduced the level of violence, but rendered brute force a less effective means of suppressing peasants (a point made well by a contemporary cartoon that had cossacks riding station behind peasants at the plow). Furthermore, in 1906 the Duma provided peasants better cover for rebellion than had the myth of Imperial approval to seize land in 1905, because the Duma really did promise land. Peasants by no means accepted the dispersal calmly, and in the immediate aftermath continued to view the Duma as an agency expressing their views and the authority for seizing land. The behavior of the Trudovik Onipko's constituents in Stavropol Province was indicative of the Duma's capacity to arouse peasants even after July 9. When they learned Onipko had been arrested in Kronstadt, they gathered by the thousands to demand the release of "the people's elect." Telegrams and petitions to Petersburg failing to secure his release, the peasants turned to the almighty, ordering up special religious services "for the health and liberation of Fedot Mikhailov" and demanding that the clergy pray for Onipko rather than the Tsar. Peasants drove recalcitrant clergymen—fifteen in the space of a few days—from the churches and told them to seek their daily bread from those for whom they prayed. Within a week, full-scale peasant rebellion was under way in Stavropol Province.[51]

Revolutionaries knew in July that peasant rebellion was mounting fast, but they misunderstood its dynamics. Both Bolsheviks and SRs assumed that peasant rebellion was a function of seasonal changes in the peasants' physical environment and rhythm of work, yet in 1905 and 1906 every forecast based on the seasonal cycle proved wrong. In 1905 peasant rebellion peaked during the winter dead season, despite the SR belief that it would not. In 1906, peasants rebelled neither at spring planting nor after the harvest. Peasant rebellion in 1905 and 1906 followed not the seasons, but events in the cities that affected the peasants' view of the regime's authority—urban disorders in 1905, the behavior of the Duma in 1906. Trudoviks, who really were peasants, understood this perfectly well. At the conference of revolutionary organizations on the night of July 20–21, a Trudovik answered the SR argument that workers should strike after peasants had risen by asserting that if the city rose so, probably, would the village. And he observed further that peasant rebellion developed irregularly, and that there would never be a moment at which one could state definitively that "the village" had risen.[52] Indeed, with news dribbling in late from rural areas, revolutionaries continued to anticipate through August that the harvest would bring full-scale agrarian rebellion and so the occasion for urban insurrection.[53] Peasants reacted to what was happening in the cities much more quickly than that, and immediately after the failure of the July general strike the number of agrarian disorders declined precipitously (see Table VII-1).

The behavior of the soldiers paralleled that of peasants in July, as it had throughout 1905 and 1906. The mutinies that began in May and continued unabated after July 9 followed from the soldiers' conviction that the Duma, first as reality and then as disembodied representative of the will of the Russian people, would overturn the existing social and military orders. Like peasants, many soldiers and sailors—in Poltava, Deshlagar, Kronstadt, Sveaborg, Revel—were willing to take up arms against the regime after July 9. Soldiers in Petersburg supported the July strike: the 200th Izhorsk regiment refused to perform guard duty at a munitions works when the workers went on strike. But when the strike collapsed, soldiers all over the city let it be known that workers had deserted them and had betrayed the mutineers of Sveaborg and Kronstadt, and after July 23 mutinies declined even more precipitously than peasant unrest: from sixteen between July 17 and 23, to two in the last week of July.[54] Suppression of the insurrections at Sveaborg and Kronstadt must have dulled the soldiers' appetite for mutiny, but news of the suppression did not deter the men of the 200th Izhorsk, and at Helsingfors harbor itself the crew of the cruiser *Kazbek* refused on July 20 to go to one of the islands to help round up surrendering artillerists. Suppression of military insurrection had not checked revolution in the army in 1905, either. What made mutiny unthinkable was the soldiers' conviction after July 23 that there was no alternative to the authority of the regime. Soldiers wished to rebel, and unlike peasants they had the means at their disposal to impose their own vision of the social order. But, like peasants, they could act only when they believed that the Duma, or an all-powerful revolutionary committee, or some other authority real or imagined, sanctioned their rebellion. By the end of July, soldiers could hardly have believed workers and revolutionaries were trustworthy, let alone that they represented an alternative to the Tsarist regime.

Mensheviks, then, had judged correctly: though they later claimed that their call for a general strike had been a mistake deriving from a conspiratorial party structure that impeded correct assessment of the popular mood, the dissolution of the Duma did provide an opportunity—perhaps the best during the entire revolution—to destroy the Tsarist regime.[55] Peasants and soldiers expected revolutionaries and workers to rise, and their behavior up to July 21 indicates that they would have supported a general strike. The condition that Bolsheviks and SRs held to be prerequisite for successful revolution—simultaneous upheaval in factory, village, and barracks—was very nearly met in July 1906. Only the workers were missing. That workers were capable of going on strike in large numbers at that point is an untestable proposition. What we do know is that the workers in small shops who were far more active throughout 1906 than in 1905 responded with alacrity to the call for a general strike in Petersburg, that the revolutionary parties had far larger organized followings in the major plants in mid-1906 than they had had at any time in 1905, that the workers in the large plants gave as their reason for not participating the arguments for delay that Bolsheviks and SRs had employed up to the very eve of the strike, and that revolutionaries almost everywhere outside the capitals refused even to attempt to promote a general strike. Had revolutionaries been preparing the workers for months to take advantage of rather than to ignore the dissolution of the Duma, had they issued a call for a strike immediately after July 9, the strike would certainly have been more impressive than it was, perhaps extensive enough to give an added boost to peasant rebellion and to trigger the final collapse of the army—and with it, of the regime.

Conclusion: Russian Society Viewed through Russian Mutiny

Once upon a time a young professor recited, in the conventional manner, the Tale of the 1905 Revolution. Industrial growth produced a large and restive working class and disrupted peasant society. The stirring of the lower classes revived the revolutionary movement and encouraged the nascent middle class, another product of Russia's socioeconomic development, to press its own claims on the regime. The regime could not manage the tension that its developmental policies generated, and its incompetence in stumbling into and then conducting war with Japan brought together all of the disparate strands of rebellion and triggered revolution. Departing somewhat from convention in order to underscore the seriousness of the revolution, the teller added that a goodly portion of the army mutinied as well. Discomfited, the audience murmured, and one of the listeners broke the thread of the narrative by asking how, in that case, the Tsarist regime survived until 1917. The teller paused. The motifs from Russian history that he had woven into his story—the disruptive effects of economic growth, the incompatibility of a static political system and a changing society—did not provide grounding for an answer. Nonetheless, he responded: the soldiers' behavior depended upon their perceptions of authority, and those perceptions changed as rapidly as the flux of events. The explanation, taken from a different tale, was utterly unconvincing.

The conventional socioeconomic analysis of Russian history is not wrong, but it does not explain the behavior of Russian soldiers in 1905 and 1906. Soldiers suppressed civilians, sometimes ferociously, from January through October 1905, mutinied from late October through early December, shot civilians again in December; they mutinied from May through July 1906, abruptly ceased to mutiny in late July. The same soldiers behaved in radically different ways in rapid succesion—two complete cycles of rebellion and submission in ten months. No changes in their own immediate situation can account for this, and the events that so dramatically and rapidly altered their behavior had in only one case an immediate bearing on the army. They were not even much alike. The October general strike, October Manifesto, and ensuing breakdown of civil government were incomparably more traumatic than the meeting of the Duma, which caused excitement but no urban upheaval. The regime's show of force and the resulting insurrections in late 1905 put considerable pressure on soldiers, the very ungeneral strike of July 1906 threatened no one. All that these events had in common was the construction that soldiers put on them: they contained, for soldiers, unambiguous messages about the authority of the Tsarist regime. When they believed the regime's writ had expired, soldiers mutinied. When they believed the regime's authority to be intact, they repressed civilians. Neither hardship, nor ill-treatment at the hands of officers, nor class consciousness goaded soldiers into rebellion; those motivations became operative only when the psychological impediment to rebellion had been removed. Repression did not check mutiny so long as soldiers disbelieved in the authority of the regime, and was not necessary when soldiers no longer detected a break in the web of authority around them.

The sudden and repeated reversals of behavior that the soldiers' sensitivity to emblems of authority produced were not unique: the soldiers' revolution of 1905 and 1906 was a special case of Russian peasant rebellion. It is widely recognized that from at least the seventeenth century through the post-Emancipation agrarian disorders, Russian peasants rebelled when they believed that the Tsar—pretend or genuine—stood with them, and that they created myths to legitimize rebellion whenever there was a noticeable perturbation in the flow of power. Though unremarked, peasant rebellion followed an identical pattern in 1905 and 1906. Peasants did not rebel, in 1905 or earlier, because of crop failure, or onerous taxation, or even because urban commercial networks disrupted the village economy, though these conditions may have increased peasant receptivity to rumors and myths. Poverty and oppression were omnipresent in the villages; peasants seldom rebelled. They rebelled in 1905 when the explosion in urban Russia manifestly shook the regime, and in 1906 when the Duma appeared to provide an authority that countervailed the regime's. Peasants ceased to rebel when they concluded that the regime had bested its enemies. Peasant and soldier rebellion thus traced nearly identical courses in 1905 and 1906. Unlike soldiers, however, peasants were not required to repress other peasants once their rebellion was over; the alteration in their behavior was, therefore, not so dramatic. The soldiers' rebellion also began and ended suddenly, without the months of slowly ascending and descending incidence of disorders characteristic of peasant rebellion. Soldiers had far more at stake than peasants in properly interpreting the signals bearing on the regime's authority. What is remarkable is that, like peasants, they lost their inhibitions and fear of reprisals so completely in brief bursts of rebellion.

That psychology of obedience and revolt was rooted in the most basic social and cultural structures of Russian society. Submissiveness was the psychological complement to the environmental and social arrangements that constricted peasant society. Personal experience and collective wisdom taught peasants that they might maneuver around, deceive, or propitiate, but never escape the powerful men who controlled their lives. And peasants were constantly reminded of their helplessness: at the slightest sign of resistance to officials or gentry, soldiers descended on the villages. Submission did not foster among Russian peasants bonds of identity with their overlords. They prized myths and legends of a world without gentry and officials. Moreover, the gulf that must naturally divide those who wield power, however limited, from those who are utterly dependent was made wider by the cultural differences between peasants, whose beliefs and customs looked back to pre-Petrine Russia, and the educated who, however much they remained Russians, took their cultural cues from Europe. The natural repulsion between peasant and official societies was nearly as strong as the bond that held them together.

Repulsion overcame submission when peasants convinced themselves that they had the backing of the Tsar or some other agency more powerful than the bearers of power around them. When they saw the system of controls break down, peasants resurrected the latent myth of the good Tsar who blessed their rebellion. Rebellion was the more determined because sanctioned from on high; it was to the same extent vulnerable, because the sanction could be disconfirmed. But rebellion always lurked just beneath the surface of Russian society, and when it came it was profoundly centrifugal: peasants wished not to improve their standing in society, but to escape from the alien society of gentry and officials. Russian society in rebellion moved rapidly toward collapse, as it did after October 17, 1905, and as it was on the way to doing in June and July 1906. After February 1917, there was no force to check disintegration, and Russian society collapsed catastrophically.

The polarity of peasant and European Russias was the dominant characteristic of Russian society, but it was not absolute. There were some small intermediate strata, of which by the early twentieth century factory workers were one and, in a different way, merchants another. But if these groups shaded the socio-cultural division, they did not efface it, or provide a bond between the two Russias. When the two Russias clashed, groups in the middle were either pulverized or pulled into the orbit of one Russia or the other.

The gulf between traditional and European Russias loomed just as wide from the European side. Liberals and revolutionaries were fully aware of the peasants' latent potential for rebellion against the institutions of official society. Liberals recoiled in fear, because they understood that peasant rebellion threatened to destroy their world; but what they took to be anarchy was in the peasants' view an orderly society in which the culture of gentlemen had no place. Revolutionaries contemplated peasant rebellion with hope, but without much understanding. One of the themes of this study has been the failure of revolutionaries to comprehend what drove soldiers and peasants to rebel. That has not been meant as belittlement, or even criticism, any more than one belittles peasants by pointing out the limitations of the peasant mentality. Here and there, in fact, one catches a glimmer of comprehension among revolutionaries—in the recognition by the spokesman for the Petersburg SR military organization, for instance, that there was something unique about the psychology that underlay soldier rebellion. But most of what revolutionaries had to say about soldiers and peasants was either wrong or beside the point. Revolutionaries did get a lot right—the regime's dependence on armed force for its existence, the naiveté of the belief that reform could be obtained without violence, the liberals' ultimate fear of the aspirations of peasants and workers. They understood their own society well. They did not understand peasant Russia.

It is of course easier to discern the great fault lines in a society from a distance than when standing on top of them, but revolutionaries did not so much fail to see, as see them through mental constructs nearly as imperfect as those of peasants. Revolutionaries placed peasants in hierarchies (the village bourgeoisie versus the village proletariat) and continua (the laboring peasantry together with other laboring classes) that they believed to be universal. They outfitted peasants with bourgeois, petit bourgeois, or socialist goals that might, with detailed codicils, have been plausible but did not immediately provide an accurate gauge of what peasants were about. The obscuring veil that this terminology produced darkened completely when revolutionaries divided the world into the "conscious" and the "unconscious." The esoteric meaning of those words had a respectable lineage in Western revolutionary theory, but applied to Russia coincided disconcertingly with the view official Russia took of the inferior classes: the revolutionary's unconscious peasant or proletarian was the nobleman's and

officer's childlike peasant and soldier. The presumption that the unconscious peasant could be led into conscious adulthood rested on the
assumption that there was only one appropriate way to see the world.
Reasonable or not, that assumption made it difficult to fathom the
thoughts and behavior of the "unconscious." But the thinking of peasants and of social groups closely linked to the peasantry was no more
obscure to the revolutionaries than it was to liberals, or officers, or
bureaucrats, or any other group of European Russians.

The practical results of mutual incomprehension appeared during the
revolution. Revolutionaries, rational calculators that they were, attempted to determine the optimal combination of variables that would
warrant calling for a general strike or insurrection. Their equations were
internally consistent but at best proved irrelevant, as in October 1905,
and at worst yielded seriously misleading solutions, as in July 1906.
Calculations premised on the assumption that (just for example) soldiers
and peasants would share the view that there was advantage in delaying
rebellion until the proletariat had taken to the streets, or the harvest
taken in, could not provide useful guidelines for revolution in Russian
society. The very assumption that revolution was calculable, that there
was a best time for rebellion and that proper selection would maximize
the chance for success, ran directly counter to the peasant assumption
that authority could not be challenged, and that rebellion was possible
only when constraining authority had been eliminated. The peasant
conception of the social order of course made no sense at all to revolutionaries, and they could not abandon their own more sophisticated
analysis just because peasants and soldiers read apocalyptic significance
into mundane events. Revolutionaries, who had many variables to consider, hesitated to act—in October and December 1905, in July 1906.
Peasants and soldiers did not hesitate once they believed the one condition for rebellion had been met. The rational calculus betrayed revolutionaries. It very nearly betrayed the regime as well: the difficulty of
finding the proper set of rational responses to the dangers besetting
them paralyzed officials, and the regime's indecisiveness was one of the
prerequisites for peasant and soldier rebellion.

The soldiers' revolution of 1905 and 1906 thus illuminates, in a small
but crucial way, the discord at the heart of Russian society. Revolutionaries and soldiers lived in different worlds, had incompatible assumptions
about the structure of the social order, and attributed to their unique
visions transcendent truth. When soldiers and revolutionaries acted on
their different assumptions at the same time, they produced neither
harmony nor counterpoint, but dissonance. Yet disconfirming evidence
did not shake the soldiers' or revolutionaries beliefs, because those beliefs were solidly grounded in their own particular social experiences.

Mutually incomprehending, soldiers and revolutionaries were bound into a single society not through a network of social or cultural linkages, but by force alone. That force depended, ultimately, on the soldiers' inability to conceive of openly challenging the powers that be. Peasants as soldiers repressed themselves, and peasant submissiveness lent the Russian empire an appearance of extreme durability. When the psychological constraint on rebellion disappeared, however, there was nothing left to hold Russian society together. The soldiers' extreme volatility in 1905 and 1906 showed how fragile the barrier between stability and decomposition really was.

Abbreviations Used in Appendix, Notes, and Bibliography

Revoliutsiia 1905–1907 gg. Dokumenty i materialy.

ViL	*Revoliutsionnoe dvizhenie v Rossii vesnoi i letom 1905 goda. Aprel'-sentiabr',* parts 1–2, M., 1957–61
VP	*Vyshii pod"em revoliutsii 1905–1907 gg. Vooruzhennye vosstaniia. Noiabr'-dekabr' 1905 goda,* parts 1–4, M., 1955–1957
VPR	*Vtoroi period revoliutsii. 1906–1907 gody,* parts 1–3, M., 1957–1963
VPS	*Vserossiiskaia politicheskaia stachka v oktiabre 1905 goda,* parts 1–2, M., 1955

FR	*Free Russia*
IISH	International Institute for Social History
IS	*Izvestiia soveta rabochikh deputatov* (Spb.)
ISM	*Izvestiia moskovskogo soveta rabochikh deputatov*
ISSR	*Istoriia SSSR*
IV	*Istoricheskii vestnik*
IZ	*Istoricheskie zapiski*
JSH	*Journal of Social History*
KA	*Krasnyi arkhiv*
KDR	*Krest'ianskoe dvizhenie v Rossii* (followed by years of coverage)
KiS	*Katorga i ssylka*
KL	*Krasnaia letopis'*
L.	Leningrad
M.	Moscow
MG	*Moskovskaia gazeta*
NZh	*Novaia zhizn'*
Pg.	Petrograd
PI	*Poslednie izvestiia*
PR	*Proletarskaia revoliutsiia*

PSS   *Polnoe sobranie sochinenii*
RDR   *Rabochee dvizhenie v Rossii v 1901–1904 gg. Sbornik dokumentov,*
           L., 1975
RI   *Russkii invalid*
RR   *Revoliutsionnaia Rossiia*
Spb.   St. Petersburg
VI   *Voprosy istorii*
VS   *Voennyi sbornik*
VVB   *Voennye vosstaniia v Baltike v 1905–1906 gg., M., 1933*
VVZh   *Varshavskii voennyi zhurnal*

Appendix I.
Mutinies in 1905

The mutinies are listed by date of commencement: some could not be dated precisely; a few have been placed somewhat arbitrarily in a half-month period (and are so identified). In some cases the units involved in mutinies have been identified from the unit listings in *Kratkoe raspisanie sukhoputnykh voisk* and MacBean, *Handbook of the Russian Army*. Sources have been kept to the minimum necessary to identify the principal characteristics of and participants in the mutiny; other sources are available on almost all the mutinies.

The mutinies have been coded to indicate how they began (0–9) and ended (10–18), and to identify their other principal characteristics (21–25). Absence of a notation for a given characteristic (e.g., the presentation of demands, or attacks on officers) may only mean that the surviving evidence is too slender to yield the details of a mutiny.

0—the way in which mutiny began is unknown. 1—soldiers began mutiny without provocation. 2—information about other mutinies triggered mutiny. 3—mutiny began when officers arrested soldiers, or were about to do so, or (in a very few cases) did violence to soldiers. 4—soldiers began mutiny when officers attempted to impose restrictions on their movements or behavior, for instance (most frequently) attempting to prevent or disperse soldier meetings. 5—mutiny began when soldiers disobeyed a routine order (which may mean that they had plotted mutiny beforehand, though in most cases that appears not to have been the case). 6—mutiny began with a conflict over the money due soldiers, the equipment issue, food (food riots themselves have not been counted as mutiny), and so forth. 7—mutiny began with an altercation between soldiers and civilians. 8—revolutionary military organizations organized mutiny. 9—mutiny began with a fight between soldiers of different units. Many mutinies had no single cause, and in some cases the cause could reasonably be changed (e.g., the trigger for the *Potemkin* mutiny might be considered a conflict over food rather than the arrest of the sailors who protested). The number of mutinies whose origin is obscure is large, the likelihood that incomplete evidence has led to misidentification of origins in a few others equally great.

10—there is no information on how the mutiny ended. 11—mutiny ended when soldiers won concessions. 12—mutiny subsided without soldiers winning concessions or officers taking action against them. 13—mutiny ended when soldiers won concessions, but officers carried out arrests shortly thereafter. 14—mutiny subsided, arrests were made shortly afterwards (but soldiers ended their mutiny without threat of arrest). 15—arrests (without the assistance of military force) brought mutiny to an end. 16—mutiny ended when a reliable unit was drawn up against mutineers. 17—mutiny ended in an exchange of gunfire between reliable and mutinous troops. 18—mutiny ended when the unit was transferred. 18a—the unit transferred also won concessions.

21—reserves played a decisive role in the mutiny. 22—mutineers presented a set of demands. 22a—some of the demands were political. 22ad—some of the demands involved the Duma. 23—mutiny had an identifiably political element. 23a—mutineers refused to repress workers or peasants. 23b—mutineers organized a political demonstration. 23c—mutineers refused to replace striking workers, or struck along with the workers. 23d—mutineers dispatched a *nakaz* to the Duma. 23e—mutineers discussed and promised to support the Duma. (To these political mutinies should be added those coded 22a, 22ad; political characteristics have not been systematically identified for 1905, because so many mutinies were linked directly to the publication of the October Manifesto: the politics in these mutinies involved the soldiers' assumptions rather than their convictions.) 24—the mutiny involved violence. 24a—mutineers attacked officers, NCOs, or (in a few cases in 1906) police. 24b—mutineers did violence to their barracks or other property. 24c—mutineers fired their weapons (often only in the air). (To these violent mutinies should be added those coded 17.) 25—mutineers held a march.

There is a different list of 195 mutinies, October–December 1905, in Petrov, *Ocherki*, pp. 387–96. Many of the disturbances Petrov counts as mutiny do not meet my test (see the discussion in Chapter IV) or are based on insufficiently persuasive evidence. Nevertheless, the list is worth consulting because Petrov identifies characteristics that I have not (though the greater the reach for fineness of detail, the more likelihood of error). Petrov claims 76 mutinies for January–September 1905, but most of the evidence he presents indicates no more than individual disobedience or revolutionary agitation, not genuine mutiny. On the other hand, there were certainly a few more than the 23 mutinies that I have listed for January–October 17.

January. Morshansk. Medics. 6, 10, Petrov, *Ocherki*, p. 117.

January 9. Kronstadt. Sailors. 1, 11, 23a. Petrov, *Ocherki*, p. 118.

January 9. Petersburg. 14th naval *équipage*. 1, 15, 23a. Petrov, *Ocherki*, p. 118.

January 11–12. 3rd Pacific Squadron. Cruiser *Admiral Nakhimov*. 6, 11. Petrov, *Ocherki*, p. 116.

January 30. 3rd Pacific Squadron. Battleship *Orel*. 6, 11, 24. Petrov, *Ocherki*, p. 117.

April 14. Novaia Aleksandriia/Pulawy. 71st Belevsk and 72nd Tula infantry. 1, 14, 23b. Petrov, *Ocherki*, pp. 126–36; *Iskra*, 15 May 1905; 1 July 1905.

April 17. Manchuria. 10th Siberian rifles. 5, 10, 24a. Poleshchuk, "Revoliutsionnoe dvizhenie v Man'chzhurskoi," p. 310.

May 24–25. Tashkent. Turkestan sapper battalion and military telegraph company. 6, 15, 22. Cherkasov, "Revoliutsionnoe dvizhenie," p. 460; Piaskovskii, *Revoliutsiia 1905–1907*, pp. 162–3.

June 14–25. Battleships *Potemkin* and *St. George,* training ship *Prut.* 3, 12, 23, 24ac. For sources, see Chapter 3, note 44.

June 15–16. Libava. 6, 9, 13, 15 naval *équipages.* 6, 16, 22, 23, 24c. *Revoliutsiia 1905–1907 gg. v Latvii. Dokumenty i materialy,* Riga, 1956, pp. 205–11, 446 fn. 65; Andreev, "Revoliutsionnoe dvizhenie," pp. 103–14; Kirilov, *Istoriia 114-go,* pp. 295–6.

June 16–17. Samarkand. 7th Turkestan rifles, 5th company. 3, 10. Soifer, *Revoliutsionnoe dvizhenie,* p. 31; Petrov, *Ocherki,* pp. 150–1.

June 20. Kherson. Disciplinary battalion, 3rd company. 0, 15, 24a. Petrov, *Ocherki,* p. 146.

June 20–25. Ust-Dvinsk fortress. Fortress artillery, mine company. 1, 11, 22, 23. Surikov, "Revoliutsionnoe dvizhenie," pp. 268–70; *ViL,* pp. 409–10.

June 22. Kolpino. Naval company. 5, 10. Petrov, *Ocherki,* p. 206.

June 25. Baltic Fleet. Cruiser *Minin.* 0, 16. Petrov, *Ocherki,* p. 147.

July 8. Kiev. 7th and 14th sapper battalions. 0, 10, 22. Petrov, *Ocherki,* p. 151.

July 11. Sukhum. 258th Sukhum infantry. 3, 10. Petrov, *Ocherki,* p. 150; *Revoliutsiia 1905–1907 gg. v Gruzii,* pp. 244–5.

July 29. Mineralnye Vody. 81st Apsheron infantry. 0, 10, 23, 24a. Steklov, "Revoliutsionnoe dvizhenie," p. 403; *Iskra,* no. 110, 10 Sept. 1905.

Summer. Mineralnye Vody. Ossetian cavalry division. 1, 10, 23a. Steklov, "Revoliutsionnoe dvizhenie," p. 382.

August 1. Chita. 18th Vologda infantry, one company. 1, 10, 23a. Petrov, *Ocherki,* p. 151.

August 26. Kars. 2nd Chernomorsk Kuban cossacks. 3, 12. *Revoliutsionnoe dvizhenie v Armenii,* pp. 339–40.

October 13. Eniseisk. Local detail. 5, 10. Petrov, *Ocherki,* pp. 302–3.

October 16. Petersburg. 14th and 18th naval *équipages.* 1, 12, 24b. "Iz bumag D. F. Trepova," pp. 460–2.

October 18. Petersburg. 8th naval *équipage.* 1, 16. *VPS,* v. 1, pp. 377, 391–2.

October 20. Baku. Caspian naval *équipage.* 1, 16, 23. *Revoliutsiia 1905 v Zakavkaz'i,* p. 85; "Napadenie matrosov kaspiiskogo ekipazha na patrioticheskuiu manifestatsiiu v 1905 g. (Na osnovanii ofits. dokumentov)," *Krasnyi baltiets,* 1921 no. 2, pp. 43–6.

October 22–23. Ust-Dvinsk fortress. 4th and 5th companies fortress artillery, sappers, miners. 4, 12, 22. *Revoliutsiia 1905–1907 gg. v Latvii,* pp. 224–5; Korol'-kov, "Revoliutsionnoe dvizhenie . . . Vilenskogo," p. 164.

October 22–27. Askhabad. 6th Turkestan rifle brigade (4 battalions), 6th Geok-Tepinsk reserve battalion, 1st Transcaspian railway battalion (3rd company), 2nd Turkestan artillery brigade (5th mountain battery). 1, 14, 22, 24, 25. Annanepesov, *Uchastie soldatskikh mass,* pp. 41–7; Piaskovskii, *Revoliutsiia 1905–1907,* pp. 225, 258–60; Petrov, *Ocherki,* pp. 266–8; *SO,* 15 Nov. 1905.

October 24–25. Kars. Fortress sapper company. 3, 15, 22. Petrov, *Ocherki,* pp. 263–5, 328, 387; *Baku,* 12 Nov. 1905.

October 25–26. Krasnovodsk, 8th Krasnovodsk Turkestan reserve battalion. 4, 12. Annanepesov, *Uchastie soldatskikh mass,* p. 51.

October 26–27. Kronstadt. 2nd, 3rd, 4th, 7th, 15th naval *équipages,* fortress artillery, fortress mine company, 2nd fortress infantry battalion (second company). 3, 17, 24c. For sources, see Chapter 4, note 31.

October 28. Merv. 7th Merv reserve battalion, 4th company. 3, 13. "K istorii revoliutsionnogo dvizheniia v Rossii (oktiabr'–noiabr' 1905 g.)," *Istoricheskii arkhiv*, 1955 no. 1, p. 129; Soifer, *Revoliutsionnoe dvizhenie*, p. 39.

October 28. Petersburg. Guard sapper battalion. 0, 10, 22. *NZh*, 29 Oct. 1905.

October 28–29. Vladivostok. Cruiser *Rossiia*. 0, 18, 22. *VP*, v. 1, pp. 250–1.

October 28–29. Vladikavkaz. 81st Apsheronsk infantry. 1, 13, 21, 22. *Severnaia Osetiia v revoliutsii*, pp. 254–60; *Novoe obozrenie*, 4 Nov. 1905; *Revoliutsiia 1905 v. Zakavkaz'i*, p. 88.

October 29–30. Sveaborg. Fortress artillery. 1, 11, 22a. Tsion, *Tri dnia*, pp. 19–33; Muratov, *Revoliutsionnoe dvizhenie*, pp. 77–81; Petrov, *Ocherki*, pp. 177–8, 268–72; Andreev, "Revoliutsionnoe dvizhenie," pp. 19–21; *NZh*, 23 Nov. 1905.

October 30–31. Vladivostok. Siberian naval *équipage*, Khabarovsk reserve regiment, 1st and 2nd Vladivostok fortress mine companies, East Siberian mine company, Novokievsk mine company, torpedo boats. 7, 12, 21, 24c. *VP*, v. 1, pp. 228–52; "Pogrom Vladivostoka 30 i 31 oktiabria," *Priroda i liudi Dal'nego Vostoka*, 1906 no. 1, pp. 9–12; Ivanov, "Revoliutsionnye dni na Vostoke," *Sibirskie voprosy*, 1907 no. 36, pp. 18–21.

October 30–November 1. Pogranichnaia station. 3rd Transamur railway battalion, 18th company. 2, 12, 23b, 24b. Poleshchuk, "Revoliutsionnoe dvizhenie v Man'chzhurskoi," p. 321; *Russkoe slovo*, 13 Nov. 1905.

October, after October 17. Moscow. 4th Nesvizh Grenadiers. 1, 11, 21, 22. Petrov, *Ocherki*, p. 387; Gavrilov, *Voennaia rabota*, pp. 62–3 (Gavrilov misidentifies the regiment).

November 2. Batum. Fortress artillery, two companies. 3, 11. *Chernomorskii vestnik*, 15 Nov. 1905; Steklov, "Revoliutsionnoe dvizhenie," p. 393.

November 2–3. Grozny. 82nd Dagestan infantry. 3, 10, 22. Steklov, "Revoliutsionnoe dvizhenie," p. 404; Petrov, *Ocherki*, p. 388; Kireev, *Rabochii klass*, p. 119.

November 2–December 16. Baranovichi. 2nd reserve railway battalion, elements of other railway battalions. 0, 16, 22, 24a. *VP*, v. 4, pp. 180–1, 189, 209, 217–8, 795–6 fn. 43; Korol'kov, "Revoliutsionnoe dvizhenie . . . Vilenskogo," pp. 170–1; *Nachalo*, 18 Nov. 1905.

November 5. Gomel. 160th depot infantry battalion. 1, 10, 21. *VP*, v. 4, pp. 268–9, 797 fn. 50.

November 4–5. Grodno. 12th and 26th artillery brigades. 2, 16, 21, 22. *VP*, v. 4, pp. 121–2; Korol'kov, "Revoliutsionnoe dvizhenie . . . Vilenskogo," pp. 168–9, 178–9; Muratov, *Revoliutsionnoe dvizhenie*, pp. 199–201; Petrov, *Ocherki*, p. 273; *Nachalo*, 29 Nov. 1905.

November 5. Petersburg. 14th naval *équipage*. 3, 11. "K istorii revoliutsionnogo dvizheniia v Rossii," *Istoricheskii arkhiv*, 1955 no. 1, p. 128.

November 5 and later. Gori. 259th Gori infantry, 263rd Novo-Baiazetsk infantry (2nd battalion), Caucasus reserve artillery brigade (8th battery). 0, 11, 22. *Tiflisskii listok*, 13 Nov. 1905; *Vozrozhdenie*, 15 Nov. 1905; 19 Nov. 1905; *Novoe obozrenie*, 12 Nov. 1905.

November 5–ca. 20. Mogilev. 314th Kadnikov infantry. 1, 18, 21, 22. *VP,* v. 4, pp. 269–70; *Novaia zaria,* 17 Nov. 1905; *SO,* 27 Nov. 1905; *Severo-zapadnyi krai,* 6 Dec. 1905.

November 6. Nizhnii Novgorod. 307th Arzamas infantry. 5, 10, 21. *VP,* v. 2, p. 93; *Nachalo,* 16 Nov. 1905; *Nizhegorodskii listok,* 10 Nov. 1905.

November 6. Goldingen. 50th Irkutsk dragoons. 0, 10, 22. Petrov, *Ocherki,* p. 289.

November 6, 9. Tiflis. Clerks at the staff of the Caucasus military district. 0, 11, 22. *Vozrozhdenie,* 20 Nov. 1905.

November 6–11. Dvinsk. 246th Griazovets infantry (elements of other units). 0, 10, 22. Korol'kov, "Revoliutsionnoe dvizhenie . . . Vilenskogo," p. 169; Petrov, *Ocherki,* p. 388; *NZh,* 9 Nov. 1905.

November 8. Samarkand. 2nd Transcaspian railway battalion (two companies). 0, 11, 22. *VP,* v. 3 book 2, pp. 941–3, 951–2; Cherkasov, "Revoliutsionnoe dvizhenie," pp. 327–8; Annanepesov, *Uchastie soldatskikh mass,* pp. 53–4.

November 8–9. Aleksandrovskoe (Irkutsk Province). Local detail. 5, 14, 24c. *Obzor revoliutsionnogo dvizhenie v okruge Irkutskoi sudovoi palaty,* p. 75; Poleshchuk, "Revoliutsionnoe dvizhenie . . . Irkutskogo," pp. 317–18.

November 9. Kremenchug. 272nd Korocha infantry. 5, 11, 22. *SO,* 17 Nov. 1905; *Severnyi golos,* 7 Dec. 1905.

November 9. Tiflis. 15th Tiflis Grenadiers. 7, 11, 21, 22. *Tiflisskii listok,* 11 Nov. 1905; *Novoe obozrenie,* 11 Nov. 1905; *Vozrozhdenie,* 15 Nov. 1905.

November 10. Aleksandrovskoe (Irkutsk Province). 2nd Sofia infantry, one battalion. 5, 11, 21. Poleshchuk, "Revoliutsionnoe dvizhenie v Man'chzhurskoi," pp. 322–3.

November 10–11. Stavropol. 249th Maikop reserve battalion. 3, 12, 22, 24c. Korol'kov, "Revoliutsionnoe dvizhenie . . . Kavkazskogo," pp. 345–6; *Tiflisskii listok,* 17 Nov. 1905; *SO,* 17 Nov. 1905; *Nachalo,* 24 Nov. 1905.

November 10–14. Petersburg. Electrotechnical company. 1, 16, 22. *VP,* v. 1, pp. 531–3; Akhun and Petrov, *Bol'sheviki,* pp. 33–43; Poluektov, "1905 g. v kazarme," pp. 112–5; *Nachalo,* 26 Nov. 1905; *NZh,* 13 Nov. 1905.

November 10–15. Riga. 115th Viazma and 177th Izborsk infantry. 0, 16, 22. Korol'kov, "Revoliutsionnoe dvizhenie . . . Vilenskogo," pp. 162–3; *SO,* 19 Nov. 1905; *Russkoe slovo,* 26 Nov. 1905; *Golos soldata* (SD, Riga), no. 4, 6 May 1906.

November 11–15. Sevastopol. 49th Brest infantry, 49th depot infantry battalion, fortress sapper company, fortress artillery, naval barracks, cruiser *Ochakov,* mine cruiser *Griden',* battleship *Panteleimon,* torpedo boat *Svirepyi,* destroyer *Zavetnyi,* destroyer *Skoryi,* destroyer *Zorkii,* torpedo boats 265, 268, 270, training ship *Dnestr,* training ship *Prut,* gun boat *Uralets.* 4, 17, 22, 24c, 25. *VP,* v. 1, pp. 266–342; Voronitsyn, *Leitenant Shmidt,* M.-L., 1925; Drobot, "Sevastopol'skoe vosstanie 1905 g.," *PR,* 1923 no. 6–7, pp. 109–63; no. 10, pp. 61–94.

November, not after the 12th. Novgorod Volynsk. 18th depot infantry battalion. 0, 10, 21. *NZh,* 12 Nov. 1905.

November 12. Vladivostok. Kvantun fortress artillery (returned POWs). 4, 16, 24a. Korol'kov. "Revoliutsionnoe dvizhenie . . . Priamurskogo," pp. 365–6; *VP,* v. 2, p. 1145 fn. 246; *Novoe vremia,* 15 Nov. 1905.

November 13. Askhabad. 1st Transcaspian railway battalion, 3rd company. 3, 12, 22. Cherkasov, "Revoliutsionnoe dvizhenie," p. 296.

November 13–14. Batum. Fortress mine company, fortress sapper company, fortress infantry battalion, fortress artillery, elements of 130th Kherson and 260th Adragansk infantry, 1st Kuban plastoon battalion. 1, 11, 22. Samoilenko, "Sredi kazakov," pp. 180–4; Steklov, Revoliutsionnoe dvizhenie," pp. 393–5; *Chernomorskii vestnik*, 15 Nov. 1905; 17 Nov. 1905.

November 13–14. Ust-Dvinsk fortress. Fortress sapper company, pontoon company, fortress artillery, mine company, fortress infantry battalion. 1, 12, 22. *VP,* v. 4, pp. 371–2, 378; *SO,* 17 Nov. 1905.

November 13–14. Chardzhui. Amu-Daria flotilla. 0, 11, 22. Cherkasov, "Revoliutsionnoe dvizhenie," p. 324; *VP,* v. 3 book 2, pp. 1006–9.

November 13–14. Tiflis. 1st Caucasus sapper battalion. 0, 11, 22. *Russkoe slovo,* 15 Nov. 1905; *Vozrozhdenie,* 15 Nov. 1905; 16 Nov. 1905; 17 Nov. 1905; Steklov, "Revoliutsionnoe dvizhenie," pp. 387–9.

November 13–14. Samara. 312th Berezina infantry. 1, 11, 21. *Samarskii kur'er,* 15 Nov. 1905; Bliumental', "Sotsial-demokratiia," pp. 266, 275.

November 13–15. Tiflis. Artillery depot. 0, 11, 22. *Revoliutsiia 1905 v Zakavkaz'i,* p. 102; *Vozrozhdenie,* 19 Nov. 1905.

November 13–14, 24–25. Petersburg. 14th and 18th naval *équipages.* 0, 16, 22. Petrov, *Ocherki,* pp. 174–5, 390; *Obnovlennaia Rossiia,* 15 Nov. 1905; *NZh,* 19 Nov. 1905; 25 Nov. 1905; *Nachalo,* 25 Nov. 1905; 26 Nov. 1905; *SO,* 26 Nov. 1905; 27 Nov. 1905; *Pravo,* 27 Nov. 1905; [Raukh], "Dnevnik," p. 88.

November, before the 14th. Kars. Fortress infantry regiment, 1st company. 0, 11. *Russkie vedomosti,* 16 Nov. 1905.

November 14–15. Rostov (Iaroslavskii). 3rd Grenadier artillery brigade. 1, 10, 22. *VP,* v. 2, pp. 240–1; *Russkoe slovo,* 21 Nov. 1905; *NZh,* 27 Nov. 1905.

November 14–16. Lagodekhi (Tiflis Province). 264th Lori infantry. 7, 11, 22, 24a. Korol'kov, "Revoliutsionnoe dvizhenie . . . Kavkazskogo," p. 355.

November 15. Kharkov. 165th Lutsk infantry (three companies). 0, 12, 21, 22. *VP,* v. 3 book 1, pp. 350–1; Tkachukov, "1905 g. v Khar'kove," *Puti revoliutsii,* 1925 no. 3, p. 10; Iakovlev, "Khar'kovskoe likholet'e," *IV,* 1910 no. 11, pp. 544–5.

November ca. 15. Dzharkent. 1st or 2nd Siberian cossacks, one squadron. 5, 10. *VP,* v. 3 book 2, pp. 959–60.

November, not after 15th. Petersburg. Clerks at the cossack administration. 0, 10, 22. *NZh,* 15 Nov. 1905.

November 15. Taiga station, Siberian railway. 3rd Narva infantry, 1st battalion. 5, 11, 21. *VP,* v. 2, 1065–6, 1094; *Samarskaia luka,* 21 Nov. 1906.

November 15–16. Tashkent. 1st Tashkent reserve battalion, Turkestan reserve artillery park, 1st Turkestan mobile artillery park. 8, 17, 22, 24c. *VP,* v. 3 book 2, pp. 980–94; Cherkasov, "Revoliutsionnoe dvizhenie," pp. 288–93, 322–4.

November 15. Karkaralinsk. Local detail. 1, 10, 23b. *Revoliutsionnoe dvizhenie v Kazakhstane,* pp. 86–7.

November 15–17. Shaugolan (Manchuria). 123rd Kozlov infantry. 0, 10, 21. Petrov, *Ocherki,* pp. 219, 239, 390.

November 15–January 21. Chita. 141st Mozhaisk infantry, 144th Kashira infantry, 3rd reserve railway battalion, 4th Transbaikal cossack foot battalion, 2nd

Chita reserve battalion, 6th East Siberian reserve battalion, Transbaikal cossack squadron, 2nd East Siberian telegraph battalion, Chita local detail, Transbaikal cossack reserve battery, 1st Transbaikal Chita cossacks. 1, 16, 22, 23b. *VP*, v. 2, pp. 948–9, 951–60, 965–7, 971–5, 1139 fn. 198; Poleshchuk, "Revoliutsionnoe dvizhenie . . . Irkutskogo," pp. 341–77; *Karatel'nye ekspeditsii*, pp. 139–40, 159; "Dvizhenie v voiskakh na Dal'nem Vostoke," pp. 332, 364; B. Rybal'skii-Bestuzhev, "V stolitse zabaikal'skoi 'respubliki'," *Volia*, 24 May 1906; 29 May 1906; 31 May 1906; 12 June 1906.

November, first half. Rembertow. Artillerists. 1, 10, 22. Korol'kov, "Revoliutsionnoe dvizhenie . . . Vilenskogo," p. 177; Pawłowski, *Wojskowa*, p. 238; *Russkie vedomosti*, 23 Nov. 1905.

November, first half (arbitrarily). Ostrov. 91st depot infantry battalion. 3, 10, 21. Korablev, "Revoliutsionnoe dvizhenie," p. 137.

November, not after 16th. Iaroslavl. 11th Fanagoriisk Grenadiers. 0, 10, 21. Petrov, *Ocherki*, p. 390; *VP*, v. 2, pp. 230–1; *NZh*, 30 Nov. 1905.

November, ca 16th. Odessa. 4th depot rifle battalion. 0, 11, 22. *VP*, v. 3 book 1, p. 501.

November 16. Krasnoiarsk. 2nd Sofia and 191st Mozhaisk infantry, one train each. 5, 11. *Karatel'nye ekspeditsii*, p. 198; Poleshchuk, "Revoliutsionnoe dvizhenie v Man'chzhurskoi," pp. 313, 323.

November 16. Voronezh. 290th Lipetsk infantry, 11th company. 0, 10, 21, 22. *Revoliutsionnoe dvizhenie v Voronezhskoi gubernii*, p. 235; *Nachalo*, 17 Nov. 1905.

November 16. Tiflis. 16th Mingrelsk Grenadiers. 0, 11, 22. *Novoe obozrenie*, 18 Nov. 1905; *Vozrozhdenie*, 19 Nov. 1906.

November 16–17. Lomzha. 16th Ladoga infantry. 1, 16, 22, 24b. *VP*, v. 4, pp. 707–9; *Russkoe slovo*, 26 Nov. 1905; Pawłowski, *Wojskowa*, p. 235; Korol'kov, "Revoliutsionnoe dvizhenie . . . Vilenskogo," p. 176.

November 16–18. Kiev. Elements of 4th and 5th pontoon battalions, 5th, 7th, and 14th sapper battalions, band of 125th Kursk infantry, 2nd horse artillery division. 2, 17, 22, 25. *VP*, v. 3 book 1, pp. 228–65; Manilov, "Kievskaia voennaia organizatsiia"; Voronitsyn, *Istoriia odnogo katorzhnika*, pp. 27–46; Sukhomlinov, *Vospominaniia*, pp. 107–9; Vanovskii, "Burnye gody," pp. 16–21; *NZh*, 26 Nov. 1905; *Nachalo*, 23 Nov. 1905.

November 16–24. Ekaterinodar. 252nd Anapa reserve battalion. 2, 11, 22, 24a. *VP*, v. 2, pp. 401–2; *Revoliutsionnoe dvizhenie na Kubani*, pp. 135–9; Korol'kov, "Revoliutsionnoe dvizhenie . . . Kavkazskogo," pp. 341–2; *Nachalo*, 24 Nov. 1905; *Pravo*, 4 Dec. 1905; 18 Dec. 1905.

November 16–late November. Kursk. 203rd Graivoron and 204th Oboian infantry, military escort detail. 0, 10, 21, 22. *Revoliutsionnye sobytiia 1905–1907 gg. v Kurskoi gubernii*, pp. 99–100; *Russkoe slovo*, 27 Nov. 1905; 28 Nov. 1905; Drozdov, *Agrarnye volneniia*, p. 145; *Zhizn'*, 27 Nov. 1905.

November 16–December 3. Central Asian railway. 1st and 2nd Transcaspian railway battalion, Kizil-Arvat military escort detail, Kushka military telegraph company. 1, 12, 22. *VP*, v. 3 book 2, pp. 927–34, 937–40, 945–6, 996–7; Soifer, *Revoliutsionnoe dvizhenie*, pp. 54, 56–7, 64; Cherkasov, "Revoliutsionnoe dvizhenie," pp. 296–8, 324–7.

November 17. Kharkov. 269th Bogodukhovsk infantry. 0, 12, 21, 22, 25. *VP*, v. 3

book 1, pp. 344, 352–4; Tkachukov, "1905 g. v Khar'kove," *Puti revoliutsii*, 1925 no. 3, pp. 10–12; Kantsel'son, "Revoliutsionnoe dvizhenie," pp. 213–4.

November 17. Warsaw. 3rd Guards artillery brigade. 0, 16, 22. Korol'kov, "Revoliutsionnoe dvizhenie . . . Vilenskogo," p. 175; *Pravo*, 27 Nov. 1905.

November 17. Zlatoust. 214th depot battalion. 0, 10, 21. *VP*, v. 2, p. 875.

November 17–18. Sukhum. 258th Sukhum infantry, 2nd Laba Kuban cossacks (one squadron). 2, 10, 22. *Chernomorskii vestnik*, 29 Nov. 1905; *Vozrozhdenie*, 4 Dec. 1905.

November 17–20. Belyi Kliuch (Tiflis Province). 14th Gruzinsk Grenadiers. 1, 11, 21, 22. *Baku*, 25 Nov. 1905; Steklov, "Revoliutsionnoe dvizhenie," pp. 249–50.

November 17–20. Taganrog. 2nd reserve artillery brigade. 0, 10, 22. *1905–1907 gody na Donu*, pp. 249–50.

November 17–28. Piatigorsk. 250th Akhulginsk reserve infantry battalion, Caucasus reserve artillery brigade (one battery). 2, 11, 22, 25. For sources, see Chapter 5, note 81.

November 18. Voronezh. Voronezh disciplinary battalion. 3, 17, 24c. *VP*, v. 1, p. 142; *VP*, v. 2, pp. 330–3; V. Shpanets, *Lobnoe mesto. Voronezhskii distsiplinarnyi batal'on*, M., 1930, pp. 33–67.

November 18. Harbin. Unidentified infantry battalion. 0, 10. *Russko-iaponskaia voina. Iz dnevnikov*, p. 116.

November 18. Petersburg. Pavlov Guards infantry. 6, 10, 22. Akhun and Petrov, *Bol'sheviki*, p. 44; Petrov, *Ocherki*, pp. 200, 289, 391.

November 18–December 9. Ekaterinoslav. 133rd Simferopol, 134th Feodosiia, 278th Berdiansk infantry. 1, 12, 21, 22. *VP*, v. 1, p. 60; *VP*, v. 3 book 1, pp. 73–4, 94, 145–6, 166; *Ekaterinoslavshchina*, pp. 198–9, 206; *Izvestiia federativnogo soveta khar'kovskikh komitetov*, no. 5, 18 Dec. 1905.

November, not after the 18th. Riga. NCO training battalion. 0, 10, 22. *Nachalo*, 20 Nov. 1905; *Russkoe slovo*, 23 Nov. 1905.

November, ca. 19. Vyborg. 7th Finland rifles. 0, 10, 22. *SO*, 22 Nov. 1905; *Novoe vremia*, 1 Dec. 1905.

November 19–24. Ostrog. 32nd artillery brigade (three batteries). 1, 13, 22. *VP*, v. 3 book 1, pp. 12–3; Kantsel'son, "Revoliutsionnoe dvizhenie," pp. 225–6.

November 20. Moscow. Clerks on the military district staff. 6, 10, 22. *Bor'ba*, 30 Nov. 1905.

November 20. Telav (Tiflis Province). Bashkadykliar reserve battalion. 0, 11, 22. *Revoliutsiia 1905 v Zakavkaz'i*, p. 105.

November 20–21. Kutais. 79th Kurinsk, 257th Poti infantry (composite company). 0, 10, 22. *Revoliutsiia 1905–1907 gg. v Gruzii*, pp. 475–7; Starosel'skii, " 'Dni svobody'," pp. 286–7.

November 20, 25. Samara. Military escort detail. 2, 11, 22. Bliumental', "Sotsial-demokratiia," pp. 267, 272.

November 20–26. Tiflis. 1st and 2nd Caucasus sapper battalions, 4th Caucasus rifles, 15th Tiflis and 16th Mingrelsk Grenadiers, 1st Caucasus railway battalion, 44th Nizhegorodsk dragoons, 2 artillery batteries (probably Caucasus Grenadier artillery brigade). 8, 12, 22, 25. *Kavkazskii rabochii listok*, 23 Nov. 1905; 27 Nov. 1905; 30 Nov. 1905; *Tiflisskii listok*, 23 Nov. 1905; *Novoe obozrenie*,

23 Nov. 1905; *Revoliutsiia 1905 v Zakavkaz'i*, pp. 107–9; Petrov, *Ocherki*, p. 298; *Vozrozhdenie*, 27 Nov. 1905.

November ca. 21. Petersburg. Okhta local detail. 6, 11, 22. *SO*, 23 Nov. 1905; 26 Nov. 1905; Petrov, *Ocherki*, p. 201.

November 21–24. Ostrolenka. 21st Murom and 22nd Nizhegorodsk infantry, 10th sapper battalion, 16th Glukhov dragoons. 0, 12, 22, 24. *VP*, v. 1, p. 107; *VP*, v. 4, pp. 709, 712; *Nachalo*, 29 Nov. 1905; Korol'kov, "Revoliutsionnoe dvizhenie . . . Vilenskogo," p. 176.

November 22. Aleksandropol. 153rd Baku infantry. 0, 11, 21, 22. *VP*, v. 3 book 2, p. 880; Korol'kov, "Revoliutsionnoe dvizhenie . . . Kavkazskogo," p. 355.

November, not after the 22nd. Volkovysk. 8th Smolensk dragoons. 0, 10, 22. *VP*, v. 4, pp. 772–3; *Russkoe slovo*, 23 Nov. 1905.

November, not after the 22nd. Warsaw. Litovsk Guards infantry. 6, 10, 22. Korol'kov, "Revoliutsionnoe dvizhenie . . . Vilenskogo," p. 175; *VP*, v. 4, p. 184; *Russkoe slovo*, 23 Nov. 1905; 25 November 1905.

November 22. Warsaw. Keksgolm Guards infantry, 4th battalion. 0, 10, 22. *Nashi dni*, 7 Dec. 1905; 8 Dec. 1905 (regimental order); *Severo-zapadnyi golos*, 6 Dec. 1905.

November, not after the 22nd. Nizhnii Novgorod. 307 Arzamas infantry, 1st reserve artillery brigade, military infirmary. 0, 10. Petrov, *Ocherki*, p. 391.

November 22–25. Bobruisk. Bobruisk disciplinary battalion. 2, 16, 22. *VP*, v. 4, pp. 213–4; *Revoliutsionnoe dvizhenie v Belorussii*, pp. 354–5; *Soldatskaia zhizn'* (SD, Moscow), no. 6, 15 March 1906.

November 22–26. Ostrovets. 23rd Nizovsk, 24th Simbirsk infantry. 1, 13, 21, 22. Pawłowski, *Wojskowa*, p. 240; *VP*, v. 4, p. 709; Korol'kov, "Revoliutsionnoe dvizhenie . . . Vilenskogo," p. 177.

November 23. Smorgon. 3rd Don cossacks, one-half squadron. 0, 10, 23a. *VP*, v. 4, p. 17; Petrov, *Ocherki*, p. 391.

November 23. Izmail. Draft board detail. 0, 10, 22. Petrov, *Ocherki*, pp. 289, 392.

November 23. Kharkov. 165th Lutsk, 201st Lebedinsk, 202nd Starobelsk, 269th Bogodukhovsk infantry. 8, 12, 22, 25. *VP*, v. 3 book 1, pp. 356–62; Iakovlev, "Khar'kovskoe litholet'e," *IV*, 1910 no. 11, pp. 557–73; Kantsel'son, "Revoliutsionnoe dvizhenie," pp. 218–23; Tkachukov, "1905 g. v Khar'kove," *Puti revoliutsii*, 1925 no. 3, pp. 15–8; *NZh*, 3 Dec. 1905; *Nachalo*, 1 Dec. 1905.

November 23. Baku. 2nd Khoper Kuban cossacks, 1st squadron. 5, 10, 22. *Baku*, no. 170, 25 Nov. 1905.

November ca. 23. Petersburg. 1st railway battalion. 0, 10, 22. Petrov, *Ocherki*, p. 289; *Severnyi golos*, no. 1, 6 Dec. 1905.

November 23–24. Kars. 14th Derbent infantry, 2nd Chernomorsk Kuban cossacks (6th squadron). 1, 15, 21, 22, 25. *VP*, v. 3 book 2, p. 705; *Vozrozhdenie*, 8 Dec. 1905; *Novoe obozrenie*, 4 Dec. 1905; Korol'kov, "Revoliutsionnoe dvizhenie . . . Kavkazskogo," p. 354.

November, not after 24th. Petersburg. 198th Aleksandr Nevskii infantry. 0, 10, 22. *NZh*, 24 Nov. 1905.

November 24–25. Kazan. Military hospital. 1, 11, 22. *Volzhskii vestnik*, 27 Nov. 1905.

November 24. Proskurov. 46th Dnepr infantry (at least the training detail). 0, 10. Akun and Petrov, *Bol'sheviki*, p. 36; *NZh*, 30 Nov. 1905.

November 24–25. Gora-Kalvariia. 6th and 7th pontoon battalions. 0, 10, 22. Petrov, *Ocherki*, pp. 368, 392; Pawłowski, *Wojskowa*, pp. 241–2.

November 24–29. Brest-Litovsk. Fortress artillery, 2nd siege artillery battalion, military hospital. 8, 11, 22. *VP*, v. 1, p. 107; *VP*, v. 4, pp. 127–30; *SO*, 26 Nov. 1905.

November 24–December. Krasnoiarsk, Viazma. 3rd railway battalion. 1, 10, 22. *Karatel'nye ekespeditsii*, p. 198; *Biulleten'* (Krasnoiarsk RSDRP), 25 Nov.; no. 2, n.d.; *Soldatskaia gazeta* (SR, Central Committee), no. 7, 5 March 1907.

November 24–December 10. Lodz. 37th Ekaterinburg infantry. 0, 10, 21, 22. *VP*, v. 4, pp. 669, 739; Petrov, *Ocherki*, p. 392.

November 24–January 3. Krasnoiarsk. 2nd railway battalion, 3rd Siberian depot battalion, Krasnoiarsk cossack division, Krasnoiarsk military escort detail, hospital staff, 10th Omsk Siberian infantry, 11th Semiplatinsk Siberian infantry, Krasnoiarsk local detail. 1, 17, 21, 22, 24c, 25. *VP*, v. 2, pp. 895–935; *Krasnoiarskii rabochii*, 10 Dec. 1905; 13 Dec. 1905; 22 Dec. 1905; *Biulleten'* (Krasnoiarsk RSDRP), no. 1, 25 Nov. 1905; no. 2, n.d.; no. 3, 2 Dec. 1905; no. 4, 4 Dec. 1905; Leskovskii, "Dvizhenie sredi voisk," pp. 59–77; Poleshchuk, "Revoliutsionnoe dvizhenie v Man'chzhurskoi," pp. 342–3; *Obzor revoliutsionnogo dvizheniia v okruge Irkutskoi sudovoi palaty*, pp. 22–5, 37–42; Cherkasov, "Revoliutsionnoe dvizhenie," pp. 242–52.

November 25. Rovno. 127th Putivl infantry. 4, 13, 22. *VP*, v. 3 book 1, p. 13; Petrov, *Ocherki*, pp. 333–4; *Bor'ba*, 7 Dec. 1905.

November 25. Vitebsk. 313th Kineshma infantry. 0, 10, 22. *VP*, v. 4, p. 58; *SO*, 27 Nov. 1905.

November 25. Bronnitsy. 1st Grenadier mobile artillery park. 0, 10, 22. *VP*, v. 1, p. 608. Konovalov, "Revoliutsionnoe dvizhenie," p. 50.

November 25–26. Moscow. 1st Don cossacks (two squadrons). 0, 11, 22. Mel'nikov, "Revoliutsionnoe dvizhenie . . . v period dekabr'skogo," p. 274; *Russkoe slovo*, 27 Nov. 1905; *Bor'ba*, 27 Nov. 1905; *Zhizn'*, 27 Nov. 1905; *SO*, 28 Nov. 1905.

November 25–December 3. Samara. 3rd reserve artillery brigade (some soldiers of military escort detail and 312th Berezina infantry). 1, 13, 22. *VP*, v. 2, pp. 692–4; Bliumental', "Sotsial-demokratiia," pp. 261–96; *Samarskii kur'er*, 29 Nov. 1905; 30 Nov. 1905; 3 Dec. 1905.

November 25–December 3. Samtredi and Kvirily stations (Kutais Province). 2nd Laba Kuban cossacks (two squadrons). 3, 10. Starosel'skii, " 'Dni svobody'," pp. 282, 290; *Kavkazskii rabochii listok*, 4 Dec. 1905; 9 Dec. 1905.

November 26–27. Saratov. 227th Balashov infantry. 0, 10, 22. *VP*, v. 2, pp. 777, 1134 fn. 138; Petrov, *Ocherki*, p. 392.

November 26–27. Nikolaev. 58th depot battalion. 5, 11, 21. *VP*, v. 3 book 1, p. 578.

November 26–27. Moscow. 3rd and 5th reserve sapper battalions, 221st Troitse-Sergiev infantry (3rd battalion). 1, 12, 22. *VP*, v. 1, pp. 609–10; Mel'nikov, "Revoliutsionnoe dvizhenie . . . v period dekabr'skogo," pp. 271–3; *Russkoe slovo*, 28 Nov. 1905; *Zhizn'*, 28 Nov. 1905; *Bor'ba*, 3 Dec. 1905.

November 26–December 2. Irkutsk. Irkutsk cossack division (two squadrons), 1st and 2nd Siberian reserve battalions, military telegraph company, military escort detail, 144th Kashira infantry, hospital staff, warehouse troops. 1, 16, 22. *VP*, v. 2, pp. 896, 1010, 1012–19, 1028–35; *Za narod*, no. 9, 5 Oct. 1907, pp. 4–7; Cherkasov, "Revoliutsionnoe dvizhenie," pp. 261–73; Mandel'berg, *Iz perezhitogo*, pp. 90–2; *Obzor revoliutsionnogo dvizheniia v okruge Irkutskoi sudovoi palaty*, pp. 75–9.

November 27. Lomzha. 13th Belozersk infantry. 0, 11, 21. *VP*, v. 4, p. 710.

November 27. Karachev. 26th artillery brigade, one battery. 0, 10, 22. Konovalov, "Revoliutsionnoe dvizhenie," pp. 50–1.

November 27. Khasav-Iurt (Terek District). 84th Shirvan infantry. 1, 10, 22. Kireev, *Rabochii klass*, pp. 119–20; Steklov, "Revoliutsionnoe dvizhenie," p. 409.

November 27. Baku. 79th Kurinsk infantry. 1, 12, 22, 25. *Revoliutsiia 1905 v Zakavkaz'i*, pp. 91, 127; *Baku*, 30 Nov. 1905; *Kaspii*, 29 Nov. 1905.

November 27. Petersburg. Fortress artillery and explosive stores. 0, 15, 22. *VP*, v. 1, p. 495; Petrov, *Ocherki*, p. 393; Korablev, "Revoliutsionnoe," p. 131.

November 28. Kielce. 23rd horse artillery battery (14th horse artillery division). 0, 11, 22. Pawłowski, *Wojskowa*, p. 242; Petrov, *Ocherki*, pp. 305, 393.

November 28–29. Belgorod. 51st artillery brigade. 2, 13, 22, 25. *VP*, v. 2, p. 347; *Revoliutsionnye sobytiia 1905–1907 gg. v Kurskoi gubernii*, pp. 101–2; *Russkoe slovo*, 1 Dec. 1905; 2 Dec. 1905; 4 Dec. 1905.

November 28–December 2. Eastern Georgia. 2nd Poltava Kuban cossacks. 0, 15, 22. *Tiflisskii listok*, 1 Dec. 1905; 3 Dec. 1905; *Vozrozhdenie*, 30 Nov. 1905; Steklov, "Revoliutsionnoe dvizhenie," pp. 389–90.

November 28–December 6. Viatka. 231st Kotel'nich reserve infantry battalion. 1, 12, 22. *VP*, v. 2, pp. 793, 797–9, 802–3, 805–6; Dubrovskii and Grave, *Agrarnoe dvizhenie*, pp. 33–7; I. Danchik, "Besporiadki v Kotel'nicheskom batal'one," *1905 g. v Viatskoi gubernii*, Viatka, 1925, pp. 137–41; P. Fabrichnyi, "Iz kazarmy—na katorgu," *V tsarskoi kazarme*, M., 1929, pp. 146–69.

November 29–30. Kazan. 229th Sviazhsk reserve battalion. 2, 11, 22. *Volzhskii vestnik*, 3 Dec. 1905; Petrov, *Ocherki*, pp. 260, 393.

November 29–30. Tsaritsyn. 226th Bobruisk infantry. 5, 13, 22, 25. *VP*, v. 2, p. 775; Semennikov, *Revoliutsiia*, pp. 176–8; *Pravo*, 28 Dec. 1905; V. Kuz'min, "Revoliutsionnaia rabota sredi soldat i vosstanie bobruitsev v 1905 g.," *1905 god v Stalingradskoi gubernii*, Stalingrad, 1925, pp. 67–82.

November 29–December 2. Moscow. 1st Ekaterinoslav, 3rd Pernov, 4th Nesvizh Grenadiers. 1, 11, 22. *VP*, v. 1, p. 613; Mel'nikov, "Revoliutsionnoe dvizhenie . . . v period dekabr'skogo," pp. 274–7; Vasin, *Armiia*, pp. 48–9; Shabrov, "Dni vosstaniia," p. 48; *Vpered*, 2 Dec. 1905; *Zhizn'*, 3 Dec. 1905; *Russkoe slovo*, 4 Dec. 1905; *Bor'ba*, 6 Dec. 1905.

November 30. Tambov. 7th reserve cavalry regiment. 8, 13, 22. *Za narod*, no. 22, Oct. 1909, pp. 7–9; *VPR*, part 2 book 2, p. 183.

November 30–December 4. Zaraisk. 2nd and 4th reserve sapper battalions. 1, 10, 22. *VP*, v. 2, p. 380; *Vpered*, 6 Dec. 1905.

November, late. Kremenchug. Artillery arsenal. 0, 11, 22. *Severnyi golos*, 7 Dec. 1905.

November, late—early December. Akhaltsyk (Tiflis Province). 77th Tenginsk infantry. 0, 12, 21, 22. *Vozrozhdenie*, 3 Dec. 1905; Steklov, "Revoliutsionnoe dvizhenie," p. 392.

November, second half (arbitrarily). Mozdok. Military clerks. 0, 10, 22. Petrov, *Ocherki*, pp. 380, 394.

November, second half (arbitrarily). Innokentevskaia station (Siberia). Elements of 1st Nevskii and 2nd Sofiia infantry. 1, 11. *Karatel'nye ekspeditsii*, p. 125; "Sibirskaia ekspeditsiia," p. 149.

November, second half (arbitrarily). Aleksandrov (Vladimir Province). 1st reserve sapper battalion. 0, 11, 22. Petrov, *Ocherki*, pp. 190, 289, 394.

November, second half (no later than 28 November). Vilna. 107th Troitsk infantry (noncombatant company). 0, 10. *VP*, v. 4, pp. 19–20.

November, second half. Mariampol. 111th Don infantry, 2nd battalion. 0, 11. Proclamations by the Mariampol Military-Revolutionary Organization, "K soldatam" (March 1906) and "Tovarishchi 2-go bataliona" (March or April 1906), Bund Archive.

November, second half (arbitrarily). Western Siberia. 4th Kopore infantry, one battalion. 0, 10. Poleshchuk, "Revoliutsionnoe dvizhenie v Man'chzhurskoi," p. 323.

November, second half–December 2. Deshlagar. 83rd Samur infantry. 0, 10, 22. *Vozrozhdenie*, 9 Dec. 1905; Steklov, "Revoliutsionnoe dvizhenie," p. 443.

November, second half–December. Zima station (Siberia). 142nd Zvenigorod infantry. 1, 10. "Sibirskaia ekspeditsiia," p. 149; *Karatel'nye ekspeditsii*, pp. 124–5.

December, no later than the 1st. Ivangorod Fortress. Fortress infantry regiment. 0, 10. Petrov, *Ocherki*, p. 394.

December 1. Ekaterinoslav. 20th Don cossacks, 6th squadron. 5, 12. *VP*, v. 1, p. 60; Petrov, *Ocherki*, p. 394.

December 1. Harbin. 2nd, 3rd, 4th Transamur railway battalions. 1, 10, 22. Stankevich, *Khronika*, p. 54.

December 1–8. Stavropol, Kavkazskaia station, Tikhoretskaia station. 2nd Kavkaz Kuban cossacks. 1, 12, 22. *VP*, v. 2, pp. 402, 406, 1126 fn. 69; *Revoliutsionnoe dvizhenie na Kubani*, pp. 207–11.

December, early. Tiflis. Personal escort of the Viceroy. 0, 11, 22. *Vozrozhdenie*, 8 Dec. 1905; *Novoe obozrenie*, 8 Dec. 1905.

December, early. Khailar (Chinese Eastern railway). 3rd Nerchinsk reserve battalion. 0, 10. *Karatel'nye ekspeditsii*, p. 193; *VP*, v. 2, p. 978.

December, early. Tiraspol. 56th depot infantry battalion. 0, 16, 21. *Czerwony Sztandar* (SDKPiL), 25/12 Dec. 1905; *Robotnik*, 23/10 Dec. 1905; *Nashi dni*, 8 Dec. 1905.

December, early–6. Novokievskoe (near Vladivostok). 6th East Siberian rifles. 0, 16, 21, 22. "Razlozhenie armii," pp. 113–4; Stankevich, *Khronika*, pp. 56–7; Poleshchuk, "Revoliutsionnoe dvizhenie . . . Irkutskogo," p. 324.

December 2–3. Archeda station (Don District). 3rd composite Don cossacks. 1, 10, 24b. *VP*, v. 1, p. 64.

December 2–4. Moscow. 2nd Rostov Grenadiers. 1, 14, 22. For sources, see Chapter 5, fn. 49.

December 2–9. Sungari (Manchuria). 3rd pontoon battalion. 1, 10, 21. [Kuropatkin], "Iz dnevnika . . . s 23 okt.," p. 63.

December ca. 2–13. Novorossiisk-Umansk Station. 17th Kuban plastoons. 1, 11. *VP*, v. 2, pp. 412, 585; Steklov, "Revoliutsionnoe dvizhenie," pp. 410–11.

December, before the 3rd. Kiev. 44th Kamchatka infantry. 0, 10. Petrov, *Ocherki*, p. 394.

December 3. Dubno. 11th artillery brigade, 2nd battery. 1, 10, 21, 22. Petrov, *Ocherki*, pp. 289, 394; *SO*, 29 Nov. 1905.

December 3. Stretensk. 1st Stretensk reserve battalion. 0, 10, 21, 22. *Karatel'nye ekspeditsii*, p. 193; *Krasnoiarskii rabochii*, 22 Dec. 1905.

December 3–5. Nikolaev. 277th Ingulsk infantry. 1, 16, 21, 22. *VP*, v. 3 book 1, pp. 567–8, 576–94.

December 3–January 21. Blagoveshchensk. Amur cossack division, Amur cossack regiment. 1, 12, 22. N.A. Obetkovskii, "Revoliutsionnoe dvizhenie Amurskogo kazachestva v 1905–1907 godov," *Zapiski Amurskogo oblastnogo muzeia kraevedeniia i o-va kraevedeniia*, v. 5, 1961, pp. 30–6; *VP*, v. 2, pp. 1038–43; M. Astaf'ev, "Amurskoe kazachestvo v 1905 godu. (Vospominaniia uchastnika)," *1905. Revoliutsionnoe dvizhenie na Dal'nem Vostoke*, Vladivostok, 1925, pp. 150–3.

December 4. Ekaterinogradskaia (Terek District). Ekaterinogradskaia disciplinary battalion. 1, 16, 25. Korol'kov, "Revoliutsionnoe . . . Kavkazskogo," p. 348.

December 4. Nerchinsk. 1st and 2nd East Siberian reserve battalions, 2nd East Siberian rifle artillery park, 5th Transbaikal cossack battalion, military escort detail, Verkhneudinsk local detail. 2, 10, 22. *Karatel'nye ekspeditsii*, pp. 193, 302; *Zabaikal'e*, 6 Dec. 1905.

December 4. Novogeorgievsk Fortress. 4th Novogeorgievsk fortress infantry regiment. 0, 10. Petrov, *Ocherki*, p. 394.

December 4. Grodno. 101st Perm and 102nd Viatka infantry. 8, 12. *VP*, v. 4, p. 130; Petrov, *Ocherki*, p. 394.

December 4–25. Elizavetpol. 1st and 2nd Caucasus sapper battalions, 261st Shemansk infantry, Aslanduzsk reserve battalion. 1, 10, 22. Steklov, "Revoliutsionnoe dvizhenie," pp. 400–1.

December 5. Revel. Military infirmary. 3, 10, 21, 24b. Korablev, "Revoliutsionnoe dvizhenie," p. 138, Petrov, *Ocherki*, pp. 260, 394.

December 6. Rostov-on-Don. 134th Feodosiia infantry (one battalion), cossacks, cossack artillery. 3, 12. Iakovlev, *Vooruzhennye vosstaniia*, p. 231; V.S., "Dekabr'skie dni v Rostove na Donu," *Otkliki sovremennosti*, 1906 no. 3, p. 65.

December 6. Medvezhii stan (near Petersburg). 200th Izhorsk infantry, 6th company. 4, 12. *VP*, v. 1, p. 496.

December 6–7. Bobruisk. 237 Kremlevsk and 238th Kliazma infantry. 0, 11, 21, 22. *VP*, v. 4, p. 215; Petrov, *Ocherki*, p. 305.

December 7–15. Vladivostok. 29th, 30th, 37th, 40th East Siberian rifles, 2nd fortress artillery regiment (8th artillery division), 1st Ussuri railway battalion, Siberian noncombat naval *équipage* (2nd company). 1, 12, 22. *VP*, v. 2, pp. 1048–52; Korol'kov, "Revoliutsionnoe dvizhenie . . . Priamurskogo," pp. 367–8; *Obzor revoliutsionnogo dvizheniia v okruge Irkutskoi sudovoi palaty*, p. 172.

December 7. Briansk. 305th Bogorodsk infantry. 0, 12, 22. *VP*, v. 2, p. 358; Zheleznov, "Revoliutsionnoe dvizhenie," p. 134.

December 8. Minsk. 55th artillery brigade, 239th Oka infantry (6th company, band). 0, 10, 21, 22. Petrov, *Ocherki*, pp. 293, 300–1.

December 8–9. Petersburg. Kronstadt fortress mine company. 1, 16, 23c. *Pravo*, 28 Dec. 1905; *VP*, v. 1, p. 486.

December 9. Van-dia-Gan (Manchuria). 21st East Siberian rifles, 5th and 6th companies. 5, 11, 21. Poleshchuk, "Revoliutsionnoe . . . v Man'chzhurskoi," pp. 339–40.

December 9. Arkhangelsk. Arkhangelogorodsk reserve battalion, 1st company. 6, 10, 22. Petrov, *Ocherki*, pp. 218–19, 289, 303.

December 11. Penza. 20th sapper battalion (also reserves and sailors from troop trains). 0, 10, 23. *VP*, v. 2, pp. 671, 673; *Karatel'nye ekspeditsii*, p. 118.

December 11. Khan-di-Ufan (Manchuria). 3rd East Siberian rifle artillery brigade. 3, 12, 22. Poleshchuk, "Revoliutsionnoe dvizhenie v Man'chzhurskoi," p. 340.

December 11–21. Northern Caucasus. 14th Kuban plastoons. 1, 11. *VP*, v. 2, pp. 407–9, 412, 414; Semennikov, *Revoliutsiia*, pp. 209–10; *Baku*, 14 Dec. 1905.

December 12. Akmolinsk. 6th Enisei reserve battalion. 0, 10, 22. Petrov, *Ocherki*, p. 395.

December 12. Odessa. 15th artillery brigade, 1st battery. 5, 12. *VP*, v. 3 book 1, pp. 555–60.

December 12. Grodno. Fortress infantry battalion (1st company). 5, 18. *VP*, v. 1, p. 180; Petrov, *Ocherki*, p. 395; *Robotnik*, 8 Jan. 1906/26 Dec. 1905.

December 12. Novokhopersk. Four troop trains with reserves. 1, 11, 23. *VP*, v. 2, p. 309.

December 12. Baku. 79th Kura, 131st Tiraspol, 132nd Bendery infantry, 53rd artillery brigade, Caspian naval *équipage*. 1, 12, 22, 25. *Baku*, 13 Dec. 1905; 15 Dec. 1905; *Kaspii*, 15 Dec. 1905; *Izvestiia soveta rabochikh deputatov* (Baku), 16 Dec. 1905; Korol'kov, "Revoliutsionnoe dvizhenie . . . Kavkazskogo," pp. 352–3 (misdated as 2 December).

December 12–16. Manchuria. 1st East Siberian balloon division. 1, 16, 21. Poleshchuk, "Revoliutsionnoe dvizhenie v Man'chzhurskoi," p. 340.

December 12–18. Vladikavkaz. Ossetian cavalry division. 7, 11, 22. *VP*, v. 2, pp. 545–6, 553, 564; *Severnaia Osetiia v revoliutsii*, pp. 271–2; Apukhtin, "Vosstanie v Osetinskom konnom divizione," *1905 g. vo Vladikavkaze. Sbornik*, Vladikavkaz, 1925, pp. 31–4.

December 13–14. Slonim. 240th Krasinsk reserve infantry battalion. 0, 10, 22. Petrov, *Ocherki*, p. 289.

December 14–17. Krimskaia station, Slavianskaia (Kuban Territory). 15th Kuban plastoons. 2, 11. *VP*, v. 2, p. 412; Semennikov, *Revoliutsiia*, pp. 209–10; *Revoliutsionnoe dvizhenie na Kubani*, pp. 197–200, 203–4.

December 15. Nikolaev. Naval barracks. 0, 16. *Pravo*, 18 Dec. 1905.

December 15. Manchuria. 59th Lublin infantry, 2nd battalion. 1, 12, 21. Poleshchuk, "Revoliutsionnoe dvizhenie v Man'chzhurskoi," p. 340.

December 15–February 7. Novorossiisk, Ekaterinodar, Maikop. 2nd Urup Kuban cossacks. 1, 17, 22. *VP*, v. 2, pp. 413–17, 420–9; L. Il'in, *Vosstanie 2-go Urupskogo kazach'ego polka v 1905 godu*, Rostov n/D, 1926.

December, first half. Elendorf (Caucasus). 1st Laba Kuban cossacks. 1, 12, 22. Steklov, "Revoliutsionnoe dvizhenie," p. 402.

December, first half. Kirensk. Local detail. 2, 10, 22. Poleshchuk, "Revoliutsionnoe dvizhenie . . . Irkutskogo," p. 324.

December ca. 15. Manchuria. XVI corps artillery park. 1, 10, 21. [Kuropatkin], "Iz dnevnika . . . s 23 okt.," p. 66.

December 16. Armavir. Caucasus reserve cavalry division. 1, 11, 22, 25. *VP*, v. 2, p. 410.

December 17–18. Vladikavkaz. 2nd Gorsko-Mozdok Terek cossacks (2nd squadron). 5, 10. *VP*, v. 2, p. 553.

December 18. Feodosiia. 52nd Vilna infantry (two companies and band). 1, 17, 22. Petrov, *Ocherki*, pp. 306, 334, 367.

December, no later than 18th. Borisov. 1st detached cavalry brigade. 0, 10, 22. Petrov, *Ocherki*, p. 395.

December 19. Kamenskoe (Ekaterinoslav Province). 278th Berdiansk infantry (one company). 1, 12, 23a. *Ekaterinoslavshchina v revoliutsii*, p. 229.

December 20. Cheliabinsk. 1st and 109th reserve hospital staffs. 1, 15. *VP*, v. 2, p. 811.

December 20. Kutais. 155th Kubinsk infantry. 0, 12. Starosel'skii, " 'Dni svobody'," p. 296; Steklov, "Revoliutsionnoe dvizhenie," p. 396; Gubernarchuk, *Ocherki istorii 129-go*, pp. 338–9.

December 25–26. Ust-Dvinsk fortress. Fortress artillery, 4th and 5th companies. 9, 16. Korol'kov, "Revoliutsionnoe dvizhenie . . . Vilenskogo," p. 165.

December 25–27. Khodzhent. Turkestan pontoon company. 3, 14, 22, 24c. *VP*, v. 3, book 2, pp. 949–50; Cherkasov, "Revoliutsionnoe," p. 329; Soifer, *Revoliutsionnoe dvizhenie*, pp. 70–2.

December 26–27. Vladivostok. 32nd East Siberian rifles. 0, 10. *VP*, v. 2, p. 1057.

December 27. Transbaikal railway. 1st Sretensk Siberian infantry. 0, 10, 22. Poleshchuk, "Revoliutsionnoe dvizhenie v Man'chzhurskoi," p. 343.

December 27–30. Manchuria. 6th East Siberian sapper battalion. 1, 16. *VP*, v. 2, pp. 1080–1.

December 28. Batum. Fortress sappers, fortress artillery. 0, 16. Korol'kov, "Revoliutsionnoe dvizhenie . . . Kavkazskogo," p. 357.

December 29. Bobruisk disciplinary battalion, 2nd company. 3, 15. Petrov, *Ocherki*, pp. 303–4.

December, late. Częstochowa. 42nd Mitava dragoons. 1, 11. Pawłowski, *Wojskowa*, p. 270.

December, second half (arbitrarily). Vilna. 1st mortar regiment. 0, 11. *Severozapadnyi golos*, 21 Dec. 1905.

Appendix II.
Mutinies in 1906

The annotation of the mutinies is the same as in Appendix I.

January 2–20. Vladivostok. 2nd fortress artillery regiment, 32nd East Siberian rifle regiment, destroyers *Besposhchadnyi* and *Bodryi*, cruisers *Rossiia*, *Terek*, and *Zhemchug*, torpedo boat *Groznyi*, transports *Argun*, *Kolyma*, *Lena*, and *Shilka*, icebreaker *Nadezhnyi*, Siberian fleet barracks, 1st Ussuri railway battalion. 1, 17, 24c. *VPR*, part 1 book 1, pp. 895–933; Korol'kov, "Revoliutsionnoe dvizhenie . . . Priamurskogo," pp. 368–73; *Chto proizoshlo vo Vladivostoke 10/23 i 11/24 ianvaria*, [Nagasaki], 1906.

January 3. Novorossiisk. 16th Kuban plastoons, 2nd company. 1, 10. *VP*, v. 2, pp. 413–4.

January 9. Mariampol. 111th Don infantry. 1, 12, 23b. Grishkunaite, "Volneniia v voiskakh," p. 125 (the regiment is misidentified as the 3rd Don).

January 10–February. Nikolaevsk-on-Amur (Fortress Chnyrrakh). 3, 12, 22, 24c. *VPR*, part 1 book 1, pp. 933–57; Stankevich, *Khronika*, pp. 79–80; *1905. Revoliutsionnoe dvizhenie na Dal'nem Vostoke*, pp. 194–6.

January 12. Novorossiisk. 17th Kuban plastoons. 1, 15. *VP*, v. 2, p. 593; Korol'kov, "Revoliutsionnoe dvizhenie . . . Kavkazskogo," pp. 356–7.

January, first half. Lodz. 37th Ekaterinburg infantry. 3, 13, 22a. Pawłowski, *Wojskowa*, p. 274.

January 19. Dzharkent. 3rd West Siberian rifle battalion, 1st or 2nd West Siberian cossacks. 0, 10, 22. *Revoliutsionnoe dvizhenie v Kazakhstane*, pp. 142–4.

January 19. Kherson Province. 135th Kerch-Enikalsk infantry, 5th company. 1, 12, 23a. *VPR*, part 1 book 2, p. 176.

January 22. Kiev. 7th sapper battalion, 2nd company. 3, 16. *VPR*, part 1 book 2, pp. 87, 644–5 fn. 33.

January 29. Odessa. Gunboat *Donets*. 3, 15. *VPR*, part 1 book 2, pp. 177–8, 651 fn. 75.

January 29. Manchuria Station. 1st Transamur railway battalion. 0, 16. Poleshchuk, "Revoliutsionnoe dvizhenie v Man'chzhurskoi," p. 348.

January, second half. Saratov province. 7th Orenburg cossacks, 2nd and 3rd squadrons. 0, 10. *VPR*, part 1 book 1, pp. 728–9.

February 10. Lukow. 3rd transport battalion, 9th and 10th companies. 5, 10. Pawłowski, *Wojskowa*, p. 275.

February 11. Baku. Caspian naval barracks, 2nd company. 1, 15, 22. S.F. Naida,

Revoliutsionnoe dvizhenie v tsarskom flote. 1825–1917, M.-L., 1948.

February 21. Mukhrovani (Tiflis Province). 17th East Siberian mountain battery. 1, 12, 22. *VPR*, part 2 book 3, p. 305.

February 27. Manchuria. 54th Minsk and 56th Zhitomir infantry. 1, 16. Poleshchuk, "Revoliutsionnoe dvizhenie v Man'chzhurskoi," p. 348.

February 28. Irkutsk. 5th Irkutsk Siberian infantry. 0, 16. Poleshchuk, "Revoliutsionnoe dvizhenie . . . Irkutskogo," p. 356.

February. Kirensk. Local detail. 3, 10. Poleschuk, "Revoliutsionnoe dvizhenie . . . Irkutskogo," pp. 356–7.

March 8. Harbin. 160th Abkhazsk infantry. 6, 17. *VPR*, part 1 book 2, p. 476; Poleshchuk, "Revoliutsionnoe dvizhenie v Man'chzhurskoi," p. 348.

March 22. Baku. 33rd artillery brigade, 6th battery. 0, 12. *VPR*, part 2 book 2, pp. 305–6.

March 21. Kiev. 44th Kamchatka infantry, 8th company. 1, 12. Kantsel'son, "Revoliutsionnoe dvizhenie," p. 233.

March 26. Tiflis. 16th Mingrelsk Grenadier infantry. 3, 17. *Revoliutsiia 1905–1907 gg. v Gruzii*, pp. 596–7, 627–32; *VPR*, part 1 book 2, pp. 364–5.

March. Port-Petrovsk. 21st mobile artillery park. 5, 10. Narushevich, "Vosstanie soldat," p. 56.

April 11–late May. Petersburg. 145th Novocherkassk infantry. 1, 18, 23. *Narodnyi vestnik*, 19 May 1906; 24 May 1906; *Kur'er*, 3 June 1906; *Ekho*, 4 July 1906.

April 13. Temir-Khan-Shury. 254th Temir-Khan-Shury reserve infantry battalion. 1, 13, 22. *VPR*, part 2 book 3, p. 302; Gadzhiev, "Revoliutsionnye vystupleniia," pp. 72–3; Narushevich, "Vosstanie soldat," p. 56.

April 16. Tver. 1st Life Dragoon regiment. 0, 11, 22. *VPR*, part 1 book 1, pp. 127–8, 465, 1005 fn. 172; Zheleznov, "Revoliutsionnoe dvizhenie," p. 135; "Materialy o pervoi voennoi konferentsii."

April 16. Brest-Litovsk. 3rd reserve artillery brigade, 2nd battery. 1, 12. *VPR*, part 1 book 2, pp. 437–8.

May 1. Petersburg. Guards naval barracks. 1, 12, 23a. *Nevskaia gazeta*, 5 May 1906.

May, early. Novgorod Province. 199th Svirsk infantry, 6th company. 1, 18, 23a. *Soldatskaia mysl'* (SD, Moscow), no. 1, June 1906; *Prizyv*, 5 May 1906; *Ekho*, 4 July 1906; "Materialy o pervoi voennoi konferentsii."

May 7–12. Tiumen. 9th Tobolsk Siberian infantry, scouting detail, 3rd and 4th companies. 1, 15, 22, 23a. Kondrikov, "Revoliutsionnye vystupleniia," p. 104; *Golos truda*, 10 June 1906; *Golos*, 9 June 1906.

May 11. Libava. Battleship *Tsesarevich*. 5, 11. *Kur'er*, 8 June 1906; *Svobodnoe slovo*, 2 June 1906.

May 11. Chernigovka (near Vladivostok). 2nd Siberian artillery regiment. 1, 15. Stankevich, *Khronika*, pp. 95–6.

May 11. Petersburg Province. 200th Izhorsk reserve infantry regiment. 6, 11. Korablev, "Revoliutsionnoe dvizhenie," p. 150; *Svetoch*, 16 May 1906.

May, first half—June 16. Orenburg. 14th Orenburg cossacks. 1, 12, 22, 23d. *Privolzhskii krai*, 21 May 1906; *Trud*, 24 May 1906; 30 May 1906; *Kur'er*, 11 June 1906; *Mysl'*, 2 July 1906; 4 July 1906; *Kurskaia vest'*, 4 July 1906.

May 18–23. Kansk. Local detail. 0, 10. Poleshchuk, "Revoliutsionnoe dvizhenie . . . Irkutskogo," p. 365.

May, second decade. Libava. Cruiser *Bogatyr.* 5, 13, 22. *Soldatskaia gazeta* (SR, Central Committee), no. 4, 5 Nov. 1906; *Soldatskaia mysl'* (SR, Petersburg), no. 3, December 1906.

May 20–June 12. Voronezh. 1st Neva infantry. 5, 11, 22. *Narodnyi vestnik,* 28 May 1906; *Golos,* 10 June 1906; *Mysl',* 29 June 1906; *Zhizn' kazarmy* (SD, Voronezh), no. 1, 25 June 1906.

May 22–28. Evpatoria. 51st Litovsk infantry, 14th company. 1, 10, 23a. *Otkliki Kryma,* 26 May 1906; 2 June 1906; 3 June 1906; *Kur'er,* 31 May 1906; *Iuzhnaia narodnaia gazeta,* 1 June 1906; *Ekho,* 23 June 1906.

May 22–late June. Kursk. 123rd Kozlov and 203rd Graivoron infantry, 68th artillery brigade, Don cossacks, Kuban cossacks. 1, 18, 22, 23d. For sources, see Chapter Seven, fn. 45.

May 24. Kherson. Disciplinary battalion. 0, 17, 24b. *VPR,* part 2 book 1, p. 230.

May ca. 25. Kostroma. 30th Don cossacks, 6th squadron. 6, 13, 22. *Kostromskaia gazeta,* 28 May 1906; *Kostromskoi krai,* 2 July 1906.

May 25–late July. Baranovichi. 1st, 2nd, 3rd railway battalions. 6, 12, 23e. *VPR,* part 2 book 3, pp. 494, 496–500, 513, 655–6 fns. 221–2; *Dvadtsatyi vek,* 5 June 1906; 23 June 1906; *Golos,* 6 June 1906.

May 26. Novyi Margelan. 2nd Transcaspian railway battalion, 6th company. 1, 11. Cherkasov, "Revoliutsionnoe dvizhenie . . . Sibirskogo," p. 330.

May 28. Pavlograd. 135th Kerch-Enikalsk infantry, 12th company. 3, 14. *VPR,* part 2 book 3, pp. 64, 625–6.

May 28–29. Poltava. 33rd Elets infantry. 4, 12, 22. *VPR,* part 2 book 3, pp. 145–9; Kantsel'son, "Revoliutsionnoe dvizhenie," pp. 237–40; Pavchinskii, *Russkaia armiia,* pp. 49–51; Sukhomlinov, *Vospominaniia,* pp. 110–1.

May 30. Voronezh. 29th Don cossacks. 1, 10, 22. *Sovremennik,* 1 June 1906; Shuliakovskii, "Deiatel'nost' voennoi organizatsii," p. 7.

May 31—ca. mid-June. Powązki (camp near Warsaw). 10th and 15th sapper battalions. 3, 15, 22a. *VPR,* part 2 book 3, pp. 583–6, 590; Pawłowski, *Wojskowa,* pp. 301, 304; *Mysl',* 28 June 1906; 2 July 1906; *Ekho,* 22 June 1906.

May, probably second half. Odessa. 210th Perekop infantry. 0, 10. *Soldatskaia mysl'* (SR, Petersburg), no. 2, Oct. 1906; *Soldatskaia beseda* (SD, Central Committee), no. 4, 12 Nov. 1906.

May, second half. Perm. 232nd Irbit reserve infantry battalion, 1st Urals cossacks. 1, 10, 23a. *Golos,* 6 June 1906 (official telegram).

May, second half. Telava (Georgia). Bashkadykliar reserve infantry battalion. 0, 10, 22, 24b. *Duma,* 1 June 1906; *Kur'er,* 9 June 1906.

May, second half. Near Rostov-on-Don. 36th Don cossacks. 5, 12, 23d. *Sovremennik,* 3 June 1906; *Dvadtsatyi vek,* 2 June 1906; *Voennyi golos,* 16 June 1906.

June 1. Novogeorgievsk fortress/Modlin. Fortress artillery workshop. 1, 10, 22. *VPR,* part 2 book 3, p. 590.

June 1–3. Abo. 3rd Finland rifle regiment, one battalion. 6, 11, 22, 23e. *Put',* 10 June 1906; *Vestnik kazarmy* (SD, Finland), no. 5, 15 June 1906.

June, early. Kusary. 275th Khotin infantry, 5th company. 1, 15, 23. *VPR,* part 2 book 3, pp. 320–1; *Baku,* 20 June 1906.

June, early—22. Petersburg. 85th Vyborg infantry. 4, 12, 22, 23a. *VPR*, part 2 book 1, pp. 324–6; *Duma*, 7 June 1906; Pavchinskii, *Russkaia armiia*, pp. 88–9, 91; *Russkoe slovo*, 22 June 1906.

June, early. Lomzha Province. 13th Belozersk, 14th Olonets infantry. 0, 10, 22. *Mysl'*, 2 July 1906.

June 4. Termez. 1st Turkestan artillery brigade, 5th battery. 5, 11. Cherkasov, "Revoliutsionnoe dvizhenie . . . Sibirskogo," pp. 330–1.

June 5. Orenburg. 6th reserve artillery park. 5, 11. *Severnaia zemlia*, 23 June 1906.

June 5–6. Kaluga. 9th Ingermanland and 139th Morshansk infantry, 29th Don cossacks (2 squadrons). 1, 12, 23a. Pavchinskii, *Russkaia armiia*, pp. 90–1; *Duma*, 6 June 1906; *Golos*, 9 June 1906.

June 5–7. Askhabad. 1st Transcaspian railway battalion, 3rd company. 1, 11, 22. Soifer, *Revoliutsionnoe dvizhenie*, p. 84; Piaskovskii, *Revoliutsiia 1905–1907*, pp. 407–8.

June 5–7. Omsk. 10th Siberian Omsk infantry, 4th East Siberian sapper battalion. 0, 16. *VPR*, part 2 book 3, pp. 408–9; Kondrikov, "Revoliutsionnye vystupleniia," pp. 104–5.

June 5–7. Sevastopol. 1st and 2nd fortress artillery battalions, mine company, sailors from the 30th *équipage*. 1, 16, 22. *VPR*, part 2 book 3, p. 278; Ovsiannikov, "Revoliutsionnoe dvizhenie," pp. 225–6; *Soldatskaia gazeta* (SR, Central Committee), no. 3, 8 October 1906.

June 5–8. Tula. 10th Novo-Ingermanland infantry. 1, 11, 22. Zheleznov, "Revoliutsionnoe dvizhenie," pp. 148–9; *Sovremennik*, 6 June 1906.

June ca. 6. Kharkov. 122nd Tambov and 124th Voronezh infantry. 0, 10. Sukhomlinov, *Vospominaniia*, p. 110; *Sovremennik*, 9 June 1906; *Ekho*, 4 July 1906.

June 6–8. Riazan. 138th Bolkhov infantry. 1, 12, 22, 24c. *Voennyi golos*, 10 June 1906; Zheleznov, "Revoliutsionnoe dvizhenie," pp. 135–6; *Dvadtsatyi vek*, 23 June 1906.

June 7. Krasnoe Selo. 198th Aleksandr Nevskii reserve infantry. 0, 10. *Vpered*, 9 June 1906; *Ekho*, 4 July 1906; *Soldatskaia mysl'* (SD, Moscow), no. 2, June 1906.

June 7–21. Krasnoiarsk. 7th Krasnoiarsk Siberian infantry, 25th East Siberian rifles, two troop trains from Manchuria. 3, 18a, 24a. Poleshchuk, "Revoliutsionnoe dvizhenie . . . Irkutskogo," p. 362; *VPR*, part 2 book 2, p. 418; *Sotsialdemokrat* (TsK RSDRP), no. 1, 17 Sept. 1906.

June 9–12. Voronezh. 224th Skopin infantry. 0, 11, 22. *Ekho*, 4 July 1906; *Sovremennik*, 15 June 1906; *Zhizn' kazarmy* (SD, Voronezh), no. 1, 25 June 1906.

June 9–ca. mid-June. Osovets. 2nd fortress infantry battalion, sappers. 1, 10, 22a. *VPR*, part 2 book 3, pp. 474–6, 479, 653–4 fns. 205 and 209; *Voennyi golos*, 15 June 1906; *Dvadtsatyi vek*, 24 June 1906.

June 9–11. Peterhof. Preobrazhensk Guards infantry, 1st battalion. 1, 15, 22ad. For sources, see Chapter 7, fn. 52.

June 10–13. Vladikavkaz. 18th East Siberian mountain battery, other artillery, local detail. 0, 16, 23e, 24c. *VPR*, part 2 book 2, pp. 215–20; *VPR*, part 2 book 3, pp. 302–4; Steklov, "Revoliutsionnoe dvizhenie," pp. 430–1; *Severnaia Osetiia v revoliutsii*, pp. 296–301; *Dvadtsatyi vek*, no. 93, 1 July 1906.

June 10–13. Batum. Fortress artillery, sappers, mine company. 1, 13, 23e. *VPR*, part 2 book 3, pp. 323–9; *Revoliutsiia 1905–1907 gg. v Gruzii*, pp. 666–7, 672–3,

680–4; Pavchinskii, *Russkaia armiia*, pp. 55–8.

June 11. Suchedniow. 71st Belevsk infantry, one company. 1, 18, 23b. Pawłowski, *Wojskowa*, p. 302.

June 12–late June. Odessa. 11th and 12th sapper battalions. 1, 10, 22, 23d. *VPR*, part 2 book 3, pp. 232–3; *Dvadtsatyi vek*, 22 June 1906; Ovsiannikov, "Revoliutsionnoe dvizhenie," pp. 196, 227; *Prizyv*, 15 June 1906; *Mysl'*, 22 June 1906.

June 12. Radom. 71st Belevsk infantry, 14th company. 1, 15, 22, 23b. *Kostromskoi krai*, 22 June 1906 (story taken from *Kurier Radomski*).

June 13–18. Askhabad. 1st, 2nd, 3rd Transcaspian rifle battalion, 1st Transcaspian railway battalion, 2nd Turkestan artillery brigade. 3, 13, 22, 23e. Piaskovskii, *Revoliutsiia 1905–1907*, pp. 407–18; Annanepesov, *Uchastie soldatskikh mass*, pp. 100–45.

June 13–14. Penza. 213th Orovaisk and 216th Insar infantry. 4, 10, 22. *VPR*, part 2 book 2, p. 268; Pavchinskii, *Russkaia armiia*, pp. 64, 88; "Materialy o pervoi voennoi konferentsii."

June 14. Tambov Province. 7th reserve cavalry regiment, one squadron. 1, 12, 23a. Dubrovskii and Grave, *Agrarnoe dvizhenie*, pp. 368–71.

June 14. Petersburg (camp). Guards sapper battalion. 1, 12, 22ad. Akhun and Petrov, *Bol'sheviki*, p. 72; Pavchinskii, *Russkaia armiia*, pp. 71–2.

June 14. Ostrovka. 6th artillery brigade. 1, 11. Pawłowski, *Wojskowa*, p. 302.

June 14–15. Petersburg. Petropavlovsk fortress artillerists. 1, 10. *Ekho*, 4 July 1906.

June 14–17. Plotsk. 1st and 2nd rifle battalions. 1, 11. Pawłowski, *Wojskowa*, p. 302; *Ekho*, 7 July 1906.

June 14–26. Samara. 215th Buzuluk and 244th Borisovsk infantry, 3rd reserve artillery brigade. 3, 11, 22a. *VPR*, part 2 book 2, pp. 286–7; *Revoliutsiia 1905–1907 godov v g. Samare*, pp. 329–32; *Privolzhskii krai*, 23 June 1906; *Mysl'*, 23 June 1906; 27 June 1906.

June 15. Grozny. 82nd Dagestan infantry, 12th company. 1, 12, 23a. *VPR*, part 2 book 3, p. 306; Kireev, *Rabochii klass*, p. 137; *Baku*, 1 July 1906.

June 15. Orel Province. 31st Don cossacks, detachment of. 1, 10, 23a. *VPR*, part 2 book 2, pp. 155, 473 fn. 121; *Prizyv*, 15 June 1906 (official telegram).

June 15. Tiflis. 156th Elizavetpol infantry. 3, 15. *Resheniia Glavnogo voennogo suda za 1907 g.*, pp. 191–5; *Trudovaia zhizn'*, 20 June 1906.

June ca. 15. Sevastopol. Fortress infantry. 1, 11, 22. *Voennyi golos*, 18 June 1906; *Mysl'*, 22 June 1906; 24 June 1906.

June, first half. Nizhnii Novgorod. 239th Oka reserve infantry battalion. 0, 10, 22. *Revoliutsionnoe dvizhenie v N. Novgorode*, p. 471; *Ekho*, 4 July 1906.

June, first half. Chernigov. 167th Ostrozhsk infantry. 0, 10. *VPR*, part 2 book 3, p. 244.

June, first half. Odessa. 57th Modlin infantry. 6, 10, 22. *VPR*, part 2 book 3, p. 234.

June, first half. Odessa. 60th Zamoste infantry. 0, 10. *VPR*, part 2 book 3, p. 234.

June, first half. Tambov Province. Unidentified infantry, one company. 1, 18, 23a. *Krest'ianskoe dvizhenie 1905–1907 gg. v tambovskoi gubernii*, pp. 113–4.

June, first half (arbitrarily). Nizhnii Novgorod Province. Unidentified infantry, one company. 1, 18, 23a. Shestovalov, "Bol'shevistskaia propaganda," p. 88.

June 17–28. Verkhnedneprovsk. 20th Don cossacks, one squadron. 0, 10, 22, 24b. *Kurskaia vest'*, 7 July 1906; *Iuzhnaia zaria*, 29 June 1906; *Golos trudy*, 5 July 1906.

June 17. Kaluga. 9th Ingermanland infantry. 6, 10, 22. Zheleznov, "Revoliutsionnoe dvizhenie," pp. 137–8; *Revoliutsionnoe dvizhenie v Kaluzhskoi gubernii*, pp. 161–2.

June 17–18. Petersburg. Tsarskoe Selo railway battalion. 0, 10. *Ekho*, 22 June 1906.

June 18. Kovna Province. 3rd Don cossacks. 1, 10, 23a. *Mysl'*, 27 June 1906 (official telegram).

June 18. Nizhnii Novgorod. 32nd Don Cossacks. 3, 18, 22, 23d. *VPR*, part 2 book 2, p. 61; Zheleznov, "Revoliutsionnoe dvizhenie," p. 147; *Soldatskaia mysl'* (SR, Petersburg), no. 3, Dec. 1905.

June 18–20. Rostov, camp near. 1st and 3rd Grenadier artillery brigades. 1, 10, 22a. *VPR*, part 2 book 1, pp. 511–2; *VPR*, part 2 book 2, pp. 82–3, 465 fn. 66; Zheleznov, "Revoliutsionnoe dvizhenie," pp. 136–7; Mel'nikov, "Revoliutsionnoe dvizhenie . . . 1906 g.," pp. 99–100, 106; Pavchinskii, *Russkaia armiia*, pp. 68–9; *Mysl'*, 30 June 1906.

June 18–27. Tambov. 7th reserve cavalry. 3, 17, 22ad, 24c. *VPR*, part 2 book 2, pp. 183–5; "Iz istorii revoliutsionnogo dvizheniia v armii v 1905–1906 gg. (Vosstanie 7-go zapasnogo kavaleriiskogo polka v Tambove)," *KA*, 1935 no. 4, pp. 39–59; Konovalov, "Revoliutsionnoe dvizhenie," pp. 83–9; Pavchinskii, *Russkaia armiia*, pp. 83–7.

June ca. 20. Kostroma. 140th Zaraisk infantry. 1, 10, 23a. *Dvadtsatyi vek*, 23 June 1906; *Ekho*, 4 July 1906.

June 20–29. Taganrog. 2nd reserve artillery brigade, 2nd battery. 0, 10, 24b. *VPR*, part 2 book 2, p. 205; *1905–1907 gody na Donu*, pp. 329–30.

June 21–22. Tiflis. Caucasus railway battalion. 5, 16, 23c, 24a. *Trudovaia zhizn'*, 22 June 1906; *VPR*, part 2 book 3, pp. 367, 374–81.

June 21–22. Petersburg. 88th Petrovsk infantry. 0, 10, 23b. *VPR*, part 2 book 1, pp. 324–5; Korablev, "Revoliutsionnoe dvizhenie," p. 114; *Ekho*, 29 June 1906.

June 21. Tara (Tobolsk Province). Local detail. 0, 15. Kondrikov, "Revoliutsionnye vystupleniia," p. 105.

June 21. Taganrog. 41st Don cossacks, 1st squadron. 1, 12, 23a. *1905–1907 gody na Donu*, pp. 329–30; *VPR*, part 2 book 2, p. 205; *Donskaia zhizn'*, 22 June 1906.

June 21. Vologda. 139th Morshansk infantry, one battalion. 4, 11. *Kostromskoe slovo*, 6 July 1906.

June 21 or 22. Iaransk (Viatka Province). Military escort. 3, 10, 24a. *Severnaia zemlia*, 23 June 1906 (semi-official telegram).

June 21–23. Iuzovka. 3rd detached Don cossack squadron. 1, 15, 23a. *VPR*, part 2 book 3, pp. 37, 39, 44–5, 65, 67–74, 156.

June 21–26. Tashkent. 2nd Transcaspian railway battalion, 6th company. 5, 18, 23c. Soifer, *Revoliutsionnoe dvizhenie*, 82–3.

June 21–26. Tiumen. 9th Tobolsk Siberian infantry. 1, 18, 22, 23e. Pavchinskii, *Russkaia armiia*, pp. 63–4; *Ekho*, 2 July 1906; 6 July 1906.

June 22–30. Kaluga Province. 6th sapper brigade (4 battalions). 3, 16, 22. For sources, see Chapter 8, fn. 18.

June 22. Tiflis. Medics. 1, 10, 23c. *VPR*, part 2 book 3, p. 301.

June 22 or 23. Moscow. 137th Nezhin infantry. 1, 11, 22. Mel'nikov, "Revoliutsionnoe dvizhenie . . . 1906 g.," p. 102; Zheleznov, "Revoliutsionnoe dvizhenie," p. 144; *Soldatskaia mysl'* (SD, Moscow), no. 2, June 1906; no. 3, 12 July 1906.

June 24. Moscow. 3rd Sumy dragoons. 0, 12, 22. Mel'nikov, "Revoliutsionnoe dvizhenie . . . 1906 g.," p. 114; *Soldatskaia mysl'* (SD, Moscow), no. 3, 12 July 1906.

June 24–28. Moscow. 1st Don cossacks, cossacks from other units. 1, 10, 22, 23c. Pavchinskii, *Russkaia armiia*, pp. 76–7; Mel'nikov, "Revoliutsionnoe dvizhenie . . . 1906 g.," p. 115; *Ekho*, 1 July 1906.

June 25. Tomsk. 8th Tomsk Siberian infantry. 3, 16, 22. *VPR*, part 2 book 2, pp. 438–9, 498–9 fns. 320–321.

June 25. Grozny. 82nd Dagestan infantry, 10th and 15th companies. 1, 15, 23ad. *VPR*, part 2 book 2, pp. 221–3; *VPR*, part 2 book 3, p. 306; Kireev, *Rabochii klass*, pp. 137, 141–3; *Baku*, 1 July 1906; *Trudovaia zhizn'*, 2 July 1906.

June 25–26. Aleksandropol. 1st and 2nd Caucasus sapper battalions. 1, 16. *VPR*, part 2 book 3, pp. 384–96; *Revoliutsionnoe dvizhenie v Armenii*, pp. 354–8, 361–4, 369.

June 27. Voronezh. 223rd Korotoiak infantry. 0, 10. Zheleznov, "Revoliutsionnoe dvizhenie," pp. 148, 379.

June 27–July 5. Orenburg. 242nd Belebei infantry. 1, 12, 22. *VPR*, part 2 book 2, pp. 357–8; *Privolzhskii krai*, 1 August 1906.

June 27–30. Kronstadt. Cruiser *Rynda*. 0, 15. Drezen, *Revoliutsiia vo flote*, p. 54.

June 28–29. Batum. 260th Adragansk infantry, fortress mine company, 1st Caucasus rifle battalion (3rd company). 3, 15. *Revoliutsiia 1905–1907 gg. v Gruzii*, pp. 696–8; Steklov, "Revoliutsionnoe dvizhenie," pp. 435–6.

June 29–July 1. Libava. 3rd fortress artillery battalion, fortress mine company. 6, 12, 22. *Soldat* (SD, Libava), no. 17, 8 July 1906.

June 30–early July. Morshansk. 219th Iukhnov and 220th Epifan infantry. 1, 18, 22a. *VPR*, part 2 book 2, pp. 165–6; Zheleznov, "Revoliutsionnoe dvizhenie," p. 159; *Proletarii* (Bolshevik, Finland-Paris), no. 3, 8 Sept. 1906.

June, second half. Kishinev. 54th Minsk infantry. 0, 10. *Russkoe slovo*, 17 June 1906; *Ekho*, 4 July 1906.

June, second half. Vinnitsa. 47th Ukrainian infantry. 0, 10, 22. *Ekho*, 22 June 1906.

June, second half. Petersburg. Guards Cuirassiers. 3, 15. *Mysl'*, 28 June 1906; *Ekho*, 4 July 1906.

June, second half. Moscow. Artillery depot. 0, 12. Mel'nikov, "Revoliutsionnoe dvizhenie . . . 1906 g.," pp. 114, 116.

June, second half. Moscow. Grenadier sapper battalion. 0, 10, 22. Mel'nikov, "Revoliutsionnoe dvizhenie . . . 1906 g.," pp. 114, 116.

June, second half (arbitrarily). Petersburg. 200th Izhorsk regiment, 1, 15, 22a. Korablev, "Revoliutsionnoe dvizhenie," p. 155.

June, second half. Warsaw. 3rd and 4th Warsaw fortress infantry regiments. 0, 10, 23b. Pawłowski, *Wojskowa*, p. 314; *Ekho*, 4 July 1906.

June, second half. Warsaw. 184th Warsaw infantry. 1, 10. Pawłowski, *Wojskowa*, p. 315; *Ekho*, 4 July 1906; 5 July 1906.

June, late. Petersburg. Horse Guards. 0, 10, 22. *Mysl'*, 4 July 1906; *Voennyi golos*,

18 July 1906.

June, late. Kiev. 132 Bendery infantry. 6, 10. *Mysl'*, 27 June 1906; *Ekho*, 4 July 1906.

July 2–19. Zlatoust. 214th Moksha infantry. 0, 16, 23, 24c. *VPR*, part 2 book 2, pp. 385–6; *Voennyi golos*, 13 July 1906; 19 July 1906.

July 3. Tashkent. Turkestan sapper battalion, Transcaspian sapper battalion, 2nd Transcaspian railway battalion (2nd company). 1, 17, 24c. Piaskovskii, *Revoliutsiia 1905–1907*, pp. 421–5; *VPR*, part 2 book 3, pp. 438–48; A. Rudyi, "Iiul'skoe vosstanie v Tashkente," *IV*, v. 116, 1909, pp. 891–900.

July 3. Zambrow. 15th Shlisselburg infantry. 0, 10, 23. Pawłowski, *Wojskowa*, p. 316.

July 5. Baltic fleet. Battleship *Slava*. 3, 13. *Soldatskaia beseda* (SD, Central Committee), no. 5, 2 Dec. 1906.

July 5. Lublin. 69th Riazan infantry (six companies). 3, 10. Pawłowski, *Wojskowa*, p. 316.

July 6. Elizavetgrad. 33rd Don cossacks. 0, 10, 23. *Mysl'*, 6 July 1906.

July, early. Kutko. 4th rifle battalion. 3, 10. *Ekho*, 7 July 1906.

July, first quarter. Aleksandropol. 80th Kabardinsk infantry. 0, 10, 22a. *Revoliutsionnoe dvizhenie v Armenii*, pp. 392–3.

July, early. Saratov. 7th Orenburg cossacks, one squadron. 0, 14, 22. *Privolzhskii krai*, 6 July 1906.

July 9. Rostov-on-Don. 41st Don cossacks, 2nd squadron. 0, 10. Ovsiannikov, "Revoliutsionnoe dvizhenie," p. 196; *1905. Armiia*, p. 379.

July 9. Taganrog. 8th detached Don cossack squadron, local cossack detail. 1, 12, 23a. *1905–1907 gody na Donu*, p. 321; *Kurskaia vest'*, 13 July 1906.

July 9–10. Brest-Litovsk. Fortress artillery, 2nd siege artillery regiment, 19th sapper battalion. 1, 16, 22, 23e, 24c. *VPR*, part 2 book 3, pp. 477–9, 654 fn. 207; Pavchinskii, *Russkaia armiia*, p. 108.

July 10. Orany. 2nd sapper brigade (4 battalions). 1, 12, 22. *VPR*, part 2 book 3, pp. 460–1; *Revoliutsiia 1905–1907 gg. v Litve*, pp. 446–8.

July 10–11. Samara. 215th Buzuluk infantry. 1, 15, 23be. *Revoliutsiia 1905–1907 godov v g. Samare*, pp. 354–60.

July 12. Amu-Daria Flotilla. Steamer *Tsesarevich*, barge *Volga*. 5, 12. Cherkasov, "Revoliutsionnoe dvizhenie," p. 335.

July 15. Poltava. 34th Sevsk infantry, 9th artillery brigade. 1, 17, 23e, 24c. *VPR*, part 2 book 3, pp. 140–2; Kantsel'son, "Revoliutsionnoe dvizhenie," pp. 240–2; G. Gruza, "Poltavskoe voennoe vosstanie," *1905 god na Poltavshchine*, Poltava, 1925, pp. 46–9.

July 15. Ekaterinodar. 2nd (?) Urup Kuban cossacks. 1, 12, 23a. *Kurskaia vest'*, 30 July 1906.

July 15. Mariampol. 111th Don infantry. 3, 13, 23e. *VPR*, part 2 book 3, pp. 613–4; *Revoliutsiia 1905–1907 gg. v Litve*, pp. 441–2.

July 15. Novyi Margelan. 4th Andizhan (Turkestan) reserve battalion, 5th company. 3, 13, 24c. Soifer, *Revoliutsionnoe dvizhenie*, pp. 101–2; Cherkasov, "Revoliutsionnoe dvizhenie," pp. 304, 335–6.

July, first half. Vologda. 86th Vilmanstrand and 139th Morshansk infantry. 0, 10, 23. Zheleznov, "Revoliutsionnoe dvizhenie," p. 150; *Soldatskaia beseda* (SD,

Central Committee), no. 3, 13 Oct. 1906.

July, first half. Askhabad. All units (see June 13–18). 1, 12, 23e. *Soldatskaia beseda* (SD, Central Committee), no. 3, 13 Oct. 1906.

July 16. Krasnovodsk. 1st Transcaspian railway battalion, 1st company. 1, 14. *VPR*, part 2 book 3, pp. 421, 425; Annanepesov, *Uchastie*, pp. 147–8.

July 16. Olty (Kars Province). Local detail, warehouse detail. 1, 10, 22. Steklov, "Revoliutsionnoe dvizhenie," p. 442.

July 17. Harbin. Unidentified units. 0, 15, 22. Stankevich, *Khronika*, p. 101.

July 17–18. Deshlagar. 83rd Samur infantry. 1, 14, 23e, 24c. Gadzhiev, "Revoliutsionnye vystupleniia," pp. 74–81; Narushevich, "Vosstanie soldat," pp. 57–60; *VPR*, part 2 book 3, pp. 334–7; *VPR*, part 2 book 2, pp. 229–31.

July 17–20. Sveaborg. Fortress artillerists, sailors, miners. 3, 17, 23e, 24c. For sources, see Chapter 8, fns. 42, 45.

July 18–20. Lyskovo (Nizhnii Novgorod Province). 238th Kliazma and 306th Kovrov reserve battalions. 3, 16, 23, 24a. Zheleznov, "Revoliutsionnoe dvizhenie," pp. 151–3; *Revoliutsionnoe dvizhenie v N. Novgorode*, p. 30; Shestovalov, "Bol'shevistskaia," pp. 88–9; *VPR*, part 2 book 2, pp. 63–6.

July 19–20. Kronstadt. Sailors, miners, sappers, battleship *Aleksandr II*. 1, 17, 23e, 24c. For sources, see Chapter 8, fns. 44, 46.

July 19–20. Revel. Cruiser *Pamiat' Azova*. 1, 17, 23e, 24c. For sources, see Chapter 8, fn. 47.

July 20. Revel. Training ship *Riga*. 0, 12, 23e, 24c. Drezen, *Revoliutsiia vo flote*, p. 66.

July 20. Temir-Khan-Shury. 21st artillery park. 1, 10. *VPR*, part 2 book 3, p. 305.

July 20. Helsingfors. Mine cruiser *Kazanets*. 5, 10. Drezen, *Revoliutsiia vo flote*, p. 65.

July 21. Petersburg. 200th Izhorsk infantry. 1, 10, 23c. TsK RSDRP, "Pis'mo k partiinym organizastiiam No. 5," July 1906, Helsinki 117 II.

July 21. Near Revel. Training ship *Evropa*. 5, 11. Drezen, *Revoliutsiia vo flote*, p. 66.

July 22. Aleksandropol. 153rd Baku infantry. 0, 16, 23. *Revoliutsionnoe dvizhenie v Armenii*, pp. 386–7.

July 22–3. Manchuria station. 19th East Siberian rifles. 3, 15. *Karatel'nye ekspeditsii*, p. 392.

July 22–24. Irkutsk. 6th East Siberian sapper battalion. 3, 16. Poleshchuk, "Revoliutsionnoe dvizhenie . . . Irkutskogo," pp. 365–6.

July, second decade. Tambov. 218th Borisoglebsk infantry. 0, 10, 24a. Zheleznov, "Revoliutsionnoe dvizhenie," pp. 143–4.

July 23–24. Chita. 2nd East Siberian sapper battalion. 3, 16, 24a. *VPR*, part 2 book 2, pp. 424–5; *Karatel'nye ekspeditsii*, p. 392; Poleshchuk, "Revoliutsionnoe dvizhenie . . . Irkutskogo," pp. 367–9.

July 26. Penza Province. 127th Putilovo infantry, one company. 1, 10, 23a. *Revoliutsionnaia bor'ba trudiashchikhsia Penzenskoi gubernii v 1905–1907 godakh. Sbornik dokumentov*, Penza, 1955, p. 128.

July 31–August 1. Tiflis Province. 2nd Poltava Kuban cossacks, 5th squadron. 5, 16. *VPR*, part 2 book 3, pp. 301–2.

August 1. Chita. 18th East Siberian rifles, 3rd company. 1, 15, 23a. *VPR*, part 2 book 2; *Karatel'nye ekspeditsii*, pp. 393–5; *Sotsial-demokrat* (TsK RSDRP), no. 4, 20

Oct. 1906.

August 3. Vitebsk. 163rd Lenkoransko-Nasheburg infantry. 6, 12, 24b. *VPR*, part 2 book 3, p. 465.

August 12. Ilovlia station (Tsaritsyn Province). 21st Don cossacks. 0, 10. *Kazarma*, 5 Sept. 1906 (official telegram).

August 14. Petrovskoe (Stravropol Province). 2nd Gorsko-Mozdok Terek cossacks. 1, 18, 23a. *VPR*, part 2 book 3, pp. 306–7; *Kazarma*, 5 Sept. 1906 (official telegram).

August 14. Kars. 1st battalion fortress infantry. 1, 11. *Revoliutsionnoe dvizhenie v Armenii*, pp. 387–91.

August, first half? Samarkand. 2nd Urals cossacks. 0, 11. Piaskovskii, *Revoliutsiia 1905–1907*, p. 427.

August 22. Konstantinovskoe (Stavropol Province). Caucasus reserve artillery brigade. 1, 16, 23a. *VPR*, part 2 book 3, p. 307.

August, late. Kars. 2nd Chernomorsk Kuban cossacks. 3, 10. *VPR*, part 2 book 3, p. 299.

September 4. Baku. Railway battalion. 3, 15, 23c. *Riadovoi* (SD, Baku), no. 2, 1906.

September 6. Kokand. 12th Turkestan rifle battalion, 3rd and 4th companies. 0, 10, 22. Piaskovskii, *Revoliutsiia 1905–1907*, p. 427.

September 10. Turinsk (Tobolsk Province). Local detail. 0, 10, 24ab. Kondrikov, "Revoliutsionnye vystupleniia," p. 111.

September. Berdichev. Unidentified Urals cossacks. 0, 15. *Soldatskaia gazeta*, (SR, Central Committee), no. 3, 8 Oct. 1906.

September. Petersburg. 145th Novocherkassk infantry, 15th company. 1, 10, 23a. *VPR*, part 2 book 1, p. 613 fn. 184.

September, second half. Lodz. 37th Ekaterinburg infantry. 0, 15. Pawłowski, *Wojskowa*, p. 331.

September, second half. Helsingfors. 23rd mountain battery. 3, 11. *Kazarma*, 26 Nov. 1906.

October 2. Iaomyn station, Chinese-Eastern railway. 2nd Transamur railway battalion. 0, 15. Stankevich, *Khronika*, pp. 103–4.

October 3–5. Vladivostok. Unidentified sappers, 4th company. 6, 11. *Volia*, 3 Nov. 1905.

October 10. Vladivostok. 5th East-Siberian mountain battery. 3, 16. *Resheniia Glavnogo voennogo suda za 1907 g.*, pp. 147–9; Stankevich, *Khronika*, p. 121.

October 13. Eniseisk. Local detail. 5, 10. Poleshchuk, "Revoliutsionnoe dvizhenie . . . Irkutskogo," p. 371.

October 17, 30. Iaomyn station, Chinese-Eastern railway. 2nd Transamur railway battalion, 11th company. 1, 15. *Volia*, 2 Dec. 1906.

October 18. Libava. 178th Venden infantry, clerks. 1, 16. *Soldat* (Libava, SD), no. 25, 18 Nov. 1906; Surikov, "Revoliutsionnoe dvizhenie," p. 283.

October 21. Krasnoiarsk. 31st East Siberian rifles, one company. 3, 16, 24a. *VPR*, part 3, pp. 313, 564 fn. 315; *Obzor revoliutsionnogo dvizheniia v okruge Irkutskoi sudovoi palaty*, p. 34.

October. Nikolsk-Ussuriisk. 4th East Siberian rifles, training detail. 5, 15. *Volia*, 2 Dec. 1906.

November 27. Moimodza station, Chinese-Eastern railway. 6th East Siberian
sapper battalion. 1, 12, 23b. Stankevich, *Khronika*, p. 105.
December 7. Nikolsk-Ussuriisk. Unidentified railway battalion. 3, 11. *Volia*, 7
January 1907.
December. Moscow. 1st Don cossacks. 0, 15. Mel'nikov, "Revoliutsionnoe
dvizhenie . . . 1906 g.," p. 126.

Notes

I. Officers and Men in the Russian Army

1. Translated as "Distsiplina v russkoi armii," *Razvedchik*, 22 Sept. 1903.

2. Walter Pintner, "Russia as a Great Power, 1709–1856: Reflections on the Problem of Relative Backwardness, with Special Reference to the Russian Army and Russian Society," Kennan Institute Occasional Paper No. 33, Washington, D.C., July 18, 1978, pp. 2–3, 48–9. Another selection of foreign comments on the eighteenth-century Russian army is provided by M. Borodkin, "Russkaia armiia pri Ekaterine II," *VS*, 1909 no. 8, pp. 18–19.

3. Fon Tettau, "Dva mesiatsa v gostiakh v russkoi armii," *Razvedchik*, 17 Feb. 1904 (emphasis presumably added by the editors of *Razvedchik*). Among the many books Von Tettau wrote on the Russian army was *Ergänzung und Organisation der Russischen Armee in Krieg und Frieden*, Berlin, 1902.

4. "Distsiplina v russkoi armii," *Razvedchik*, 22 Sept. 1903.

5. "Otchet po prizyvu k ispolneniiu voinskoi povinnosti naseleniia Imperii za 1903 god," *VS*, 1905 no. 1, pp. 264–5. In the infantry, cavalry, and artillery in 1910, 60–65% were agriculturalists, 16–19% artisans and tradesmen; in engineering units 27% and in railroad units 8% were agriculturalists, while in both 46% were artisans and tradesmen; *Voenno-statisticheskii ezhegodnik armii za 1910 god*, Spb., 1911, p. 279.

6. Two officers made this connection intelligently: A. Rittikh, *Russkii voennyi byt v deistvitel'nosti i mechtakh*, Spb., 1893, pp. 257–9, and Veselovskii, *K voprosu o vospitanii soldat*, Spb., 1900, pp. 7–10.

7. On the Petrine officer corps, see M. D. Rabinovich, "Sotsial'noe proiskhozhdenie i imushchestvennoe polozhenie ofitserov reguliarnoi russkoi armii v kontse Severnoi voiny," *Rossiia v period reform Petra I*, M., 1973, pp. 133–71; I have recombined his social categories to arrive at the figure 17% non-noble. For the rest of the eighteenth and early nineteenth century, see the well-reasoned speculation in Pintner, "Russia as a Great Power," pp. 36–7. The figure on class background for the mid-nineteenth century is from John Shelton Curtiss, *The Russian Army under Nicholas I, 1825–1855*, Durham, N.C., 1965, p. 177. For the late nineteenth century, see P. A. Zaionchkovskii, *Samoderzhavie i russkaia armiia na rubezhe XIX–XX stoletii*, M., 1973, pp. 203–12, and A. P. Korelin, *Dvorianstvo v poreformennoi Rossii 1861–1904 gg.*, M., 1979, p. 86.

8. Zaionchkovskii, *Samoderzhavie*, pp. 213, 220–27; Hans-Peter Stein, "Der Offizier des russischen Heeres im Zeitabschnitt zwischen Reform und Revolution, 1861–1905," *Forschungen zur osteuropäischen Geschichte*, v. 13, 1967, pp. 409–

11, 415–18; John Bushnell, "The Tsarist Officer Corps, 1881–1914: Customs, Duties, Inefficiency," *American Historical Review*, v. 86 no. 4, Oct. 1981, pp. 757–8.

9. For a more detailed discussion, see Bushnell, "Tsarist Officer Corps," pp. 755–63. See also William C. Fuller, Jr., *Civil-Military Conflict in Imperial Russia*, Chapter 1, forthcoming, Princeton University Press.

10. Nikolai A. Epanchin, "Na sluzhbe trekh imperatorov," typescript, 1939, Bakhmeteff Archive, Columbia University, p. 70.

11. Alexander Herzen, "The Russian People and Socialism. An Open Letter to Jules Michelet," in Herzen, *From the Other Shore*, New York, 1956, p. 182.

12. George Foster, "Peasant Society and the Image of Limited Good," *American Anthropologist*, v. 67 no. 2, 1967, pp. 293–315.

13. A. G. Rashin, "Gramotnost' i narodnoe obrazovanie v XIX i nachale XX v.," *IZ*, v. 37, 1951, p. 45.

14. Ben Eklof, "Peasant Sloth Reconsidered: Strategies of Education and Learning in Rural Russia before the Revolution," *JSH*, Spring 1981, pp. 355–85.

15. V. A. Nikonov, *Imia i obshchestvo*, M., 1974, pp. 66, 172–3.

16. For a useful review of the literature on the Miliutin reforms, see Peter Von Wahlde, "Dmitrii Miliutin: Appraisals," *Canadian Slavic Studies*, v. 3, no. 2, Summer 1969, pp. 400–414. The best study is P. A. Zaionchkovskii, *Voennye reformy 1860–1870 godov v Rossii*, M., 1952.

17. For a brief account of the traditional leave-taking ritual, and a sample of the laments recited over the conscripts, see E. V. Barsov, *Prichitan'ia severnogo kraia*, v. 2, *Plachi, zavoennye, rekrutskie i soldatskie*, M., 1882, pp. 262–75. Sources from other regions describe much the same ritual.

18. A. N. Radishchev, *Puteshestvie iz Peterburga v Moskvu*, M., 1966, p. 174.

19. Barsov, *Prichitan'ia*, v. 2, p. 220.

20. A superficial survey is provided by E. N. Pushkarev, "Soldatskaia pesnia—istochnik po istorii voennogo byta russkoi reguliarnoi armii XVIII–pervoi polviny XIX v.," *Voprosy voennoi istorii Rossii. XVIII i pervaia polovina XIX vekov*, M., 1969, pp. 422–32.

21. For Miliutin's general thoughts on military reform, see P. A. Zaionchkovskii, "D. A. Miliutin. Biograficheskii ocherk," in D. A. Miliutin, *Dnevnik D. A. Miliutina 1873–1875*, v. 1, M., 1947, pp. 23–6; Zaionchkovskii, *Voennye reformy*, pp. 49–50, 52, 58; Edwin Willis Brooks, "D. A. Miliutin. Life and Activity to 1856," Ph.D. dissertation, Stanford University, 1970, pp. 162–3. For Miliutin's observations on military life as he knew it in the artillery, see D. A. Miliutin, *Vospominaniia*, Tomsk, 1919, reprinted with an introduction by Bruce Lincoln, Newtonville, Mass., 1979, pp. 80, 86–7, 90–93. Miliutin's remarks on the treatment of soldiers are in "Suvorov kak polkovodets," *Otechestvennye zapiski*, 3 part 2, April 1839, pp. 24, 27–8, 31.

22. Brooks, "Miliutin," pp. 14, 28, 37, 45–6, 50–51, 67, 88–9, 99–100, 112–23, 134, 142, 147–8, 160 and passim; Zaionchkovskii, "D. A. Miliutin," pp. 7, 21, 32, 36, 37, 57–9, 63–4; Zaionchkovskii, *Voennye reformy*, pp. 54–5, 82, 258–9.

23. Zaionchkovskii, *Voennye reformy*, pp. 82–3, 104; "O rekrutskom nabore v 1863 godu," *VS*, v. 28, 1862, pp. 385–92.

24. M. Grulev, *Zloby dnia v zhizni armii*, [Brest-Litovsk], 1911, p. 75; Zaion-

chkovskii, *Voennye reformy,* pp. 210–13; Forrestt A. Miller, *Dmitrii Miliutin and the Reform Era in Russia,* Nashville, Tenn., 1968, pp. 210–13; Rashin, "Gramotnost'," p. 44. In the late 1850s and 1860s, *Voennyi sbornik* published numerous articles emphasizing the advantages of literacy.

25. Quoted in Nicholas Golovine, *The Russian Army in the World War,* New Haven, 1931, pp. 1–2. Miller, *Dmitrii Miliutin,* pp. 182–225; P. A. Zaionchkovskii, "Podgotovka voennoi reformy 1874 goda," *IZ,* v. 27, 1948, pp. 170–201; Miliutin, *Dnevnik,* v. 1, pp. 77–80, 83, 105–11, 119–20.

26. In fact, literacy instruction was made optional in 1880, during Miliutin's tenure; Grulev, *Zloby dnia,* pp. 75–8. I have seen no discussion of this, but it is likely that Miliutin yielded to the pressure of colonels and generals who complained that schooling cut into drill, the standard excuse officers gave for not educating illiterate soldiers. On the post-Miliutin attitude toward educating soldiers, see John Bushnell, "Peasants in Uniform: The Tsarist Army as a Peasant Society," *JSH,* Summer 1980, pp. 566, 573 n. 4. In addition: N. Butovskii, "Shkola gramotnosti i prepodavanie ustavov v voiskakh," *VS,* 1886, no. 6, pp. 301–5; K. Shavrov, "Gramotnost' v voiskakh," *VS,* 1892 no. 2, pp. 191–6; F. A. Arnol'dov, "Sovremennoe znachenie voinskoi povinnosti," *Ezhemesiachnye literaturnye prilozheniia k zhurnalu "Niva,"* May–Aug. 1902, pp. 271–2; P. Kochergin, *Nuzhdy russkogo soldata,* Saratov, 1905, pp. 11–12, 16–17; L.S., "Vospominaniia studenta-soldata," *Byloe,* 1906, no. 5, pp. 180–81; A. I. Denikin, *Staraia armiia,* v. 2, Paris, 1931, p. 165. A. I. Denikin, *Put' russkogo ofitsera,* New York, 1953, p. 123, claims that at least after 1902 hundreds of thousands of Russian soldiers did become literate while in the army, but the statistics do not bear him out. In 1910, 46% of all soldiers in the army were literate, 22% were semiliterate (probably meaning they could read but not write); *Voenno-statisticheskii ezhegodnik armii za 1910 god,* p. 276. The combined figure is just slightly higher than the average rate of literacy of the conscript classes of 1907–1909: 61.9, 64.1, 62.9. Rashin, "Gramotnost'," p. 45. There would in any case be a tendency for army literacy to be slightly above conscript literacy even in the complete absence of schooling in the army, since the few NCO reenlistees would necessarily have been literate.

27. N. Wrangel, *From Serfdom to Bolshevism. The Memoirs of Baron N. Wrangel 1847–1920,* Philadelphia, 1927, pp. 121, 123.

28. Fedor Stepun, *Byvshee i nesbyvsheesia,* v. 1, 1956, pp. 65, 67–71, 73, 75, 79, 81, 86; *Golos iz russkoi armii. Razoblacheniia,* Berlin, 1902, pp. 5, 7–8, 20, 23, 28, 30, 36, 50–51, 53, 58–61; M. Grulev, *Zapiski generala-evreia,* Paris, 1930, pp. 92–3; *V tsarstve shtykov,* Nizhnii Novgorod, 1908, p. 9; Captain Ivanko, "Sluzhba v polku," *Na sluzhbe otechestva,* San Francisco, 1963, p. 290; L.S., "Vospominaniia studenta-soldata," pp. 170–71, 173–6, 178–9, 182–3.

29. A. Denikin, "Soldatskii byt," *Razvedchik,* 24 June 1903.

30. *Ustav vnutrennei sluzhby,* Spb., 1902, pp. 13–16; K. A. Piatin, *Spravochnik. Polnyi i podrobnyi alfavitnyi ukazatel' prikazov po voennomu vedomstvu, tsirkuliarov, predpisanii i otzyvov Glavnogo shtaba i prochikh Glavnykh upravlenii i prikazov, prikazanii i tsirkuliarov po vsem voennym okrugam. Za 52 goda, s 1859 po 1911 g.,* Book 2, 3rd ed., Spb., 1911.

31. The evidence on this point is conclusive. Tsarist officers themselves pro-

vide ample testimony: E. I. Martynov, *Iz pechal'nogo opyta russko-iaponskoi voiny,* Spb., 1906, p. 72; Aleksei Ignatyev, *A Subaltern in Old Russia,* London, 1944, p. 95; A. I. Denikin, *Staraia armiia,* v. 1, Paris, 1929, pp. 46–7; A. Lobanov-Rostovsky, *The Grinding Mill. Reminiscences of War and Revolution in Russia, 1913–1920,* New York, 1935, pp. 6–7; Kochergin, *Nuzhdy,* p. 14.

32. For a summary of the controversy over the form of address, see Grulev, *Zloby dnia,* pp. 1–4.

33. "Bran' v voiskakh," *Razvedchik* no. 560, 10 July 1901.

34. *Golos iz russkoi armii,* pp. 7–8, 49, 62; P. N. Krasnov, *Ot Dvuglavogo Orla k krasnomu znameni,* v. 1, New York, 1960, pp. 46–8. Officers knew that soldiers came into the army expecting to be beaten; Zenchenko, *Obuchenie i vospitanie soldata. (Soobshchenie),* Spb., 1902, p. 74.

35. Rittikh, *Russkii,* p. 20, also pp. 38, 263. For a similar view, see Arnol'dov, "Sovremennoe znachenie voinskoi povinnosti," pp. 266–72.

36. Daniel Lerner and Richard D. Robinson, "Swords and Plowshares: The Turkish Army as a Modernizing Force," *World Politics,* v. 13, Oct. 1960, p. 32. The same thought has been expressed by others who have studied third world armies.

37. Fuller, *Civil-Military Conflict,* Chapter II. The comparison of course is of total military expenditures divided by the number of soldiers. Comparison of the money actually devoted to the upkeep of soldiers would be even less favorable to Russia—see Kochergin, *Nuzhdy,* pp. 62–3. Unfortunately, Kochergin compares provisions for Russian and Western soldiers in real rather than monetary terms.

38. See the sources in Bushnell, "Tsarist Officer Corps," p. 766, and Bushnell, "Peasants in Uniform," p. 573 n. 9.

39. A. Gerua, *Posle voiny. O nashei armii,* 2nd ed., Spb., 1907, p. 51; Vs. Sakharov, "Mysli po sovremennym voprosam," *VS,* 1907, no. 6, pp. 64–7. Similar estimates are provided by Grulev, *Zloby dnia,* p. 154; Denikin, *Staraia armiia,* v. 2, pp. 179–80; and A. Petrov, "Prakticheskie zaniatiia pekhoty v letnyi period," *VS,* 1905 no. 10, pp. 72–3.

40. Petrov, "Prakticheskie zaniatiia," pp. 65–82; V. M. Dragomirov, "Podgotovka russkoi armii k velikoi voine," *VS,* v. 5, 1924, pp. 199, 204; A. Voronetskii, "K vospitaniiu voisk," *VS,* 1913 no. 11, p. 90.

41. Gerua, *Posle voiny,* p. 52.

42. Bushnell, "Tsarist Officer Corps," pp. 768–9 and notes.

43. On *vol'nye raboty* generally, see B. V. Gerua, *Vospominaniia, o moei zhizni,* v. 1, Paris, 1969, pp. 71–2; A. Gerua, *Posle voiny,* pp. 108–11; Grulev, *Zapiski,* p. 93; *V tsarstve shtykov,* p. 29; Denikin, *Staraia armiia,* v. 2, pp. 178–9; Rittikh, *Russkii,* pp. 51–2; Kochergin, *Nuzhdy,* pp. 34–5; *Polozhenie o khoziastve v rote,* Spb., 1878, pp. 44–8; and "Vol'nye raboty," *Razvedchik,* 1 May 1901.

44. Quoted in Zaionchkovskii, *Samoderzhavie,* pp. 272–3.

45. *Razvedchik,* 13 Feb. 1901.

46. *Razvedchik,* 12 Dec. 1902; Rittikh, *Russkii,* p. 52; Zaionchkovskii, *Samoderzhavie,* p. 275; F. A. Maksheev, *Voennoe khoziaistvo v mirnoe vremia v armiiakh: russkoi, germanskoi, avstriiskoi i frantsuzskoi. (Sravnitel'nyi ocherk sovremennogo ustroistva ego),* Spb., 1904, pp. 683–4. K. Kononovich, "Nuzhdy soldata i ego ras-

khody," *VS*, v. 25, 1862, p. 157, puts the earnings of an average Guards regiment at 11,880 rubles. V. Andro-de-Biui Gingliatt, "O rotnom khoziastve i neobkhodimykh denezhnykh sredstvakh dlia nego," *VS*, 1909, no. 8, p. 152, asserts that a company earned 600–1,000 rubles per year (a regiment, thus, 9,600–16,000) from *vol'nye raboty*, the hiring out of horses, and the sale of vegetables from the company garden.

47. Kochergin, *Nuzhdy*, pp. 32–3, 35–6, 39, 42. A selection of articles on the subject: *Razvedchik*, 13 Feb. 1901; 1 May 1901; 7 May 1902; 9 July 1902; 17 June 1903.

48. *Razvedchik*, 13 Feb. 1901; 7 May 1902; *VVZh*, 1902 no. 1; 1903 no. 5; Kochergin, *Nuzhdy*, pp. 39–42.

49. "Otriad generala Renenkampfa v 1900 godu," *VVZh*, 1902 no. 8, p. 755.

50. *Razvedchik*, 16 Oct. 1901.

51. F. Maksheev, "Zhalovan'e i pensii nizhnym chinam," *Intendantskii zhurnal*, 1903 no. 5, pp. 44–7; E. N. Sysoev, "Vol'nye raboty," *Razvedchik*, 1 May 1901; K. K. Piatnitskii, "Vol'nye raboty," *Razvedchik*, 14 Aug. 1901; "Po povodu proekta Podpolkovnika Derevitskogo ob otmene zhalovan'ia riadovym," *VVZh*, 1902 no. 5, sets the soldier's monthly budget at 147 kopeks. For the early 1860s, K. Kononovich, "Nuzhdy soldata i ego raskhody," set the monthly budget at 226 kopeks.

52. *Razvedchik*, 7 May 1902; 3 June 1903; 17 June 1903; *VVZh*, 1902 no. 1; A. M. Volgin, *Ob armii*, 3rd ed., Spb., 1908, p. 111; Kononovich, "Nuzhdy soldata," p. 159; Grulev, *Zapiski*, p. 94; B. V. Rechenberg-Linten, *Russische Soldaten und Offiziere aus der Zarenzeit. Nach selbsterlebnissen in einer russischen Garnison*, Bern-Leipzig, 1924, p. 16; Kochergin, *Nuzhdy*, p. 43; V. A. Petrov, *Ocherki po istorii revoliutsionnogo dvizheniia v Russkoi armii v 1905 g.*, M.-L., 1964, p. 150 (citing a Kostroma police source on soldier begging); and V. E. Poleshchuk, "Revoliutsionnoe dvizhenie v chastiakh Irkutskogo voennogo okruga," *Revoliutsionnoe dvizhenie v armii v gody pervoi russkoi revoliutsii. Sbornik statei*, M., 1955, p. 300 (begging reported in 1904 by the Irkutsk local brigade).

53. Bushnell, "Peasants in Uniform," p. 566.

54. Rittikh, *Russkii*, pp. 44–7, 54, 100, 143, 146, 153; Arnol'dov, "Sovremennoe znachenie voinskoi povinnosti," pp. 276–88.

55. Gerua, *Posle voiny*, p. 66; *Stoletie voennogo ministerstva, 1802–1902*, vol. 5, *Glavnoe intendantskoe upravlenie: Istoricheskii ocherk*, part 1, *Vvedenie i tsarstvovanie Imperatora Aleksandra I*, Spb., 1903, pp. 1–129; Beskrovnyi, *Russkaia armiia i flot v XVIII veke*, pp. 111–25, 375–82; V. Anichkov, *Voennoe khoziaistvo. Sravnitel'noe issledovanie polozhitel'nykh zakonodatel'stv Rossii, Frantsii, Prussii, Avstrii, Sardinii, Bel'gii i Bavarii*, Spb., 1860, pp. 456–8, 471–2, 543–6, 550–51, 556–60, 576–81, and passim; Curtiss, *Russian Army*, pp. 212–15, 246–48; Richard Pipes, "The Russian Military Colonies, 1810–31," *Journal of Modern History*, v. 12 no. 2, June 1950, pp. 205–19; Kononovich, "Nuzhdy soldata," pp. 156–8; Armeiskii rotnyi komandir, "Temnaia summa. Po povodu stat'i g. Klugina: Russkaia soldatskaia artel'," *VS*, v. 23, 1862, pp. 172–3; Zaionchkovskii, *Samoderzhavie*, pp. 270–71; V. F. Borzunov, *Proletariat Sibiri i Dal'nego Vostoka nakanune pervoi russkoi revoliutsii. (Po materialam stroitel'stva transsibirskoi magistrali, 1891–1904 gg.)*, M., 1965, pp. 36–7, 67–71.

56. *RI*, 28 Oct. 1900.

57. "Esche o vol'nykh rabotakh," *VVZh*, 1902 no. 1.

58. Denikin, *Staraia armiia*, v. 1, p. 93; General P. I. Zalesskii, *Vozmezdie. Prichiny russkoi katastrofy*, Berlin, 1925, pp. 62–4; A. Gerua, *Posle voiny*, pp. 48–9; Aleksandr Bragin, "Vospominaniia. Zhizni mysh'ia begotnia," typescript, 1941, Bakhmeteff Archive, Columbia University; v. 1, pp. 63–4. *Golos iz russkoi armii*, p. 5; Grulev, *Zloby dnia*, 228–9, 237–8, 269–70; N. Butovskii, *Stat'i na sovremennye temy*, Spb., 1907, pp. 62–65.

59. *V tsarstve shtykov*, pp. 13, 23; P. N. Krasnov, *Nakanune voiny*, Paris, 1937, pp. 14–15; P. N. Krasnov, *Na rubezhe Kitaia*, Paris, 1939, p. 66; Bragin, "Vospominaniia," v. 1, pp. 33–4, 64–6; v. 2, pp. 66–7; G. Mannerheim, *Erinnerungen*, Zurich, 1952, pp. 20–21; Petr Pil'skii, "Armiia i obshchestvo: Elementy vrazhdy i prepiatsvii," *Mir bozhii*, 1906 no. 7, pp. 223–4; Grulev, *Zloby dnia*, p. 23; V. Sukhomlinov, *Vospominaniia*, Berlin, 1924, pp. 94–5. As is made clear by D. A. Iuzefovich, "Neskol'ko slov ob ustroistve polkovogo i rotnogo khoziaistva," *VS*, v. 23, 1862, pp. 465–6, commanders did not always seek personal gain by acting as middlemen, they might instead be amassing funds for other needs of the unit; yet suspicion that they were profiting personally was, as Iuzefovich recognized, inevitable.

60. Zaionchkovskii, *Samoderzhavie*, pp. 274–5; *VVZh*, 1902 no. 1.

61. *Soldatskimi mozoliami ofitsery syto zhivut*: L. Voitolovskii, "Soldatskie pesni i skazki. (Iz knigi 'Po sledam voiny')," *Krasnaia nov'*, 1923 n. 5, p. 130.

62. A. P. Voznesenskii, "O voennom khoziaistve," *Obshchestvo revnitelei voennykh znanii*, 1906 no. 4, pp. 111–12, 122; Armeiskii rotnyi komandir, "Temnaia summa," pp. 171–2, 192; Lt. Col. Sul'menev, "Nedostatki nashego voiskovogo khoziaistva," *VS*, 1906 no. 5, pp. 190, 193; Staryi, "Kaveleriiskie mysli i nabroski," *VS*, 1906 no. 6, p. 133.

63. Barsov, *Prichitan'ia*, v. 2, p. 203.

64. A. Rediger, *Unter-ofitserskii vopros v glavnykh evropeiskikh armiiakh*, Spb., 1880, pp. 8–10, 145–7, 151–64 and passim; Grulev, *Zapiski*, pp. 92, 98; Zenchenko, *Obuchenie*, p. 59; A. Gerua, *Posle voiny*, p. 83; Col. Mamontov, "Sovremennoe polozhenie 'untr-ofitserskogo voprosa' v Rossii i za granitseiu," *Obshchestvo revnitelei voennykh znanii*, 1906 no. 4, pp. 97, 101–2; V. M. Dragomirov, "Podgotovka russkoi armii," v. 5, pp. 196–7; Zaionchkovskii, *Samoderzhavie*, pp. 120–23.

65. On the territorial basis of assignment to units, see A. Rediger, *Komplektovanie i ustroistvo vooruzhennoi sily*, 3rd ed., Spb., 1900, pp. 115–16; A. Gerua, *Posle voiny*, pp. 86, 88. Direct evidence on the existence of *zemliachestva* in army units is scant, but in August of 1907 a conference of SR military organizations resolved to use *zemliachestva* as a means of drawing soldiers into their organizations because of the very strong bonds among *zemliaki*; "Protokoly chastnogo soveshchaniia predstavitelei Vyborgskoi, Peterburgskoi, Kronshtadtskoi i Revel'skoi voennykh organizatsii P.S.R. 2 avgusta 1907," manuscript, IISH, SR Archive, Dossier 700, no. 4 [pp. 3–4]. There is very good evidence on *zemliachestva* in the Black Sea Fleet: I. Iakhnovskii, "Iz istorii revoliutsionnoi raboty v Chernomorskom flote," *PR*, 1930 no. 11, pp. 90–91; A. P. Platonov, *Vosstanie v chernomorskom flote v 1905 g.*, L., 1925, p. 31.

66. Iuzefovich, "Neskol'ko slov," pp. 466–7; "Trudy komiteta vysochaishee utverzhdennogo dlia opredeleniia dovol'stviia armeiskikh voisk," *VS*, v. 28, 1862, pp. 299–306; Armeiskii rotnyi komandir, "Temnaia summa," pp. 169–70, 188–9; Anichkov, *Voennoe khoziaistvo*, pp. 543–5, 557, 577–8; *Polozhenie o khoziaistve v rote*, pp. 24–37, 45, 47; *V tsarstve shtykov*, p. 13; [A. Sil'vin,] *V kazarme. Iz nabliudenii sots.-demokrata*, Geneva, 1903, pp. 9–10; Capt. I. D. Mikhailov, "Dovol'stvie voisk," *Voennaia entsiklopediia*, v. 9, Spb., 1912, pp. 150–51.

67. *V tsarstve shtykov*, pp. 23–4; Veselovskii, *K voprosu o vospitanii*, pp. 11–12; Krasnov, *Ot Dvuglavogo Orla*, p. 316.

68. I. Voronitsyn, *Istoriia odnogo katorzhanina*, M.-L., 1926, pp. 20–26; Denikin, *Staraia armiia*, v. 2, p. 151.

69. Konstantin Nikolaevich Rozen, "Vospominaniia o sluzhbe v polku, 1902–1917," Paris, 1928, typescript, Bakhmeteff Archive, p. 33; N. Voronovich, *Vechernyi zvon. Ocherki proshlogo*, v. 1, *1891–1917*, New York, 1955, pp. 160–64; B. V. Gerua, *Vospominaniia*, v. 1, p. 65; Zaionchkovskii, *Samoderzhavie*, pp. 227–8; N. A. Petrovskii, "Vospominaniia Fligel'-Ad"iutanta Polkovnika Nikolaia Aleksandrovicha Petrovskogo," in N. M. Devlet-Kil'deev, ed., *Kirasiry Ego Velichestva, 1902–1914. Poslednye gody mirnogo vremeni*, Washington, D.C., 1959, p. 35; F. N. Buak, "Vospominaniia starogo kavalergarda 1885–1902 goda," n.p., n.d., typescript, Bakhmeteff Archive, MsColl/Rozen Box 2, pp. 19, 86–7; *Istoriia L.Gv. Konnogo polka 1730–1930*, v. 3, Paris, 1964, pp. 28, 78; Epanchin, "Na sluzhbe," p. 33; M. A. Svechin, *Zapiski starogo generala o bylom*, Nice, 1964, p. 18; Ignatyev, *Subaltern*, pp. 14–15, 64–5, 68, 91–2.

70. Anichkov, *Voennoe khoziaistvo*, pp. 576, 579–80; Svechin, *Zapiski*, pp. 56–7; Buak, "Vospominaniia," p. 13.

71. Al. Akkerman, "Iz svetlogo proshlogo. Rozhdestvenskaia elka v batarei," *Vestnik L.-Gv. 2-i artilleriiskoi brigady*, no. 1, 3/16 Feb. 1935, pp. 19–23; Rozen, "Vospominaniia," pp. 23–9; Ignatyev, *Subaltern*, pp. 86–7, 89, 144; Petrovskii, "Vospominaniia," pp. 65–7; Paul Rodzianko, *Tattered Banners. An Autobiography*, London, 1939, p. 86; *Istoriia L.Gv. Konnogo polka*, v. 3, pp. 78–9.

72. Data on the involvement of members of the Imperial family in the Guards regiments is available in *Imperatorskaia gvardiia. Po 1 maia 1899 g. Spravochnaia knizhka*, Spb., 1899. See also D. Podshivalov, *Vospominaniia kavalergarda*, Tver, 1904, passim (Podshivalov was a Sgt. Major); N. V. Nagaev, "Leib-Gvardii 2-i Strelkovyi batalion—Leib-Gvardii 2-i strelkovyi Tsarskosel'skii polk. Ocherki byta i sluzhby Tsariu i Rodine za period ot Iaponskoi do Mirovoi voiny. Iz vospominanii Tsarskosel'skogo strelka," in E. A. Vertsinskii, ed., *Pamiatnye dni. Iz vospominanii Gvardeiskikh strelkov*, [v. 2], Tallinn, 1937, pp. 23–8, 44–6; Svechin, *Zapiski*, pp. 38–40; Rodzianko, *Tattered Banners*, p. 89; *Istoriia L.Gv. Konnogo polka*, v. 3, p. 77.

73. Petrovskii, "Vospominaniia," p. 73.

74. B. V. Gerua, *Vospominaniia*, p. 67; General P. A. Polovtsoff, *Glory and Downfall: Reminiscences of a Russian General Staff Officer*, London, 1935, p. 11; Svechin, *Zapiski*, p. 57; Rodzianko, *Tattered Banners*, pp. 89–90; Ivanko, "Sluzhba v polku," p. 258.

75. Krasnov, *Ot Dvuglavogo Orla*, p. 144.

76. Ibid., p. 205.

77. W. Barnes Steveni, *The Russian Army from Within*, London, 1914, pp. 36, 46; Zenchenko, *Obuchenie*, pp. 70–71; Rittikh, *Russkii*, p. 19; Rodzianko, *Tattered Banners*, pp. 84–6; Veselovskii, *K voprosu o vospitanii*, p. 23; "Report of Lt. Col. Walter S. Schuyler," and "Report of Capt. Carl Reichman," U.S. War Dept. Gen. Staff G-2, *Reports of Military Observers Attached to the Armies in Manchuria*, v. 1, Washington, D.C. 1906, pp. 138, 244–5.

78. V. N. Birkin, *Osinoe gnezdo. Povesti minuvshikh let*, v. 4, Berlin, 1930, p. 134.

79. Maxim Gorky, *On Literature*, Seattle, 1973, p. 300.

II. Enemies Domestic

1. *Krest'ianskoe dvizhenie v Rossii v 1857-mae 1861 gg. Sbornik dokumentov*, M., 1963, p. 15 (henceforth *KDR*).

2. S. V. Tokarev, "O chislennosti krest'ianskikh vystuplenii v Rossii v gody pervoi revoliutsionnoi situatsii," *Revoliutsionnaia situatsiia v Rossii v 1859–1861 gg.*, v. I, M., 1960, pp. 124–32; *KDR* (1857–1861), pp. 15–16, 736; P. A. Zaionchkovskii, *Otmena krepostnogo prava v Rossii*, 3rd ed., M., 1968, pp. 63–124; Zaionchkovskii, *Provedenie v zhizni krest'ianskoi reformy 1861 g.*, M., 1958, pp. 64–81; I. I. Ignatovich, "Volneniia pomeshchich'ikh krest'ian ot 1854 po 1863 g.," *Minuvshie gody*, 1908 no. 5–6, pp. 93–127; no. 7, pp. 45–92; no. 8, pp. 181–208; no. 9, pp. 152–173; no. 10, pp. 227–253; no. 11, pp. 189–211; Terence Emmons, "The Peasant and the Emancipation," in Wayne S. Vucinich, ed., *The Peasant in Nineteenth-Century Russia*, Stanford, 1968, pp. 41–71; Daniel Field, *Rebels in the Name of the Tsar*, Boston, 1976, pp. 31–111.

3. See the statistics and lists in *KDR* (1861–1869), M., 1964, pp. 798–800; *KDR* (1870–1880), M., 1968, pp. 521–9; *KDR* (1881–1889), M., 1960, pp. 788–830; *KDR* (1890–1900), M., 1959, pp. 601–648. The data are mostly from the central archives and of course are incomplete.

4. See the breakdown of causes and characteristics of peasant disturbances prepared by the Ministry of Interior's Department of Police, "Krest'ianskoe dvizhenie v kontse XIX v. (1881–1894 gg.)," *KA*, 1938, v. 4–5 (89–90), pp. 219–21. For the incidents referred to, see *KDR* (1890–1900), pp. 36–9, 44–5, 102–8, 272, 332.

5. In a file of 872 disorders 1865–1884, troops were used 219 times: *KDR* (1861–1869), pp. 798–800; *KDR* (1870–1880), pp. 521–9; P. A. Zaionchkovskii, *Krizis samoderzhaviia na rubezhe 1870–1880 godov*, M., 1964, p. 10. (Zaionchkovskii counts 189 disorders and 51 instances of military intervention, 1881–84; *KDR* [1881–1889], pp. 788–830, lists 308 disturbances in the same four years, but does not provide a good record of the number of times troops intervened.) Unfortunately, the volumes of *KDR* for 1881–1900 do not provide a complete record of the intervention of the army in peasant disorders. For some examples of the use of troops against peasants in the 1880s, see *KDR* (1881–1889), pp. 43–52, 58–60, 66–7, 108–17, 121–5, 130–33, 169–73, 176–8, 192–4, 197–203, 209–13, 221, 233–7, 275–7, 343–9, 354–64, 381–4, 386, 428–34, 461–4, 466–9, 475–7, 480–83, 486, 564,

566–7, 573–7, 586–90, 594–5, 671, 710–11, 721–4. This sample is no different than in the other volumes of *KDR*.

6. The idea that a "black repartition" was an age-old peasant dream is firmly established but wrong, as shown by B. A. Litvak, *Opyt statisticheskogo izucheniia krest'ianskogo dvizheniia v Rossii XIX v.*, M., 1967, pp. 18–21. On the emergence of such rumors in the 1870s and their dissemination by peasants in contact with the cities, see V. A. Vinogradov, "Istochniki dlia izucheniia mirovozreniia poreformennogo krest'ianstva," *Istochnikovedenie otechestvennoi istorii. Sbornik statei. 1979*, M., 1980, pp. 163–169; Vl. Gorn, "Krest'ianskoe dvizhenie do 1905 g.," in L. Martov, et al., eds., *Obshchestvennoe dvizhenie v Rossii v nachale XX-go veka*, v. 1, Spb., 1909, pp. 234–7; and Daniel Field, *Rebels*, pp. 122, 126, 132–3.

7. Alexander Gerschenkron, "The Rate of Growth of Industrial Production in Russia since 1885," *Journal of Economic History*, Supplement to v. 7, 1947, p. 149; Raymond W. Goldsmith, "The Economic Growth of Tsarist Russia, 1860–1913," *Economic Development and Cultural Change*, v. 9 no. 3, April 1961, p. 471.

8. The number of workers has been calculated from data in A. G. Rashin, *Formirovanie rabochego klassa v Rossii*, M., 1958, pp. 61, 117, 181. The latest results of the combing of archives for information on strikes (correctly distinguished from mere "disturbances") are provided by A. S. Trofimov, *Proletariat Rossii i ego bor'ba protiv tsarizma, 1861–1904 gg.*, M., 1979, pp. 107–9, 112. Figures compiled by the Factory Inspectorate of the Ministry of Finance for strikes in industries subject to its jurisdiction are lower, but only 50% of all industrial enterprises and 70% of industrial workers were subject to the factory inspectorate: V. E. Varzar, *Statisticheskie svedeniia o stachkakh rabochikh na fabrikakh i zavodakh za desiatiletie 1895–1904 goda*, Spb., 1905, pp. 1, 22; A. S. Amalrik, "K voprosu o chislennosti i geograficheskom razmeshchenii stachechnikov v Evropeiskoi Rossii v 1905 godu," *IZ*, v. 52, 1955, pp. 142, 144.

9. Between 1895 and 1904, troops intervened against 340 of the 1,765 strikes at factories under the jurisdiction of the factory inspectorate; Varzar, *Statisticheskie svedeniia . . . 1895–1904 gg.*, p. 78. For a discussion (really little more than a sample) of the use of troops against workers, see A. F. Vovchik, *Politika tsarizma po rabochemu voprosu v predrevoliutsionnyi period (1895–1904)*, L'vov, 1964, pp. 283–94.

10. Data on use of troops against workers are in Vovchik, *Politika tsarizma*, p. 284. Ministry of War figures on the use of troops against all civil disorders are in William C. Fuller, Jr., *Civil-Military Conflict in Imperial Russia*, forthcoming from Princeton University Press, Chapter 3.

11. Fuller, *Civil-Military Conflict*, Chapter 3; S. I. Potolov, *Rabochie Donbassa v XIX veke*, M.-L., 1963, pp. 212–14.

12. Potolov, *Rabochie Donbassa*, pp. 204–7, 210–11, 215–16, 229, 233–4; V.Ia. Laverychev, *Tsarizm i rabochii vopros v Rossii (1861–1917)*, M., 1972, pp. 118–19; V. Kuz'min, "Revoliutsionnaia rabota sredi soldat i vosstanie bobruitsev v 1905 g.," *1905 god v Stalingradskoi gubernii*, Stalingrad, 1925, pp. 67–8.

13. Fuller, *Civil-Military Conflict*, Chapter 3; Laverychev, *Tsarizm*, pp. 119–20; Vovchik, *Politika tsarizma*, p. 294.

14. Laverychev, *Tsarizm*, p. 118; Fuller, *Civil-Military Conflict*, Chapter 3.

15. P. S. Gusiatnikov, *Revoliutsionnoe studencheskoe dvizhenie v Rossii, 1899–*

1907, M., 1971, pp. 13–93; Lewis S. Feuer, *The Conflict of Generations: The Character and Significance of Student Movements*, New York, 1969, pp. 135–43; Fuller, *Civil-Military Conflict*, Chapter 3.

16. L. S., "Vospominaniia studenta-soldata," *Byloe*, 1906 no. 5, pp. 163–9, 179–83; the Kiev military district circular of 22 October 1899 is in *Rabochee delo*, Geneva, no. 6, April 1900, pp. 59–62.

17. Allan Wildman, *The Making of a Workers' Revolution. Russian Social Democracy, 1891–1903*, Chicago, 1967, pp. 116–17, 150–51, 213–21 and passim; "Events in Kharkov," *FR*, 1 Feb. 1902, pp. 14–15; "The Battle in Ekaterinoslav," ibid., p. 15; *Rabochee dvizhenie v Rossii v 1901–1904 gg. Sbornik dokumentov* (henceforth *RDR*), L., 1975, pp. 63–4, 130–32, 157–9, 239–41, 385–6, 404, 408, 410–11.

18. Wildman, *Making of a Workers' Revolution*, pp. 150–51, 246; *RDR*, pp. 28–31, 110–20, 132; "Rabochee dvizhenie na zavodakh Peterburga v mae 1901 g.," *KA*, 1936 no. 3, pp. 54–8; [Meer Iakovlevich Lukomskii], *Obukhovskaia oborona*, Geneva, 1902; *Iskra*, no. 20, 1 May 1902; *Iz Materialov "Revoliutsionnoi Rossii"*, no. 38, 19/6 April 1902; *PI*, no. 65, 17 April 1902. For an account of the Batum events written in 1925 by one of the officers involved, see D. S. Kldiashvili, *Izbrannye sochineniia*, translated from the Georgian by N. Chkheidze, v. 2, Tbilisi, 1952, pp. 210–17.

19. The latest Soviet count for 1901 is 353 strikes, for 1902 285 strikes; Iu. I. Kir'ianov, "Statistika stachechnykh vystuplenii rabochikh Rossii nakanune revoliutsii 1905–1907 gg.," *Rabochii klass Rossii v period burzhuazno-demokraticheskikh revoliutsii*, M., 1978, pp. 28–47 (Kir'ianov argues convincingly that even this count is incomplete). Permanently detailed units and standing orders on troop disposition in the event of disorders are reported for Batum (Kldiashvili, *Izbrannye*, v. 2, p. 211), Tiflis (*RDR*, pp. 63–4), and Poltava (*Iz materialov "Revoliutsionnoi Rossii"*, no. 43, 1 May/18 April 1902). There is no reason to doubt the same was true elsewhere.

20. Maureen Perrie, *The Agrarian Policy of the Russian Socialist-Revolutionary Party. From Its Origins through the Revolution of 1905–1907*, New York, 1976, pp. 53–7; F. Volkhovsky, "The Rebellious Peasantry," *FR*, 1 June 1902, pp. 62–4; Gorn, "Krest'ianskoe dvizhenie," pp. 243–45; Fuller, *Civil-Military Conflict*, Chapter 3.

21. *RDR*, pp. 220–27, 244–7, 253–64, 267–70, 272–4, 280–95, 450, 478–91; Vovchik, *Politika tsarizma*, pp. 300–302; "K istorii vseobshchei stachki na iuge Rossii v 1903 g.," *KA*, 1938 no. 3, pp. 76–122; Kir'ianov, "Statistika," pp. 28–47; Jeremiah Schneiderman, *Sergei Zubatov and Revolutionary Marxism. The Struggle for the Working Class in Tsarist Russia*, Ithaca, 1976, pp. 143–53, 185–9, 238–42, 246–52, 305–38; Fuller, *Civil-Military Conflict*, Chapter 3.

22. Fuller, *Civil-Military Conflict*, Chapter 3; Petrov, "Tsarskaia armiia v bor'be s massovym revoliutsionnym dvizheniem v nachale XX v.," *IZ*, v. 34, 1950, p. 325; *Vsepoddanneishii otchet Voennogo ministerstva za 1903 g.*, "Otchet po Glavnomu shtabu," Spb., 1905, p. 37; Zaionchkovskii, *Samoderzhavie i russkaia armiia*, p. 34.

23. A. N. Kuropatkin, *Zapiski Generala Kuropatkina o russko-iaponskoi voine. Itogi voiny*, Berlin, 1909, pp. 166–7; Fuller, *Civil-Military Conflict*, Chapter 3; Vovchik, *Politika tsarizma*, pp. 303–9.

24. [A. N. Kuropatkin], "Dnevnik A. N. Kuropatkina (17 noiabria 1902 g.–7 fevralia 1904 g.)," *KA*, 1922 no. 2, p. 27.

25. Quoted in Zaionchkovskii, *Samoderzhavie*, p. 43; Fuller, *Civil-Military Conflict*, Chapter 3.

26. Quoted in Zaionchkovskii, *Samoderzhavie*, p. 34.

27. *Iskra*, no. 51, 22 Oct. 1903; *RDR*, pp. 266–70, 370 n. 4.

28. L. T. Senchakova, *Revoliutsionnoe dvizhenie v russkoi armii i flote v kontse XIX–nachale XX v.*, M., 1972, pp. 154–5; *RR*, no. 8, 25 June 1902; no. 19, 1 March 1903; *Letuchii listok* (Ekaterinoslav SD), no. 2, April 1902; *PI*, no. 117, 10 April (28 March) 1903.

29. [Kuropatkin], "Dnevnik . . . 17 noiabria," pp. 13, 40, 53.

30. L. G. Beskrovnyi, *Russkaia armiia i flot v XIX veke*, M., 1973, pp. 214–78; S. S. Volk, *Narodnaia volia, 1879–1882*, M., 1966, pp. 139, 141, 148, 315–18, 320–22, 329, 331–2; Senchakova, *Revoliutsionnoe*, pp. 42–54; "Programma voenno-revoliutsionnoi organizatsii," *Literatura partii 'Narodnaia Volia'*, M., 1930, pp. 314–16; M.Iu. Ashenbrenner, "Voennaia organizatsiia partii 'Narodnoi Voli'," *Byloe*, 1906 no. 7, pp. 4, 9–10, 18, and passim.

31. *Vestnik russkoi revoliutsii*, no. 1, July 1901, p. 11; *Iskra*, no. 14, 1 Jan. 1902; no. 45, 1 Aug. 1903; *RR*, no. 6, May 1902; no. 21, 1 April 1903; V. I. Lenin, *PSS*, 5th ed., v. 6, M., 1972, p. 129; v. 7, M., 1972, p. 14; and *Vtoroi s"ezd RSDRP. Iiul'-avgust 1903 goda. Protokoly*, M., 1959, p. 432. French secret police agents observing Russian emigrés in England and Switzerland took careful note of the revolutionaries' interest in the Russian army—shipments of revolutionary brochures for the army, reports on the army in the revolutionary press, and rumors. See the reports in Archives Nationales, F 7 1251 beginning 31 March (Annemasse) and 9 April (London) 1902.

32. The circular is in *Iskra*, no. 27, 1 Nov. 1902. The commander of the Caucasus military district also noted a surge of revolutionary propaganda directed at the army in 1902; V. A. Petrov, "Revoliutsionnaia propaganda v tsarskoi armii nakanune revoliutsii 1905 goda," *VI*, 1949 no. 6, pp. 33–4; Senchakova, *Revoliutsionnoe*, pp. 157–8.

33. A. V. Ushakov, *Bor'ba partii za gegemoniiu proletariata*, M., 1974, p. 87, finds 21 SD organizations conducting military work in 1902 and 45 in 1903; these figures are probably about right—always remembering that "military work" usually entailed nothing more than producing a leaflet or two for soldiers. No similar figures are available for the SRs, but there is no reason to doubt that they were as active as SDs. SR organizations producing leaflets for the army are listed in *RR*, no. 6, May 1902; no. 25, 1 June 1903; no. 31, 1 Sept. 1903; and in other issues. SR interest in the army is also noted in a secret police survey, *Letopis' revoliutsionnogo dvizheniia v Rossii za 1902 g.*, Saratov, 1924, pp. 37, 45, 115, 161. For the revolutionaries' thinking on the structure and purpose of military organizations, see *RR*, no. 31, 1 April 1903; Martov, *Militarizm i rabochii klass*, Geneva, 1903, p. 30; Lenin, *PSS*, v. 6, p. 129; v. 7, pp. 81, 103; *Vtoroi s"ezd RSDRP*, p. 49; Russkii Sotsialist [F. I. Somov], *K voprosu o tseli revoliutsionnoi raboty v voiskakh* [London, 1903]. On the pseudo-reincarnation of the Military Revolutionary Organization in 1903, see *Iskra*, no. 35, 1 March 1903; no. 51, 22 Oct. 1903; *PI*, no.

107, 12 Feb./30 Jan. 1903; no. 108, 19/6 Feb. 1903; no. 138, 18/5 June 1903; *Osvobozhdenie*, no. 8, 2/15 Oct. 1903; *RR*, no. 20, 15 March 1903; A. I. Spiridovich, *Revoliutsionnoe dvizhenie v Rossii v period imperii. Partiia sotsialistov-revoliutsionerov i ee predshestvenniki. 1886–1916*, 2nd ed., Pg., 1918, p. 98.

34. Ivan Volnyi [V. Dmitreva], *Za Veru, Tsaria i Otechestvo*, n.p., 1902; K. Mironov, *Soldatskii podvig*, n.p., 1902; [N. A. Rubakin], *K soldatam ot rabochikh sotsialistov-revoliutsionerov*, n.p., 1903; A. Mashitskii, *Unter-ofitser. Rasskaz*, Geneva, 1903. Only one story offers a broader perspective—mutiny leading to successful revolution; A. Mashitskii, *Iz zhizni soldata (skazka-pravda)*, Geneva, 1903.

35. L. N. Tolstoi, *Ofitserskaia pamiatka*, Christchurch, 1902; Tolstoi, *Soldatskaia pamiatka*, Christchurch, 1902; Tolstoi, *Pis'mo k fel'dfebeliu*, Christchurch, 1902. Tolstoi began writing these pamphlets in 1901, after the street demonstrations that had attracted the attention of revolutionaries, too, to the army. Reports of the distribution of these pamphlets by revolutionaries are very frequent, for example: *Letopis' revoliutsionnogo dvizheniia*, p. 165; *Perepiska V. I. Lenina i redaktsii gazety "Iskra" s sotsial-demokraticheskimi organizatsiiami v Rossii 1900–1903 gg.*, v. 2, *Iiun'-dekabr' 1902*, M., 1969, p. 407; V. Manilov, "Kievskaia voennaia organizatsiia RSDRP i vosstanie saper v 1905 g.," *LR*, 1925 no. 5–6, pp. 176–7; Senchakova, *Revoliutsionnoe*, p. 140; *Iskra*, no. 27, 1 Nov. 1902; no. 98, 23 April 1905; *RR*, no. 14, Dec. 1902; no. 25, 1 June 1903; no. 30, 20 Aug. 1903; *Listki "Zhizni"*, no. 2, 17/30 May 1902.

36. The best sources on the Alshanskii case are the revolutionary newspapers, which carried many of the official documents: *Osvobozhdenie*, no. 4, 2/15 Aug. 1903; no. 5, 19 Aug./1 Sept. 1903; *Iskra*, no. 27, 1 Nov. 1902; no. 44, 15 June 1903; *RR*, no. 25, 1 June 1903; *PI*, no. 128, 17/44 May 1903.

37. *RR*, no. 25, 1 June 1903.

38. On Bund distribution of proclamations among draftees in Vitebsk in 1899, see *Rabochee delo*, no. 6, April 1900; and *Vpered. Kievskaia rabochaia gazeta*, no. 8–9, Nov. 1899–March 1900. On subsequent Bund activity among draftees: *PI*, no. 95, 20 Nov. 1902; no. 154, 23/10, Nov. 1903; *Iz materialov "Revoliutsionnoi Rossii"*, no. 80, 30/17 Nov. 1902; *Iskra*, no. 11, 20 Nov. 1901; *Vtoroi s"ezd RSDRP*, p. 506; *Letopis' revoliutsionnogo dvizheniia*, p. 133. On the SD and SR campaigns among draftees in 1902, see Senchakova, *Revoliutsionnoe*, pp. 141–2; *Listovki revoliutsionnykh sotsial-demokraticheskikh organizatsii Ukrainy, 1896–1904*, Kiev, 1963, pp. 583–5; A. P. Steklov, "Revoliutsionnoe dvizhenie v voiskakh na Kavkaze nakanune pervoi russkoi revoliutsii (do russko-iaponskoi voiny)," *Trudy Tbilisskogo gos. ped. in-ta*, v. 10, 1955, pp. 86–8; *Iskra*, no. 54, 1 Dec. 1903; V. A. Petrov, "Revoliutsionnaia propaganda v tsarskoi armii nakanune revoliutsii 1905 goda. (Do russko-iaponskoi voiny)," *VI*, 1949 no. 6, pp. 36–7; Spiridovich, *Revoliutsionnoe dvizhenie*, p. 98; *Letopis' revoliutsionnogo dvizheniia*, pp. 115, 161; *Iz materialov "Revoliutsionnoi Rossii"*, no. 77, 2 Nov. 1902; no. 80, 30/17 Nov. 1902; *RR*, no. 14, Dec. 1902.

39. *PI*, no. 94, 13 Nov. 1902.

40. A. P. Steklov, "Revoliutsionnoe dvizhenie v voiskakh na Kavkaze," pp. 90–92; *Proletarii*, no. 11, 9 Aug./27 July 1905.

41. I. Iakhnovskii, "Iz istorii revoliutsionnoi raboty," *PR*, 1930 no. 11, pp. 90–97; I. Iakhnovskii, "Revoliutsionnaia rabota v Chernomorskom flote," *KiS*, 1925

no. 5, pp. 24–7; Denisenko, "Potemkinskoe vosstanie," *KiS*, 1925 no. 5, p. 28;
I. A. Lychev, *Vospominaniia potemkintsa*, M.-L., 1924, p. 18; *Listki "Zhizni"*, no. 2,
17/30 May 1903; *Sotsial'demokrat*, no. 2, 18 Aug. 1905; no. 13, 1 Sept. 1905; *Iskra*,
no. 105, 15 July 1905; *RR*, no. 10, Aug. 1902; no. 40, 15 Jan. 1904. According to
"Revoliutsionnaia rabota v Chernomorskom flote. (Vospominaniia byvshego
matrosa sotsialdemokrata)," *Sotsial'demokrat*, no. 13, 1 Sept. 1905, in 1903 SRs
had circles in 3 barracks, SDs in 6 barracks. According to *RR*, no. 70, 1 July 1905,
as of August 1903 SR circles were attended by more than 100 sailors—so the total
of all sailors in circles must have been around 300 at that point. There were
anywhere from 600 to 900 sailors in circles in late 1904. From 200 to 300 sailors at
a time attended meetings in March 1905 (the numbers of sailors voting for
resolutions were counted), and probably no more than one-third to one-half of
the organized sailors attended these meetings at one time; *Iskra*, no. 98, 23 April
1905. According to the somewhat confused testimony of K. F[el'dman], "Chernomorskii flot i revoliutsiia (1905–1917)," *Voenmor*, Baku, 1920 no. 46, p. 3, 800
armed sailors could be sent from Sevastopol to take part in a demonstration in
Odessa in late 1904. The story itself is unlikely, but the figure sounds as though it
was mentioned at the time as the number of sailors considered to be "organized."

42. D. A. Garkavenko, "Sotsial'nyi sostav matrosov russkogo flota v epokhu
imperializma," *ISSSR*, 1968 no. 5, pp. 39–41, 45.

43. SRs in 1903 were in contact with soldier and sailor groups in Kiev, Moscow, Petersburg, and Samara; Spiridovich, *Revoliutsionnoe dvizhenie*, pp. 98–9; *Za
narod!*, no. 25, Jan. 1910. In 1903 SDs were in contact with groups of soldiers in
Pskov, Rovno, Saratov, Irkutsk, Vilna, and possibly in Minsk; Senchakova, *Revoliutsionnoe*, pp. 146, 176; Ushakov, *Bor'ba*, pp. 88, 90; E. D. Stasova, *Stranitsy
zhizni i bor'by*, M., 1957, p. 42; V. E. Poleshchuk, "Revoliutsionnoe dvizhenie v
chastiakh Irkutskogo voennogo okruga," *Revoliutsionnoe dvizhenie v armii v gody
pervoi russkoi revoliutsii. Sbornik statei*, M., 1955, pp. 304–5; *Revoliutsiia 1905–1907
gg. v Litve. Dokumenty i materialy*, Vil'nius, 1961, pp. 31–3, 37; *Perepiska V. I.
Lenina*, v. 2, pp. 435, 551.

44. *PI*, 23/10 Nov. 1903.

45. The first 51 issues of the SD's *Iskra* (Dec. 1900–Oct. 1903) contained 20 or
so references to soldiers and the army. The same 51 issues contained 88 letters,
reports, articles, and proclamations from, about, or to students; Gusiatnikov,
Revoliutsionnoe studencheskoe, p. 11. In the first 38 issues (to the end of 1903) of the
SR's *Revoliutsionnaia Rossiia*, there was one major article on the army, two on the
student movement; there were 23 items of correspondence on the army, against
66 on students; "Polnyi sistematicheskii ukazetel' 'Revoliutsionnoi Rossii',"
Pamiatnaia knizhka sotsialista-revoliutsionera [Paris], 1914, pp. 59–88.

46. *Ob ulichnykh besporiadkakh* [Geneva], 1901; Richard Eiter, "Organizational
Growth and Revolutionary Tactics: Unity and Discord in the Socialist Revolutionary Party," Ph.D. dissertation, University of Pittsburgh, 1978, pp. 198–208..

47. Engels' pronouncement is in his 1895 introduction to Marx's *Die Klassen-
kampfe in Frankreich*. The introduction was bowdlerized by the German Social
Democrats, and Engels took offense at that, fearing that he might appear too
moderate. The first published version dropped a paragraph stressing that street

fighting was still possible, though more at the end of a period of revolution than at the beginning. Since the text as Engels wrote it was not published until 1930, the 1895 version was what Russian SDs had to go by. Alexander Fischer, *Russische Sozialdemokratie und bewaffneter Aufstand im Jahre 1905*, Wiesbaden, 1967, p. 3; *Voennye organizatsii rossiiskogo proletariata i opyt ego vooruzhennoi bor'by*, M., 1974, p. 33. For a good discussion of Engels' thoughts on the army, see Martin Berger, *Engels, Armies and Revolution*, Hamden, 1977, pp. 154–70 and passim.

48. Zaionchkovskii, *Samoderzhavie*, p. 119; Senchakova, *Revoliutsionnoe*, p. 155; Petrov, "Revoliutsionnaia propaganda," pp. 42–3; A. Drezen, *Armiia i flot v revoliutsii 1905 g.*, M. 1931, p. 9.

49. *Osvobozhdenie*, no. 9, 19 Oct./1 Nov. 1903; no. 7, 18 Sept./1 Oct., 1903; *PI*, no. 100, 18/5 Dec. 1902; no. 118, 16/3 April 1903; no. 122, 6 May/23 April 1903; no. 148, 15/2 Oct. 1903; *RR*, no. 25, 1 July 1903; Drezen, *Armiia i flot*, pp. 9–10; Senchakova, *Revoliutsionnoe*, pp. 161–4, 166; S. F. Naida, *Revoliutsionnoe dvizhenie v tsarskom flote. 1825–1917*, M.-L., 1948, pp. 74–5, 85.

50. A. S. Suvorin, *Dnevnik A. S. Suvorina*, M.-Pg., 1923, p. 327.

51. Surveys of the emergence of the liberal movement and of regime activities are Shmuel Galai, *The Liberation Movement in Russia*, Cambridge, England, 1973, pp. 34–193; Bernard Pares, *The Fall of the Russian Monarchy. A Study of the Evidence*, New York, 1939/1961, pp. 58–63, 130–32 and passim; and L. G. Zakharova, "Krizis samoderzhaviia nakanune revoliutsii 1905 goda," *VI*, 1972 no. 8, pp. 119–40. For reaction to assassinations, see Suvorin, *Dnevnik*, p. 291; and V. I. Gurko, *Features and Figures of the Past. Government and Opinion in the Reign of Nicholas II*, Stanford, 1939, pp. 6, 88, 176.

52. Andrew Malozemoff, *Russian Foreign Policy 1881–1904. With Special Emphasis on the Causes of the Russo-Japanese War*, Berkeley and Los Angeles, 1958; Gurko, *Features and Figures*, pp. 259–91; Shumpei Okamoto, *The Japanese Oligarchy and the Russo-Japanese War*, New York, 1970, pp. 57–102.

53. A selection of the vast literature on the war: M. Svechin, "Strategicheskii ocherk russko-iaponskoi voiny ot nachala kampanii do srazheniia pod Liaoianom vkliuchitel'no," *VS*, 1907 no. 2, pp. 59–78; 1907 no. 3, pp. 47–63; 1907 no. 4, pp. 47–69; N. Kozlovskii, "K voprosu o sootnoshenii chislennogo sostava russkikh i iaponskikh voisk i ikh boevykh poter' v voinu 1904–1905 gg.," *VS*, 1914 no. 4, pp. 79–86; Dennis and Peggy Warner, *The Tide at Sunrise. A History of the Russo-Japanese War 1904–1905*, New York, 1974; V. A. Apushkin, *Russko-iaponskaia voina, 1904–5 gg.*, 2nd ed., M., 1911; I. I. Rostunov, ed., *Istoriia russko-iaponskoi voiny 1904–1905 gg.*, M., 1977.

54. Galai, *Liberation Movement*, pp. 196–219; P. N. Miliukov, *Vospominaniia (1859–1917)*, v. 1, New York, 1955, pp. 242–5; N. S. Rusanov, *V emigratsii*, M., 1929, pp. 278–80; V. M. Chernov, *Pered burei. Vospominaniia*, New York, 1953, pp. 206–12.

55. Gurko, *Features and Figures*, pp. 292–302, 309–13; S.Iu. Vitte, *Vospominaniia*, v. 2, M., 1960, pp. 321–4; Roberta Manning, *The Crisis of the Old Order in Russia. Gentry and Government*, Princeton, 1982, pp. 68–88; Galai, *Liberation Movement*, pp. 224–36; Terence Emmons, "Russia's Banquet Campaign," *California Slavic Studies*, v. 10, 1977, pp. 45–86.

56. Gurko, *Features and Figures*, pp. 303–4, 315–17; Galai, *Liberation Movement*, pp. 237–8; Vitte, *Vospominaniia*, v. 2, pp. 327–9, 331–5. The text of the public rebuke to the marshal of the nobility is in Suvorin, *Dnevnik*, p. 329.

57. From the *Daily News* (London), reprinted in *FR*, 1 Jan. 1905, pp. 6–7 (I have modernized the transliteration).

58. *Russko-iaponskaia voina 1904–1905 gg. Rabota voenno-istoricheskoi komissii*, v. 7, Spb., 1910, pp. 26–30; V. A. Petrov, *Ocherki po istorii revoliutsionnogo dvizheniia v russkoi armii v 1905 g.*, M.-L., 1964, pp. 57–8; *Vsepoddanneishii otchet Voennogo ministerstva za 1904 god*, Spb., 1906, "Otchet po Glavnomu shtabu za 1904 god," p. 70; V. E. Poleshchuk, "Revoliutsionnoe dvizhenie v Man'chzhurskoi armii," *IZ*, v. 49, 1954, p. 303.

59. *Russko-iaponskaia voina 1904–1905 gg.*, v. 7, pp. 31–3; Petrov, *Ocherki*, pp. 35–7, 51; M.N., *Na voinu. (Iz zapisok zapasnogo soldata)*, n.p., 1904, pp. 2–4; *Iskra*, no. 74, 20 Sept. 1904; Grulev, *Zloby dnia*, pp. 189–91.

60. On the depot battalions: *Russko-iaponskaia voina 1904–1905 gg.*, v. 7, p. 37. Peacetime strength of infantry regiments was set at 70 officers and 1,786 men, wartime strength at 79 officers and 3,830 men: *Svod shtatov voenno-sukhoputnogo vedomstva. Izdanie 1893 goda*, book 2, Spb., 1893, pp. 29–30. The 50th Belostok regiment lost 44 officers and 1,594 men to the Far East; E. P. Nikolaev, *Istoriia 50-go pekhotnogo Belostokskogo polka*, v. 2, Odessa, 1909, p. 376. The 179th Ust-Dvinsk regiment lost 31 officers and about 1,100 men through transfers; S. E. Charnetskii, *Istoriia 179-go pekhotnogo Ust'-Dvinskogo polka*, Spb., 1911, pp. 138–44. The 114th Novotorzhok regiment lost only one-third of its officers; E. A. Kirilov, *Istoriia 114-go pekhotnogo Novotorzhokskogo polka*, Mitava, 1913, p. 286.

61. Iakovlev, "Khar'kovskoe likholet'e," *IV*, 1910 no. 11, p. 554. See also: *Russko-iaponskaia voina 1904–1905 gg.*, v. 7, p. 36; Charnetskii, *Istoriia 179-go*, p. 144; "Volneniia v voiskakh," *RI*, no. 258, 10 Dec. 1905; and *Z Pola Walki*, no. 7, 29 March 1905 (an order to a garrison in Poland dealing with reserve officers).

62. V. Ul'ianinskii, "Vosstanie Rostovskogo polka v dekabre 1905 goda," *KiS*, 1925 no. 6, p. 36; Byvshii zapasnoi, "Vospominanie o zapasnoi pulemetnoi komande," *Pervaia revoliutsiia v Peterburge*, v. 2, L., 1925, pp. 131–2; M. A. Iakovlev, "Khar'kovskoe likholet'e," *IV*, 1910 no. 11, p. 554.

III. Failing to Contain Revolution

1. The text of the petition is in Walter Sablinsky, *The Road to Bloody Sunday. Father Gapon and the St. Petersburg Massacre of 1905*, Princeton, 1976, pp. 344–9.

2. Sablinsky, *Road to Bloody Sunday*; Gerald D. Suhr, "Petersburg's First Mass Labor Organization: The Assembly of Russian Workers and Father Gapon," *Russian Review*, v. 40 no. 3, July 1981, pp. 241–62, and v. 40 no. 4, Oct. 1981, pp. 412–41.

3. V. E. Varzar, *Statistika stachek rabochikh na fabrikakh i zavodakh za 1905 god*, Spb., 1908, p. 5; S. M. Dubrovskii, *Krest'ianskoe dvizhenie v revoliutsii 1905–1907 gg.*, M., 1956, pp. 46–51, 70–73; L. K. Erman, *Intelligentsiia v pervoi russkoi revoliutsii*, M., 1966, pp. 46–67; Robert Byrnes, "Kliuchevskii and the Revolution of

1905," Colloque la révolution de 1905, Sorbonne, 1981; V. Nevskii, "Ianvarskie dni 1905 g. v provintsii," *KL*, v. 4, 1922, pp. 52–132.

4. Kevin R. Cox and George J. Demko, "Conflict Behavior in a Spatio-Temporal Context," *Sociological Focus*, v. 1 no. 3, Spring 1968, pp. 55–67, treat the spread of agrarian disorders as the result of a peasant-to-peasant demonstration effect. However, peasant disturbances spread north from the Caucasus and east from Poland, the centers of the January rebellion, and the timing of peasant activization appears to fit well the intensity and temporal-geographical spread of strikes. Compare the maps in Cox and Demko with the maps and tables in Varzar, *Statistika stachek . . . 1905*, pp. 15, 103–4. For official reports on the rumors that circulated among peasants in early 1905, see S. Dubrovskii and B. Grave, compilers, *Agrarnoe dvizhenie v 1905–1907 gg.*, v. 1, M.-L., 1925, pp. 237, 264–5, 385–6. For general discussions of the peasant disorders, see Petr Maslov, *Krest'ianskoe dvizhenie v Rossii v epokhu pervoi revoliutsii*, 2nd edition, M., 1924, pp. 3–47, 65–9; Perrie, *Agrarian Policy*, pp. 118–39; Cox and Demko, "Agrarian Structure and Peasant Discontent in the Russian Revolution of 1905," *The East Lakes Geographer*, v. 3, Oct. 1967, pp. 4–20.

5. On peasant social and political psychology, see Field, *Rebels in the Name of the Tsar*, pp. 1–26; Eugene Vinogradoff, "The Political Consciousness of the Peasantry of Central Russia during the 'Period of Reaction' (1907–1914)," (unpublished paper); E. J. Hobsbawm, "Peasants and Politics," *Journal of Peasant Studies*, v. 1 no. 1, Oct. 1973, pp. 3–22; George Foster, "Peasant Society and the Image of Limited Good," *American Anthropologist*, v. 67 no. 2, 1965, pp. 293–315.

6. Kathleen Prevo, "Worker Reaction to Bloody Sunday in Voronezh," Colloque la révolution de 1905, Sorbonne, 1981; Gerald Dennis Suhr, "Petersburg Workers in 1905: Strikes, Workplace Democracy, and the Revolution," Ph.D. dissertation, University of California, Berkeley, 1979, pp. 237–44, 381–2.

7. Sablinsky, *Road to Bloody Sunday*, pp. 216, 243.

8. Varzar, *Statistika stachek . . . 1905*, p. 7; Varzar, *Statisticheskie svedeniia*, pp. 30–31, and "Prilozheniia," p. 11.

9. Varzar, *Statistika stachek . . . 1905*, p. 7; D. Kol'tsov, "Rabochie v 1905–1907 gg.," in L. Martov, et al., eds., *Obshchestvennoe dvizhenie v Rossii v nachale XX-go veka*, v. 2, part 1, Spb., 1910, pp. 191–3, 200–25; *Rabochii klass v pervoi russkoi revoliutsii 1905–1907 gg.*, M., 1981, pp. 87–98, 123–37.

10. The only statistical source (and that incomplete) on SR Party membership dates from October 1906 and records 34,200 members; based on that source, the estimate by Manfred Hildermeier, *Die Sozialrevolutionäre Partei Russlands. Agrarsozialismus und Modernisierung in Zarenreich (1900–1914)*, Köln-Wien, 1978, p. 267, for late 1906 is 42–45,000. Bolsheviks and Mensheviks together had approximately 76,000 members in October 1906, around 15,000 in late 1905; David Lane, *The Roots of Russian Communism. A Social and Historical Study of Russian Social-Democracy, 1898–1907*, pp. 12–14. Assuming the ratio of SRs to SDs was the same in 1905 as in 1906, SR membership in late 1905 would be 8–9,000. The Bund membership estimate in 1903 was 30,000; Henry Tobias, *The Jewish Bund in Russia. From Its Origins to 1905*, Stanford, 1972, p. 239. Latvian SDs numbered 3,400 in 1904, 9,000 by June 1905, 18,200 by October 1905; Ernest O. F. Ames, ed., *The Revolution in the Baltic Provinces of Russia. A Brief Account of the Activity of the Lettish*

Social Democratic Workers' Party, By an Active Member, London, 1907, pp. 11, 20, 22. As of early 1907, the Bund and the SDKPiL each claimed 25,000 members, the Latvian SDs 13,000; Lane, *Roots*, p. 13.

11. Eiter, "Organizational Growth," pp. 222, 227–9; Hildermeier, *Die Sozial-revolutionäre Partei*, pp. 142–5, 153–4; Perrie, *Agrarian Policy*, pp. 101–13; "Predverie revoliutsii," *RR*, no. 58, 20 Jan. 1905, pp. 1–2; "Boevoi moment," *RR*, no. 59, 10 Feb. 1905, pp. 1–2; J. L. H. Keep, *The Rise of Social Democracy in Russia*, London, 1963, pp. 187–202; Solomon Schwarz, *The Russian Revolution of 1905*, Chicago, 1967, pp. 8–28, 131–4; Alexander Fischer, *Russische Sozialdemokratie*, pp. 41–81, 102–108.

12. Galai, *Liberation Movement*, pp. 243–53; Shmuel Galai, "The Role of the Union of Unions in the Revolution of 1905," *Jahrbücher für Geschichte Osteuropas*, 1976 no. 4, pp. 512–25; Manning, *Crisis of the Old Order*, pp. 90–127.

13. Gurko, *Features and Figures*, pp. 355–72, 376–80; V. N. Kokovtsov, *Out of My Past. The Memoirs of Count Kokovtsov*, translated by Laura Matveev, Stanford, 1935, pp. 38–41, 44–5, 50–51; Vitte, *Vospominaniia*, v. 2, pp. 346–8, 368–70, 375–8; E. D. Chermenskii, *Burzhuaziia i tsarizm v pervoi russkoi revoliutsii*, 2nd ed., M., 1970, pp. 52–61, 70–88; R.Sh. Ganelin, "Ukaz 18 fevralia 1905 g. o petitsiiakh i pravitel'stvennaia politika," *Vspomogatel'nye istoricheskie distsipliny*, v. 14, L., 1983, pp. 170–85.

14. "Konets russko-iaponskoi voiny. (Voennoe soveshchanie 24 maia 1905 g. v Tsarskom Sele)," *KA*, 1928 no. 3 (28), pp. 182–204; Raymond A. Esthus, "Nicholas II and the Russo-Japanese War," *Russian Review*, v. 40 no. 4, Oct. 1981, pp. 397–406; Vitte, *Vospominaniia*, v. 2, pp. 383–8, 573–5; Kokovtsov, *Out of My Past*, pp. 49–50.

15. "Zapiski A. S. Ermolova," *KA*, 1925 no. 1, p. 51.

16. Orders to local garrisons and military districts: *Prikaz po voiskam ekaterinoslavskogo garnizona s prilozheniem stat'i "Pravitel'stvo gotovitsia,"* Geneva, 1905; *Pravo*, 6 Feb. 1905; *Revoliutsiia 1905–1907 gg. v Litve*, pp. 97–101, 107–8; *Kaluzhskaia guberniia v 1905 godu. Sbornik statei, vospominanii i materialov*, Kaluga, 1925, pp. 363–9; *Proletarii* (Geneva), no. 19, 3 Oct./20 Sept., 1905. The methods by which units operated, and local policy on placement of troops on estates and at factories, and to reinforce police patrols, are detailed in "Pribaltiiskii krai v 1905 godu," *KA*, 1925 no. 4–5, p. 274; S. E. Charnetskii, *Istoriia 179-go*, pp. 144–5; A. Pokrovskii, *3-i Donskoi kazachii polk*, Vilna, 1910, pp. 89–90; M. K. Sokolovskii, *Istoricheskii ocherk 10-go Ulanskogo polka*, Spb., 1912, pp. 398–400; E. A. Kirilov, *Istoriia 114-go*, pp. 292–5; and many other regimental histories.

17. The figures on units deployed are from a report by Minister of War Rediger to the Tsar: *Revoliutsiia 1905–1907 gg. v Rossii. Dokumenty i materialy. Vysshii pod"em Revoliutsii 1905–1907 gg. Vooruzhennye vosstaniia. Noiabr'–dekabr' 1905 goda* (henceforth: *VP*), vol. 1, M., 1955, p. 172. The authorized strength of an infantry company was 107 men, of a cavalry squadron 100 men; the strength of these and other types of units listed in Rediger's report can be found in *Svod shtatov voenno-sukhoputnogo vedomstva*, vol. 2, Spb., 1893. Of course, not all companies were at authorized strength, and not all men in a company went out on every assignment.

18. Troop strength has been calculated from *Vsepoddanneishii otchet Voennogo*

ministerstva za 1905 god, "Obshchii obzor," pp. 2–3, 11–13, 34. The figures therein do not take account of the 60,000-odd cossacks in the field as of October. *Kratkoe raspisanie sukhoputnykh voisk, ispravlennoe po 1-e avgusta 1905 g.,* Spb., 1905, lists 61½ cossack regiments and 6 plastoon (foot) battalions in the field as of 1 August. One other regiment was mobilized in August. For that and the dates of the earlier mobilization of cossack regiments for internal service, see *Tsirkuliary Glavnogo shtaba,* [Spb., 1905,] No. 115, 29 March 1905; No. 196, 8 July 1905; No. 247, 2 Sept. 1905. Four cossack regiments had been mobilized for internal service in the Caucasus in late 1904: *Tsirkuliary Glavnogo shtaba,* [Spb., 1904,] No. 360, 27 Dec. 1904; and *Vsepoddanneishii otchet Voennogo ministerstva za 1905 god,* "Otchet Glavnogo upravleniia kazach'ikh voisk," pp. 10–11.

19. I. Burskii, *Istoriia 8-go gusarskogo Lubenskogo polka,* Odessa, 1913, pp. 520–21, 523–4. The 24th dragoons were rechristened the 8th hussars after 1905 as part of an army-wide effort to restore unit morale with distinctive uniforms and trappings.

20. Fuller, *Civil-Military Conflict,* Chapter 5.

21. Quoted in Pereverzev, "Karatel'naia ekspeditsiia Gen.-leit. P. K. Rennenkampfa v Zabaik. Ob.," *Byloe,* 1907 no. 4, pp. 134–5.

22. *RI,* 24 Nov. 1905, 10 Dec. 1905, 17 Dec. 1905, and 18 Dec. 1905; Rozen, "Vospominaniia," p. 26.

23. *PI,* no. 243, 2 August/20 July 1905; Ul'ianinskii, "Vosstanie Rostovskogo polka," p. 34.

24. A Trepov letter of 28 June 1905, quoted in Petrov, *Ocherki,* p. 55; the incident cited is in I. G. Drozdov, *Agrarnye volneniia i karatel'nye ekspeditsii v chernigovskoi gubernii v gody pervoi revoliutsii 1905–1906 gg.,* M.-L., 1925, p. 27.

25. *PI,* no. 243, 2 Aug./20 July 1905.

26. See the report on the Plotsk garrison in *Proletarii,* no. 15, 5 Sept./23 Aug. 1905; Ul'ianinskii, "Vosstanie Rostovskogo polka," p. 36; Shabrov, "Dni vosstaniia v Rostovskom polku," *Krasnoe znamia* (Paris), 1906 no. 4, p. 24.

27. Ul'ianinskii, "Vosstanie Rostovskogo polka," p. 38; *VP,* v. 2, p. 428; *Vserossiiskaia politicheskaia stachka v oktiabre 1905 goda* (henceforth: *VPS*), v. 2, M., 1955, p. 149; P. Cherkasov, "Revoliutsionnoe dvizhenie v voiskakh Sibirskogo i Turkestanskogo voennykh okrugov," *1905. Armiia v pervoi revoliutsii,* M.-L., 1927, pp. 296, 327; Ia. Leskovskii, "Dvizhenie sredi voisk v Krasnoiarske v 1905 g.," *PR,* 1925 no. 10, p. 60; Iak. Novogreshnov, *1905 god v Krasnoiarske. Populiarnyi ocherk,* Krasnoiarsk, 1925, p. 19; *Samarskii kur'er,* 29 Nov. 1905; [Mariampol SD/ Bund Military Revolutionary Organization,] "Otkrytoe pis'mo soznatel'nykh soldat 112 Ural'skogo i 111 Donskogo pekhotnykh polkov ko vsem tovarishchim soldatam," hectograph, late 1905, Bund Archive; A. P. Steklov, "Revoliutsionnoe dvizhenie v voiskakh Kavkazskogo voennogo okruga," *Revoliutsionnoe dvizhenie v armii v gody pervoi russkoi revoliutsii,* M., 1955, p. 404.

28. Evidence on midsummer indiscipline is voluminous. On the Smolensk incident, see D. I. Budaev, "Rabochee i krest'ianskoe dvizhenie v Smolenskoi gubernii v period pervoi russkoi revoliutsii," *Revoliutsionnoe dvizhenie v Smolenskoi gubernii v 1905–1907 gg.,* Smolensk, 1956, p. 47, and Budaev, "Khronika osnovnykh revoliutsionnykh sobytii v Smolenskoi gubernii v period pervoi russ-

koi revoliutsii (1905–1907 godov)," ibid., p. 120. The Main Staff circular is in *Revoliutsionnoe dvizhenie v Rossii vesnoi i letom 1905 goda. Aprel'–sentiabr'*, part 1, M., 1957, p. 395. The situation in the Moscow camp is reported in ibid., pp. 397–400; General A. I. Spiridovich of the secret police reports the surprise of the generals in Kiev when told of midsummer plots in the Kiev sapper camp; A. I. Spiridovich, "Pri tsarskom rezhime," *Arkhiv russkoi revoliutsii*, v. 15, 1924, pp. 203–5.

29. A report in the liberal newspaper *Rus'* reprinted in *Proletarii*, no. 23, 31/18 Oct. 1905.

30. See Appendix I.

31. *Pravo*, no. 22, 8 June 1905; Petrov, *Ocherki*, p. 137; A. Belen'kaia, "O rabote Kievskoi organizatsii v 1905 g.," *PR*, 1926 no. 2, p. 260; *Proletarii*, no. 8, 17 (4) July 1905; *PI*, no. 238, 27/14 June 1905; S. M. Dubnow, *History of the Jews in Russia and Poland from the Earliest Times until the Present Day*, v. 3, Philadelphia, 1920, pp. 119–20.

32. *RI*, 10 Sept. 1905.

33. John Bushnell, "Mutineers and Revolutionaries. Military Revolution in Russia, 1905–1907," Ph.D. dissertation, Indiana University, 1977, pp. 53–7.

34. Kh. A. Vermishev, *Iz nedavnego proshlogo. 29 avgusta 1905 g. na Tiflisskoi gorodskoi dume*, Baku, 1917; *1905 god v Tiflise*, Tiflis, 1926, pp. 70–75; *Sotsial'demokrat*, no. 14, 15 Sept. 1905.

35. *Pravo*, 18 Sept. 1905; V. P. Semennikov, ed., *Revoliutsiia 1905 goda i samoderzhavie*, M.-L., 1928, pp. 99–103; Budaev, "Rabochee i krest'ianskoe dvizhenie," p. 120.

36. *Pravo*, 10 July 1905; *PI*, no. 239, 4 July/21 June 1905, and no. 240, 10 July/27 June 1905; *Lodzinskii listok*, 14/27 June 1905.

37. S. Mstislavskii, "Otryvki o piatom gode," *KiS*, 1928 no. 2, pp. 12–23; Plekhanov, "Vroz' itti, vmeste bit'!" *Iskra*, no. 87, 10 Feb. 1905; *Tretii s"ezd RSDRP. Protokoly*, M., 1959, p. 112 (Bogdanov).

38. Plekhanov, "Vroz' itti, vmeste bit'!" *Iskra*, no. 87, 10 Feb. 1905.

39. *Tretti s"ezd RSDRP*, pp. 109, 111–13, 117, 122–3, 127, 131, 143–4, 153.

40. *Pervaia obshcherusskaia konferentsiia partiinykh rabotnikov*, Geneva, 1905, pp. 29–30.

41. Chuzhak, "Chto delaetsia v voiskakh," *Proletarii*, no. 6, 3 July/20 June 1905.

42. For a fuller discussion, see Bushnell, "Mutineers and Revolutionaries," pp. 187–93. Somewhat inaccurate statistics on SD military organization formation, and a list of SD military organization with date of formation and documentation, are in ibid., pp. 442–52.

43. Lenin, "Nachalo revoliutsii v Rossii," *Vpered*, no. 4, 31/18 Jan. 1905; V.S., "Rol' organizatsii v narodnykh dvizheniiakh," *Vpered*, no. 18, 18/5 May 1905; Esper Serebriakov, "What Will the Army Do?" *FR*, 1 March 1905. On SD combat organizations: *1905. Boevaia gruppa pri Tsk RSDRP(b). 1905–1907 gg.*, M.-L., 1927; *Iskra*, no. 87, 10 Feb. 1905; no. 89, 24 Feb. 1905; no. 90, 3 March 1905; no. 95, 25 March 1905; Fischer, *Russische Sozialdemokratie*, pp. 82–124. SRs: Nat. Blinova, "Delo o revoliutsionnom dvizhenii v armii," *Sbornik materialov i statei. Redaktsiia*

zhurnala "Istoricheskii arkhiv," v. 1, M., 1921, p. 202; Eiter, "Organizational Growth," pp. 223–4.

44. Discussion of the *Potemkin* mutiny is based substantially on *Iskra,* no. 81, 23 Dec. 1904; no. 98, 23 April 1905; no. 103, 21 June 1905; no. 105, 15 July 1905; *Sotsial'demokrat,* no. 10, 21 July 1905; no. 13, 1 Sept. 1905; no. 14, 15 Sept. 1905; *RR,* no. 70, 1 July 1905; no. 75, 15 Sept. 1905; A. P. Berezovskii, *Odinnadtsat' dnei na Potemkine,* Spb., 1907; Constantine Feldman, *The Revolt of the "Potemkin,"* London, 1908; Denisenko, "Potemkinskoe vosstanie. (Vospominaniia matrosa'-potemkintsa')," *KiS,* 1925 no. 5, pp. 28–42; Startsev-Shishkarev, "Vosstanie na bronenostse 'Potemkin'," *Puti revoliutsii,* 1925, no. 1, pp. 7–14; *Revoliutsionnyi bronenosets. Vosstanie v Chernomorskom flote. (Po materialam "Iskry" i "Sotsialdemo-krata"),* Geneva, 1905; *Matrosy Chernogo moria,* n.p., 1905; N. Rostotskaia, *Potemkinskie dni v Odesse,* Spb., 1906; I. A. Lychev, *Vospominaniia potemkintsa,* M.-L., 1925; M. Morshanskaia, "Matros Chernomorskogo flota A. M. Petrov," *PR,* 1925 no. 4, pp. 138–48; B.I. Gavrilov, "K istorii vosstaniia na bronenostse 'Potemkin'," *IZ,* v. 95, 1975, pp. 284–313.

45. *Iskra,* no. 98, 23 April 1905.

46. Ibid.; "Pis'ma matrosa A. M. Petrova," *PR,* 1925 no. 12, p. 93.

47. A letter of 8/21 July 1905 from the Department of Police in St. Petersburg to the Sûreté Générale, a letter of 28 July from Paris to the Sûreté agent in An-nemasse keeping tabs on Russian revolutionaries in Switzerland, a report from Annemasse on revolutionary activity in the Russian armed forces, and other correspondence are in the Archives Nationales, F7 12521.

48. E. Genkin, *Po tiurmam i etapam,* P., 1922, p. 6; M. Vasil'ev-Iuzhin, "Vos-stanie na bronenostse 'Potemkine' i t. Lenin," *Molodaia gvardiia,* 1924 no. 2–3, pp. 54–7; Vasil'ev-Iuzhin, "V ogne pervoi revoliutsii," *PR,* 1926 no. 4, pp. 223–31; *Revoliutsiia 1905–1907 godov v g. Samare i Samarskoi gubernii. Dokumenty i materialy,* Kuibyshev, 1955, p. 96; *RR,* no. 70, 1 July 1905; Filatov, "Kniaz' Potemkin Tav-richeskii," *Proletarii,* no. 8, 17/4 July 1905; Lenin, "Revoliutsionnaia armiia i re-voliutsionnyi narod," *Proletarii,* no. 7, 10 July/27 June 1905; Martov, "Voennaia sila na sluzhbe revoliutsii," *Sotsial'demokrat,* no. 8, 24 June 1905; *Dnevnik sotsial-demokrata Plekhanova,* no. 2, Aug. 1905.

49. *Revoliutsiia 1905–1907 godov v g. Samare,* p. 96; *Proletarii,* no. 10, 2 Aug./20 July 1905; no. 20, 10 Oct./27 Sept. 1905. For documentation on central and local appeals to soldiers after the *Potemkin* mutiny, see Bushnell, "Mutineers," p. 225 n. 21; on SD military organization formation and documentation thereof, ibid., pp. 442–52 (the totals therein are incomplete).

50. Martov, "Respublika i voisko," *Sotsial'demokrat,* no. 9, 7 July 1905; Martov, "Ofitsery i soldaty v revoliutsii," *Sotsial'demokrat,* no. 13, 1 Sept. 1905; "Revoliut-siia i kontr-revoliutsiia," *Rabochii,* no. 1, Aug. 1905; "Voennaia khitrost' pravitel'stva," *Rabochii,* no. 2, 3 Aug. 1905; "Put' revoliutsii. Narodnoe vos-stanie," *Rabochii,* no. 3, 15 Oct. 1905; "K voprosu o taktike," *RR,* no. 74, 1 Sept. 1905; "Kniaz' Potemkin Tavricheskii," *Dnevnik sotsial-demokrata Plekhanova,* no. 2, Aug. 1905; Lenin, "Revoliutsionnaia armiia i revoliutsionnyi narod," *Proletarii,* no. 7, 10 July/27 June 1905.

51. "Kniaz' Potemkin Tavricheskii," *Dnevnik sotsial-demokrata Plekhanova,* no. 2, Aug. 1905.

52. See note 49.

53. Lenin, *PSS*, v. 10, M., 1967, pp. 335–45, 401–4; v. 11, pp. 133–43, 170–71, 185, 188–93, 246–8, 336–8, 339–43, 365, 410–11.

54. "Iz dnevnika chitatelia," *RR*, no. 70, 1 July 1905, p. 12; attribution to Gots is from Maureen Perrie, "The Socialist Revolutionaries on 'Permanent Revolution'," *Soviet Studies*, Jan. 1973, p. 411. Local reports in the revolutionary press provide evidence of the revolutionaries' euphoria.

55. "Narodnaia revoliutsiia," *RR*, no. 69, 15 June 1905, pp. 1–2; "Krest'ianskie s"ezdy," *RR*, no. 72, Aug. 1905, pp. 20–21; Viktor Chernov, "Ot 'Revoliutsionnoi Rossii' k 'Synu otechestva'," *Letopis' revoliutsii*, v. 1, 1923, pp. 69–71; Perrie, *Agrarian Policy*, pp. 105–6; L. M. Ivanov, "Boikot bulyginskoi dumy i stachka v oktiabre 1905 g. (K voprosu o rasstanovke boriushchikhsia sil)," *IZ*, v. 83, 1969, pp. 138–48; *Pis'ma P. B. Aksel'roda i Iu.O. Martova 1901–1916*, Berlin, 1924, pp. 123–8, 131–2; Iu. Martov, *Istoriia Rossiiskoi Sotsial-Demokratii*, 2nd edition, M.-Pg., 1923, pp. 125–8.

56. Galai, *Liberation Movement*, pp. 254–60; P. N. Miliukov, *Vospominaniia (1859–1917)*, v. 1, New York, 1955, pp. 299–305; Chermenskii, *Burzhuaziia i tsarizm*, pp. 108–120; Manning, *Crisis of the Old Order*, pp. 133–7.

57. Quoted in Sidney Harcave, *First Blood. The Russian Revolution of 1905*, New York, 1964, p. 169.

58. Voitinskii, *Gody pobed i porazhenii*, v. 1, Berlin-Pg.-M., 1923, pp. 52–63; Laura Engelstein, *Moscow, 1905. Working Class Organization and Political Conflict*, Stanford, 1982, p. 72.

59. M. Balabanov, "Promyshlennost' v 1904–1907 gg.," in L. Martov, et al., eds., *Obshchestvennoe dvizhenie v Rossii v nachale XX-go veka*, v. 4 pt. 1, Spb., 1912, pp. 69–73; Suhr, "Petersburg Workers," p. 381; Engelstein, *Moscow*, pp. 36, 76, 83; Varzar, *Statisticheskie svedeniia . . . 1894–1904*, p. 31 and "Prilozheniia," p. 18.

60. Engelstein, *Moscow*, pp. 73–96; P. A. Garvi, *Vospominaniia sotsialdemokrata*, New York, 1946, pp. 539–45.

61. Henry Frederick Reichman, "Russian Railwaymen and the Revolution of 1905," Ph.D. dissertation, University of California, Berkeley, 1977, pp. 364–410; I. M. Pushkareva, *Zheleznodorozhniki Rossii v burzhuazno-demokraticheskikh revoliutsiiakh*, M., 1975, pp. 144–75; A. Shestakov, "Vseobshchaia oktiabr'skaia stachka 1905 g.," in M. N. Pokrovskii, ed., *1905. Istoriia revoliutsionnogo dvizheniia v otdel'-nykh ocherkakh*, v. 2, M.-L., 1925, pp. 264–352; Engelstein, *Moscow*, pp. 105–35; Suhr, "Petersburg Workers," pp. 400–22. On the attitudes of revolutionaries: Voitinskii, *Gody pobed i porazhenii*, v. 1, pp. 92–6, 128–9, 134; Schwarz, *Russian Revolution*, pp. 138–40, 172; Engelstein, *Moscow*, p. 106; Garvi, *Vospominaniia*, pp. 556, 559–60; Shestakov, "Vseobshchaia oktiabr'skaia," pp. 279, 285; *Proletarii*, no. 24, 7 Nov/25 Oct. 1905.

62. Galai, *Liberation Movement*, pp. 262–3; Engelstein, *Moscow*, pp. 115–29, 133–4; Chermenskii, *Burzhuaziia i tsarizm*, pp. 133–5; Erman, *Intelligentsiia*, pp. 155–66; Cherkasov, "Revoliutsionnoe dvizhenie," p. 262; *Obzor revoliutsionnogo dvizheniia v okruge Irkutskoi sudovoi palaty za 1897–1907 gg.*, Spb., 1908, pp. 68–70; *VPS*, v. 1, pp. 363–4; *Pravo*, 8 Nov. 1905.

63. On total troop strength, see note 18 above. On the mobilization of reserves for the Caucasus: *Vsepoddanneishii otchet Voennogo ministerstva za 1905 god*, "Otchet po Glavnomu shtabu," p. 108.

64. [A. F. Rediger], "Zapiski A. F. Redigera o 1905 g.," *KA*, 1931 no. 2, p. 97;

V. E. Poleshchuk, "Revoliutsionnoe dvizhenie v Man'chzhurskoi armii," p. 317; *VPS*, v. 2, pp. 242–3; *VP*, v. 2, pp. 1082–3, 1108.

65. *VPS*, v. 1, pp. 87–8, 215, 271–2, 274, 280, 345, 356, 453–4, 537, 565, 642–4; *VPS*, v. 2, pp. 149–50, 156–61.

66. *VPS*, v. 1, pp. 239–40; *VPS*, v. 2, pp. 103–9; *Ekaterinoslavshchina v revoliutsii 1905–1907 gg. Dokumenty i materialy*, Dnepropetrovsk, 1975, pp. 167–77, 181–5, 187–90; *Novaia zhizn'*, 8 Nov. 1905; Shestakov, "Vseobshchaia oktiabr'skaia," pp. 307–11.

67. *VPS*, v. 1, pp. 354, 429, 432; *VPS*, v. 2, pp. 148–9; *Ekaterinoslavshchina*, p. 171; "Iz bumag D. F. Trepova," *KA*, 1925, no. 4–5, p. 455; *The Secret Letters of the Last Tsar. Being the Confidential Correspondence between Nicholas II and His Mother, Dowager Empress Maria Feodorovna*, edited by Edward J. Bing, New York-Toronto, 1938, pp. 183–4.

68. *VPS*, v. 2, pp. 247, 250–55; *Tsarizm v bor'be s revoliutsiei 1905–1907 gg. Sbornik dokumentov*, M., 1936, p. 161; "Revoliutsionnye sobytiia v Pribaltike v 1905 g.," *KA*, 1940 no. 5, p. 144; *Novaia zhizn'*, 1 Nov. 1905.

69. *Kratkoe raspisanie sukhoputnykh voisk* lists only 3 railroad battalions in Europe as of August; in addition there was the 4th reserve railroad battalion in Petersburg (see *VP*, v. 1, pp. 430–32), and a battalion in the Caucasus. On the use of these troops to move trains between Moscow and Petersburg, and around Irkutsk and Tiflis, see *VPS*, v. 1, pp. 228, 250, 253, 272; and *RI*, no. 234, 8 Nov. 1905. See also the information on the railway strike, and the helplessness of authorities to deal with it, drawn up by the Department of Police: *VPS*, v. 1, pp. 210–37. On the use of technical troops to run public utilities: Engelstein, *Moscow*, p. 132; *VP*, v. 1, p. 499; V. N. Poluektov, "1905 g. v kazarmakh, kreposti i tiur'me," *Po tiur'mam. Sbornik vospominanii iz epokhi pervoi revoliutsii*, M., 1925, pp. 113–4.

70. *VPS*, v. 1, pp. 213–4, 430, 679, fn. 200; *VPS*, v. 2, p. 250; Vitte, *Vospominaniia*, v. 3, p. 34; [Vitte], "Spravka o Manifeste 17 Oktiabria 1905 g.," and "Pis'mo A. Redigera k S.Iu. Vitte, 28 ianvaria 1907 g.," in "Manifest 17 Oktiabria," *KA*, 1925 no. 4–5, pp. 79, 82–3 (Witte's original recollection of the meeting, and Rediger's amplification); Shestakov, "Vseobshchaia oktiabr'skaia," p. 294; "Iz bumag D. F. Trepova," pp. 456–8.

71. *Secret Letters*, p. 185.

72. Vitte, *Vospominaniia*, v. 3, pp. 20, 34, 37–8.

73. Howard D. Mehlinger and John M. Thompson, *Count Witte and the Tsarist Government in the 1905 Revolution*, Bloomington, Ind., 1972, pp. 31–8; Vitte, *Vospominaniia*, v. 2, pp. 544–59, and v. 3, pp. 10–12, 19–20, 23–26; "Dnevnik A. A. Polovtseva," *KA*, no. 4, 1923, pp. 63–76; Kokovtsov, *Out of My Past*, pp. 65–8; N. G. Koroleva, *Pervaia rossiiskaia revoliutsiia i tsarizm. Sovet ministrov Rossii v 1905–1907 gg.*, M., 1982, pp. 29–37; *VPS*, v. 1, pp. 213–4.

74. *Secret Letters*, p. 185; "Dnevnik A. A. Polovtseva," p. 76; Vitte, *Vospominaniia*, v. 3, pp. 14–17, 26–31, 35–53; Mehlinger and Thompson, *Count Witte*, pp. 40–6; "Manifest 17 Oktiabria," pp. 80–82; A. V. Ostrovskii, M. M. Safonov, "Manifest 17 Oktiabria 1905 g.," *Vspomogatel'nye istoricheskie distsipliny*, v. 12, 1981, pp. 168–88.

75. Vitte, *Vospominaniia*, v. 3, pp. 31, 34.

76. "K istorii Manifesta 17 oktiabria 1905 goda. Sekretnaia perepiska," *Byloe*, no. 14, 1919, pp. 109–11; Chermenskii, *Burzhuaziia i tsarizm*, p. 144.

77. Shestakov, "Vseobshchaia oktiabr'skaia," pp. 330–33; Voitinskii, *Gody pobed i porazhenii*, v. 1, pp. 159–61; Engelstein, *Moscow*, pp. 132–3.

78. *Dnevnik Imperatora Nikolaia II*, Berlin, 1923, p. 222.

IV. Revolution in the Army

1. Suhr, "Petersburg Workers," pp. 423–31, 440–47, 501–5; Engelstein, *Moscow*, pp. 149–74; Leon Trotsky, *1905*, New York, 1972, pp. 103–12, 123–30, 140–56, 166–78; Oscar Anweiler, *The Soviets. The Russian Workers, Peasants and Soldiers Councils 1905–1921*, New York, 1974, pp. 43–83; *Rabochii klass v pervoi*, pp. 187–8, 243–51; Schwarz, *Russian Revolution*, pp. 171–95, 331–4, 339–54; M. Rafes, *Ocherki po istorii "Bunda"*, M., 1923, pp. 169–73; A. A. Voskresenskii and I.Sh. Chernomazov, "Federativnyi Sovet khar'kovskikh komitetov RSDRP (noiabr' 1905–ianvar' 1906 gg.)," *Vestnik Khar'kovskogo universiteta*, 1964 no. 1, pp. 125–6.

2. *VP*, v. 2, pp. 37–8, 215, 287, 328, 680; *VP*, v. 3 part 1, p. 306; *VPS*, v. 2, pp. 375, 379, 384, 388–9, 406–7, 417, 439, 445–6; Dubrovskii and Grave, *Agrarnoe dvizhenie*, pp. 63, 66, 170, 243–4, 296–7; *VP*, v. 4, pp. 44–5, 74, 167, 194, 199, 204–5, 207, 377–9; Maslov, *Krest'ianskoe dvizhenie*, pp. 79–100.

3. A good survey of events in the Baltic provinces is provided by "Pribaltiiskii krai v 1905 godu"; see also the sources in Chapter 4 n. 86, and Chapter 5 n. 17. On the Caucasus: Varl. Kalandadze and Vl. Mkheidze, *Ocherki revoliutsionnogo dvizhenie v Gruzii*, Spb., 1906, pp. 11–77; and *Vsepoddanneishaia zapiska po upravleniiu kavkazskim kraem gen.-ad"iutanta grafa Vorontsova-Dashkova*, n.p., 1907, pp. 6–7, 17, 23–30.

4. "Voinskii ustav o nakazaniiakh," st. 110, *Voinskii ustav o nakazaniiakh i Ustav distsiplinarnyi*, Spb., 1905, pp. 37–8. (Other Tsarist military crimes that were covered by mutiny articles in other armies are in st. 105, 107, 108, and 111.) On the interpretation of article 110 by the Military Supreme Court in 1883: *Resheniia Glavnogo Voennogo Suda za 1907*, [Spb., 1907], p. 148. On its application to mutinies in 1905 and 1906, see ibid., pp. 147–9, 191–5; *VP*, vol. 1, pp. 334, 641; *VP*, vol. 2, p. 429.

5. The number of units and their location have been calculated from *Kratkoe raspisanie sukhoputnykh voisk*; Major W. W. MacBean, *Handbook of the Russian Army*, 4th ed., London, 1905, pp. 250–95; and *Vsepodanneishii otchet Voennogo ministerstva za 1905 god*, "Obshchii obzor," p. 10. There were mutinies in 3 of the 4 unbrigaded reserve battalions, 1 of 8 Finland rifle regiments, 1 of 8 Caucasus rifle regiments, and 6 of 27 fortress infantry regiments and battalions; for all categories, there were mutinies in 92 of 282 infantry units in European Russia. I have not taken depot battalions into account, as they were formed only to ready replacements for the army in Manchuria and were rapidly disbanded after the conclusion of peace.

6. There is good evidence of widespread indiscipline and unreliability (as

government officials put it) in 24 other line infantry regiments; in some of these cases there may have been mutiny, but there is not enough evidence to be sure. It is harder to find reliable than unreliable units.

7. From October 18 through December 31, there were mutinies in 12 of 46 Guards, Grenadier, and line artillery brigades in European Russia; if reserve brigades, mortar regiments, and the like are added, there were mutinies in 19 of 65 artillery units. (I have not counted fortress artillery, because it has been difficult to identify formations.) For technical (excluding fortress) units, there were mutinies in 13 of 15 sapper battalions, 4 of 6 railway units (including one that returned from Siberia in late 1905), and 4 of 7 pontoon companies. There were 10 mutinies in the 65 line, reserve and native cavalry regiments, in none of the 13 Guards cavalry regiments. There were mutinies in 12 of the 71 mounted cossack regiments in Europe, in 4 of the 12 plastoon (foot) battalions. For sources on the number and location of artillery, technical and cavalry regiments, see note 5 above. For the cossacks, *Kratkoe raspisanie* lists a total of 62½ regiments and 6 plastoon battalions in the fields as of 1 August. One more cossack regiment was called up in August, and 8 regiments and 6 battalions were mobilized for use in European Russia in November and early December (I have converted individual cossack squadrons into regiments at a rate of 6 to 1; I have not counted a cossack regiment mobilized on December 30, or another mobilized for use in Central Asia); *Tsirkuliary Glavnogo shtaba*, [Spb., 1905], No. 247, 27 Sept. 1905; No. 335, 5 Dec. 1905; No. 336, 7 Dec. 1905; No. 343, 13 Dec. 1905; *Tsirkuliary Glavnogo shtaba*, [Spb., 1906]., No. 2, 4 Jan. 1906; No. 64, 21 Feb. 1906.

8. It is difficult to quantify naval mutinies, because sailors were assigned both to ships and to shore barracks *(ekipazhi)*. On the discussion of mothballing the navy, see [Rediger], "Zapiski," pp. 95–6; *Novoe vremia*, 1 Dec. 1905; and *RI*, 11 Dec. 1905.

9. *Vsepoddanneishii otchet Voennogo ministerstva za 1905*, "Otchet po Glavnomu shtabu," p. 95; *VP*, v. 2, pp. 363–73, 698–9, 1083, 1091–3; Pereverzev, "Karatel'-naia ekspeditsiia," pp. 137–8; *Karatel'nye ekspeditsii v Sibiri v 1905–1906 gg. Dokumenty i materialy*, M.-L., 1932, p. 150; A. B. Mel'nikov, "Revoliutsionnoe dvizhenie v Moskovskom garnizone v 1906 g.," *IZ*, v. 56, 1956, p. 96 note 2. Nicholas II wrote his mother on December 1 that the first units of XIII corps had arrived in Moscow; *Secret Letters*, p. 194. All the other evidence contradicts this. Nicholas likely mistook commanders for units. As General Meller-Zakomelskii, who led a punitive detachment into Siberia and had to restore order to XIII corps troop trains, reported, "The entire command structure of this corps, from the corps commander to the regimental commanders, left with their staffs for their permanent quarters in Russia," leaving their men behind them; "Sibirskaia ekspeditsiia barona Meller-Zakomel'skogo," *Byloe*, 1917 no. 3, p. 149. On XIII corps mutinies, see note 44 below.

10. Maureen Perrie, *Agrarian Policy*, p. 117.

11. Mehlinger and Thompson, *Count Witte*, p. x (the conclusion is Thompson's). Michael Perrins, "Russian Military Policy in the Far East and the 1905 Revolution in the Russian Army," *European Studies Review*, v. 9 no. 3, July 1979, pp. 344–5, offers a similar assessment. Allan Wildman provides the best picture of the ferment in the army in 1905 and 1906, but he does not assess the impact of

the mutinies on the course of the revolution; Wildman, *The End of the Russian Imperial Army. The Old Army and the Soldiers' Revolt (March–April 1917)*, Princeton, 1980, pp. 47–64.

12. *Revoliutsiia 1905–1907 godov v Rossii*, M., 1975, p. 369. See also Kh.I. Muratov, *Revoliutsionnoe dvizhenie v russkoi armii v 1905–1907 gg.*, M., 1955, p. 38; and A. V. Piaskovskii, *Revoliutsiia 1905–1907 gg.*, M., 1966, p. 288.

13. *VPS*, v. 2, pp. 15–16.

14. *VPS*, v. 1, pp. 600–601; *VPS*, v. 2, pp. 30–32, 99, 231–2; Engelman, *Moscow*, p. 137; *VP*, v. 1, pp. 240–41.

15. *VPS*, v. 1, pp. 375, 377, 381; *VPS*, v. 2, pp. 124–7, 138–40, 224, 229–31, 332–3; F. Kasatkin-Rostovskii, *Pamiatka Semenovtsa*, Spb., 1909, p. 79; "Iz bumag D. F. Trepova," pp. 458–60.

16. Shlomo Lambroza, "The Pogrom Movement in Tsarist Russia, 1903–1906," Ph.D. dissertation, Rutgers University, 1981, pp. 114–223, 278–94; Dubnow, *History of the Jews*, v. 3, pp. 125–30; Mehlinger and Thompson, *Count Witte*, pp. 57–64; Zionistischen Hilfsfonds, *Die Judenpogrome in Russland*, Cologne-Leipzig, 1910, vol. 1, pp. 190–191, and vol. 2, pp. 109–132, and passim.

17. Engelman, *Moscow*, pp. 139–44; Zenzinov, *Perezhitoe*, New York, 1953, pp. 218–9; Mark Vishniak, *Dan' proshlomu*, New York, 1954, pp. 109–10; *VPS*, v. 1, p. 641; Shestakov, "Vseobshchaia oktiabr'skaia," pp. 244–6; Zionistischen Hilfsfonds, *Die Judenpogrome*, v. 2, pp. 504–11.

18. *VPS*, v. 2, p. 398; Mehlinger and Thompson, *Count Witte*, pp. 66–9; *VP*, v. 1, p. 61; *VP*, v. 2, p. 295; *VP*, v. 4, pp. 172–3, 231; *Pravo*, 20 Nov. 1905, and 24 Dec. 1905; *Secret Letters*, pp. 185, 192; *Karatel'nye ekspeditsii*, p. 52.

19. *VPS*, v. 2, pp. 135, 201, 203–8, 236, 332–3; *Pravo*, 27 Nov. 1905; *Severozapadnoe slovo*, 1 Nov. 1905; Ignacy Pawłowski, *Wojskowa dzialność SDKPiL w Rewolucji 1905–1907*, Warsaw, 1956, pp. 219–20; *Revoliutsiia 1905–1907 gg. v. Litve*, p. 185.

20. *VPS*, v. 1, pp. 554–5; Nemanov, "Kievskaia i Ekaterinoslavskaia voennye organizatsii v 1905 g.," *PR*, 1926 n. 4, pp. 205–7; Zionistischen Hilfsfonds, *Die Judenpogrome*, v. 1, pp. 294–6; v. 2, pp. 184–188 and passim.

21. *VPS*, v. 2, pp. 43–5, 264–6; A. V. Piaskovskii, *Revoliutsiia 1905–1907 godov v Turkestane*, M., 1958, p. 225; *Vozrozhdenie*, 30 Oct. 1905; *Novoe obozrenie*, 13 Nov. 1905 and 15 Nov. 1905; V. Potto, *Istoriia 17 dragunskogo Nizhegorodskogo polka*, v. 11, Tiflis, 1908, pp. 182–3.

22. *VPS*, v. 2, pp. 48–52; *RI*, 17 Nov. 1905; W.G., "Ocherki sovremennogo revoliutsionnogo dvizheniia v Rossii. Tomsk," *Krasnoe znamia*, 1906 no. 3, pp. 113–17; *Oktiabr'skie dni v Tomske*, Tomsk, 1905.

23. D. I. Soifer, *Revoliutsionnoe dvizhenie soldat v Turkestane*, Tashkent, 1969, pp. 39–40; Budaev, "Rabochee i krest'ianskoe dvizhenie," p. 48; N. A. Obetkovskii, "Revoliutsionnoe dvizhenie Amurskogo kazachestva v 1905–1907 godakh," *Zapiski Amurskogo oblastnogo muzeia kraevedeniia i obshchestva kraevedeniia*, v. 5, 1961, p. 29.

24. Baku: for sailors, see Appendix I, October 20, Baku, Caspian Naval Barracks; on the behavior of soldiers, *VPS*, v. 2, pp. 279–80; *Kaspii*, 26 Oct. 1905 and 24 Nov. 1905; *Baku*, 4 Nov. 1905; 13 Nov. 1905; 24 Nov. 1905; and 26 Nov. 1905. Tiflis: *Vozrozhdenie*, 10 Nov. 1905; *Novoe obozrenie*, 2 Nov. 1905 and 9 Nov. 1905.

25. See the 25 Oct. 1905 order to the Moscow military district in *MG*, 20 Nov. 1905, and a 31 Oct. 1905 circular to the Moscow military district in *VP*, v. 1, p. 607. A 6 Nov. 1905 order to the Samara garrison is in *Samarskii kur'er*, 19 Nov. 1905. Most of the sources in Appendix I document rampant indiscipline prior to mutiny.

26. *Razvedchik*, no. 785, 10 Nov. 1905.

27. *RI*, 25 Nov. 1905.

28. *NZh*, 18 Nov. 1905.

29. *MG*, 18 Nov. 1905.

30. For a 26 Oct. 1905 order to the Warsaw fortress district, see *Vestnik voennogo dukhovenstva*, no. 3, 1 Feb. 1906. Vladivostok: *VP*, v. 1, pp. 233, 250–51; *SO*, 17 Nov. 1905. Saratov: *Privolzhskii krai*, 19 Nov. 1905. Rembertow: *Russkie vedomosti*, 23 Nov. 1905; Korol'kov, "Revoliutsionnoe dvizhenie v voiskakh Vilenskogo," p. 177. Kars: Petrov, *Ocherki*, pp. 263–5. Appendix I: October 22–27, Askhabad; October 25–6, Krasnovodsk, 8th reserve Turkestan battalion; October 28, Vladivostok, Cruiser *Rossiia*.

31. My reconstruction of the Kronstadt mutiny is based substantially on *VP*, v. 1, pp. 191–227; *Voennye vosstaniia v Baltike v 1905–1906 gg.*, M., 1933, pp. 29–58, 70; S. Ivanov, "Kronshtadtskoe podpol'e (1905–1906 gg.)," *PR*, 1924 no. 12, pp. 138–43; A. K. Drezen, *Revoliutsiia vo flote. Baltiiskie moriaki v vosstaniiakh 1905–1906 gg.*, L., 1926, pp. 7–29, 43; K. S. Zharnovetskii, "Kronshtadtskie vosstaniia v 1905–1906 gg.," *KL*, 1925 no. 3, pp. 52–4; V. Amosov, "V 1905 g.," *KL*, 1925 no. 3, p. 109; "Vosstanie 26–27 oktiabria 1905 g. v Kronshtadte," *Krasnyi baltiets*, 1920 no. 1, pp. 36–40; Iv. Egorov, "Voennye organizatsii RSDRP(b)," *1905. Vosstaniia v Baltiiskom flote v 1905–1906 gg. Sbornik*, L., 1926, p. 57; Ottoson-Nikolaev, "Iz vospominanii o Kronshtadte i Sveaborge 1905 g.," ibid., p. 101; Kal', "Iz vospominanii matrosa A. Koltova o vosstanii v Kronshtadte v 1905 godu," ibid., pp. 24–33; L. I. Andreev, "Revoliutsionnoe dvizhenie v voiskakh severozapadnogo okruga," *1905. Armiia v pervoi revoliutsii*, M.-L., 1927, pp. 4–14; *IS*, 3 Nov. 1905; *NZh*, 1 Nov. 1905; *Pravo*, 8 Nov. 1905. There is a lengthy reconstruction, somewhat different from my own, in Joseph Hartgrove, "Red Tide: The Kronstadters in the Russian Revolutionary Movement, 1901–1917," Ph.D. dissertation, University of North Carolina at Chapel Hill, 1975, pp. 47–92.

32. *NZh*, 1 Nov. 1905.

33. *VP*, v. 1, p. 191.

34. *NZh*, 1 Nov. 1905.

35. *VP*, v. 1, p. 193.

36. Drezen, *Revoliutsiia*, p. 30; Mehlinger and Thompson, *Count Witte*, p. 140; *IS*, 20 Oct. 1905 and 3 Nov. 1905; Trotsky, *1905*, pp. 174–5, 258; Andreev, "Revoliutsionnoe," pp. 15–18; *RI*, 6 Nov. 1905.

37. Cited in *NZh*, 25 Nov. 1905.

38. *VPS*, v. 2, p. 87; *VP*, v. 1, pp. 233, 239–41; *VP*, v. 2, p. 1089; "Dvizhenie v voiskakh na Dal'nem Vostoke," *KA*, 1925 no. 4–5, pp. 309–10, 315; Pereverzev, "Karatel'naia ekspeditsiia," pp. 148–9; M. Ivanov, "Revoliutsionnye dni na vostoke," *Sibirskie voprosy*, 1907 no. 25, p. 7, and 1907 no. 36, pp. 18–19; *Karatel'nye ekspeditsii*, pp. 77–8; V. S., "V polose otchuzhdeniia (1905–1906 gg. po materialam

Dal'istparta)," *1905. Revoliutsionnoe dvizhenie na Dal'nem Vostoke. Sbornik statei*, Vladivostok, 1925, p. 86; V. E. Poleshchuk, "Revoliutsionnoe dvizhenie v Man'chzhurskoi armii," p. 323; [A. N. Kuropatkin], "Iz dnevnika A. N. Kuropatkina (s 23 okt. po 23 dek. 1905)," *KA*, 1924 no. 7, pp. 56, 66; *Russko-iaponskaia voina. Iz dnevnikov A. N. Kuropatkina i N. P. Linevicha*, L., 1925, p. 115; M[ashin], "Iz Man'chzhurii v Rossiiu," *Otkliki sovremennosti*, 1906 no. 4, pp. 47–9; A. A. Ignatyev, *A Subaltern in Old Russia*, London, 1944, p. 278; N. Voronovich, *Russko-iaponskaia voina. Vospominaniia*, New York, 1952, pp. 63–6.

39. *RI*, 26 Oct. 1905; *VP*, v. 2, pp. 1083–5, 1090, 1096; *Karatel'nye ekspeditsii*, pp. 77–8; Poleshchuk, "Revoliutsionnoe dvizhenie v Man'chzhurskoi armii," pp. 317, 321–2; Pereverzev, "Karatel'naia ekspeditsiia," pp. 137–8; "Dvizhenie v voiskakh," pp. 290, 323, 383; Cherkasov, "Revoliutsionnoe dvizhenie," pp. 239–40; [A. N. Kuropatkin], "Iz dnevnika A. N. Kuropatkina. (S 23 dekabria 1905 goda po 12 marta 1906 goda)," *KA*, 1925 no. 1, p. 78.

40. *VP*, v. 2, pp. 1091, 1095–7, 1099–1102, 1106–7; Pereverzev, "Karatel'naia ekspeditsiia," pp. 145–8; "Dvizhenie v voiskakh," pp. 290, 292–3, 298, 300, 308, 310, 318–19, 321, 325–7, 338; M. Ivanov, "Revoliutsionnye dni," *Sibirskie voprosy*, 1907 no. 35, p. 13 and 1907 no. 37, p. 14; "Razlozhenie armii v 1905 g. na Dal'nem Vostoke," *Byloe*, 1925 no. 4 (32), pp. 110–16; [Kuropatkin], "Iz dnevnika . . . 23 dekabria," pp. 71–2, 75–6; [Rediger], "Zapiski," pp. 108–9; [A. F. Rediger], "Iz zapisok A. F. Redigera," *KA*, 1933 no. 5 (60), pp. 100, 102–4; *Zabaikal'skii rabochii*, 7 Dec. 1905; Poleshchuk, "Revoliutsionnoe dvizhenie v Man'chzhurskoi armii," p. 327; [Kuropatkin], "Iz dnevnika . . . 23 oktiabria," pp. 62–3; *Russko-iaponskaia voina. Iz dnevnikov*, pp. 116, 127, 156; Mashin, "V manchzhurskikh armiiakh," *Otkliki sovremennosti*, 1906 no. 2, pp. 121–2, and 1906 no. 3, pp. 48–58; M[ashin], "Iz Manchzhurii," pp. 47–8; Denikin, *Staraia armiia*, v. 1, pp. 47, 136–7; Svechin, *Zapiski*, p. 83.

41. "Dvizhenie v voiskakh," p. 327; "Sibirskaia ekspeditsiia," pp. 136–7, 140, 146; V. Mandel'berg, *Iz perezhitogo*, Davos, 1910, pp. 96–8; Cherkasov, "Revoliutsionnoe dvizhenie," pp. 240–41; *VP*, v. 2, pp. 892, 898, 1062; *Karatel'nye ekspeditsii*, pp. 49, 83–4, 118, 121; P. K-v, "Krasnoiarsk v kontse 1905 goda. (Nabroski po vospominaniiam)," *Byloe*, 1907 no. 6, pp. 26–7, 33; M. Trigoni, "Posle Shlissel'burga," *Byloe*, 1906 no. 9, p. 62; M[ashin], "Iz Manchzhurii," pp. 57–61; Denikin, *Put'*, pp. 224–6; Denikin, *Staraia armiia*, v. 1, pp. 133–4; Voronovich, *Russko-iaponskaia voina*, p. 73; *Novoe vremia*, 9 Nov. 1905; *Istoriia sviiazhtsev*, Spb., 1913, p. 122.

42. [Rediger], "Zapiski," p. 98; "Razlozhenie armii," p. 110; *VP*, v. 2, pp. 1095, 1097.

43. *VP*, v. 2, pp. 304, 671–3.

44. For general complaints about XIII corps: *VP*, v. 2, pp. 896, 1094–5; *Karatel'nye ekspeditsii*, pp. 124–5; "Sibirskaia ekspeditsiia," p. 149; [Kuropatkin], "Iz dnevnika . . . 23 dekabria," p. 97. For mutinies, see Appendix I: Nov. 10, Aleksandrovskoe, 2nd Sofia; 15 Nov., Chita, 141st Mozhaisk, 144th Kashira; 15 Nov., Taiga station, 3rd Narva; 16 Nov., Krasnoiarsk, 2nd Sofia, 141st Mozhaisk; 26 Nov., Irkutsk, 144th Kashira; second half of Nov., Innokentev'skaia station, 1st Nevskii, 2nd Sofia; second half of November, near Tomsk, 4th Khopersk; second

half of November, Zima station, 142nd Zvenigorod. On indiscipline that apparently did not turn into mutiny in the 143rd Dorogobuzh infantry: "Sibirskaia ekspeditsiia," pp. 149–50.

45. Mandel'berg, *Iz perezhitogo*, p. 90. On the mutinies, see Appendix I.

46. [Rediger], "Zapiski," p. 94; *RI*, 26 Oct. 1905; 4 Nov. 1905; 20 Nov. 1905; *Vsepoddanneishii otchet Voennogo ministerstva za 1905 god*, "Obshchii obzor," pp. 33–4; Petrov, *Ocherki*, p. 53; "Kratkii obzor," *Voina i mir*, 1906 no. 1, p. 159.

47. [Rediger], "Zapiski," p. 94; *RI*, 20 Nov. 1905; *VP*, v. 2, p. 393; *VP*, v. 4, p. 521; "Nikolai Romanov o revoliutsionnom dvizhenii," *KA*, 1930 no. 1, p. 217; "Pribaltiiskii krai," p. 278; Iakovlev, "Khar'kovskoe likholet'e," *IV*, 1910 no. 11, pp. 554–5; *Severo-zapadnyi krai*, 27 Nov. 1905 and 29 Nov. 1905; *Samarskii kur'er*, 8 Nov. 1905; *Baku*, 16 Nov. 1905; *Privolzhskii krai*, 16 Nov. 1905; V. M. Kantsel'son, "Revoliutsionnoe dvizhenie v voiskakh Kievskogo voennogo okruga," *Revoliutsionnoe dvizhenie v armii*, p. 216; *Kaspii*, 27 Nov. 1905. Troop strength has been calculated from *Vsepoddanneishii otchet Voennogo ministerstva za 1905 god*, "Obshchii obzor," pp. 2–3, 11–13, 34.

48. *Revoliutsiia 1905 v Zakavkaz'i. Khronika sobytii, dokumentov i materialov*, Tiflis, 1926, pp. 88–9, 91, 93. See also the order to the Caucasus military district on the subject of these reserves in *Tiflisskii listok*, 19 Nov. 1905.

49. *VP*, v. 3 part 1, pp. 350–51; *VP*, v. 4, 268; *Nizhegorodskii listok*, 10 Nov. 1905; *Volzhskii vestnik*, 12 Nov. 1905.

50. Petrov, *Ocherki*, p. 384, claims that reserves participated in 60 of the 195 mutinies he counts in the last three months of 1905. I have found that reserves played a prominent (not necessarily a controlling) part in only 43 of the 211 mutinies I have documented between October 18 and December 31, but reserves may have been prominent in a few more than that. The total of 43 includes mutinies in identifiable units in Manchuria and Siberia (but not the mass stampede of reserves from the field army).

51. Muratov, *Revoliutsionnoe dvizhenie*, p. 78.

52. S. A. Tsion, *Tri dnia vosstaniia v Sveaborge*, Helsingfors, 1907, p. 20.

53. Ibid., p. 24. For other sources on the mutiny, see Appendix I.

54. *PI*, no. 137, 12 Feb. 1903; no. 234, 7 June/25 May 1905; no. 245, 9 Aug./27 July 1905; no. 252, 10 Oct./27 Sept. 1905; G. Korol'kov, "Revoliutsionnoe dvizhenie v voiskakh Vilenskogo i Varshavskogo voennykh okrugov," *1905. Armiia v pervoi revoliutsii*, M.-L., 1927, pp. 168–9.

55. *VP*, v. 4, pp. 124–5; Muratov, *Revoliutsionnoe dvizhenie*, pp. 199–201; *Revoliutsionnoe dvizhenie v Belorussii 1905–1907 gg. Dokumenty i materialy*, Minsk, 1955, pp. 313–4; Korol'kov, "Revoliutsionnoe dvizhenie v voiskakh Vilenskogo," pp. 168–9 (Korol'kov misidentifies the Bund military organization as SR).

56. *VP*, v. 4, pp. 128–9. For the mutinies on December 4 and 12, see Appendix I. The single source on the possible mutiny in the 4th sapper battalion is *Robotnik* (PPS), no. 70, 8 Jan. 1906 (i.e., 26 Dec. 1905 o.s.). *Robotnik* does not give the number of the sapper battalion, but it was the 4th that was garrisoned in Grodno: MacBean, *Handbook*, p. 254.

57. On clashes between civilians and the 229th Sviiazhsk battalion on October 17, see *Istoriia sviiazhtsev*, p. 123; *VPS*, v. 2, pp. 593–4; and *Volzhskii vestnik*, 26 Nov. 1905.

58. *VP,* v. 3 part 2, p. 1007.

59. Petrov, *Ocherki,* pp. 269–73, counts 22 mutinies during which the Grodno demands were mentioned, but three were not in fact mutinies. The Grodno demands were frequently mentioned favorably in other units. On the Samarkand demands, see Petrov, *Ocherki,* pp. 173–4. The 258th Sukhum reserve battalion (Sukhum) copied demands adopted by the Batum garrison, and the Sukhum demands were in turn copied by the 2nd Urupsk Kuban cossack regiment: *Chernomorskii vestnik,* 29 Nov. 1905; and *VP,* v. 2, p. 422. The 16th Mingrelian grenadiers copied the demands of the 15th Tiflis grenadiers; *Novoe obozrenie,* 18 Nov. 1905.

60. For statistics and sources, see Bushnell, "Mutineers and Revolutionaries," pp. 442–459. The material there is somewhat incomplete. Unfortunately, there is little good information on SR military organizations prior to October 17, and probably too little information on SR military organizations even in late 1905, to obtain a true picture of SR activity in the army in that period.

61. Petrov, *Ocherki,* pp. 347, 384, claims 10 "insurrections" and a total of 62 mutinies in which arms were used either in insurrection or to emphasize the seriousness of the soldiers' intent. 52 instances of brandishing arms is a likely figure, though the data I have examined does not directly confirm it.

62. Ibid., p. 385, identifies 31 such cases in his list of 195 mutinies. That figure is exaggerated by the inclusion of some nonmutinous incidents, including some meetings, and even a few letters by "groups of soldiers."

63. Ibid., p. 385, identifies 95 mutinies in which meetings were held. Almost all mutinies that did not begin as a spontaneous outburst of anger, and for which enough information is available to chart their course, were either preceded or accompanied by meetings. For mutinies the sources for which reveal particularly well the character of the meetings, see Appendix I: Oct. 22–27, Askhabad; and Nov. 2–Dec. 16, Baranovichi.

64. Petrov, *Ocherki,* pp. 266, 328; M. Annanepesov, *Uchastie soldatskikh mass v revoliutsii 1905–1907 godov v Turkmenistane,* Ashkhabad, 1966, pp. 41–5; Iakovlev, "Khar'kovskoe likholet'e," *IV,* 1910 no. 11, pp. 557–61; *VP,* v. 1, pp. 625–41; *VP,* v. 3, part 1, pp. 239–41, 245–6.

65. The testimony of Mikhail Bonch-Bruevich, given to Aleksandr Vanovskii in 1907; Aleksandr Vanovskii, "Burnye gody. (Vospominaniia uchastnika revoliutsii 1905 goda)," typescript, 1954, p. 21, Bakhmeteff Archive, Columbia University. The march grew out of a mutiny beginning 16 November. See Appendix I.

66. Korol'kov, "Revoliutsionnoe dvizhenie v voiskakh Vilenskogo," pp. 178–9.

67. M. Grulev, *Zloby dnia,* p. 4.

68. Petrov, *Ocherki,* pp. 186–254, analyzes the various demands made in 1905; a tabular summary of frequency is in ibid., pp. 250–51. The sample is slightly biased toward political demands because Petrov included a few lists of demands compiled by SD military organizations but not known actually to have been adopted by soldiers.

69. Ibid., pp. 200–1, 209, 250–51.

70. Ibid., pp. 199–200, 250–51.

71. Birkin, *Osinoe gnezdo*, pp. 89–90 and passim; *VPS*, v. 2, pp. 203–8, 1052; *VP,* v. 3, pp. 1014–9, 1029; *VP,* v. 4, pp. 143, 669–70; Manilov, "Kievskaia," p. 186; [Kuropatkin], "Iz dnevnika . . . s 23 okt. po 22 dek. 1905," p. 56; "Dvizhenie v voiskakh," pp. 313, 345–6; Mashin, "V manchzhurskikh armiiakh," *Otkliki sovremennosti,* 1906 no. 3, pp. 49–58; Okuntsov, "Chitinskii voenno-ofitserskii soiuz v 1905–1906 gg. (Vospominaniia uchastnika)," *1905. Revoliutsionnoe dvizhenie na Dal'nem Vostoke. Sbornik statei,* Vladivostok, 1925, pp. 38–42.

72. Chita: Cherkasov, "Revoliutsionnoe dvizhenie," p. 255; *Zabaikal'skii rabochii,* 18 Dec. 1905. Samara: *Samarskii kur'er,* 30 Nov. 1905; I. I. Bliumental', "Sotsial-demokratiia i revoliutsionnoe dvizhenie 1905 goda v Samarskom krae," *1905 god v Samarskom krae. Materialy po istorii R.K.P.(b) i revoliutsionnogo dvizheniia,* Samara, 1925, pp. 279, 282–7, 290–94. See also Birkin, *Osinoe gnezdo,* pp. 217, 221 and passim; and *VPR,* part 1 book 2, M., 1959, p. 611.

73. See Appendix I: Nov. 5, Gomel, 160th depot infantry battalion; Nov. 28, Viatka, 231st Kotelnich infantry battalion; Nov. 18, Voronezh, Voronezh disciplinary battalion.

74. Petrov, *Ocherki,* pp. 250, 384; I. Voronitsyn, *Istoriia odnogo katorzhnika,* M.-L., 1926, pp. 31–2; N. Znamenskii, *Voennaia organizatsiia pri Kazanskom komitete RSDRP,* Kazan, 1926, p. 69. For hostility toward civilians during mutinous meetings and marches, see Appendix I: Nov. 13, Batum; Nov. 16, Ekaterinodar; Nov. 17, Piatigorsk; Nov. 23, Kharkov; Nov. 29, Tsaritsyn.

75. Bliumental', "Sotsial-demokratiia," p. 292. See also Mandel'berg, *Iz perezhitogo,* p. 94; Shabrov, "Dni vosstaniia," pp. 60–61; N. Rozhkov and A. Sokolov, *O 1905 gode. Vospominaniia,* M., 1925, pp. 51–2; Vanovskii, "Burnye gody," p. 16.

76. For the Moscow and Ekaterinodar mutinies, see Appendix I. Similar protestations of loyalty were made by the 2nd Khopersk Kuban cossack regiment, Baku, 23 November, and by the Convoy of the Viceroy of the Caucasus, Tiflis, early December.

77. For Ekaterinograd, see Appendix I, Dec. 4. Among other examples: November 18 march by the Kiev sappers (mutiny beginning November 16); Nov. 23, Kharkov; 12 November march in Sevastopol (mutiny beginning November 11).

78. Chalmers Johnson, *Revolutionary Change,* Boston, 1966, p. 138.

79. *VP,* v. 2, pp. 281, 531, 589, 642–4; *VP,* v. 4, pp. 18, 27, 75, 171, 180, 187, 230, 234–7, 241–4; Semennikov, *Revoliutsiia,* p. 105; "Revoliutsionnye sobytiia v Pribaltike," pp. 155–6; V. Starosel'skii, " 'Dni svobody' v Kutaisskoi gubernii," *Byloe,* 1907 no. 7, p. 291.

80. 130 of the 254 infantry regiments and brigaded battalions in the nine European districts were in the Warsaw, Vilna, and Caucasus districts. Of the 130 cavalry and cossack regiments, 72 were in those three districts. MacBean, *Handbook,* pp. 250–95. MacBean lists the regiments in IX, XIII, and XIX corps subsequently shipped to Manchuria; I have subtracted them from the totals.

81. *VP,* v. 2, p. 393.

82. [Rediger], "Zapiski," p. 91. A sampling of civilian appeals for troops in the central regions: *VP,* v. 2, pp. 8, 18, 21–2, 49, 59, 76, 87, 95, 104, 206, 210, 227, 228, 240, 254, 256–8, 266–7, 288–9, 319–24, 376, 384, 387, 393, 652, 782, 799, 868.

83. Vitte, *Vospominaniia*, v. 3, p. 147; Semennikov, *Revoliutsiia*, p. 34; Iakovlev, "Khar'kovskoe likholet'e," *IV*, 1910 no. 11, p. 561.

84. *VP*, v. 2, pp. 642–4; *VP*, v. 3, part 1, pp. 74, 91–3, 151–2; *VP*, v. 3, part 2, pp. 774–5; *VP*, v. 4, pp. 64, 71–2; Starosel'skii, " 'Dni svobody'," pp. 296–7.

85. *Dokumenty po istorii revoliutsionnogo dvizheniia sel'skikh rabochikh v Pribaltike*, M.-L., 1957, pp. 131–2; [Rediger], "Zapiski," p. 99; *VP*, v. 2, pp. 227, 358, 361–2, 364–5, 367; Starosel'skii, " 'Dni svobody'," p. 292.

86. N. N. Iakovlev, *Vooruzhennye vosstaniia v dekabre 1905 goda*, M., 1957, pp. 429–30; *RI*, no. 267, 21 Dec. 1905; *Dokumenty po istorii revoliutsionnogo dvizhenie sel'skikh rabochikh*, pp. 247–50; *VP*, v. 1, pp. 51, 56–7, 63, 65; *VP*, v. 4, pp. 416–7, 438; "Pribaltiiskii krai," pp. 274, 278; Semennikov, *Revoliutsiia*, p. 176.

87. Appendix I. Moscow: Nov. 25, Nov. 26, Nov. 29, Dec. 2. Ekaterinoslav: Nov. 18, Dec. 1. Kharkov: Nov. 17, Nov. 23. Tiflis: Nov. 20 and early Dec. Baku: Nov. 23, Nov. 27, Dec. 12. Riga: Nov. 10. Lodz: Nov. 24 (see also *VP*, v. 4, p. 669). Saratov: Nov. 26 (see also *Protokoly pervoi konferentsii voennykh i boevykh organizatsii Rossiiskoi Sotsial-Demokraticheskoi Rabochei Partii sostoiavsheisia v noiabre 1906 g.*, Spb., 1907, p. 42; *Privolzhskii krai*, 16 Nov. 1905; 17 Nov. 1905; 19 Nov. 1905; 8 Dec. 1905; 9 Dec. 1905). Kazan: Nov. 24, Nov. 29 (see also *Volzhskii vestnik*, 25 Nov. 1905). Rostov: Dec. 6 (see also N. N. Iakovlev, *Vooruzhennye vosstaniia v dekabre 1905 goda*, M., 1957, pp. 225, 230–31; V.S., "Dekabr'skie dni v Rostove na Donu," *Otkliki sovremennosti*, 1906 no. 3, p. 65; *Russkoe slovo*, 30 Nov. 1905).

88. Appendix I. Vilna: Second half of November (see also *VP*, v. 4, pp. 19–20, 22; *Severo-zapadnyi golos*, 21 Dec. 1905; *Novaia zaria*, 22 Nov. 1905; *Severo-zapadnoe slovo*, 17 Nov. 1905; *Revoliutsiia 1905–1907 gg. v Litve*, pp. 429–30). Kiev: Nov. 16, Dec. before the 3rd (see also Vanovskii, "Burnye gody," p. 21). Tashkent: Nov. 15. Odessa: ca. Nov. 16, Dec. 12 (see also *Russkoe slovo*, 15 Nov. 1905; *Russkie vedomosti*, 25 Nov. 1905; *VP*, v. 3, part 1, p. 502). Warsaw: Nov. 17, Nov. 22, not after Nov. 22. On Astrakhan and Tula, see *VP*, v. 2, pp. 210, 211, 215, 652.

89. *NZh*, 29 Nov. 1905; 3 Dec. 1905; Iu. I. Korablev, "Revoliutsionnoe dvizhenie v voiskakh Peterburgskogo voennogo okruga," *Revoliutsionnoe dvizhenie v armii*, p. 133; M. Akhun and V. A. Petrov, *Bol'sheviki i armiia v 1905–1917 gg.*, L., 1929, p. 25; *Severnyi golos*, no. 1, 6 Dec. 1905; no. 2, 7 Dec. 1905.

90. [Rediger], "Zapiski," p. 91.

V. December 1905

1. On cossack mobilization prior to October, see Chapter 3 n. 18. On subsequent mobilizations: *VP*, v. 1, pp. 138–41; Petrov, *Ocherki*, p. 344; [Rediger], "Zapiski," pp. 91, 98; *Tsirkuliary Glavnogo shtaba*, 1905, No. 335, 5 Dec.; No. 337, 7 Dec.; No. 343, 13 Dec.; *Tsirkuliary Glavnogo shtaba*, 1906, No. 2, 4 Jan.; No. 5, 6 Jan.; No. 7, 7 Jan.; No. 24, 23 Jan.; No. 27, 27 Jan.; No. 56, 20 Feb.; No. 64, 21 Feb.

2. For a brief discussion of the village background to mutiny, see Bushnell, "Mutineers and Revolutionaries," pp. 121–3.

3. On the Don cossack mutinies, see Appendix I: Nov. 23, Smorgun, 3rd Don; Nov. 24, Moscow, 1st Don; Dec. 1, Ekaterinoslav, 20th Don (mobilized in March);

Dec. 2, Archeda station, 3rd composite Don (mobilized in November); Dec. 6, Rostov-on-Don, unidentified Don cossack unit.

4. Appendix I, Dec. 2–3, Archeda station; [Rediger], "Zapiski," p. 98.

5. In addition to the mutinies in notes 6, 7 and 8, see Appendix I: Nov. 13, Batum, 1st plastoon; Nov. 17, Sukhum, and Nov. 25, Samtredi, 2nd Laba; Nov. 23, Kars, 2nd Chernomorsk; Dec., first half, Elendorf, 1st Laba. The non-mutinous but restive plastoon battalion was the 13th; *VP,* v. 2, p. 425; *Revoliut-sionnoe dvizhenie na Kubani v 1905–1907 gg. Sbornik dokumentov i materialov,* Krasnodar, 1956, pp. 140–41.

6. *VP,* v. 2, p. 403. On the regiments demanding cancellation of debts, see Appendix I: Nov. 23, Baku, 2nd Khoper; Nov. 28, Eastern Georgia, 2nd Poltava.

7. Appendix I; Nov. 25, Samtredi, 2nd Laba; Dec. 2, Novorossiisk, 17th plas-toon; Dec. 11, North Caucasus, 14th plastoon; Dec. 14, Ekaterinodar, Krymskaia station, 15th plastoon; Dec. 15, Novorossiisk, Ekaterinodar, 2nd Urup.

8. For sources, see Appendix I: Dec. 2, Novorossiisk, 17th plastoon; Dec. 14, Ekaterinodar, 15th plastoon; Dec. 15, Novorossiisk, 2nd Urup; and Nov. 16, Ekaterinodar, 252nd Anapa reserve battalion.

9. [Rediger], "Zapiski," pp. 93–4; Petrov, *Ocherki,* p. 209; *RI,* 4 Nov. 1905; 6 Dec. 1905; *Razvedchik,* 10 Nov. 1905; 24 Jan. 1906; 14 March 1906; [Rediger], "Iz zapisok," pp. 104–5.

10. See Appendix I: November 28, Viatka; December 6, Rostov.

11. Mehlinger and Thompson, *Count Witte,* pp. 47–131.

12. *VPS,* v. 2, p. 451; "Agrarnoe dvizhenie v Chernigovskoi gub.," *KA,* 1925 no. 4, pp. 113–4; *VP,* v. 1, p. 137; *Vsepoddanneishii otchet Voennogo ministerstva za 1905 god,* "Otchet po Glavnomu shtabu," p. 48; Vitte, *Vospominaniia,* v. 3, pp. 144–5.

13. *RI,* 2 Nov. 1905; "Ob"ezd satrapa," *KA,* 1935 no. 2–3, pp. 40–71; Sem-menikov, *Revoliutsiia,* pp. 105–6; Drozdov, *Agrarnye volneniia,* pp. 109–21, 145 and passim; "Agrarnoe dvizhenie v Chernigovskoi gub.," pp. 116–8, 121. For reports on the operations of other plenipotentiaries: *VP,* v. 1, pp. 141–4, 170–1; *VP,* v. 2, pp. 395–7, 685–7, 758–61, 769–74; Semmenikov, *Revoliutsiia,* pp. 175, 191–3; *RI,* 11 Dec. 1905; *Privolzhskii krai,* 13 Nov. 1905.

14. Semennikov, *Revoliutsiia,* pp. 25–6; *VP,* v. 1, p. 157; Koroleva, *Pervaia ros-siiskaia,* pp. 62–4.

15. *VP,* v. 2, p. 342; Drozdov, *Agrarnye volneniia,* pp. 117–8.

16. A. K. Drezen, ed., *Tsarizm v bor'be s revoliutsiei 1905–1907 gg. Sbornik dokumentov,* M., 1936, pp. 116–17, 119; Drozdov, *Agrarnye volneniia,* pp. 110–14, 132–9; "Agrarnoe dvizhenie v Chernigovskoi gub.," pp. 121–5; Vladimir Korolenko, *Sorochinskaia tragediia,* Spb., 1907; *Novoe vremia,* 1 Dec. 1905; *Revoliut-siia 1905 goda v Zakavkaz'i,* p. 89.

17. There is an extensive literature on the revolution in the Baltic. Two good short surveys are "Pribaltiiskii krai," pp. 263–88; and Iakovlev, *Vooruzhennye,* pp. 431–53. See also: *VP,* v. 1, pp. 71, 84; *VP,* v. 4, pp. 241, 287–8, 381; Ames, *Revolution in the Baltic Provinces,* pp. 41–64; K. P. Berzin, "Tukkumskoe vos-stanie," *Iz epokhi bor'by s tsarizmom,* 1924 no. 1, pp. 33–8; *Dokumenty po istorii revoliutsionnogo dvizheniia sel'skikh rabochikh,* pp. 11, 155–6.

18. *Dokumenty po istorii revoliutsionnogo dvizheniia sel'skikh rabochikh*, p. 11; "Revoliutsionnye sobytiia v Pribaltike," pp. 145–6; [Rediger], "Iz zapisok," p. 99; *VP*, v. 1, p. 63; *VP*, v. 4, pp. 36–7, 416–17, 800 n. 68.

19. "Pribaltiiskii krai," p. 281; "Morskie karatel'nye batal'ony v Pribaltiiskom krae," *KA*, 1930 no. 1, p. 165; [G. O. Raukh], "Dnevnik G. O. Raukha," *KA*, 1926 no. 6, p. 84.

20. "Morskie karatel'nye batal'ony," p. 165; Vitte, *Vospominaniia*, v. 3, p. 157.

21. [Raukh], "Dnevnik," pp. 86, 88, 90; *Dokumenty po istorii revoliutsionnogo dvizheniia sel'skikh rabochikh*, pp. 191–2; "Revoliutsionnye sobytiia v Pribaltike," pp. 155–6; *VP*, v. 1, p. 173; P. Sadikov, "Karatel'naia ekspeditsiia v Pribaltike v 1905 godu," *KA*, 1925 no. 2, p. 108; "Dnevnik otriada grafa Grabbe," *KA*, 1925 no. 2, pp. 119, 125, 130.

22. "Pribaltiiskii krai v 1905 godu," pp. 282, 285; *Dokumenty po istorii revoliutsionnogo dvizheniia sel'skikh rabochikh*, p. 170; *VP*, v. 4, p. 588; F. F. Iushkevich, *Kratkaia istoriia 15-go pekhotnogo Shlissel'burgskogo polka. 1700–1909*, [Warsaw, 1909], pp. 72–3; K. K. Agafonov, *Letopis' Novotroitsko-Ekaterionoslavskikh dragun*, part 3, Spb., 1908, pp. 469–71.

23. [Raukh], "Dnevnik," p. 95; "Revoliutsionnye sobytiia v Pribaltike," p. 134; Semennikov, *Revoliutsiia*, p. 166.

24. *Dokumenty po istorii revoliutsionnogo dvizheniia sel'skikh rabochikh*, pp. 194–7, 209; *VP*, v. 4, pp. 326–8, 593–5; "Morskie karatel'nye batal'ony," p. 167; "Dnevnik otriada grafa Grabbe," pp. 130–31; Drezen, *Tsarizm*, p. 156.

25. *Dokumenty po istorii revoliutsionnogo dvizheniia sel'skikh rabochikh*, pp. 205–6, 214–26; Semennikov, *Revoliutsiia*, p. 44; [Raukh], "Dnevnik," pp. 93, 100; Ames, ed., *Revolution in the Baltic Provinces*, pp. 66–89; Vasilii Klimkov, *Raspravy i rasstrely*, M., 1906, pp. 99–102, 105–6, 119–123, 129–151; V. P. Obninskii, *Polgoda russkoi revoliutsii*, part 1, M., 1906, pp. 170–72; V. P. Obninskii, *Letopis' russkoi revoliutsii*, v. 3 part 1, M., 1907, "Khronika," pp. 91–2, 103; "Morskie karatel'nye batal'ony," pp. 168–9; "Revoliutsionnye sobytiia v Pribaltike," p. 156.

26. [Rediger], "Zapiski," p. 104; "K istorii karatel'nykh ekspeditsii v Sibiri," *KA*, 1922 no. 1, pp. 330–36; Semennikov, *Revoliutsiia*, pp. 30–31, 165–6; Vitte, *Vospominaniia*, v. 3, pp. 149, 152–3; *VP*, v. 1, pp. 151–2; *Karatel'nye ekspeditsii*, pp. 95–7, 100–101, 107–11, 116–7, 204, 207–8; "Sibirskaia ekspeditsiia," pp. 135–6, 142; Kanukov, *Doblestnaia sluzhba L.-Gv. S.-Peterburgskogo polka v smutnye 1904–1907 gg.*, Warsaw, n.d., pp. 38–9.

27. *Karatel'nye ekspeditsii*, pp. 83–4, 116–20; *VP*, v. 2, pp. 1085–6, 1090, 1100; Poleshchuk, "Revoliutsionnoe dvizhenie v Man'chzhurskoi armii," pp. 347–8; [Kuropatkin], "Iz dnevnika A. N. Kuropatkina (s 23 okt. po 23 dek. 1905)," p. 66.

28. *Karatel'nye ekspeditsii*, p. 50; *VP*, v. 2, pp. 895–7, 926, 931–4, 1030–32, 1035; *Obzor revoliutsionnogo dvizheniia v okruge Irkutskoi sudovoi palaty*, p. 79; Cherkasov, "Revoliutsionnoe dvizhenie v voiskakh Sibirskogo," pp. 242–52, 270–72; Iak. Novogreshnov, *1905 god v Krasnoiarske. Populiarnyi ocherk*, Krasnoiarsk, 1925, pp. 38–42; F. Romanov, "Krasnoiarskaia respublika," *Sibirskie voprosy*, 1907 no. 2, pp. 56–62.

29. *Karatel'nye ekspeditsii*, pp. 111, 119, 130–35, 153–72, 209, 212–17, 222–4, 250–337; "Sibirskaia ekspeditsiia," pp. 136, 138, 140, 142; *VP*, v. 2, pp. 966, 972,

989–1001; P. Klark, "V dni Rennenkampfa," *KiS*, 1925 no. 3, pp. 51–67; no. 4, pp. 50–62; Obninskii, *Letopis'*, v. 3 part 1, pp. 86–91; Semennikov, *Revoliutsiia*, pp. 14–15, 56, 213–14.

30. *VP*, v. 4, pp. 240–42.

31. Dan, "Obshchaia politika pravitel'stva i izmeneniia v gosudarstvennoi organizatsii v period 1905–1907 gg.," in L. Martov, et al., eds., *Obshchestvennoe dvizhenie v Rossii v nachale XX-go veka*, v. 4, part 1, Spb., 1912, pp. 362–4; Koroleva, *Pervaia rossiiskaia revoliutsiia*, pp. 61, 64–5, 89–90; Engelstein, *Moscow*, pp. 174–9; Mehlinger and Thompson, *Count Witte*, pp. 89, 105–6; *VP*, v. 1, pp. 128, 145, 147–50.

32. Miliukov's articles of 8 and 9 December 1905, in P. Miliukov, *God bor'by. Publitsisticheskaia khronika*, Spb., 1907, pp. 170–74.

33. [Viktor Chernov], "Proshloe i nastoiaschee," *Biulleten' Tsentral'nogo komiteta Partii Sotsialistov-Revoliutsionerov*, no. 1, March 1906, p. 2; *Dobavlenie k protokolam pervogo s"ezda Partii Sotsialistov-Revoliutsionerov*, n.p., 1906, pp. 16–40.

34. *IS*, 7 Nov. 1905; Trotsky, *1905*, pp. 170–74, 308; Lenin, *PSS*, v. 12, M., 1968, pp. 106–7, 448–9 n. 59; Lenin, "Neudavshaisia provokatsiia," *NZh*, 15 Nov. 1905; [Viktor Chernov], "K voprosu o blizhaishikh zadachakh nashikh sotsialisticheskikh partii," *Otdel'nyi ottisk iz No. 77 Revoliutsionnoi Rossii*, no. 3, Dec. 1905, pp. 1–7; Chernov, "Ot 'Revoliutsionnoi Rossii'," pp. 74–6, 86, 92, 94–6; Vladimir Zenzinov, *Iz zhizni revoliutsionera*, Paris, 1919, p. 16; V. Zenzinov, *Perezhitoe*, pp. 225–26.

35. Trotsky, *1905*, pp. 180–84; Suhr, "Petersburg Workers," pp. 477–87, 490–91, 499–500; G. Khrustalev-Nosar, "Istoriia Soveta Rabochikh Deputatov (do 26-go noiabria 1905 g.)," *Istoriia Soveta rabochikh deputatov*, Spb., 1906, pp. 106–43.

36. *Proletarii*, no. 25, 15/3 Nov. 1905; *NZh*, 1 Nov. 1905; 8 Nov. 1905; 11 Nov. 1905; *Syn otechestva*, 18 Nov. 1905.

37. *Syn otechestva*, 18 Nov. 1905; 19 Nov. 1905; 24 Nov. 1905; 29 Nov. 1905; *Nachalo*, 15 Nov. 1905; 20 Nov. 1905; 23 Nov. 1905; 24 Nov. 1905; 29 Nov. 1905; *Volzhskii vestnik*, 24 Nov. 1905; *Privolzhskii krai*, 2 Dec. 1905; *NZh*, 18 Nov. 1905; 19 Nov. 1905; 23 Nov. 1905; 24 Nov. 1905; *Kavkazskii rabochii listok*, 23 Nov. 1905; 27 Nov. 1905; 1 Dec. 1905; 13 Dec. 1905; *Severnyi golos*, 7 Dec. 1905; *Robotnik*, 26 Dec. 1905 (n.s.).

38. *Proletarii*, no. 24, 7 Nov./25 Oct. 1905; *NZh*, 8 Nov. 1905; 12 Nov. 1905; 16 Nov. 1905; 23 Nov. 1905; *Kavkazskii rabochii listok*, 23 Nov. 1905; 1 Dec. 1905; *Nachalo*, 20 Nov. 1905; *Syn otechestva*, 24 Nov. 1905.

39. "Vseobshchaia stachka soldat i matrosov," *Nachalo*, 2 Dec. 1905.

40. Engelstein, *Moscow*, pp. 162–80; Garvi, *Vospominaniia*, p. 605; Robert Slusser, "The Moscow Soviet of Workers' Deputies of 1905: Origin, Structure, and Policies," Ph.D. dissertation, Columbia University, 1963, pp. 41–82.

41. There was one mutiny before late November; see Appendix I, October, after the 17th, 4th Nesvizh Grenadiers. On indiscipline, see *VP*, v. 1, p. 607; A. B. Mel'nikov, "Revoliutsionnoe dvizhenie v moskovskom garnizone v period dekabr'skogo vooruzhennogo dvizheniia," *IZ*, no. 49, 1954, pp. 270–1; *MG*, 18 Nov. 1905 and 20 Nov. 1905; "V sude," *Voprosy dnia*, no. 3, 25 Nov. 1906, pp. 22–3; Joseph Sanders, "The Moscow Uprising of December 1905: A Background

Study," Ph.D. dissertation, University of Washington, 1980, pp. 444–50. There are unconfirmed reports of mutinies among clerks in the military district staff (*Bor'ba*, 30 Nov. 1905) and in a penal guards unit (*Zhizn'*, 27 Nov. 1905). Revolutionary comments: *MG*, 15 Nov. 1905; 20 Nov. 1905; *Bor'ba*, 27 Nov. 1905; 29 Nov. 1905; 3 Dec. 1905.

42. Bushnell, "Mutineers and Revolutionaries," pp. 208–10, 447–8, 456.

43. *VP*, v. 1, p. 608.

44. On the cossack and sapper mutinies, see Appendix I. See also *VP*, v. 1, pp. 609–10; *Pravo*, 4 Dec. 1905; Mel'nikov, "Revoliutsionnoe dvizhenie v moskovskom garnizone v period," pp. 270–71, 274; *Russkoe slovo*, 28 Nov. 1905.

45. On the mutinies, see Appendix I, Nov. 29 and Dec. 2. On the Tauride regiment, see *NZh*, 2 Dec. 1905; on disturbances of an unspecified nature in an artillery brigade, see *Russkoe slovo*, 4 Dec. 1905, and *Pravo*, 4 Dec. 1905.

46. The source for the sappers' offer is Vasil'ev-Iuzhin, who repeats it in more or less the same terms in all of his various memoirs, e.g., *Moskovksii soviet rabochikh deputatov v 1905 g., i podgotovka im vooruzhennogo vosstaniia, po lichnym vospominaniiam i dokumentam*, M., 1925, pp. 54, 59. He consistently confuses the dates and sequence of the sappers' mutiny and the subsequent mutiny of the Rostov Grenadiers. On the meeting of the Presnia-Khamovniki district soviet: *Bor'ba*, 6 Dec. 1905.

47. On the SRs in Moscow: V. M. Chernov, *Pered burei. Vospominaniia*, New York, 1953, pp. 257–8; Hildermeier, *Die Sozialrevolutionäre Partei*, pp. 131–3. On the SR military organization plan and the Bolshevik response: Ul'ianinskii, "Vosstanie," p. 40; Shabrov, "O vosstanii Rostovskogo polka v dekabre 1905 goda," *KiS*, 1926 no. 1, p. 124; M. Liadov, *Iz zhizni partii v 1903–1907 gg.*, M., 1926, pp. 121–2.

48. Ul'ianinskii, "Vosstanie," p. 38; Shabrov, "O vosstanii," pp. 125–6; Mel'nikov, "Revoliutsionnoe dvizhenie v moskovskom garnizone v period," pp. 273, 278–9; A. Fridman, "Vospominaniia o minuvshikh dniakh. (Iz epokhi pervoi revoliutsii)," *KiS*, 1931 no. 2, p. 151; N. A. Snegul'skii, "Vosstanie grenaderov," *Na barrikadakh*, M., 1955, p. 166; *VP*, v. 1, p. 625; *Zhizn'*, 28 Nov. 1905; Sanders, "Moscow Uprising," pp. 453–6, 459–61.

49. Snegul'skii, "Vosstanie," pp. 166–176; Mel'nikov, "Revoliutsionnoe dvizhenie v moskovskom garnizone v period," pp. 279–87; Zheleznov, "Revoliutsionnoe dvizhenie," pp. 31–7; *VP*, v. 1, pp. 613, 616–41; Ul'ianinskii, "Vosstanie," pp. 40–48; Shabrov, "O vosstanii," pp. 125–30; "V sude," *Voprosy dnia*, no. 3, 25 Nov. 1906; Polk. Simanskii, "Volnenie Rostovtsev, *Razvedchik*, 31 Jan. 1906; *Bor'ba*, no. 6, 3 Dec. 1905; [Rediger], "Zapiski," p. 100; Petrov, *Ocherki*, p. 172; I. N. Vasin, *Armiia i revoliutsii*, M., 1973, p. 52; Shabrov, "Dni vosstaniia," pp. 38–64; *Vpered*, 4 Dec. 1905; 6 Dec. 1905; Sokolov, "O 1905 gode," in Rozhkov and Sokolov, *O 1905 gode*, pp. 51–2; Fridman, "Vospoiminaniia," p. 153.

50. Engelstein, *Moscow*, pp. 187–92; Trotsky, *1905*, p. 231; Pushkareva, *Zheleznodorozhniki*, pp. 197–8; V. N. Pereverzev, "Pervyi vserossiiskii zheleznodorozhnyi soiuz 1905 goda," *Byloe*, 1925 no. 4, pp. 62–4; Reichman, "Russian Railwaymen," pp. 478–80; V. Zvezdin, "Poslednie dni Soveta (26 noiabria–3 dekabria)," *Istoriia Soveta Rabochikh Deputatov g. S-Peterburga*, Spb., 1906, pp. 174–

5, 197–200; Garvi, *Vospominaniia*, pp. 606–9, 611–12; Vasil'ev-Iuzhin, *Moskovskii Sovet*, pp. 66–78; Liadov, *Iz zhizni partii*, pp. 122–4; Sokolov, "O 1905 gode," in Rozhkov and Sokolov, *O 1905 gode*, p. 52; Zenzinov, *Iz perezhitogo*, pp. 225–6; Chernov, *Pered burei*, pp. 258–9; Vishniak, *Dan' proshlomu*, p. 114.

51. *Vpered*, 3 Dec. 1905; Mel'nikov, "Revoliutsionnoe dvizhenie v moskovskom garnizone v period," p. 293; *Bor'ba*, 6 Dec. 1905; *ISM*, 8 Dec. 1905; *VP*, v. 1, p. 599; P. N. Kokhmanskii, *Moskva v dekabre 1905 g.*, M., 1906, p. 192; Sokolov, "O 1905 gode," in Rozhkov and Sokolov, *O 1905 gode*, p. 52; Iakovlev, *Vooruzhennye vosstaniia*, pp. 152–4; Em. Iaroslavskii, "Dekabr'skoe vosstanie," in M. N. Pokrovskii, ed., *1905. Istoriia revoliutsionnogo dvizheniia v otdel'nykh ocherkakh*, v. 3 part 2, M.-L., 1925, pp. 98–9, 102, 124–6; Liadov, *Iz zhizni partii*, pp. 126–7; Slusser, "Moscow Soviet," pp. 113–4; M. Vladimirskii, "Moskovskii Komitet RSDRP," in *Dekabr'skoe vosstanie v Moskve 1905 g.*, M., 1919, p. 42; Druzhinik, "Moskovskoe vosstanie," *Volia*, 1 May 1906; Sanders, "Moscow Uprising," pp. 500–11.

52. Sokolov, "O 1905 gode," in Rozhkov and Sokolov, *O 1905 gode*, p. 50.

53. *Bor'ba*, 3 Dec. 1905; *Vpered*, 6 Dec. 1905; Kokhmanskii, *Moskva*, pp. 7, 9; Vladimirskii, "Moskovskii komitet," p. 42; Liadov, *Iz zhizni partii*, pp. 122–4, 126–7; Sokolov, "O 1905 gode," in Rozhkov and Sokolov, *O 1905 gode*, pp. 52–3; Vasil'ev-Iuzhin, *Moskovskii sovet*, pp. 66–78, 80–81; Chernov, *Pered burei*, p. 259; Slusser, "Moscow Soviet," pp. 122–4; Garvi, *Vospominaniia*, pp. 609–10; Engelstein, *Moscow*, p. 192.

54. Iakovlev, *Vooruzhennye vosstaniia*, pp. 161–3; *ISM*, 7 Dec. 1905.

55. Vasin, *Armiia*, pp. 43, 64; Kokhmanskii, *Moskva*, p. 195; *VP*, v. 1, pp. 728–9; V. Strozhev, "Dekabr'skoe vooruzhennoe vosstanie (po arkhivnym materialam)," *Dekabr'skoe vosstanie v Moskve*, pp. 172–4. F. I. Zubarev, *Pamiatka 12 grenaderskogo Astrakhanskogo polka*, M., 1910, p. 87, mentions that on December 2 there were only 62 soldiers in one of the regiment's battalions, which would make 15–16 men per company, approximately what the garrison average would be if in fact only 1,850 infantry were available.

56. Iakovlev, *Vooruzhennye vosstaniia*, p. 164; Mel'nikov, "Revoliutsionnoe dvizhenie v moskovskom garnizone v period," p. 296; Semennikov, *Revoliutsiia*, pp. 31, 181; [Raukh], "Dnevnik," p. 90; Vasin, *Armiia*, p. 64; *VP*, v. 1, pp. 676–7; Drezen, *Tsarizm*, pp. 7–8.

57. Mel'nikov, "Revoliutsionnoe dvizhenie v moskovskom garnizone v period," pp. 296–8; Vasin, *Armiia*, p. 65; *VP*, v. 1, p. 723; Iakovlev, *Vooruzhennye vosstaniia*, p. 166; Kokhmanskii, *Moskva*, pp. 196–8, 200–1; Zubarev, *Pamiatka*, passim.

58. *VP*, v. 1, p. 660; *ISM*, 10 Dec. 1905; Kokhmanskii, *Moskva*, pp. 142, 192, 198, 205; Zheleznov, "Revoliutsionnoe dvizhenie," p. 124; Garvi, *Vospominaniia*, pp. 632–3; Zenzinov, *Perezhitoe*, pp. 239–40.

59. On the behavior of the troops, see Vasin, *Armiia*, pp. 62–3; "Khronika vooruzhennoi bor'by," pp. 164–5; Kokhmanskii, *Moskva*, pp. 192, 197–8, 202; *ISM*, 9 Dec. 1905 and 11 Dec. 1905; Iakovlev, *Vooruzhennye vosstaniia*, p. 171; *VP*, v. 1, pp. 681, 684, 720–21, 724–6; Vasilii Klimkov, *Raspravy i rasstrely*, M., 1906, pp. 13–33. On the Bolsheviks' 12 December decision: Slusser, "Moscow Soviet," p. 167; Kokhmanskii, *Moskva*, pp. 142–3. General accounts of the insurrection:

Engelstein, *Moscow*, pp. 197–219; Zenzinov, *Perezhitoe*, pp. 229–59; Iaroslavskii, "Dekabr'skoe vosstanie," pp. 135–76.

60. Kokhmanskii, *Moskva*, pp. 147–8; Slusser, "Moscow Soviet," pp. 176–7, 179–80; Zenzinov, *Perezhitoe*, pp. 257–9.

61. *VP*, v. 1, pp. 687–8, 690–92, 726, 729–35; Kasatkin-Rostovskii, *Pamiatka Semenovtsa*, Spb., 1909, pp. 84–6; Iakovlev, *Vooruzhennye vosstaniia*, p. 208; Semennikov, *Revoliutsiia*, pp. 186–7; S. Ivanov, "Karatel'naia ekspeditsiia polk. Rimana," *KA*, 1925 no. 4–5, pp. 398–420; Iaroslavskii, "Dekabr'skoe vosstanie," pp. 177–94; Klimkov, *Raspravy*, pp. 34–43, 48–55, 64–73; V. Vladimirov, *Karatel'-naia ekspeditsiia otriada leib-gvardii Semenovskogo polka v dekabr'skie dni na Moskovsko-kazanskoi zhel. dor.*, M., 1906, pp. 11–149; Garvi, *Vospominaniia*, pp. 662–77; Engelstein, *Moscow*, pp. 219–21, 286 n. 99.

62. *Listovki moskovskikh bol'shevikov v period Pervoi russkoi revoliutsii*, M., 1955, pp. 365–7. An identical argument is made in a Menshevik proclamation of about the same date (*1905. Bol'shevistskie proklamatsii i listovki po Moskve i Moskovskoi gubernii*, M.-L., 1926, pp. 446–8), so that Slusser, "Moscow Soviet," pp. 180–81, is probably correct in assuming that the Executive Committee proclamation was authored by Mensheviks. Their view of the matter is not likely to have differed from the Bolshevik view.

63. Varzar, *Statistika stachek . . . 1905*, Prilozheniia, pp. 101–2; Varzar, *Statistika stachek . . . 1906–1908*, Prilozheniia, p. 72.

64. Reichman, "Russian Railwaymen," pp. 511–45; *Rabochii klass v pervoi rossiiskoi revoliutsii*, pp. 212–29; Iakovlev, *Vooruzhennye vosstaniia*, passim.

65. My account is based on Iakovlev, *Vooruzhennye vosstaniia*, pp. 225–58; *VPS*, v. 1, p. 641; *VP*, v. 2, pp. 454–73; *Novoe vremia*, 9 Nov. 1905; *1905–1907 gody na Donu. Sbornik dokumentov*, Rostov n/D, 1955, pp. 147–8, 156–7; V.S., "Dekabr'skie dni v Rostove na Donu," *Otkliki sovremennosti*, 1906 no. 3, pp. 61–78; *Russkoe slovo*, 30 Nov. 1905; "Dekabr'skoe vosstanie v osveshchenii Okhranogo otdeleniia," *Proletarskaia revoliutsiia na Donu*, 1922 no. 1, pp. 19, 23–4.

66. Iakovlev, *Vooruzhennye vosstaniia*, pp. 386–7, 391–5; *VP*, v. 2, pp. 108, 112, 115–8, 122.

67. *VP*, v. 2, pp. 585, 572, 580–81, 605; Iakovlev, *Vooruzhennye vosstaniia*, pp. 269, 271–2; "Vooruzhennaia bor'ba novorossiiskikh rabochikh v dekabre 1905 g.," *KA*, 1940 no. 2, p. 83.

68. Iakovlev, *Vooruzhennye vosstaniia*, pp. 294–5, 325, 339–41; "Khronika vooruzhennoi bor'by. Reliatsiia general'nogo shtaba samoderzhaviia o boevykh deistviiakh v dekabre 1905 g.," *KA*, 1925 no. 4–5, pp. 173–4; Nemanov, "Kievskaia i Ekaterinoslavskaia voennye organizatsii v 1905 g.," *PR*, 1926 no. 4, pp. 205–7; *VP*, v. 3 book 1, pp. 73–4, 79–81, 94–5, 166; *Ekaterinoslavshchina v revoliutsii*, pp. 210–11, 232; *Izvestiia federativnogo soveta khar'kovskikh komitetov Rossiiskoi Sotsial-Demokraticheskoi Rabochei Partii*, 18 Dec. 1905.

69. Matushanskaia, "1905 god v Khar'kove," *VI*, 1965 no. 1, pp. 209–10; Iakovlev, *Vooruzhennye vosstaniia*, pp. 354–8; M. A. Iakovlev, "Khar'kovskoe likholet'e," *IV*, 1910 no. 12, pp. 1008–20; *Izvestiia federativnogo soveta*, Dec. 13, 1905; *VP*, v. 3 book 1, pp. 372, 381–2, 388–9, 397–9.

70. *Vsepoddanneishaia zapiska po upravleniiu kavkazskim kraem*, pp. 18–9, 30–33;

Kalandadze and Mkheidze, *Ocherki revoliutsionnogo dvizheniia*, pp. 77–84. The number of units in the Caucasus has been calculated from MacBean, *Handbook*, pp. 389–94; mutinies have been calculated from Appendix I. On the 33rd infantry division: *Vsepoddanneishii otchet Voennogo ministerstva za 1905 god*, "Obshchii obzor," p. 10; Gubernchuk, *Ocherk istorii 129-go pekhotnogo Bessarabskogo polka. 1806–1863–1906 gg.*, Kiev, 1909, p. 309.

71. *Revoliutsiia 1905 goda v Zakavkaz'i*, pp. 88–9, 91, 93, 100, 122; *Revoliutsiia 1905–1907 gg. v Gruzii. Sbornik dokumentov*, Tbilisi, 1956, pp. 102–5, 325–7, 331, 409, 537; Semennikov, *Revoliutsiia*, pp. 168, 178–80; *Revoliutsionnoe dvizhenie v Armenii 1905–1907 gg. Sbornik dokumentov i materialov*, Erevan, 1955, p. 166; Iakovlev, *Vooruzhennye vosstaniia*, p. 426; *Secret Letters*, p. 204.

72. Starosel'skii, "Dni svobody," pp. 287–8, 302; *Revoliutsiia 1905–1907 gg. v Gruzii*, pp. 463–5.

73. On the mutiny, see Appendix I: Nov. 13, Batum. Starosel'skii, "Dni svobody," p. 288; *Revoliutsiia 1905–1907 gg. v Gruzii*, pp. 512–14; A. Mgebrov, *Vospominaniia artilleriiskogo ofitsera*, M., 1929, pp. 43–56; *VP*, v. 3 book 2, pp. 770–9, 781; *Tiflisskii listok*, 2 Dec. 1905.

74. Appendix I: Nov. 20–21, Kutais. Iakovlev, *Vooruzhennye vosstaniia*, p. 420; Starosel'skii, "Dni svobody," pp. 280, 284–7; *Revoliutsiia 1905–1907 gg. v Gruzii*, pp. 437, 465–8, 475–7; *VP*, v. 3 book 2, pp. 704, 789–91; *Chernomorskii vestnik*, 29 Nov. 1905; *Tiflisskii listok*, 6 Dec. 1905; *Novoe obozrenie*, 1 Dec. 1905; Gubernchuk, *Ocherk istorii 129-go*, pp. 326–36.

75. Appendix I: Nov. 20–26, Tiflis. Iakovlev, *Vooruzhennye vosstaniia*, pp. 426–8; *VP*, v. 1, p. 105; *VP*, v. 3 book 2, pp. 705, 857–8, 861–2; Potto, *Istoriia 17 dragunskogo*, v. 11, pp. 189–90; *Novoe obozrenie*, 2 Dec. 1905; *Kavkazskii rabochii listok*, 6 Dec. 1905.

76. Obninskii, *Letopis'*, v. 3 part 1, pp. 100–110, and "Khronika," pp. 99–101; *Rech'*, 27 Feb. 1906 and 12 March 1906; Semennikov, *Revoliutsiia*, pp. 200–1, 206; *Revoliutsiia 1905–1907 gg. v Gruzii*, pp. 535–7, 539–42, 573–6; Kalandadze and Mkheidze, *Ocherki revoliutsionnogo dvizheniia*, pp. 84–94; Klimkov, *Raspravy*, pp. 223–37; Potto, *Istoriia 17 dragunskogo*, pp. 194–9, 202–4; Gubernchuk, *Ocherk istorii 129-go*, pp. 352–5; G. E. Startsev, *Krovavye dni na Kavkaze*, Spb., 1907, pp. 61–71.

77. On the mutinies, see Appendix I: Nov. 17, Piatigorsk, 250th Akhulginsk; Nov. 27, Khasav-Iurt, 84th Shirvansk; Dec. 17, Vladikavkaz, 2nd Gorsko-Mozdok Terek cossacks. On the punitive expedition: *Sluzhba Shirvantsev Ego Velichestva za period 1904–1911 godov*, Piatigorsk, 1912, pp. 6–7; Obninskii, *Letopis'*, v. 3 part 1, pp. 116–7; *Severnaia Osetiia v revoliutsii 1905–1907 godov. Dokumenty i materialy*, Ordzhonikidze, 1955, pp. 244–50.

78. Semennikov, *Revoliutsiia*, pp. 166–7; *Revoliutsiia 1905–1907 gg. v Gruzii*, pp. 619–20.

79. *Izvestiia federativnogo soveta khar'kovskikh komitetov*, 24 Dec. 1905. On the mutinies, see Appendix I: Nov. 15 and Nov. 23. On Dec. 12: *VP*, v. 3 book 1, p. 388.

80. Appendix I, Nov. 15, Kharkov; *VP*, v. 3 book 1, p. 388.

81. *VP*, v. 2, pp. 567–8; Korol'kov, "Revoliutsionnoe dvizhenie v voiskakh

Kavkazskogo voennogo okruga," *1905. Armiia v pervoi revoliutsii*, M.-L., 1927, pp. 349–50; *Severnaia Osetiia*, pp. 103–4; Petrov, *Ocherki*, pp. 341–3.

82. *VP*, v. 1, pp. 72–3; *VP*, v. 2, pp. 547–9, 555, 559–62; Dr. Kobylin, "O revoliutsionnykh dniakh v Piatigorske," *Baku*, 16 June 1906; 22 June 1906; 25 June 1906.

83. *VP*, v. 2, pp. 925–7; Piaskovskii, *Revoliutsiia*, pp. 311–12, 316.

84. *VP*, v. 4, pp. 662–3, 676–8, 716–8, 742–3, 757–8, 770–71, 782–4, and passim; Pawłowski, *Wojskowa działaność*, pp. 207–29.

85. This assessment of the revolution in the Ukraine and Belorussia is based on a reading of *VP*, v. 1, pp. 122–3, 135–6; *VP*, v. 3 book 1, pp. 47–9, 73–4, 79–81, 89–90, 94–5, 106–8, 113–5, 145–57, 202–3, 211–2, 304–5, 308–10, 368–9, 446, 450–64, 546, 574, 594–6, 609–10, 616–9; *VP*, v. 4, pp. 63–5, 71–2, 77–8, 80, 98–100, 175, 179, 180–91, 230–42, 257–8.

86. Drezen, *Tsarizm*, pp. 7–8.

VI. Preparations for the Second Round

1. Keep, *Rise of Social Democracy*, pp. 265, 267, 283 and passim; Mehlinger and Thompson, *Count Witte*, pp. 153, 169, 175–6; Harcave, *First Blood. The Russian Revolution of 1905*, New York, 1964, pp. 242–3; Richard Charques, *The Twilight of Imperial Russia*, London, 1958, pp. 139–40, 159; Lionel Kochan, *Russia in Revolution*, New York, 1966, pp. 101–3, 109, 112–13.

2. V. I. Bovykin, *Revoliutsiia 1905–1907 gg.*, M., 1965, pp. 73–89; A. V. Piaskovskii, *Revoliutsiia 1905–1907 gg.*, M., 1966, pp. 234–85; *Revoliutsiia 1905–1907 gg. v Rossii*, M., 1975, pp. 287–363; K. F. Shatsillo, *1905–i god*, M., 1980, PP. 173–5.

3. *Nash golos*, 18 Dec. 1905; F. I. Dan, "Armiia s 9 ianvaria 1905 g.," *Knizhka za knizhkoi*, no. 1, 1906, pp. 14–16; Parvus, *Rossiia i revoliutsiia*, Spb., 1906, pp. 220–4; Plekhanov, "Esche o nashem polozhenii," *Dnevnik sotsial-demokrata*, no. 4, Dec. 1905 (but probably written in early January); Lenin, "Rabochaia partiia i ee zadachi pri sovremennom polozhenii," *Molodaia Rossiia*, no. 1, 4 Jan. 1906; Lenin ("Bol'shevik"), "Sovremennoe polozhenie Rossii i taktika rabochei partii," *Partiinye izvestiia* (TsK RSDRP), no. 1, 7 Feb. 1906; articles by N. Rozhkov, M. N. Pokrovskii ("M-yi") and Chernomordik ("P. Larionov") in *Tekushchii moment*, M., 1906; Voitinskii, *Gody pobed i porazhenii*, v. 2, Berlin, 1924, pp. 13–4, 23–4, 37; "Pirovaia pobeda," *Evreiskii rabochii* (TsK Bund), no. 1, 28 Dec. 1905; *Protokoly pervogo s"ezda Partii Sotsialistov-Revoliutsionerov* [Helsingfors], 1906, pp. 307–9, 315–6, 325.

4. *Protokoly pervogo "s"ezda*, p. 314; [Chernov], "Proshloe i nastoiaschee," *Biulleten' Tsentral'nogo Komiteta Partii Sotsialistov-Revoliutsionerov*, no. 1, March 1906, p. 2; *Materialy k krest'ianskomu voprosu. Otchet o zasedaniiakh delegatskogo s"ezda Vserossiiskogo krest'ianskogo soiuza 6–10 noiabria 1905 g.*, Rostov/Don, 1905, pp. 38, 54, 56, 59–60, 64–6, 68, 83–5.

5. *Protokoly pervogo s"ezda*, pp. 307–32; *Dobavlenie k protokolam pervogo s"ezda Partii Sotsialistov-Revoliutsionerov*, n.p., 1906, pp. 17–40.

6. V. K. Agafonov, "Na rasputi," *Nakanune*, no. 2, 26 Feb. 1906, p. 50.

7. Lenin, "Rabochaia partiia i ee zadachi pri sovremennom polozhenii," *Molodaia Rossiia*, no. 1, 4 Jan. 1906; Lenin ("Bol'shevik"), "Sovremennoe polozhenie Rossii i taktika rabochei partii," *Partiinye izvestiia* (TsK RSDRP), no. 1, 7 Feb. 1906, pp. 2–4; Martov ("Meshkovskii"), "K voprosu o takticheskikh zadachakh momenta," ibid., pp. 6–7; P. Garvi, *Vospominaniia*, Part 2, New York, 1961, p. 14.

8. [Chernov], "Proshloe i nastoiashchee," *Biulletin' Tsentral'nogo Komiteta Partii Sotsialistov-Revoliutsionerov*, no. 1, March 1906. The same issue has the resolution of the southern conference of SR organizations.

9. London report of the Sûreté agent, dated 3 April 1906 (21 March by the Russian calendar), Archives Nationales, F7 12521.

10. *VP*, v. 2, p. 863; *VP*, v. 3 book 1, p. 688; Semennikov, *Revoliutsiia*, p. 33; Koroleva, *Pervaia rossiiskaia revoliutsiia*, p. 97.

11. *VP*, v. 1, pp. 158–61; "Bor'ba S.Iu. Vitte s agrarnoi revoliutsii," *KA*, 1928 no. 6, pp. 83, 100; Semennikov, *Revoliutsiia*, pp. 47–8; Drezen, *Tsarizm v bor'be*, pp. 121–2.

12. [Rediger], "Iz zapisok," pp. 94–5.

13. *Razvedchik*, 28 Feb. 1906; *RI*, 19 Feb. 1906.

14. Drezen, *Tsarizm v bor'be*, pp. 101–3; "Instruktsiia dlia formirovaniia i dvizheniia okhranogo poezda Nikolaevskoi zh.d.," IISH, SR, D. 606, no. 5; *Trud*, no. 23, 24 May 1906; *Karatel'nye ekspeditsii*, pp. 388–90; *VPR*, part 1 book 2, pp. 60–1; *Ekho*, 27 June 1906.

15. Semennikov, *Revoliutsiia*, pp. 27, 30–32; Vitte, *Vospominaniia*, v. 3, p. 144.

16. Semennikov, *Revoliutsiia*, pp. 30–3, 38, 108; *VP*, v. 1, pp. 170–71; Mehlinger and Thompson, *Count Witte*, p. 129; [Rediger], "Iz zapisok," pp. 94–5.

17. "Bor'ba S.Iu. Vitte s agrarnoi revoliutsiei," pp. 81–102; Mehlinger and Thompson, *Count Witte*, p. 158; [Rediger], "Iz zapisok," pp. 96, 127; K. Rozenblium, *Voennye organizatsii bol'shevikov 1905–1907 gg.*, M.-L., 1931, p. 48; *VPR*, part 1 book 1, pp. 151–3; Fuller, *Civil-Military Conflict*, Chapter 5.

18. Kokovtsov, *Out of My Past*, pp. 126–7; Gurko, *Features and Figures*, pp. 450–8, 467–8, 480; Vitte, *Vospominaniia*, v. 3, pp. 195–217, 288–307; Mehlinger and Thompson, *Count Witte*, pp. 163–4, 166, 168, 176, 201–7, 209–40, 289–312; Koroleva, *Pervaia rossiiskaia revoliutsiia*, pp. 75–86, 95–106, 113–15.

19. Lenin, "Novyi pod"em," *Volna*, 6 May 1906; Lenin, "Ob organizatsii mass i o vybore momenta bor'by," *Ekho*, 4 July 1906; [Chernov], "Proshloe i nastoiashchee," *Biulleten' Tsentral'nogo Komiteta Partii Sotsialistov-Revoliutsionerov*, no. 1, March 1906, p. 7; "Materialy o pervoi voen[noi] konfer[entsii]. 29 iiunia 1906 g. v Teriokakh," IISH, SR, D. 700, no. 1 (these "Materialy" consist of scribbled, unorganized, unpaginated notes on the discussion).

20. Voitinskii, *Gody pobed i porazhenii*, v. 2, pp. 21–32, 37–8; *Pis'ma P. B. Aksel'roda i Iu.O. Martova*, pp. 147–51; G. I. Zaichikov, *Dumskaia taktika Bol'shevikov (1905–1917 gg.)*, M., 1975, pp. 37–43; Garvi, *Vospominaniia*, part 2, pp. 14–6, 23–6, 28–9, 36–7; Martov, *Istoriia Rossiiskoi Sotsial-Demokratii*, pp. 175–9; *VPR*, part 1 book 2, pp. 67–8, 108–12, 117–9; *Protokoly pervogo s"ezda*, pp. 10–23; *Robotnik*, 19 Jan. 1906; no. 84, 1 April 1906; *1905. Evreiskoe rabochee dvizhenie. Obzor, materialy,*

dokumenty, M.-L., 1928, pp. 369–70; *Chetvertyi (Ob"edinitel'nyi) s"ezd RSDRP. Aprel' (aprel'-mai) 1906 goda. Protokoly*, M., 1959, pp. 277–8, 293–5, 319.

21. Gr. Nestroev, *Dnevnik maksimilista*, Paris, 1910, pp. 48–53 and passim; Hildermeier, *Die Sozialrevolutionäre Partei*, pp. 126–40; Eiter, "Organizational Growth," pp. 245–51; Allison Blakely, "The Socialist Revolutionary Party, 1901–1907: The Populist Response to the Industrialization of Russia," Ph.D. dissertation, University of California, Berkeley, 1971, pp. 175–99.

22. For party membership figures, see Chapter 3 n. 10. On the mood of workers (the sources are best for Petersburg and, secondarily, Moscow, spotty for other cities): Voitinskii, *Gody pobed i porazhenii*, v. 2, pp. 11, 13–14, 16–20, 26–7; Garvi, *Vospominaniia*, part 2, pp. 7, 12–3, 39–42; *Istoriia rabochikh Leningrada*, v. 1, L., 1972, pp. 314–7; *Rabochii klass v pervoi rossiiskoi revoliutsii*, pp. 268–70, 274, 281–94; Kol'tsov, "Rabochie v 1905–1907 gg.," pp. 264–70, 277–88.

23. Mehlinger and Thompson, *Count Witte*, pp. 251–88; Terrence Emmons, "Russia's First National Elections," Colloque la révolution de 1905, Sorbonne, 1981; Judith E. Zimmerman, "The Kadets and the Duma, 1905–1907," in Charles E. Timberlake, ed., *Essays on Russian Liberalism*, Columbia, Mo., 1972, pp. 120–7; Miliukov, *Vospominaniia*, pp. 359–63; Voitinksii, *Gody pobed i porazhenii*, v. 2, pp. 30–1; V. A. Maklakov, *Vlast' i obshchestvennost' na zakate staroi Rossii. (Vospominaniia sovremennika)*, Paris, 1936, pp. 543–56; Chermenskii, *Burzhuaziia i tsarizm*, pp. 250–4; *Pravo*, no. 1, 1906, pp. 4–7; 22 Jan. 1906; 29 Jan. 1906; 9 April 1906; 6 May 1906; V. D. Kuz'min-Karavaev, *Iz epokhi osvoboditel'nogo dvizheniia*, v. 2, Spb., 1907, pp. 104–19, 125–32, 153–9, 192–205, 265–9, 278–80.

24. Maslov, *Krest'ianskoe dvizhenie*, pp. 109–29; *Krest'ianskie nakazy Samarskoi gubernii*, Samara, 1906; Zaichikov, *Dumskaia taktika*, pp. 45–53; D. A. Kolesnichenko, "Iz istorii bor'by rabochego klassa za krest'ianskie massy v 1906 g.," *IZ*, v. 95, 1975, pp. 258–63; 11 April report of the agent of the Sûreté Générale in Annemasse, Archives Nationales, F7 12521 (reporting that both SRs and SDs in Switzerland had been persuaded by reports from local organizations that the boycott had been a mistake); Hildermeier, *Die Sozialrevolutionäre Partei*, pp. 176–7; *Bericht der Russischen Sozial-Revolutionären Partei an den Internationalen Sozialistenkongress zu Stuttgart (August 1907)*, Gand, 1907, pp. 37–9; A. Argunov, "Azef v Partii S.-R." *Na chuzhoi storone. Istoriko-literaturny sbornik*, v. 6, 1924, p. 186; D. A. Kolesnichenko, "K voprosu o politicheskoi evoliutsii trudovikov v 1906 g.," *IZ*, v. 92, 1973, pp. 96–8.

25. Bushnell, "Mutineers and Revolutionaries," pp. 194–206.

26. *Golos soldata* (SD, Riga), no. 9–10, 8 June 1906. For a discussion of the number of military organizations, newspapers, and membership, see Bushnell, "Mutineers and Revolutionaries," pp. 442–468. Because of incomplete data, the figures therein are somewhat lower than those given here.

27. E. Samoilenko, "Sredi kazakov chernomor'ia," *V tsarskoi kazarme. Soldaty i matrosy v pervoi revoliutsii*, M., 1929, pp. 98–9; *Khar'kov i Khar'kovskaia guberniia v pervoi russkoi revoliutsii 1905–1907 godov. Sbornik dokumentov*, Kharkov, 1955, pp. 366; E. Chistiakov, "Voennaia organizatsiia RSDRP v Kovne," *PR*, 1927 no. 5, p. 220; "Pis'mo Rostovtsa iz Tiur'my," Izd. Moskovskogo Voennogo Soiuza, Feb.

1906, IISH, SR, D.690, the first extant proclamation from the Maximalist military organization; *VPR*, part 2 book 1, p. 514; *Mysl'*, 20 June 1906; "Protokoly konferentsii voennykh rabotnikov Baltiiskogo flota. 21 iiulia 1907 goda," p. 10 ob., IISH, SR, D. 700, no. 3.

28. The sources on these organizations can be found in Bushnell, "Mutineers and Revolutionaries," pp. 442–452.

29. *Pervaia konferentsiia voennykh i boevykh organizatsii RSDRP*, M., 1932, pp. 336–7 fn. 11; O. A. Ivanova, "Moskovskoe voenno-tekhnicheskoe biuro RSDRP (1906–1907 gg.)," *IZ*, no. 55, 1956, pp. 215–6, 221, 228–9; IISH, SR, D. 690, DMVO, order of 8 June 1906; *Soldatskaia zhizn'* (M., Bolshevik), no. 1, 5 Feb. 1906; *Soldatskii golos* (M., Menshevik), no. 4, 15 March 1906; *Protokoly pervoi konferentsii voennykh*, p. 36; A. B. Mel'nikov, "Revoliutsionnoe dvizhenie v Moskovskom garnizone v 1906 g.," *IZ*, no. 56, 1956, pp. 94–5; Zheleznov, "Revoliutsionnoe dvizhenie," p. 154.

30. Ivanova, "Moskovskoe voenno-tekhnicheskoe biuro," pp. 231–2; Mel'nikov, "Revoliutsionnoe dvizhenie . . . v 1906 g.," p. 95; B. Gavrilov, *Voennaia rabota moskovskikh bol'shevikov v gody pervoi russkoi revoliutsii*, M., 1950, p. 106; Zharnovetskii, "Kronshtadtskie vosstaniia," pp. 66–7; E. Iaroslavskii, "Podpol'-naia rabota v armii v 1906 g.," *PR*, 1922 no. 5, pp. 167–9, 172, 174–5, 179, 181; Iur. Novin, "O Vilenskoi s.-d voennoi organizatsii 1906 g.," *PR*, 1922 no. 9, pp. 308–9.

31. The conflict between the military organizations and the Bolshevik and Menshevik leaders came to a head in the second half of 1906; see Bushnell, "Mutineers and Revolutionaries," pp. 356–79.

32. For a lengthier analysis, see ibid., pp. 256–62.

33. *Chetvertyi (Ob"edinitel'nyi) s"ezd*, p. 526.

34. Ibid., pp. 196–7, 244–5, 292, 313, 321–3, 370–3, 390–2, 478–82, 625 n. 98.

35. Ibid., pp. 23, 17, 21, 22; I. V. Shaurov, "Pervaia konferentsiia voennykh i boevykh organizatsii RSDRP," *Istoricheskii arkhiv*, 1959 no. 1, p. 162.

36. *Chetvertyi (Ob"edinitel'nyi) s"ezd*, pp. 373, 387, 389–90, 394–9, 527, 535; *Protokoly pervoi konferentsii voennykh*, p. 151; N. Chuzhak, *Ideia vooruzhennogo vosstaniia i bol'shevistskaia rabota v armii. Po dokumentam i po pamiati uchastnika*, M., 1929, p. 62; O. A. Ermanskii, *Iz perezhitogo*, M.-L., 1927, pp. 99–100.

37. *Protokoly pervogo s"ezda*, p. 313. The police noted a switch from workers' militia to military organizations in 1906, and their references seem primarily to the SRs: Nat. Blinov, "Delo o revoliutsionnom dvizhenii v armii," *Sbornik materialov*, M., 1921, no. 1, p. 202. S. Mstislavskii, "Iz istorii voennogo dvizhenia. (Po lichnym vospominaniiam)," *Katorga i ssylka*, 1929 no. 6, p. 11, claims that military work in all parties really got under way only in 1906, but his primary point of reference is the SR Party.

38. "Protokoly chastnogo soveshchaniia Tsentral'nogo Komiteta [PSR] i gruppy voennykh rabotnikov . . . Nachalo noiabria 1907 g.," IISH, SR, D. 5, p. 5.

39. Ibid.; Iu. Zubelevich, *Kronshtadt. Vospominaniia revoliutsinerki*, v. 2, Kronstadt, [1918?], pp. 137, 142.

40. Zubelevich, *Kronshtadt*, v. 1, p. 11; v. 2, pp. 72–8; *Za narod*, no. 54, March 1913, pp. 4–7.

41. Attendance has been reconstructed from "Materialy o pervoi voennoi

konferentsii," IISH, SR, D. 700, no. 1. There is a short summary of the reports by a delegate, Zubalevich, *Kronshtadt*, v. 2, pp. 103–9. See also *Partiinye izvestiia* (SR), no. 1, 23 Oct. 1906, which published the resolutions.

42. *Voina i mir*, 1906 no. 10–11, pp. 33–42; *Voennyi golos*, 2 March 1906; *RI*, 10 Dec. 1905 and 4 Jan. 1906; Garvilov, *Voennaia rabota*, pp. 130–1.

43. *Soldatskaia zhizn'* (M., Bolshevik), no. 2–3, 16 Feb. 1906; Gavrilov, *Voennaia rabota*, p. 130; I. Engel'man, "Zametki po vospitaniiu lichnogo sostava flota," *Morskoi sbornik*, 1908 no. 10, pp. 61–2; "O lektsionnom komitete v porte Imperatora Aleksandra III," *Morskoi sbornik*, 1907 no. 10, pp. 75–81; *Voennyi golos*, 4 July 1906; Denikin, *Staraia armiia,*v. 1, pp. 115.

44. *Vestnik russkoi konnitsy*, 1906 no. 8; *Voina i mir*, 1907 no. 2; *Razvedchik*, 28 Feb. 1906 and 27 June 1906; I Kazal, "Revoliutsionnaia rabota v voiskakh," *Iz epokhi bor'by s tsarizmom*, 1924 no. 1, pp. 41–2; Akhun and Petrov, *Bol'sheviki i armiia*, pp. 120–21; *Svetoch*, 14 May 1906; *Vpered*, 26 May 1906; *Ekho*, 28 June 1906; *Mysl'*, 28 June 1906; 6 July 1906; *Kazarma*, 8 March 1906; *Volna*, 7 May 1906; Denikin, *Staraia armiia*, v. 1, p. 115; *Soldat* (SD, Libava), no. 4, 3 March 1906; N. D. Butovskii, *Stat'i na sovremennye temy*, Spb., 1907, pp. 76–7, 82–5; *Duma*, 22 May 1906; *Severo-zapadnyi golos*, 24 June 1906.

45. Rozenblium, *Voennye*, pp. 201–3; "Iz istorii 'ideologicheskoi' bor'by samoderzhaviia s revoliutsionnym dvizheniem v armii," *KA*, 1931 no. 1, pp. 165–70.

46. The two literary journals for soldiers were *Chtenie dlia soldat* and *Dosug i delo*. For analysis of the stories, see K. Oberuchev, " 'Dukhovnaia pishcha' russkogo soldata," *Russkoe bogatstvo*, 1906 no. 6, pp. 1–18. On their lack of appeal: Denikin, *Staraia armiia*, v. 1, p. 118.

47. *Tsirkuliary Glavnogo shtaba*, 1906, No. 15, 15 Jan.; No. 26, 25 Jan.; No. 82, 2 March; No. 199, 2 June; No. 430, 30 Nov.; No. 467, 29 Dec.; Akhun and Petrov, *Bol'sheviki i armiia*, pp. 122–3; Drezen, *Tsarizm v bor'be*, p. 252 n. 46; "Iz istorii 'ideologicheskoi' bor'by samoderzhaviia," p. 166.

48. *Kazarma*, no. 4, 8 May 1906; *Kostromskoi krai*, 24 June 1906; Soifer, *Revoliutsionnoe dvizhenie soldat*, p. 68; Mel'nikov, "Revoliutsionnoe dvizhenie . . . v 1906 g.," p. 97; [Raukh], "Dnevnik," p. 86.

49. *Nevskaia gazeta*, 13 May 1906; *Prizyv*, 1 June 1906; *Ekho*, 28 June 1906; *Soldat* (SD, Libava), no. 13, 3 June 1906; V. Vladimirov, *Ocherki sovremennykh kaznei*, M., 1906, pp. 30–31.

50. *Voennyi golos*, 14 March 1906; Pavchinskii, *Russkaia armiia i revoliutsii*, n.p., 1907, p. 104; G. P. Marina, "Pechatnaia propaganda Bol'shevikov v voiskakh Omskogo voennogo okruga v 1906–1907 gg.," *Revoliutsionnoe dvizhenie v Sibiri i na Dal'nem Vostoke*, Tomsk, 1960, p. 124; Gavrilov, *Voennaia rabota*, p. 131; *Kostromskaia gazeta*, 26 May 1906; Petr Pil'skii, "Armiia i obshchestvo. (Elementy vrazhdy i prepiatstvii)," *Mir bozhii*, 1906 no. 8, pp. 217–8.

51. On the military-political periodicals in general, see *RI*, 9 March 1906. The earliest periodicals were *Vilenskii voennyi listok*, *Turkestanskaia voennaia gazeta*, *Russkii voin* (Odessa), and *Varshavskii voennyi vestnik*. Anti-revolutionary sermons in *Vestnik voennogo dukhovenstva* can be found in issues of 1 Feb. 1906, 1 March 1906, 15 April 1906, 1 Aug. 1906, 1 Sept. 1906, and 15 Sept. 1906.

52. Circular of 11 May 1906, in IISH, SR, D. 690, DMVO.

53. Drezen, *Tsarizm v bor'be*, p. 252 fn. 46; V-skii, *Tolkovanie Vysochaishego Manifesta 17-go Oktiabria 1905 goda. Sostavil dlia nizhnikh chinov*, Spb. 1905. See also *Voennaia reforma. Sbornik statei*, Spb., 1906, pp. 58–75; Novyi, "O gumanosti v voiskakh," *Voina i mir*, 1906 no. 12, pp. 86–90.

54. *Razvedchik*, 4 July 1906 and 1 Aug. 1906; *Voennyi golos*, 23 March 1906; *RI*, 28 March 1906.

55. *Razvedchik*, 21 March 1906; 4 April 1906; 11 April 1906; 11 July 1906; 4 Jan. 1908; *RI*, no. 91, 26 April 1906 and no. 93, 28 April 1906; *Svetoch*, 16 May 1906; *Vpered*, 26 May 1906; *Soldatskaia zhizn'* (SD, Moscow), no. 6, 15 March 1906; *Soldatskaia mysl'* (SD, Moscow), no. 2, June 1906.

56. *Soldat* (SD, Sevastopol), no. 4, May 1906.

57. Sukhomlinov, *Vospominaniia*, pp. 110, 152; [Rediger], "Iz zapisok," pp. 129–31; *Voennyi golos*, 14 July 1906; *Soldatskaia mysl'* (SR, Spb.), no. 2, Oct. 1906; *Soldat* (SD, Sevastopol), no. 4, May 1906; *Soldatskaia gazeta* (SR, Tsk), no. 1, May 1906; *Proletarii*, 8 Sept. 1906.

58. Bund Archive, New York.

59. *Voennyi listok* (SR, Simferopol), no. 3, 20 July 1906; no. 4, 1 Sept. 1906; no. 5, 1 Oct. 1906; *Soldat* (SD, Sevastopol), no. 3, April 1906.

60. For an explanation of membership statistics, see Bushnell, "Mutineers and Revolutionaries," pp. 460–2. The totals therein are lower than those given here because of new data on the SRs.

61. *Protokoly pervoi konferentsii voennykh*, p. 13.

62. Samoilenko, "Sredi kazakov," pp. 198–9.

63. See Bushnell, "Mutineers and Revolutionaries," pp. 246–7, 265–7.

64. "Materialy o pervoi voennoi konferentsii"; *Protokoly pervoi konferentsii voennykh*, p. 36; Gavrilov, *Voennaia rabota*, p. 122; Iaroslavskii, "Podpol'naia rabota," pp. 169, 172.

65. For a list of organizations with soviet structure, see Bushnell, "Mutineers and Revolutionaries," p. 282 n. 8.

66. Zubelevich, *Kronshtadt*, v. 1, pp. 42–7; *Soldatskaia mysl'* (TsK PSR), no. 2, 22 Sept. 1906; Ottoson-Nikolaev, "Iz vospominanii," p. 101; Ivanov, "Kronshtadtskoe podpol'e," pp. 140–1; Zharnovetskii, "Kronshtadtskie vosstaniia," p. 72.

67. "Materialy o pervoi voennoi konferentsii"; Rozenblium, *Voennye*, pp. 185–6; *Protokoly pervoi konferentsii voennykh*, p. 22; *Pervaia konferentsiia voennykh*, p. 187.

68. Zubelevich,*Kronshtadt*, v. 1, pp. 45–7; v. 2, pp. 95–6.

69. Zubelivich, *Kronshtadt*, v. 2, pp. 29–31.

VII. "These Words Pleased Us Very Much"

1. *Voinskii ustav o nakazaniiakh i Ustav distsiplinarnyi*, Spb., 1906, st. 75, pp. 22–3. For a list of commanders who were sacked, see "Chistka komsostava tsarskoi armii v 1906 g.," *KA*, 1932 no. 1–2, pp. 211–25.

2. Figures for 1905 based mostly on reports compiled by the Ministry of War are provided in *1905. Armiia v pervoi revoliutsii. Ocherki i materialy*, M.-L., 1927,

p. xi. The Ministry of War figures for 1906 are provided by Rozenblium, *Voennye organizatsii*, p. 45.

3. For instance, Sukhomlinov, then commander of the Kiev military district, reports that in 1906 there was both disorder *(razval)* and disaffection in X corps (Kharkov), particularly in the 122nd Tambov regiment; Sukhomlinov, *Vospominaniia*, p. 110. A report in *Sovremenik*, 9 June 1906, of a large open-air soldier meeting in Kharkov on June 6, a letter from a Kharkov revolutionary intercepted by the police reporting that in June the soldiers were on the verge of insurrection *(VPR*, part 2 book 3, p. 159), and a list of "disorders" under investigation by the Ministry of War that included the 124th Voronezh infantry, quartered in Kharkov *(Ekho*, 4 July 1906) makes it likely though not certain that there were mutinies as defined by military law in the Tambov and Voronezh infantry.

4. At mid-year the list of units whose disorders were being investigated by the Ministry of War included the Sestroretsk and Kiev local details, the 1st pontoon battalion, the 18th sapper battalion, the Nezhinsk dragoons, the 279th Ialta infantry, the 120th Serpukhov infantry, the 9th Siberian Grenadiers, the 141st Mozhaisk infantry, the Finland, Grenadier and Pavlovsk Guards infantry, and the 12th East Siberian rifles; *Ekho*, 4 July 1906. In the Petersburg military district, gendarme sources and commanders' reports relate disorders in the 23rd infantry division, the 23rd artillery brigade, the 37th artillery brigade, the 96th Omsk infantry, the 147th Samara infantry, and the Vyborg fortress artillery; Iu. Korablev, *Voennaia rabota peterburgskikh bol'shevikov v revoliutsii 1905–1907 gg.*, M., 1955, p. 117. No other information being available, they have not been counted among the mutinous.

5. Twenty-five of 43 pontoon, railroad, and sapper battalions in Europe and Central Asia experienced mutiny, as did 20 of 75 cossack regiments in Europe, 11 of 71 Guards, Grenadier, Caucasus, Turkestan, line, and reserve artillery brigades, and 5 of 80 Guards, dragoon, Dagestan and reserve cavalry regiments. Siberian units—other than infantry—and cossacks in Central Asia have been omitted because it has been difficult to establish the number of such formations in 1906 (though mutinies occurred in all of them). The number of units has been established from the sources listed in Chapter 4, ns. 5 and 7, and—for identification of units disbanded in 1906 (it has been assumed that any unit disbanded by July 1906 was unavailable for mutiny; most were disbanded by April) and units left in Manchuria throughout 1906 (and thus assumed to be unavailable for mutiny due to the special conditions under which they served)— "Obzor voennykh sobytii," in *Voennyi sbornik*, 1906 no. 8, pp. 191, 194, 207; 1906 no. 11, p. 232; 1906 no. 12, pp. 243, 265–6, 271; 1907 no. 2, pp. 280–2; 1907 no. 4, p. 278; 1907 no. 7, p. 272.

6. Alexander Iswolsky, *Recollections of a Foreign Minister. (Memoirs of Alexander Iswolsky)*, Garden City, N.Y., 1921, p. 282.

7. Ibid., pp. 74–8, 82–94, 169–74, 180–2; Gurko, *Features and Figures*, pp. 459–74; Kokovtsov, *Out of My Past*, pp. 138–43; Koroleva, *Pervaia rossiiskaia revoliutsiia*, pp. 113–27; S. M. Sidel'nikov, *Obrazovanie i deiatel'nost' pervoi gosudarstvennoi dumy*, M., 1962, pp. 204–22, 224–36, 239–74; Kuz'min-Karavaev, *Iz epokhi*, v. 2, pp. 313–20, 324–32, 409–23. See also the weekly analysis of the Duma from the Kadet point of view in *Pravo*.

8. Manning, *Crisis of the Old Order*, pp. 212–17.

9. Sidel'nikov, *Obrazovanie i deiatel'nost'*, p. 311.

10. Izwolsky, *Recollections*, p. 179; Gurko, *Features and Figures*, pp. 474–80; Koroleva, *Pervaia rossiiskaia revoliutsiia*, pp. 92–8, 122–5; Maslov, *Krest'ianskoe dvizhenie*, pp. 129–43; Manning, *Crisis of the Old Order*, pp. 218–28, 244–5; Sidel'-nikov, *Obrazovanie i deiatel'nost'*, pp. 191–6, 201, 286–8, 292–303, 306–19; D. A. Kolesnichenko, "Agrarnye proekty Trudovoi gruppy v I Gosudartsvennoi dume," *IZ*, v. 82, 1968, pp. 40–88; D. A. Kolesnichenko, "Vozniknovenie i deiatel'nost' 'Trudovoi gruppy'," *ISSSR*, 1967 no. 4, pp. 78–89; Kolesnichenko, "K voprosu o politicheskoi evoliutsii trudovikov," pp. 84–95; Scott J. Seregny, "Politics and the Rural Intelligentsia in Russia: A Biographical Sketch of Stepan Anikin, 1869–1919," *Russian History*, v. 7 pts. 1–2, 1980, pp. 187–91; V. Sh., *Trudovaia gruppa v Gosudarstvennoi dume*, M., 1906, pp. 1–16.

11. Manning, *Crisis of the Old Order*, pp. 239–45; Sidel'nikov, *Obrazovanie i deiatel'nost'*, pp. 222–3, 232–3, 281–2, 286–8; Maslov, *Agrarnoe dvizhenie*, pp. 143–53; P. N. Pershin, *Agrarnaia revoliutsiia v Rossii*, v. 1, *Ot reformy k revoliutsii*, M., 1966, pp. 252–62; Kolesnichenko, "Iz istorii bor'by rabochego klassa za krest'-ianskie massy," pp. 265–72; *VPR*, part 2 book 1, pp. 23–4, 32, 368–9, 561, 571–2; *VPR*, part 2 book 2, pp. 68, 97–8, 112–14, 115–20, 140, 143, 153–5, 157–9, 162–3, 167–8, 177, 215–6, 263–4, 267–8, 281–3, 313–5, 329–30, 414–5; Dubrovskii and Grave, *Agrarnoe dvizhenie*, pp. 18–20, 49, 70–3, 204, 208, 255, 586, 624–5.

12. Sidel'nikov, *Obrazovanie i deiatel'nost'*, p. 238; *VPR*, part 2 book 1, p. 74; Kokovtsov, *Out of My Past*, p. 137; Mary Schaeffer Conroy, *Peter Arkad'evich Stolypin. Practical Politics in Late Tsarist Russia*, Boulder, Colo., 1977, pp. 153, 179 fns. 12–13.

13. Tsion, *Tri dnia*, p. 22; *VP*, v. 1, p. 286; *VP*, v. 3 book 2, pp. 927–9.

14. *Revoliutsiia 1905–1907 gg. v. Gruzii*, p. 711.

15. Girshgorn, "Revoliutsionnoe dvizhenie v armii v 1905–1907 gg. (Doku-menty)," *Bor'ba klassov*, 1935 no. 10, p. 30.

16. A. P. Steklov, "Revoliutsionnoe dvizhenie v chastiakh Kavkazskogo voen-nogo okruga," pp. 430–1. *Revoliutsiia 1905–1907 gg. v Gruzii*, p. 711; Pavchinskii, *Russkaia armiia i revoliutsiia*, pp. 103–4; *Duma*, 20 May 1906.

17. *Mysl'*, 1 July 1906.

18. *Russkii voin*, 1 Feb. 1906; 8 Feb. 1906; *Varshavskii voennyi vestnik*, 1 June 1906; 8 June 1906; *Mysl'*, 2 July 1906; *Vpered*, 22 May 1906; *Ekho*, 25 June 1906.

19. Akhun and Petrov, *Bol'sheviki i armiia*, p. 59; *Duma*, 1 June 1906; *Golos*, 10 June 1906; *Soldat* (SD, Sevastopol), no. 6, [June] 1906; *Soldat* (SD, Libava), no. 11, 27 May 1906; Ia. Davtian, "Tiflisskaia voennaia organizatsiia v 1905–1907 gg.," *PR*, 1923 no. 4, p. 144.

20. *Soldatskii golos* (SD-Menshevik, Moscow), no. 4, 15 March 1906; *Soldatskaia zhizn'* (SD-Bolshevik, Moscow), no. 6, 15 March 1906; *Soldatskaia volia* (SD, Grodno), no. 1, 25 April 1906; *Soldat* (SD, Sevastopol), no. 4, May 1906; no. 5, 23 May 1906; *Soldat* (SD, Libava), no. 9, 10 May 1906; "Voenno-revoliutsionnyi golos No. 1," March 1906, and "1-oe maia," both hectographed leaflets produced by the Mariampol SD-Bundist military organization, Bund Archive; *Soldatskaia gazeta* (SR, Tsk), no. 1, [May] 1906.

21. *Golos soldata* (SD, Riga), no. 7–8, 18 May 1906.

22. Rozenblium, *Voennye organizatsii*, pp. 75–7; *Soldatskaia volia* (SD, Grodno), no. 2, 14 May 1906; *Golos truda*, 4 July 1906.

23. *Voennyi listok* (SR, Simferopol), no. 1, 15 June 1906.

24. *Soldatskaia mysl'* (SD, Moscow), no. 1, June 1906. Other examples: *Revoliutsiia 1905–1907 gg. v Gruzii*, pp. 668–70, 717–20; *Revoliutsionnye sobytiia v Gomele i Gomel'skoi oblasti v gody pervoi russkoi revoliutsii 1905–1907 gg. Sbornik dokumentov i materialov*, Gomel, 1955, pp. 141–3; untitled leaflet issued by the Mariampol SD-Bundist military organization in June, Bund Archive; *Golos soldata* (SD, Riga), no. 9–10, 8 June 1906.

25. *Narodnyi vestnik*, 30 May 1906.

26. *Narodnyi vestnik*, 28 May 1906; *Golos*, 8 June 1906; *Kur'er*, 2 June 1906; *Mysl'*, 22 June 1906; *Soldatskii listok* (SD, Riga), nos. 1 and 2, May 1906; Pavchinskii, *Russkaia armiia*, pp. 79–80; Marina, "Pechatnaia propaganda," p. 118.

27. Gosudarstvennaia duma, *Stenograficheskie otchety 1906 goda. Sessiia pervaia*, v. 2, Spb., 1906, pp. 1371–2, 1550–1; *Ekho*, 27 June 1906; *Golos*, 7 June 1906; *Mysl'*, 5 July 1906. Identification of deputies and political affiliation is based on *Chleny pervoi gosudarstvennoi dumy*, M., 1906.

28. *Trudovaia Rossiia*, 10 June 1906; 2 June 1906; 7 June 1906; 8 June 1906, 9 June 1906; *Izvestiia krest'ianskikh deputatov*, 20 May 1906; *Krest'ianskii deputat*, 5 July 1906.

29. Zubelevich, *Kronshtadt*, v. 2, pp. 21–6, 69–70, 99–102; "Materialy o pervoi voennoi konferentsii," IISH; Akhun and Petrov, *Bol'sheviki i armiia*, pp. 46, 60–1; Pavchinskii, *Russkaia armiia*, p. 77; *Mysl'*, 20 June 1906; *Krest'ianskii deputat*, 5 July 1906.

30. *Golos*, 6 June 1906.

31. *Narodnyi vestnik*, 30 May 1906.

32. *Prizyv*, no. 97, 4 June 1906; *Duma*, no. 36, 9 June 1906.

33. *Ekaterinoslavshchina v revoliutsii 1905–1907 gg.*, pp. 300–1, 303.

34. *Voennyi listok* (SR, Simferopol), no. 2, 27 June 1906.

35. *Ekaterinoslavshchina v revoliutsii*, pp. 300–1, 303; *Ekho*, 2 July 1906 and 4 July 1906.

36. *Golos truda*, 5 July 1906.

37. *Golos*, 6 June 1906; *Vpered*, 6 June 1906; *Ekho*, 22 June 1906; 25 June 1906; 1 July 1906; *Severnaia zemlia*, 28 June 1906; Korablev, "Revoliutsionnoe dvizhenie v voiskakh Peterburgskogo voennogo okruga," *Revoliutsionnoe dvizhenie v armii v gody pervoi russkoi revoliutsii. Sbornik statei*, M., 1955, p. 154; *VPR*, part 2 book 1, p. 615 n. 194.

38. *Soldat* (SD, Sevastopol), no. 4, May 1906; *Sovremennik*, 18 June 1906; *Kostromskoi krai*, 27 June 1906; Mel'nikov, "Revoliutsionnoe dvizhenie . . . 1906," p. 101; an order of 7 April 1906, IISH, SR, DMVO; *Iuzhnaia narodnaia gazeta*, 26 May 1906.

39. *Mysl'*, 22 June 1906; 24 June 1906; *Otkliki Kryma*, 28 June 1906.

40. V. V. Kir'iakov, "Iz derevenskikh vpechatlenii: soldatchina i rekrutchina," *Soznatel'naia Rossiia*, no. 3, 1906, pp. 5–6.

41. *Privolzhskii krai*, 8 July 1906.

42. There had been 203 line infantry units in Europe in late 1905, but 24 had been demobilized by the end of July and have been considered unavailable for mutiny in 1906; 96 line regiments had been sent to Manchuria, but 4 were left until early 1907 and were unavailable for mutiny. Nineteen percent of the former mutinied, and 34 percent of the latter mutinied, in 1906. However, it is reasonable to move the 8 regiments of XIII corps (1 of which mutinied in 1906) from the "Manchurian" to the "European" category, because they never fought in Manchuria, experienced the same indiscipline and mutiny as the European regiments in late 1905, and of course did not winter in Manchuria. The percentages in the text are based on that transferral.

43. *VPR*, part 2 book 3, pp. 232–3, 494; Zheleznov, "Revoliutsionnoe dvizhenie v voiskakh Moskovskogo voennogo okruga," p. 137.

44. For just two of many possible examples: On the Voronezh camp: *Protokoly pervoi konferentsii*, p. 30; E. G. Shuliakovskii, "Deiatel'nost voennoi organizatsii pri Voronezhskom komitete RSDRP v 1906 godu," *Trudy Voronezhskogo gos. un-ta*, v. 51 no. 1, 1958, p. 7; *Revoliutsionnoe dvizhenie v Voronezhskoi gubernii 1905–1907 gg. (Sbornik dokumentov i materialov)*, Voronezh, 1955, p. 395; *VPR*, part 2 book 2, p. 136. On the work of SRs in the Penza camp: "Materialy pervoi voennoi konferentsii," IISH. On the isolation of the sapper camp in Kaluga province: Mel'nikov, "Revoliutsionnoe dvizhenie . . . 1906 g.," p. 99.

45. The analysis is based on *Kurskaia zhizn'*, 24 May 1906; 25 May 1906; 27 May 1906; 28 May 1906; 30 May 1906; 31 May 1906; 7 June 1906; *Izvestiia krest'ianskikh deputatov*, 30 May 1906; *Revoliutsionnye sobytiia 1905–1907 gg. v Kurskoi gubernii. Sbornik dokumentov i materialov*, Kursk, 1955, pp. 161–5; V. M. Kantsel'son, "Revoliutsionnoe dvizhenie," pp. 236–7; *Svetoch*, 25 May 1906; "Materialy o pervoi voennoi konferentsii," IISH; *Narodnyi vestnik*, 23 May 1906; 24 May 1906; 25 May 1906; 31 May 1906; *Put'*, 7 June 1906; *Kur'er*, 3 June 1906; *Mysl'*, 28 June 1906; Pavchinskii, *Russkaia armiia*, p. 75; *Sovremennik*, 22 June 1906; *Ekho*, 2 July 1906; 4 July 1906; *Russkoe slovo*, 24 June 1906; Sukhomlinov, *Vospominaniia*, p. 110; *Kurskaia vest'*, 25 June 1906; 29 June 1906; 7 July 1906; 9 July 1906; 11 July 1906; 12 July 1906; 13 July 1906.

46. *Ekho*, 2 July 1906. See Appendix II for other sources on the mutiny.

47. *Revoliutsionnoe dvizhenie v Kaluzhskoi gubernii v period pervoi russkoi revoliutsii 1905–1907 godov. Sbornik dokumentov*, Kaluga, 1955, pp. 142–3. On the mutinies, see Appendix II: June 5, June 17.

48. *Krest'ianskoe dvizhenie 1905–1907 gg. v Tambovskoi gubernii. Sbornik dokumentov*, Tambov, 1957, pp. 113–4.

49. *Mysl'*, 21 June 1906. On the mutinies, see Appendix II: June 14, June 18, July after dissolution of Duma.

50. Dubrovskii and Grave, *Agrarnoe dvizhenie*, p. 589. On the mutinies, see Appendix II: 13 June, 26 July.

51. A number of Guards regiments not known to have mutinied appeared on the list of units whose "disorders" the Ministry of War was investigating: *Ekho*, 4 July 1906. For other reports on restiveness among the Guards: [Rediger], "Iz zapisok," p. 118; *Vpered*, 6 June 1906; 9 June 1906; 10 June 1906; *Svetoch*, 31 May 1906; *Kur'er*, 4 June 1906; 8 June 1906; Pavchinskii, *Ruskaia armiia*, pp. 71–2;

Akhun and Petrov, *Bol'sheviki i armiia*, p. 61; Epanchin, "Na sluzhbe trekh im-peratorov," p. 299; Svechin, *Zapiski starogo generala*, p. 88; "Vospominaniia pol-kovnika kniazia Nikolaia Mikhailovicha Devlet-Kil'deev," in M. M. Devlet-Kil'deev, ed., *Kirasiry ego velichestva, 1902–1914. Poslednye gody mirnogo vremeni*, Washington, D.C., 1959, p. 142.

52. My account is based on Akhun and Petrov, *Bol'sheviki i armiia*, pp. 54–70; [Rediger], "Iz zapisok," pp. 117–118; Svechin, *Zapiski starogo generala*, pp. 88–89; *Golos*, 29 April 1906; *Narodnyi vestnik*, 27 May 1906; *Vpered*, 10 June 1906; *VPR*, part 2 book 1, pp. 320–21; "Trebovaniia 1-go batal'ona Preobrazhenskogo polka," Spb., 1906, Helsinki 117 N; D. Khodnev, "Preobrazhenskii intsident. Iz vos-pominanii 1906 g.," 1937, manuscript, Bakhmeteff Archive, Ms Coll/Finliandskii Polk, Box 15.4.7.1, pp. 1–16.

53. Akhun and Petrov, *Bol'sheviki i armiia*, p. 59.

54. On the Guards cavalry mutinies, see Appendix II: June, second half (two different entries). [Rediger], "Iz zapisok," p. 118; Pavchinskii, *Russkaia armiia*, pp. 71, 92, 102; *Mysl'*, 22 June 1906; 6 July 1906; *Dvadtsatyi vek*, 23 June 1906; Korablev, "Revoliutsionnoe dvizhenie v voiskakh Peterburgskogo voennogo ok-ruga," p. 150; "Materialy o pervoi voennoi konferentsii," IISH.

55. For the mutinies, see Appendix II. For sources on the number of cossack regiments in the field as of summer 1906, see note 5 above.

56. *Gosudarstvennaia duma, Stenograficheskie otchety*, v. 2, pp. 1321, 1323–4, 1327; *Mysl'*, 24 June 1906; 1 July 1906; 6 July 1906; *Dvadtsatyi vek*, 2 June 1906; *Sovremennik*, 3 June 1906; *Ekho*, 28 June 1906; *Privolzhskii krai*, 8 June 1906; 8 July 1906; *Trudovaia zhizn'*, 4 July 1906; *Soldatskaia mysl'* (SD, Moscow), no. 3, 12 July 1906; "Materialy o pervoi voennoi konferentsii," IISH.

57. M. N. Korin, *Donskoe kazachestvo (Iz proshlogo)*, Rostov n/D, 1949, pp. 41–2. Other sources on the unrest in cossack villages: *1905–1907 gody na Donu*, pp. 316–8; *Duma*, 1 June 1906; *Severnaia zemlia*, 28 June 1906; *VPR*, part 2 book 2, pp. 191, 204; *Donskaia zhizn'*, 21 May 1906; 16 June 1906; 4 July 1906; 6 July 1906.

58. *Mysl'*, no. 15, 6 July 1906; *Gosudarstvennaia duma, Stenograficheskie otchety*, v. 2, pp. 961–7, 1307–39; *Severo-zapadnyi golos*, 28 June 1906.

59. *Gosudarstvennaia duma, Stenograficheskie otchety*, v. 2, p. 1321; *Krest'ians-koe dvizhenie 1905–1907 gg. v Tambovskoi gubernii. Sbornik dokumentov*, Tambov, 1957, pp. 98–9.

60. *Gosudarstvennaia duma, Stenograficheskie otchety*, v. 2, pp. 1328, 1331; *Donskaia zhizn'*, 14 June 1906; 28 June 1906; 8 July 1906; *Voennyi golos*, 25 June 1906; 4 July 1906.

61. Order of 31 May 1906, IISH, SR, DMVO; *Revoliutsiia 1905–1907 gg. v Gruzii*, pp. 703–6; *Voennyi golos*, 18 July 1906.

62. *Duma*, 31 May 1906; *Voennyi golos*, 16 June 1906; 4 July 1906; 9 July 1906; *Ekho*, 2 July 1906; 4 July 1906; 5 July 1906; *Mysl'*, 4 July 1906; *Golos truda*, 5 July 1906.

63. Fuller, *Civil-Military Conflict*, Chapter 5.

64. *Ekho*, 27 June 1906; *Voennyi golos*, 7 July 1906.

65. *Vsepoddanneishii otchet Voennogo ministerstva za 1905*, Spb., 1907, "Otchet po Glavnomu shtabu," pp. 96–7; *Vsepoddanneishii otchet Voennogo ministerstva za*

1906, Spb., 1908, "Otchet po Glavnomu shtabu," pp. 72–3; *Vsepoddanneishii otchet Voennogo ministerstva za 1907*, Spb., 1909, "Otchet po Glavnomu shtabu," p. 89. Figures on units deployed have been translated into men on the basis of authorized strengths detailed in *Svod shtatov voenno-sukhoputnogo vedomstva*, v. 2, Spb., 1893, except that infantry deployed against civilians in November and December has been counted at 50 rather than 107 men per company; for deployment through October, see Chapter 3 n. 17. See the discussion of the figures for 1907 in Fuller, *Civil-Military Conflict*, Chapter 5.

66. Fuller, *Civil-Military Conflict*, Chapter 5 and passim.

VIII. July 1906

1. Kuz'min-Karavaev, *Iz epokhi*, v. 2, pp. 403–6 (quotation from p. 404).
2. Kokovtsov, *Out of My Past*, p. 149.
3. Manning, *Crisis of the Old Order*, pp. 244–58; Kokovtsov, *Out of My Past*, pp. 146–51; Iswolsky, *Recollections*, pp. 183–94; Gurko, *Features and Figures*, pp. 482–4; Chermenskii, *Burzhuaziia i tsarizm*, pp. 283–302; Miliukov, *Vospominaniia*, pp. 377–87; P. N. Miliukov, *Tri popytki. (K istorii russkogo lzhekonstitutsionalizma)*, Paris, 1921, pp. 26–60; [Rediger], "Iz zapisok," p. 114; V. I. Startsev, *Russkaia burzhuaziia i samoderzhavie v 1905–1917 gg.*, L., 1977, pp. 71–100; Sidel'nikov, *Obrazovanie i deiatel'nost'*, pp. 332–5, 337–9; Bernard Pares, *Russia and Reform*, London, 1907, pp. 553–7, 559; Maurice Baring, *A Year in Russia*, 2nd ed. New York, [1917], pp. 240–1, 254–6; Hans Heilbronner, "Piotr Khristianovich von Schwanebach and the Dissolution of the First Two Dumas," *Canadian Slavonic Papers*, v. 11 no. 1, Spring 1969, pp. 33–6; *The Times* (London), 6 July 1906; 7 July 1906, 9 July 1906, 10 July 1906; *New York Times*, 1 July 1906; 4 July 1906; 7 July 1906.
4. *Golos truda*, 5 July 1906. The Menshevik position is spelled out in the lead editorials in *Kur'er*, 2 June 1906; 9 June 1906; 10 June 1906; 11 June 1906. See also Martov, *Istoriia Rossiiskoi Sotsial-Demokratii*, pp. 195–8; Garvi, *Vospominaniia*, part two, pp. 31, 33–4; Voitinskii, *Gody pobed i porazhenii*, v. 2, p. 66.
5. The SR position was summed up by a member of the Central Committee at the June SR military organization conference; "Materialy pervoi voennoi konferentsii." The Bolshevik position on the Duma is summarized in a series of articles by Lenin: *Vpered*, 10 June 1906; 11 June 1906; *Ekho*, 22 June 1906. See also Garvi, *Vospominaniia*, part two, pp. 34–8, 74; Voitinskii, *Gody pobed i porazhenii*, v. 2, pp. 64–72.
6. M. Egorov, "Chernaia i belaia kost' v armii," *Ekho*, 6 July 1906.
7. "Dukh vremeni," *Nakanune* (Poltava Menshevik), 5 June 1906.
8. V. Ch[ernov], "Volneniia v armii," *Mysl'*, 20 June 1906.
9. *Ekho*, 2 July 1906; *Golos*, 10 June 1906; *Kur'er*, 3 June 1906; *Trud*, 31 May 1906; 9 June 1906.
10. *Soldat* (SD, Sevastopol), no. 3, April 1906.
11. *Vestnik kazarmy* (SD, Finland), no. 4, 8 June 1906; No. 5, 15 June 1906; *Narodnyi vestnik*, 27 May 1906; *Mysl'*, 29 June 1906; *Russkii nabat*, 9 June 1906; K.

Troitskii, "Rabota s.-d. sredi voisk v 1906–1907 godov," *Materialy po istorii revoliutsionnogo dvizheniia,* Nizhnii Novgorod, v. 4, 1922, pp. 127–8; Davtian, "Tiflisskaia," p. 144; Znamenskii, *Voennaia,* p. 56; *Ekaterinoslavshchina v revoliutsii 1905–1907,* p. 308; *Listovki peterburgskikh bol'shevikov 1902–1917,* M.-L., 1939, v. 1, pp. 412–3; Imas, "Put' v emigratsiiu," *KiS,* 1928 no. 8–9, p. 144; "Materialy o pervoi voennoi konferentsii."

12. Appendix II: Abo, June 1; Samara, June 14 (and "Materialy o pervoi voennoi konferentsii"); Nizhnii Novgorod, June 18 (and Troitskii, "Rabota s.-d. sredi voisk," p. 127).

13. Zubelevich, *Kronshtadt,* v. 1, p. 142; v. 2, pp. 87–90; A. Argunov, "Azef v Partii S.R.," p. 188; "Materialy o pervoi voennoi konferentsii."

14. "Materialy o pervoi voennoi konferentsii"; Basalygo, "O partiinoi rabote v Sevastopole v 1906 godu," *PR,* 1922 no. 9, p. 193.

15. Andreev, "Revoliutsionnoe dvizhenie," p. 35.

16. Andreev, "Revoliutsionnoe dvizhenie," pp. 36, 53; Zubelevich, *Kronshtadt,* v. 2, pp. 8–16, 21–26; *Soldatskaia gazeta* (SR, Central Committee), no. 2, 22 Sept. 1906; *Voennye vosstaniia v Baltike,* p. 59; "Kronshtadtskoe vosstanie 1906 g.," *KA,* 1936 no. 4, p. 94; Argunov, "Azef v Partii S.-R.," p. 188; "Materialy o pervoi voennoi konferentsii."

17. Mel'nikov, "Revoliutsionnoe dvizhenie . . . 1906," pp. 108–13; Zheleznov, "Revoliutsionnoe dvizhenie," pp. 145–6.

18. "Materialy o pervoi voennoi konferentsii"; Zubelevich, *Kronshtadt,* v. 2, pp. 87–92; Troitskii, "Rabota s.-d. sredi voisk," p. 126; *Revoliutsiia 1905–1907 gg. v Gruzii,* pp. 717–20; *VPR,* part 2 book 2, pp. 324–5.

19. "Materialy o pervoi voennoi konferentsii"; Zubelevich, *Kronshtadt,* v. 2, pp. 103–9; *Partiinye izvestiia* (SR, Central Committee), no. 1, 22 Oct. 1906.

20. [Rediger], "Iz zapisok," p. 115; Heilbronner, "Piotr Khristianovich Schwanebach," p. 36; Iswolsky, *Recollections,* pp. 194–201; Kokovtsov, *Out of My Past,* pp. 150–6; Startsev, *Russkaia burzhuaziia,* pp. 101–4; Gurko, *Features and Figures,* pp. 483–8; Sidel'nikov, *Obrazovanie i deiatel'nost',* pp. 341–61; *Padenie tsarskogo rezhima. Stenograficheskie otchety doprosov i pokazanii, dannykh v 1917 g. v Chrezvychainoi sledstvennoi komissii Vremenogo Pravitel'stva,* ed. P. E. Shchegolov, v. 7, M.-L., pp. 95–9 (testimony of Kokovtsov).

21. M. E. Bakai, "Iz vospominanii M. E. Bakaia o chernykh kabinetakh v Rossii," *Byloe,* 1908 no. 8, pp. 104–6; Iswolsky, *Recollections,* pp. 207–8.

22. Bakai, "Iz vospominanii," p. 105; Iswolsky, *Recollections,* pp. 195–6; Sidel'nikov, *Obrazovanie i deiatel'nost',* pp. 361–3; Chermenskii, *Burzhuaziia i tsarizm,* p. 311; *Revoliutsionnoe dvizhenie v Tul'skoi gubernii v 1905–1907 gg. Sbornik dokumentov i materialov,* Tula, 1956, p. 219; *Voennyi golos,* 8 July 1906; 12 July 1906; G. M. Derenkovskii, "Vseobshaia stachka i sovety rabochikh deputatov v iiule 1906 g.," *IZ,* v. 77, 1965, pp. 123, 130; Argunov, "Azef v Partii S.-R.," pp. 189–90, 192.

23. Startsev, *Russkaia burzhuaziia,* pp. 105–6; Kokovtsov, *Out of My Past,* p. 156; Gurko, *Features and Figures,* pp. 485–6; Chermenskii, *Burzhuaziia i tsarizm,* pp. 310–11.

24. Kokovtsov, *Out of My Past,* p. 155; Sidel'nikov, *Obrazovanie i deiatel'nost',* pp. 371–2; Voitinskii, *Gody pobed i porazhenii,* v. 2, p. 84; Baring, *A Year in Russia,*

pp. 261, 268, 279–80; Bernard Pares, *My Russian Memoirs*, London, 1931, pp. 123, 127–8; M. Vinaver, "V ozhidanii rospuska i posle rospuska. (Otryvki iz vospominanii)," *K 10-letiiu l-oi Gosudarstvennoi dumy*, Pg., 1916, p. 98.

25. Pares, *Russia and Reform*, pp. 561–2.

26. Dubrovskii and Grave, *Agrarnoe dvizhenie*, pp. 222, 214; Baring, *A Year in Russia*, p. 269.

27. Sidel'nikov, *Obrazovanie i deiatel'nost'*, pp. 364–70; Chermenskii, *Burzhuaziia i tsarizm*, pp. 314–9; Vinaver, "V ozhidanii rospuska," pp. 96–113; Miliukov, *Vospominaniia*, pp. 401–6; Miliukov, *Tri popytki*, pp. 63–6; *VPR*, part 2 book 1, pp. 33–4; "Pervaia Gosudarstvennaia duma v Vyborge," *KA*, 1933 no. 2, pp. 86–99.

28. "Izveshchenie ot Komiteta Trudovoi Gruppy," *Vesti s rodiny* (SR, n.p.), 1906, pp. 10–12; "Pervaia Gosudarstvennaia duma v Vyborge," pp. 86–7, 89; Chermenskii, *Burzhuaziia i tsarizm*, pp. 314, 316, 320; Sidel'nikov, *Obrazovanie i deiatel'nost'*, pp. 324, 372–3; Kolesnichenko, "Iz istorii," pp. 278–81; Kolesnichenko, "K voprosu," pp. 101–6; *VPR*, part 2 book 2, pp. 269–72, 327–8, 491 n. 255; St. An[iki]n, "S"ezd trudovoi gruppy," *Narodnyi trud*, no. 1, 1906, pp. 40–3.

29. *VPR*, part 2 book 1, pp. 34–6, 42–7; TsK RSDRP, "Pis'mo k partiinym organizatsiiam No. 5," July 1906, Helsinki 117 II; Martov, *Istoriia Rossiiskoi Sotsial-Demokratii*, p. 204; *Listovki bol'shevistskikh organizatsii v pervoi russkoi revoliutsii 1905–1907 gg.*, v. 3, M., 1956, pp. 40–43, 69–70, 333–4; *Partiinye izvestiia* (SR, Central Committee), no. 1, 22 Oct. 1906; Lenin, *PSS*, v. 13, pp. 305–27; Derenkovskii, "Vseobshchaia stachka," pp. 113–6, 121–2.

30. *Listovki bol'shevistkikh organizatsii*, v. 3, pp. 133–4, 421–3, 518–20; *VPR*, part 2 book 1, pp. 392–3, 405–6; *VPR*, part 2 book 2, pp. 48, 81, 199–201; *VPR*, part 2 book 3, pp. 84–6; Derenkovskii, "Vseobshchaia stachka," pp. 109–13, 124–5; Federativnyi Komitet rizhskikh sots.-dem. rabochikh organizatsii, "Revoliutsiia idet svoim putem," July 1906, Bund Archive; M. Vinitskii, "Ne vo vremia," *Nashe slovo* (Vilna, Bund), no. 7, pp. 1–6.

31. Argunov, "Azef v Partii S.-R.," pp. 190–1; Zenzinov, *Perezhitoe*, p. 224; *Bericht der Russischen Sozial-Revolutionären Partei an dem Internationalen Sozialisten Kongress zu Stuttgart (August 1907)*, n.p., 1907, pp. 40–41; TsK PSR, "K partiinym organizatsiiam," July 1906, Helsinki 117 N; "Boevaia taktika partii posle razgona Dumy," *Partiinye izvestiia* (SR, Central Committee), no. 1, 22 Oct. 1906, pp. 3–6, 11; *VPR*, part 2 book 1, pp. 37–8, 40–2.

32. The SR appeal to the peasants was signed by the Trudoviks, the SD Duma deputies, the SD Central Committee, and the Railway Union. There was no independent Bolshevik organization to sign, but Bolsheviks on the SD Central Committee approved; *VPR*, part 2 book 1, p. 58.

33. Zubelevich, *Kronshtadt*, v. 3, p. 7; *Soldat* (SD, Libava), no. 19, 3 Aug. 1906; *Kostromskoe slovo*, no. 8, 13 July 1906. The cossack mutiny in Kostroma is not confirmed by official sources and so has not been counted as mutinous, but it is likely that the cossacks did mutiny on July 11 as they had mutinied earlier.

34. *Revoliutsionnoe dvizhenie na Kubane*, p. 314.

35. Troitskii, "Rabota s.-d. sredi voisk," pp. 126, 128; Derenkovskii, "Vseob-

shchaia stachka," p. 127; I. Iurenev, "Dvinsk (1904–1906 gg.)," *PR*, 1922 no. 12, p. 144.

36. Appendix II: Poltava, July 15. The Poltava SRs' plan is reported in G. Gruza, "Poltavskoe voennoe vosstanie," *1905 god na Poltavshchine*, Poltava, 1925, p. 46.

37. On the mutiny, see Appendix II. See also *Vestnik voennogo dukhoventstva*, 1 Sept. 1906.

38. A. Piskarev, "Kronshtadtskoe vosstanie 20 iiulia 1906 goda," *Krasnyi baltiets*, 1920 no. 4, p. 37; Zubelevich, *Kronshtadt*, v. 2, pp. 130–2, and v. 3, pp. 5–6; Ivanov, "Kronshtadtskoe podpol'e," p. 144; *Soldatskaia gazeta* (SR, Central Committee), no. 2, 22 Sept. 1906; *Voennye vosstaniia v Baltike*, p. 78; V. M. Mitrofanov, *V pamiat' zhizni. Vospominaniia minera-uchastnika kronshtadtskogo vosstaniia v iiule 1906 goda*, L., 1930, p. 63; "Kronshtadtskoe vosstanie 1906 g.," p. 97.

39. Zubelevich, *Kronshtadt*, v. 3, pp. 8–12, 14–17; Ottoson-Nikolaev, "Iz vospominanii," p. 103; *Protokoly pervoi konferentsii voennykh*, p. 73; Zhenevskii, "Vokrug sveaborgskogo vosstaniia (po dannym departamenta politsii)," *KL*, 1925 no. 3, p. 111; Viktor Voennyi, "K voprosu o prichinakh neudach voennykh vosstanii," *Sotsialist-revoliutsioner*, 1910 no. 2, pp. 198–204; Tsion, *Tri dnia*, pp. 41–2.

40. "Boevaia taktika partii posle razgona Dumy," *Partiinye izvestiia* (SR, Central Committee), no. 1, 22 Oct. 1906, p. 4; Ol'shanskii, "Sveaborgskoe vosstanie," *KL*, 1922 no. 2–3, p. 199; Andreev, "Revoliutsionnoe dvizhenie," p. 55; *Voennye vosstaniia v Baltike*, pp. 65–6; Zubelevich, *Kronshtadt*, v. 3, pp. 8, 20–25; *VPR*, part 2 book 1, pp. 126–9.

41. Zubelevich, *Kronshtadt*, v. 3, p. 28.

42. *Vestnik kazarmy* (SD, Finland), no. 2, 15 May 1906; *Soldatskaia gazeta* (SR, Central Committee), no. 2, 22 Sept. 1906; *Mysl'*, 6 July 1906; *Listok* (SR, Petersburg Committee), no. 1, Aug. 1906; Tsion, *Tri dnia*, pp. 42–76; Ol'shanskii, "Sveaborgskoe vosstanie," passim; *VPR*, part 2 book 1, pp. 87–94, 108–13, 590–91; Andreev, "Revoliutsionnoe dvizhenie," pp. 42–4; *Kazarma*, 12 Aug. 1906; V. N. Sokolov, *Sveaborg. Voennoe vosstanie v 1906 g.*, M., 1933, pp. 26–31; *Protokoly pervoi konferentsii voennykh*, pp. 73–7; N. M. Fedorovskii, "Sveaborgskoe vosstanie," *Krasnaia nov'*, 1926 no. 3, pp. 162–71; Derenkovskii, "Vseobshchaia stachka," pp. 128–9; Lenin, *PSS*, v. 13, p. 328; Zhenevskii, "Vokrug sveaborgskogo," p. 114; L. P. Vorob'ev, "Odna iz avtobiografii," *1905. Vosstaniia v Baltiiskom*, pp. 87–8; Egorov, "Finliandskaia sots.-dem. voennaia organizatsiia v osveshchenii provokatora," ibid., p. 90.

43. Zubelevich, *Kronshtadt*, v. 3, pp. 39–46; Andreev, "Revoliutsionnoe dvizhenie," p. 55; Zharnovetskii, "Kronshtadtskie vosstaniia," p. 85; Ottoson-Nikolaev, "Iz vospominanii," p. 104; *Voennye vosstaniia v Baltike*, pp. 72–4; "Rasskaz Nikolaia Egorova o Kronshtadtskom vosstanii, zapisannyi ego tovarishchem," *Byloe*, 1908 no. 8, p. 72.

44. Vishniak, *Dan proshlomu*, p. 131; Zenzinov, *Perezhitoe*, p. 340; Garvi, *Vospominaniia*, part 2, pp. 77–8; *Piatyi (londonskii) s"ezd RSDRP Aprel'-mai 1907 goda. Protokoly*, M., 1963, pp. 76–7, 95, 146, 157–8; Derenkovskii, "Vseobshchaia stachka," p. 149; "Boevaia taktika partii posle razgona Dumy," *Partiinye izvestiia*

(SR, Central Committee), no. 1, 22 Oct. 1906, p. 5; Zubelevich, *Kronshtadt*, v. 3, pp. 48–52; Akhun and Petrov, *Bol'sheviki*, p. 73; Zharnovetskii, "Kronshtadtskie," pp. 82, 85; I. Teodorovich, "Zametki chitatelia," *PR*, 1924 no. 7, p. 175; Voitinskii, *Gody pobed i porazhenii*, v. 2, p. 89; *Kazarma*, 12 Aug. 1906; "Rasskaz Nikolaia Egorova," pp. 72–3, 75; Mitrofanov, *V pamiat' zhizni*, p. 64; Vikhrev, "Tragediia vooruzhennogo vosstaniia v Kronshtadte," *Bor'ba* (SDLK, Central Committee), no. 1, 9 Sept. 1906.

45. Tsion, *Tri dnia*, pp. 68–73; Sokolov, *Sveaborg*, pp. 66–7, 72–3, 75–7; Mikhail Svechin, "Bunt v kreposti Sveaborg," *Chasovoi*, May 1950, pp. 11–12.

46. *Voennye vosstaniia v Baltike*, pp. 63–4, 79; "V Kronshtadte vo noch' na 20 iiulia 1906 goda (po arkhivnym dannym)," *1905. Vosstaniia v Baltiiskom*, pp. 119–22; *Soldatskaia gazeta* (SR, Central Committee), no. 2, 22 Sept. 1906; Ol'shanskii, "Kronshtadtskoe vosstanie," pp. 191–4; "Kronshtadtskoe vosstanie," pp. 97–112; Vikhrev, "Tragediia"; Mitrofanov, *V pamiat' zhizni*, pp. 65–75; Fon-Essen, "Chetvert' veka tomu nazad," *Opoveshchenie po Obshchestvu Gg. ofitserov Leib-Gvardii 1-i artilleriiskoi brigady*, no. 2, May 1932, pp. 26–31; *VPR*, part 2 book 1, pp. 123–5, 129–58.

47. Spiridovich, *Revoliutsionnoe dvizhenie*, p. 272; *Voennye vosstaniia v Baltike*, pp. 256–61; I. A. Shablin, *Vosstanie i kazn' moriakov s "Pamiati Azova"*, Revel, 1917; Drezen, *Revoliutsiia vo flote*, pp. 62–3; *Soldatskaia gazeta* (SR, Central Committee), no. 1, Sept. 1906; *Soldatskaia mysl'* (SR, Petersburg), no. 1, Sept. 1906; N. Kryzhanovskii, "Vosstanie na kreisere 'Pamiat' Azova'," *Morskie zapiski*, v. 6 no. 3–4, Dec. 1948, pp. 6–18; v. 7 no. 1, March 1949, pp. 3–8; *VPR*, part 2 book 1, pp. 176–9, 183–209; *Revoliutsiia 1905–1907 gg. v Estonii*, pp. 517–21.

48. *Listovki bol'shevistskikh organizatsii*, v. 3, pp. 40–3; Voitinskii, *Gody pobed i porazhenii*, v. 2, p. 88; TsK RSDRP, "Pis'mo k partiinym organizatsiiam No. 5"; Teodorovich, "Zametki chitatelia," pp. 174–6; Ia. Brandenburgskii, "Iz vospominanii," *PR*, 1922 no. 5, pp. 222–3; *Piatyi (londonskii) s"ezd*, pp. 157–8; Derenkovskii, "Vseobshchaia stachka," pp. 130–33; *VPR*, part 2 book 1, pp. 271–2.

49. Tsk RSDRP, "Pis'mo k partiinym organizatsiiam No. 5"; M. Vinitskii, "Ne vo vremia," *Nashe slovo* (Vilna, Bund), 1906 no. 7, p. 5; Derenkovskii, "Vseobshchaia stachka," pp. 133–4; *VPR*, part 2 book 1, pp. 50–1.

50. Tsk RSDRP, "Pis'mo k partiinym organizatsiiam No. 5"; Voitinskii, *Gody pobed i porazhenii*, v. 2, pp. 90, 92; Derenkovskii, "Vseobshchaia stachka," pp. 134–52; *VPR*, part 2 book 1, pp. 273–6, 278–80, 285, 288, 395–8, 465, 471–8; *Piatyi (londonskii) s"ezd*, p. 158; Eiter, "Organizational Growth," pp. 239–43; Hildermeier, *Die Sozialrevolutionäre Partei Russlands*, pp. 159–60.

51. An[iki]n, "S"ezd trudovoi gruppy," pp. 39–40; "V stavropol'skoi gubernii (karatel'naia ekspeditsiia Gen. Litvinova)," *Soznatel'naia Rossiia*, no. 2, 1906, pp. 72–9; Dubrovskii and Grave, *Agrarnoe dvizhenie*, pp. 672, 676–7.

52. TsK RSDRP, "Pis'mo k partiinym organizatsiiam No. 5."

53. Tsentral'naia Krest'ianskaia Komissiia pri TsK PSR, "Izveshchenie o predstoiashchem s"ezde krest'ianskikh rabotnikov P.S.R.," 17 August 1906, Helsinki 117 N; "O sovetakh rabochikh deputatov," *Listok* (SR, Petersburg Committee), no. 1, Aug. 1906, p. 4; "Postanovlenie III konferentsii predstavitelei zheleznikh dorog sozvannoi dlia resheniia voprosa o vseobshchei zabastovke v sviazi s

rospuskom Gosudarstvennoi dume," ibid., pp. 6–7; Pushkareva, *Zheleznodorozh-niki Rossii*, p. 259; "Chego zhdat'," *Volia*, no. 54, 25 Aug. 1906; *VPR*, part 2 book 1, pp. 379, 399, 401–2, 553–4; *VPR*, part 2 book 3, pp. 143–4, 214–6, 294–5.

54. TsK RSDRP, "Pis'mo k partiinym organizatsiiam No. 5."

55. *Piatyi (londonskii) s"ezd*, pp. 76–7.

Bibliography

This is less a bibliography than a guide for deciphering the notes. With very few exceptions, only those sources that have been cited three or more times are listed; most sources cited only in a single chapter in proximate notes have also been omitted. Consequently, the large body of documentary, memoir, and secondary sources that touch on only one issue or event have been excluded. By the same token, the listing of newspapers is a reasonable sample of those used, since newspapers cover many events. The notes themselves are generally abbreviated, omitting all but the most essential literature. Almost entirely missing are the sources on the activity of revolutionaries seeking to subvert the armed forces: they can be found in Bushnell, "Mutineers and Revolutionaries," as can many other works that did not manage to squeeze either into the notes or bibliography of this study.

Unpublished Documents

Archives Nationales, Paris

Reports by the agents of the Sûreté Générale at London and Annemasse, 1901–1906. F7 12521.

Bakhmeteff Archive, Columbia University, New York

Epanchin, Nikolai A., "Na sluzhbe trekh imperatorov," 1939, typescript.
Rozen, Konstantin Nikolaevich, "Vospominaniia o sluzhbe v polku, 1902–1917," 1928, typescript.
Vanovskii, Alexander, "Burnye gody. (Vospominaniia uchastnika revoliutsii 1905 goda)," 1954, typescript.

Bund Archive, New York

Twenty-nine proclamations from the Mariampol Military-Revolutionary Organization, 1905–1906, 1908, hectograph.

International Institute for Social History, Amsterdam, SR Party Archive (IISH, SR)

DMVO ["Dokumenty Moskovskogo voennogo okruga"], 1903–1906, typescript. Dossier 690.
"Materialy o pervoi voennoi konferentsii. 29 iiunia 1906 g. v Teriokakh." Dossier

700, no. 1. (A collection of stenographer's notes, draft resolutions and other materials. Notebooks and separate pieces of paper.)

"Protokoly chastnogo soveshchaniia predstavitelei Vyborgskoi, Peterburgskoi, Kronshtadtskoi i Revel'skoi voennykh organizatsii P.S.R.," 2 Aug. 1907, manuscript. Dossier 700, no. 4.

Other manuscript memoirs, protocols, proclamations, and questionnaires located in the above institutions and in the Russian Collection of the Helsinki University Library, the Houghton Library at Harvard University, and the Rare Book Division of the Lenin Library in Moscow have been cited.

Published Documentary Materials

Dokumenty po istorii revoliutsionnogo dvizheniia sel'skikh rabochikh i krest'ian v Pribaltike v period russkoi revoliutsii 1905–1907 gg., M.-L., 1957.

Drezen, A. K., ed., *Tsarizm v bor'be s revoliutsiei 1905–1907 gg. Sbornik dokumentov*, M., 1936.

Dubrovskii, S., and B. Grave, comps., *Agrarnoe dvizhenie v 1905–1907 gg.*, v. 1, M.-L., 1925.

"Dvizhenie v voiskakh na Dal'nem Vostoke," *KA*, 1925 no. 4–5, pp. 289–386.

Ekaterinoslavshchina v revoliutsii 1905–1907 gg. Dokumenty i materialy, Dnepropetrovsk, 1975.

Gosudarstvennaia duma, *Stenograficheskie otchety 1906 goda. Sessiia pervaia*, vv. 1–2, Spb., 1906.

"Iz bumag D. F. Trepova," *KA*, 1925 no. 4–5, pp. 448–66.

"K istorii revoliutsionnogo dvizheniia v Rossii (oktiabr'–noiabr' 1905 g.)," *Istoricheskii arkhiv*, 1955 no. 1, pp. 117–33.

Karatel'nye ekspeditsii v Sibiri v 1905–1906 gg. Dokumenty i materialy, M.-L., 1932.

Kratkoe raspisanie sukhoputnykh voisk, ispravlennoe po l-e avgusta 1905 g., Spb., 1905.

Krest'ianskoe dvizhenie 1905–1907 gg. v Tambovskoi gubernii. Sbornik dokumentov, Tambov, 1957.

"Kronshtadtskoe vosstanie 1906 g.," *KA*, 1936 no. 4, pp. 91–116.

[Kuropatkin, A. N.], "Dnevnik A. N. Kuropatkina [17 noiabria 1902 g.–7 fevralia 1904 gg.]," *KA*, 1922 no. 2, pp. 6–112.

[Kuropatkin, A. N.], "Iz dnevnika A. N. Kuropatkina. (S 23 dekabria 1905 goda po 12 marta 1906 goda)," *KA*, 1925 no. 1, pp. 70–100.

[Kuropatkin, A. N.], "Iz dnevnika A. N. Kuropatkina. (S 23 okt. po 23 dek. 1905)," *KA*, 1924 no. 7, pp. 55–69.

Obzor revoliutsionnogo dvizheniia v okruge Irkutskoi sudovoi palaty za 1897–1907 gg., Spb., 1908.

Pervaia konferentsiia voennykh i boevykh organizatsii RSDRP. Noiabr' 1906 goda, M., 1932.

Pis'ma P.B. Aksel'roda i Iu.O. Martova, Berlin, 1924.

"Pribaltiiskii krai v 1905 godu," *KA*, 1925 no. 4–5, pp. 263–88.

Protokoly pervogo s"ezda Partii Sotsialistov-Revoliutsionerov, Helsingfors, 1906.

Protokoly pervoi konferentsii voennykh i boevykh organizatsii Rossiiskoi Sotsial-Demokraticheskoi Rabochei Partii sostoiavsheisia v noiabre 1906 g., Spb., 1907.

[Raukh, G. O.], "Dnevnik G. O. Raukha," *KA*, 1926 no. 6, pp. 83–109.

[Rediger, A. F.], "Iz zapisok A. F. Redigera," *KA*, 1933 no. 5, pp. 92–133.

[Rediger, A. F.], "Zapiski A. F. Redigera o 1905 g.," *KA*, 1931 no. 2.

Resheniia Glavnogo voennogo suda za [1906–1908 gg.], [Spb., 1906–1908].

Revoliutsiia 1905–1907 gg. v Gruzii. Sbornik dokumentov, Tbilisi, 1956.

Revoliutsiia 1905–1907 gg. v Litve. Dokumenty i materialy, Vilnius, 1961.

Revoliutsiia 1905–1907 gg. v Rossii. Dokumenty i materialy.

Revoliutsionnoe dvizhenie v Rossii vesnoi i letom 1905 goda. Aprel'-sentiabr', parts 1–2, M., 1957–61.

Vserossiiskaia politicheskaia stachka v oktiabre 1905 goda, parts 1–2, M., 1955.

Vtoroi period revoliutsii. 1906–1907 gody, parts 1–3, M., 1957–1963.

Vysshii pod"em revoliutsii 1905–1907 gg. Vooruzhennye vosstaniia. Noiabr'–dekabr' 1905 goda, parts 1–4, M., 1955–1957.

Revoliutsiia 1905–1907 godov v g. Samare i Samarskoi gubernii. Dokumenty i materialy, Kuibyshev, 1955.

Revoliutsiia 1905 goda v Zakavkaz'i. Khronika sobytii, dokumenty i materialy. Po materialam Muzeia Revoliutsii Gruzii, Tiflis, 1926.

Revoliutsionnoe dvizhenie na Kubani v 1905–1907 gg. Sbornik dokumentov i materialov, Krasnodar, 1956.

Revoliutsionnoe dvizhenie v Armenii. 1905–1907 gg. Sbornik dokumentov i materialov, Erevan, 1955.

Revoliutsionnoe dvizhenie v Belorussii 1905–1907 gg. Dokumenty i materialy, Minsk, 1955.

Revoliutsionnoe dvizhenie v Kaluzhskoi gubernii v period pervoi russkoi revoliutsii 1905–1907 godov. Sbornik dokumentov, Kaluga, 1955.

Revoliutsionnoe dvizhenie v Kazakhstane v 1905–1907 godakh. (Sbornik dokumentov i materialov), Alma-Ata, 1953.

Revoliutsionnoe dvizhenie v N.-Novgorode i Nizhegorodskoi gubernii v 1905–1907 gg. Sbornik dokumentov i materialov, Gorkii, 1955.

Revoliutsionnoe dvizhenie v Voronezhskoi gubernii 1905–1907 gg. (Sbornik dokumentov i materialov), Voronezh, 1955.

Revoliutsionnye sobytiia 1905–1907 gg. v Kurskoi gubernii. Sbornik dokumentov i materialov, Kursk, 1955.

"Revoliutsionnye sobytiia v Pribaltike v 1905 g.," *KA*, 1940 no. 5, pp. 114–56.

Russko-iaponskaia voina. Iz dnevnikov A. N. Kuropatkina i N. P. Linevicha, L., 1925.

The Secret Letters of the Last Tsar. Being the Confidential Correspondence between Nicholas II and His Mother, Dowager Empress Maria Feodorovna, ed. Edward J. Bing, New York-Toronto, 1938.

Semennikov, V. P., ed., *Revoliutsiia 1905 goda i samoderzhavie*, M.-L., 1928.

Severnaia Osetiia v revoliutsii 1905–1907 godov. Dokumenty i materialy, Ordzhonikidze, 1955.

"Sibirskaia ekspeditsiia barona Meller-Zakomel'skogo," *Byloe*, 1917 no. 3, pp. 134–53.

Stankevich, A. P., comp., *Khronika revoliutsionnykh sobytii 1903–1908 gg. na Dal'nem Vostoke*, Khabarovsk, 1930.

Tsirkuliary Glavnogo shtaba za [1905–1907 gg.], [Spb., 1905–1907].

1905. Vosstaniia v Baltiiskom flote v 1905–1906 gg. v Kronshtadte, Sveaborge i na korable "Pamiat' Azova." Sbornik statei, vospominanii, materialov i dokumentov, L., 1926.

1905–1907 gody na Donu. Sbornik dokumentov, Rostov-na-Donu, 1955.

Voennye vosstaniia v Baltike v 1905–1906 gg., M., 1933, ed. A. K. Drezen.

Vsepoddanneishaia zapiska po upravleniiu kavkazskim kraem gen.-ad"iutanta grafa Vorontsova-Dashkova, n.p., 1907.

Vsepoddanneishii otchet Voennogo ministerstva za [1903–1908 gg.], Spb., 1905–1910.

Newspapers and Other Periodicals

Baku, Baku.

Biulleten' Tsentral'nogo Komiteta Partii Sotsialistov-Revoliutsionerov, n.p., No. 1, March 1906.

Bor'ba (legal Bolshevik), Moscow, Nos. 1–9, 27 Nov.–7 Dec. 1905.

Chernomorskii vestnik, Batum.

Dnevnik sotsial'demokrata G. V. Plekhanova, Geneva-Spb., Nos. 1–16, March 1905– April 1911.

Donskaia zhizn' (Kadet), Novocherkassk.

Duma (moderate Kadet), Spb., Nos. 1–39, 27 April–13 June 1906.

Dvadtsatyi vek, Spb., Nos. 1–120, 25 March–1 Aug. 1906.

Ekho (legal Bolshevik), Spb., Nos. 1–14, 22 June–7 July 1906.

Free Russia, London.

Golos (legal SR), Spb., Nos. 1–9, 27 April–7 May 1906; Nos. 10–17, 2–10 June 1906.

Golos soldata (illegal SD), Riga, Nos. 1–28, Dec. 1905–March 1907.

Golos truda (legal Menshevik), Spb., Nos. 1–16, 21 June–7 July 1907.

Iskra (SD), Geneva.

Iz materialov "Revoliutsionnoi Rossii" (SR), n.p., Nos. 1–84, 1901–1903. Hectograph.

Izvestiia federativnogo soveta khar'kovskikh komitetov Rossiiskoi Sotsial-Demokraticheskoi Rabochei Partii, Kharkov, Nos. 1–7, Nov.–Dec. 1905.

Izvestiia moskovskogo soveta rabochikh deputatov, Moscow, Nos. 1–6, 7–12 Dec. 1905.

Izvestiia soveta rabochikh deputatov, Spb., Nos. 1–10, Oct.–Dec. 1905.

Kaspii, Baku.

Kavkazskii rabochii listok (legal Bolshevik), Tiflis, Nos. 1–17, 20 Nov.–14 Dec. 1905 (Nos. 16–17 published as *Elisavetpol'skii vestnik*).

Kazarma (illegal SD), Spb., Nos. 1–13, Feb. 1906–March 1907.

Kostromskoi krai (legal Menshevik), Kostroma, Nos. 1–10, 22 June–4 July 1906.

Kur'er (legal Menshevik), Spb., Nos. 1–25, 17 May–13 June 1906.

Kurskaia vest', Kursk, Nos. 1–34, 24 June–4 Aug. 1906.

Moskovskaia gazeta (legal Menshevik), Moscow, Nos. 1–10, 10–20 Nov. 1905.

Mysl' (legal SR), Spb., Nos. 1–15, 20 June–6 July 1906.

Nachalo (legal Menshevik), Spb., Nos. 1–16, 13 Nov.–2 Dec. 1905.

Narodnyi vestnik (legal SR), Spb., Nos. 8–20, 17–31 May 1906.

Nevskaia gazeta (legal Menshevik), Nos. 1–10, 2–13 May 1906.

Novaia zhizn' (legal Bolshevik), Spb., Nos. 1–28, 27 Oct.–3 Dec. 1905.

Novoe obozrenie, Tiflis.
Novoe vremia (conservative), Spb.
Osvobozhdenie (Union of Liberation), Stuttgart-Paris, Nos. 1–79, 1902–1905.
Partiinye izvestiia (TsK PSR), Nos. 1–10, Oct. 1906–May 1907.
Poslednie izvestiia (Bund), London-Geneva, 1901–1906.
Pravo (liberal weekly), Spb.
Privolzhskii krai (legal Menshevik in late 1905), Saratov, 1903–1907.
Prizyv (legal Bolshevik), Spb., Nos. 1–106, January–June 1906.
Proletarii (Bolshevik), Geneva, Nos. 1–26, May–Nov. 1905.
Razvedchik (semi-official officers' weekly), Spb.
Revoliutsionnaia Rossiia (SR), Geneva, Nos. 1–76, 1900–1905.
Robotnik (illegal PPS), Warsaw.
Russkie vedomosti, Moscow.
Russkii invalid (official military daily), Spb.
Russkoe slovo, Moscow.
Samarskii kur'er (Kadet), Samara.
Severnaia zemlia (legal Bolshevik), Nos. 1–5, 23–28 June 1906.
Severnyi golos (legal Bolshevik-Menshevik), Spb., Nos. 1–3, 6–8 Dec. 1905.
Severo-zapadnyi golos, Vilna.
Soldat (illegal SD), Libava, Nos. 1–23, Feb. 1906–Feb. 1907.
Soldat (illegal SD), Sevastopol, Nos. 1–12, March 1906–Dec. 1907.
Soldatskaia beseda (TsK RSDRP), Nos. 1–9, Sept. 1906–March 1907.
Soldatskaia gazeta (TsK PSR), Nos. 1–7, May 1906–May 1907.
Soldatskaia mysl' (illegal Bolshevik), Moscow, Nos. 1–3, June–July 1906.
Soldatskaia zhizn' (illegal Bolshevik), Moscow, Nos. 1–6, Feb.–March 1906.
Sovremennik (liberal), Moscow, 1906–1907.
Svetoch (legal Bolshevik), Moscow, Nos. 1–17, 11–31 May 1906.
Syn otechestva (legal SR in November and December 1905), Spb.
Tiflisskii listok, Tiflis.
Vestnik kazarmy (illegal SD), Finland, Nos. 1–9, May–Sept. 1906.
Voennyi golos (liberal), Spb., Jan.–Sept. 1906.
Voina i mir (officers' journal), Moscow, 1906–1907.
Volia (SR), Nagasaki, Nos. 1–98–99, April 1906–Feb. 1907.
Volna (legal Bolshevik), Spb., Nos. 1–25, 26 April–24 May 1906.
Volzhskii vestnik, Kazan.
Vozrozhdenie, Tiflis, 1905–1906.
Vpered (legal Bolshevik), Moscow, Nos. 1–4, 2–6 Dec. 1905.
Vpered (legal Bolshevik), Spb., Nos. 1–17, 26 May–14 June 1906.
Za Narod (TsK PSR), Paris, Nos. 1–60, April 1907–May 1914.
Zhizn' (left Kadet), Moscow, 1905–1906.

Memoirs

Argunov, A., "Azef v Partii S.-R.," *Na chuzhoi storone. Istoriko-literaturnyi sbornik*, v. 6, 1924, pp. 157–200.
Birkin, V. N., *Osinoe gnezdo. Povesti minuvshikh let*, v. 4, Berlin, 1930.

Chernov, Viktor, "Ot 'Revoliutsionnoi Rossii' k 'Synu otechestva'," *Letopis' rev-oliutsii*, v. 1, 1923, pp. 66–98.

Chernov, V. M.,*Pered burei. Vospominaniia*, New York, 1953.

Davtian, Ia., "Tiflisskaia voennaia organizatsiia v 1905–1907 gg.," *PR*, 1923 no. 4, pp. 143–8.

Denikin, A. I., *Put' russkogo ofitsera*, New York, 1953.

Denikin, A. I., *Staraia armiia*, vv. 1–2, Paris, 1929–1931.

Garvi, P. A., *Vospominaniia*, part 2, New York, 1961.

Garvi, P. A., *Vospominaniia sotsialdemokrata. Stat'i o zhizni i deiatel'nosti P. A. Garvi*, New York, 1946.

Gerua, B. V., *Vospominaniia o moei zhizni*, v. 1, Paris, 1969.

Golos iz russkoi armii. Razoblacheniia, Berlin, 1902.

Grulev, M., *Zapiski generala-evreia*, Paris, 1930.

Gurko, V. I., *Features and Figures of the Past. Government and Opinion in the Reign of Nicholas II*, Stanford, 1939.

Iakovlev, M. A., "Khar'kovskoe likholet'e. (Otryvki iz vospominanii)," *IV*, 1910 no. 11, pp. 542–73; no. 12, pp. 1003–33.

Ignatyev, Aleksei, *A Subaltern in Old Russia*, London, 1944.

Iswolsky, Alexander, *Recollections of a Foreign Minister. (Memoirs of Alexander Is-wolsky)*, Garden City, N.Y., 1921.

Ivanov, S., "Kronshtadtskoe podpol'e (1905–1906 gg.)," *PR*, 1924 no. 12, pp. 138–44.

Kokovtsov, V. N., *Out of My Past. The Memoirs of Count Kokovtsov*, Stanford, 1935.

L. S., "Vospominaniia studenta-soldata," *Byloe*, 1906 no. 5, pp. 163–84.

Mandel'berg, V., *Iz perezhitogo*, Davos, 1910.

Miliukov, P. N., *Vospominaniia (1859–1917)*, v. 1, New York, 1955.

Ottoson-Nikolaev, "Iz vospominanii o Kronshtadte i Sveaborge 1905 goda," *1905. Vosstaniia v Baltiiskom flote v 1905–1906 gg. Sbornik*, L., 1926, pp. 98–104.

Pereverzev, P. N., "Karatel'naia ekspeditsiia General-Leitenanta P. K. Rennen-kampfa v Zabaikal'skoi oblasti," *Byloe*, 1907 no. 4, pp. 132–63.

Poluektov, V. N., "1905 g. v kazarmakh, kreposti i tiur'me," *Po tiur'mam. Sbornik vospominanii iz epokhi pervoi revoliutsii*, M., 1925, pp. 112–28.

Rozhkov, N. and A. Sokolov, *O 1905 gode. Vospominaniia*, M., 1925.

Samoilenko, E., "Sredi kazakov chernomor'ia," *V tsarskoi kazarme. Soldaty i mat-rosy v pervoi revoliutsii. Stat'i i vospominaniia uchastnikov dvizheniia*, M., 1929, pp. 177–202.

Shabrov, I., "Dni vosstaniia v Rostovskom polku," *Krasnoe znamia* (Paris), 1906 no. 4, pp. 24–67.

Shabrov, I., "O vosstanii Rostovskogo polka v dekabre 1905 goda," *KiS*, 1926 no. 1, pp. 123–30.

Starosel'skii, V. A., "'Dni svobody' v Kutaisskoi gubernii," *Byloe*, 1907 no. 7, pp. 278–306.

Sukhomlinov, V. A., *Vospominaniia*, Berlin, 1924.

Svechin, M. A., *Zapiski starogo generala o bylom*, Nice, 1964.

Tsion, S. A., *Tri dnia vosstaniia v Sveaborge*, Helsingfors, 1907.

Ul'ianinskii, V., "Vosstanie Rostovskogo polka v dekabre 1905 goda," *KiS*, 1925 no. 6, pp. 28–51.

V tsarstve shtykov, Nizhnii Novgorod, 1908.

Vishniak, Mark, *Dan' proshlomu*, New York, 1954.

Vitte, S. Iu., *Vospominaniia*, vv. 1–3, M., 1960.

Voitinskii, Vl., *Gody pobed i porazhenii*, vv. 1–2, Berlin-Pg.-M., 1923–1924.

Zenzinov, V., *Perezhitoe*, New York, 1953.

Zubelevich, Iu., *Kronshtadt. Vospominaniia revoliutsionerki*, vv. 1–3, Kronstadt, [1918?].

Other

Akhun, M. and V. A. Petrov, *Bol'sheviki i armiia v 1905–1917 gg. Voennaia organizatsiia pri Peterburgskom komitete RSDRP(b) i revoliutsionnoe dvizhenie v voiskakh Peterburga*, L., 1929.

Ames, Ernest O. F., ed., *The Revolution in the Baltic Provinces of Russia. A Brief Account of the Activity of the Lettish Social Democratic Workers' Party by an Active Member*, London, 1907.

Andreev, L. I., "Revoliutsionnoe dvizhenie v voiskakh severo-zapadnykh okrugov," *1905. Armiia v pervoi revoliutsii. Ocherki i materialy*, M.-L., 1927, pp. 1–120.

Annanepesov, M., *Uchastie soldatskikh mass v revoliutsii 1905–1907 godov v Turkmenistane*, Ashkhabad, 1966.

Bliumental', I. I., "Sotsial-demokratiia i revoliutsionnoe dvizhenie 1905 goda v Samarskom krae," *1905 god v Samarskom krae. Materialy po istorii R.K.P.(b) i revoliutsionnogo dvizheniia*, Samara, 1925, pp. 3–375.

D. I. Budaev, "Rabochee i krest'ianskoe dvizhenie v Smolenskoi gubernii v period pervoi russkoi revoliutsii," *Revoliutsionnoe dvizhenie v Smolenskoi gubernii v 1905–1907 gg.*, Smolensk, 1956, pp. 22–58.

Bushnell, John, "Mutineers and Revolutionaries: Military Revolution in Russia, 1905–1907," Ph.D. dissertation, Indiana University, 1977.

Cherkasov, P., "Revoliutsionnoe dvizhenie v voiskakh Sibirskogo i Turkestanskogo voennykh okrugov," *1905. Armiia v pervoi revoliutsii. Ocherki i materialy*, M.-L., 1927, pp. 234–337.

Chermenskii, E. D., *Burzhuaziia i tsarizm v pervoi russkoi revoliutsii*, 2nd ed., M., 1970.

Drezen, A., *Armiia i flot v revoliutsii 1905 g.*, M., 1931.

Drezen, A., *Revoliutsiia vo flote. Baltiiskie moriaki v vostanii 1905–1906 gg.*, L., 1926.

Drozdov, I. G., *Agrarnye volneniia i karatel'nye ekspeditsii v Chernigovskoi gubernii v gody pervoi revoliutsii. 1905–1906 gg.*, M.-L., 1925.

Eiter, Richard, "Organizational Growth and Revolutionary Tactics: Unity and Discord in the Socialist Revolutionary Party," Ph.D. dissertation, University of Pittsburgh, 1978.

Engelstein, Laura, *Moscow, 1905. Working-Class Organization and Political Conflict*, Stanford, 1982.

Field, Daniel, *Rebels in the Name of the Tsar*, Boston, 1976.

Fischer, Alexander, *Russische Sozialdemokratie und bewaffneter Aufstand im Jahre 1905*, Wiesbaden, 1967.

Fuller, William C., Jr., *Civil-Military Conflict in Imperial Russia, 1881–1914*, forthcoming, Princeton.

Gadzhiev, A., "Revoliutsionnye vystupleniia soldat v Dagestane v period pervoi russkoi revoliutsii," *Uchenye zapiski In-ta istorii, iazyky i literatury Dagestanskogo filiala AN SSSR*, v. 12, 1964, pp. 64–89.

Galai, Shmuel, *The Liberation Movement in Russia, 1900–1905*, Cambridge, England, 1973.

Gavrilov, B., *Voennaia rabota moskovskikh bol'shevikov v gody pervoi russkoi revoliutsii*, M., 1950.

Gerua, A., *Posle voiny. O nashei armii*, 2nd ed., Spb., 1907.

Grishkunaite, E. V., "Volneniia v voiskakh garnizonov, raspolozhennykh v Litve, v 1905–1907 gg.," *Trudy AN Litovskogo SSR*, 1960, Seriia A, v. 2, pp. 119–31.

Grulev, *Zloby dnia v zhizni armii*, [Brest-Litovsk], 1911.

Gubernchuk, *Ocherk istorii 129-go pekhotnogo Bessarabskogo polka. 1806–1863–1906 gg.*, Kiev, 1909.

Hildermeier, Manfred, *Die Sozialrevolutionäre Partei Russlands. Agrarsozialismus und Modernisierung in Zarenreich (1900–1914)*, Köln-Wien, 1978.

Iakovlev, N. N., *Vooruzhennye vosstaniia v dekabre 1905 goda*, M., 1957.

Kalandadze, Varl. and Vl. Mkheidze, *Ocherki revoliutsionnogo dvizheniia v Gurii*, Spb., 1906.

Kantsel'son, V. M., "Revoliutsionnoe dvizhenie v voiskakh Kievskogo voennogo okruga," *Revoliutsionnoe dvizhenie v armii v gody pervoi russkoi revoliutsii. Sbornik statei*, M., 1955, pp. 178–250.

Keep, J. L. H., *The Rise of Social Democracy in Russia*, London, 1963.

Kireev, E. P., *Rabochii klass i bol'shevistskaia organizatsiia groznenskogo neftepromyshlennogo raiona v revoliutsii 1905–1907 gg.*, Groznyi, 1950.

Kirilov, E. A., *Istoriia 114-go pekhotnogo Novotorzhskogo polka. (1763–1913)*, Mitava, 1913.

Klimkov, Vasilii, *Raspravy i rasstrely*, M., 1906.

Kochergin, P., *Nuzhdy russkogo soldata*, Saratov, 1905.

Kokhmanskii, P. N., *Moskva v dekabre 1905 g.*, M., 1906.

Kolesnichenko, D. A., "Iz istorii bor'by rabochego klassa za krest'ianskie massy v 1906 g.," *IZ*, v. 95, 1975, pp. 254–83.

Kolesnichenko, D. A., "K voprosu o politicheskoi evoliutsii trudovikov v 1906 g.," *IZ*, v. 92, 1973, pp. 84–108.

Kol'tsov, D., "Rabochie v 1905–1907 gg.," *Obshchestvennoe dvizhenie v Rossii v nachale XX-go veka*, ed. L. Martov et. al., v. 2 part 1, Spb., 1910, pp. 185–341.

Kondrikov, B. V., "Revoliutsionnye vystupleniia soldat v zapadnoi sibiri v gody pervoi russkoi revoliutsii," *Uchenye zapiski Omskogo gos. ped. in-ta*, v. 22, 1965, pp. 90–118.

Konovalov, V. I., "Revoliutsionnoe dvizhenie v voiskakh Moskovskogo voennogo okruga," *Revoliutsionnoe dvizhenie v armii v gody pervoi russkoi revoliutsii. Sbornik statei*, M., 1955, pp. 26–101.

Korablev, Iu.I., "Revoliutsionnoe dvizhenie v voiskakh Peterburgskogo voennogo okruga," *Revoliutsionnoe dvizhenie v armii v gody pervoi russkoi revoliutsii. Sbornik statei*, M., 1955, pp. 102–77.

Koroleva, N. G., *Pervaia rossiiskaia revoliutsiia i tsarizm. Sovet ministrov Rossii v 1905–1907 gg.*, M., 1982.

Korol'kov, G., "Revoliutsionnoe dvizhenie v voiskakh Kavkazskogo voennogo okruga," *1905. Armiia v pervoi revoliutsii. Ocherki i materialy*, M.-L., 1927, pp. 338–57.

Korol'kov, G., "Revoliutsionnoe dvizhenie v voiskakh Priamurskogo voennogo okruga," *1905. Armiia v pervoi revoliutsii. Ocherki i materialy*, M.-L., 1927, pp. 358–74.

Korol'kov, G., "Revoliutsionnoe dvizhenie v voiskakh Vilenskogo i Varshavskogo voennykh okrugov," *1905. Armiia v pervoi revoliutsii. Ocherki i materialy*, M.-L., 1927, pp. 160–79.

Kuz'min-Karavaev, V. D., *Iz epokhi osvoboditel'nogo dvizheniia*, vv. 1–2, Spb., 1907.

Lenin, V. I., *Polnoe sobranie sochinenii*, 5th ed., M., 1961– .

Leskovskii, Ia., "Dvizhenie sredi voisk v Krasnoiarske v 1905 g.," *PR*, 1925 no. 10, pp. 59–77.

MacBean, W. A., *Handbook of the Russian Army*, 4th ed., London, 1905.

Manilov, V., "Kievskaia voennaia organizatsiia RSDRP i vosstanie saper v 1905 g.," *Letopis' revoliutsii*, 1925 no. 5–6, pp. 176–225.

Manning, Roberta, *The Crisis of the Old Order in Russia. Gentry and Government*, Princeton, 1982.

Marina, G. P., "Pechatnaia propaganda bol'shevikov v voiskakh Omskogo voennogo okruga v 1906–1907 gg.," *Revoliutsionnoe dvizhenie v Sibiri i na Dal'nem Vostoke*, Tomsk, 1960, pp. 111–33.

Martov, Iu., *Istoriia Rossiiskoi Sotsial-Demokratii*, 2nd ed., M.-P., 1923.

Maslov, Petr, *Krest'ianskoe dvizhenie v Rossii v epokhu pervoi revoliutsii*, 2nd ed., M., 1924.

Mehlinger, Howard D. and John M. Thompson, *Count Witte and the Tsarist Government in the 1905 Revolution*, Bloomington, Ind., 1972.

Mel'nikov, A. B., "Revoliutsionnoe dvizhenie v moskovskom garnizone v period dekabr'skogo vooruzhennogo vosstaniia," *IZ*, v. 49, 1954, pp. 265–300.

Mel'nikov, A. B., "Revoliutsionnoe dvizhenie v moskovskom garnizone v 1906 g.," *IZ*, v. 56, 1956, pp. 91–128.

Muratov, Kh. I., *Revoliutsionnoe dvizhenie v russkoi armii v 1905–1907 gg.*, M., 1955.

Narushevich, I. N., "Vosstanie soldat 83 Samurskogo pekhotnogo polka v Deshlagare," *Uchenye zapiski Dagestanskogo gos. ped. in-ta*, v. 2, 1956, pp. 51–61.

Obninskii, V. P., *Letopis' russkoi revoliutsii*, v. 3, *Duma i revoliutsiia*, parts 1–2, M., 1907.

Ovsiannikov, P. I., "Revoliutsionnoe dvizhenie v voiskakh Kievskogo i Odesskogo voennykh okrugov," *1905. Armiia v pervoi revoliutsii. Ocherki i materialy*, M.-L., 1927, pp. 180–233.

[Pavchinskii, E. I.] "Er. Molot," *Russkaia armiia i revoliutsiia*, [M.], 1907.

Pawłowski, Ignacy, *Wojskowa dzialność SDKPiL w Rewolucji 1905–1907*, Warsaw, 1956.

Perrie, Maureen, *The Agrarian Policy of the Russian Socialist-Revolutionary Party from Its Origins through the Revolution of 1905–1907*, New York and London, 1976.

Petrov, V. A., *Ocherki po istorii revoliutsionnogo dvizheniia v russkoi armii v 1905 g.*, M.-L., 1964.

Piaskovskii, A. V., *Revoliutsiia 1905–1907 godov v Turkestane*, M., 1958.

Poleshchuk, V. E., "Revoliutsionnoe dvizhenie v chastiakh Irkutskogo voennogo okruga," *Revoliutsionnoe dvizhenie v armii v gody pervoi russkoi revoliutsii. Sbornik statei*, M., 1955, pp. 296–372.

Poleshchuk, V. E., "Revoliutsionnoe dvizhenie v man'chzhurskoi armii v 1905 g.," *IZ*, v. 49, 1954, pp. 301–51.

Potto, V., *Istoriia 17 dragunskogo Nizhegorodskogo polka*, v. 11, Tiflis, 1908.

Pushkareva, I. M., *Zheleznodorozhniki Rossii v burzhuazno-demokraticheskikh revoliutsiiakh*, M., 1975.

Rabochii klass v pervoi russkoi revoliutsii 1905–1907 gg., M., 1981.

Reichman, Henry Frederick, "Russian Railwaymen and the Revolution of 1905," Ph.D. dissertation, University of California, Berkeley, 1977.

Rozenblium, K., *Voennye organizatsii bol'shevikov 1905–1907 gg.*, M.-L., 1931.

Schwarz, Solomon, *The Russian Revolution of 1905. The Workers' Movement and the Formation of Bolshevism and Menshevism*, Chicago, 1967.

Senchakova, L. T., *Revoliutsionnoe dvizhenie v russkoi armii i flote v kontse XIX-nachale XX v.*, M., 1972.

Shestovalov, N. I., "Bol'shevistskaia propaganda v chastiakh Nizhegorodskogo garnizona v gody pervoi russkoi revoliutsii," *Uchenye zapiski Gor'kovskogo universiteta*, no. 165, 1973, pp. 74–91.

Shuliakovskii, E. G., "Deiatel'nost' voennoi organizatsii pri Voronezhskom komitete RSDRP v 1906 godu," *Trudy Voronezhskogo gos. un-ta*, v. 51 part 1, 1958, pp. 3–9.

Sidel'nikov, S. M., *Obrazovanie i deiatel'nost' Pervoi Gosudarstvennoi dumy*, M., 1962.

Soifer, D. I., *Revoliutsionnoe dvizhenie soldat v Turkestane*, Tashkent, 1969.

Spiridovich, A. I., *Revoliutsionnoe dvizhenie v Rossii v period imperii. Partiia sotsialistov-revoliutsionerov i ee predshestvenniki. 1886–1916*, 2nd ed., Pg., 1918.

Steklov, A. P., "Revoliutsionnoe dvizhenie v voiskakh Kavkazskogo voennogo okruga," *Revoliutsionnoe dvizhenie v armii v gody pervoi russkoi revoliutsii. Sbornik statei*, M., 1955, pp. 373–447.

Suhr, Gerald Dennis, "Petersburg Workers in 1905: Strikes, Workplace Democracy, and the Revolution," Ph.D. dissertation, University of California, Berkeley, 1979.

Surikov, V. P., "Revoliutsionnoe dvizhenie soldat i matrosov v Latvii," *Revoliutsionnoe dvizhenie v armii v gody pervoi russkoi revoliutsii. Sbornik statei*, M., 1955, pp. 251–95.

Troitskii, K., "Rabota s.-d. sredi voisk v 1906–1907 godakh," *Materialy po istorii revoliutsionnogo dvizheniia*, v. 4, Nizhnii Novgorod, 1922, pp. 123–30.

Trotsky, Leon, *1905*, New York, 1972.

1905 Armiia v pervoi revoliutsii. Ocherki i materialy, M.-L., 1927.

Varzar, Vasilii Egorovich, *Statisticheskie svedeniia o stachkakh rabochikh na fabrikakh i zavodakh za desiatiletie 1895–1904 goda*, Spb., 1905.

Varzar, Vasilii Egorovich, *Statistika stachek rabochikh na fabrikakh i zavodakh za trekhletie 1906–1908*, Spb., 1910.

Varzar, Vasilii Egorovich, *Statistika stachek rabochikh na fabrikakh i zavodakh za 1905 god*, Spb., 1908.

Voronitsyn, I. P., *Istoriia odnogo katorzhanina*, M.-L., 1926.

Zaionchkovskii, P. A., *Samoderzhavie i russkaia armiia na rubezhe XIX–XX stoletii. 1881–1903*, M., 1973.

Zharnovetskii, K. S., "Kronshtadtskie vosstaniia v 1905–1906 gg.," *KL*, 1925 no. 3, pp. 48–102.

Zheleznov, G. I., "Revoliutsionnoe dvizhenie v voiskakh Moskovskogo voennogo okruga v 1905 godu," *1905. Armiia v pervoi revoliutsii. Ocherki i materialy*, M.-L., 1927, pp. 121–59.

Znamenskii, N., *Voennaia organizatsiia pri Kazanskom komitete RSDRP i revoliutsionnoe dvizhenie v voiskakh Kazanskogo voennogo okruga v 1905–1907 gg.*, Kazan, 1926.

Index